CRIMMIGRANT NATIONS

Crimmigrant Nations

RESURGENT NATIONALISM AND THE CLOSING OF BORDERS

Robert Koulish and
Maartje van der Woude
EDITORS

FORDHAM UNIVERSITY PRESS NEW YORK 2020

Maartje van der Woude's co-editorship of and contributions to this volume are part of her five-year research project "Getting to the Core of Crimmigration" (project number 452-16-003), which is financed through the VIDI research scheme by the Dutch Research Council (NWO).

Visit us online at www.fordhampress.com.

Library of Congress Cataloging-in-Publication Data available online at https://catalog.loc.gov.

Printed in the United States of America

22 21 20 5 4 3 2 1

First edition

Contents

Introduction

The "Problem" of Migration

Robert Koulish and Maartje van der Woude

As the distinction between domestic and international is increasingly blurred, along with the line between internal and external borders, irregular migrants have become emblematic of the hybrid threat both to national security and sovereignty and to safety and order *inside* the state.[1] The evocation of fear and the practice of pointing to a real or imagined enemy of color that must be hated and fought against is common among populist demagogues in the United States and Europe. As Claudia Postelnicescu has observed, while Donald Trump rages against Mexican immigrants and Muslims, in Europe the refugee has rapidly been identified as the enemy.[2] This increasing influence of populism and nationalism over immigration has come to dominate politics in the United States and Europe, so much so that immigration law and policy are leading nationalist turns on both sides of the Atlantic. *Crimmigrant Nations* critically examines how the United States, Britain, and the EU advance nationalist and populist politics through immigration policy, law, and public and political discourse.

By looking at debates, practices, and policies on migration and migration control in the United States, Europe, and Britain, we aim to show not only how anti-immigrant sentiments and nationalist discourse are on the rise in various Western liberal democracies, but also how these sentiments are being translated into actual policies and practices that contribute to a merger of crime control and migration control, with devastating effects for those falling under its reach. This merger has been referred to as the phenomenon of "crimmigration."[3] Various authors have drawn attention to increasingly harsh criminal penalties that the U.S. Congress has authorized for immigration violations, to the growing category of criminal convictions for which noncitizens face discretionary or — more and more often — mandatory deportation, to the increasingly punitive feel of immigration proceedings, and to the expanding participation of state and local police agencies in immigration enforcement.[4] Although scholars provide different explanations for the crimmigration trend, they are unanimous in concluding that it creates an ever-expanding population of outsiders, making aliens into criminals without the protections that citizens enjoy.[5]

By combining these frames with scholarship on nationalism and populism, we will discuss the *how* (what measures are taken), the *why* (the rationale behind these measures and policies), and the *who* (who is subjected to exclusion as a result of these measures) of immigration and border control. As argued by Weber and McCulloch, an integration of theoretical concepts and perspectives can contribute to a more holistic understanding of the dynamics and dialectics of immigration and border control.[6] This holistic approach is necessary to make sense of the atrocities happening in the Mediterranean Sea, where thousands of refugees risk their lives trying to cross the rough waters to get into Europe, the violence depicted against the Central American migration caravan(s), the building of the new wall on the U.S.-Mexico border, the introduction of no-fly lists, and the election of hardline governments throughout Europe who are resisting refugees and opposing any EU quota system. By collecting different country case studies that pay attention to the multiscalar character of debates, decision-making, and practices of migration and border control in which local, national, and supranational actors, tensions, and interests play a role, this book looks beyond the level of the local or the national to the relational dynamics among different actors on different levels and among different institutions.[7]

Setting the Scene

Although it is easy in the light of recent events concerning migration and migration policies and debates in the countries and continents represented in this book to focus predominantly on the present, for a proper understanding of the seriousness of current times, it is necessary to briefly sketch the larger story of fears and concerns of immigration that predate the election of Trump, the Brexit vote, and the fortification of Europe's external borders.

The Lifting of Borders and Growing Concerns about Migration in Europe

To understand the current debates on migration and border control in different European countries, it is necessary to go back to the creation of the

European Union and, more importantly, the signing and implementation of the Schengen Agreement. First, under the scope of the European Union, member states to the Union have agreed to work together on several areas. One of these areas is the area of freedom, security, and justice.[8]

The Schengen Agreement effectively realized the fundamental EU principle of freedom of movement of goods, services, and people that was crucial to the success of the predominantly economic drivers behind the creation of the European Union. By signing the agreement, member states promised to eliminate border controls that, before the agreement, would be enforced while crossing borders between member states. In addition, the agreement included sections dealing with the harmonization of visa and asylum policies, the introduction of the European Arrest Warrant, the common fight against cross-border crime, and increased controls at the EU's external borders for which the European Border and Coast Guard Agency Frontex was created in 2005. These sections of the agreement increased controls of the EU's external borders and the creation of the necessary European databases to monitor entry and exit as well to exchange police information. The process has led to the reintroduction of the term "Fortress Europe."[9] In its recent use the term refers to immigration and external border fortification policies and practices that help prevent undocumented immigration into the European Union.[10] Concerns about the "security deficit" that would rise after the abolition of internal border controls in Europe have been present from the very beginning of the European Union, with specific concerns (initially) about the possibility for undocumented third-country nationals being able to move through Europe without any hindrances. Nevertheless, the economic benefits of an actual "open" market and the compensatory measures taken to fortify Europe's external border and to enhance European-wide surveillance were able to appease government leaders at the time.[11] This brief reflection on the creation of the European Union and the Schengen Agreement shows us in the light of this edited collection that (1) economic interests are central to the European Union and (2) concerns about migration to Europe from third-country nationals were present from the very beginning and were linked to concerns of international crime and abuse of (social) welfare systems in various European countries.[12]

Given the presence of these serious concerns from the very start of Schengen, it is no surprise that the external borders of the European Union could always count on high levels of scrutiny by the member states, especially those located in (north)west Europe, countries that were seen to have more pull factors for (undocumented) migrants than European countries in the south and east. In the past decades, two factors in particular have contributed to growing concerns about migration in relation to external border control in Europe.[13] The first factor is the successive periods of enlargement of the EU in 2004, 2007, and 2013, leading to the movement of the EU external border to the East of Europe and the extension of the number of member states from fifteen to twenty-eight.[14] Indeed, in the late 1990s, the EU membership of countries from Central and Eastern Europe caused a number of concerns centered in particular on the perceived difficulties that these countries would face in guarding the EU external border. The second factor has been the "war on terror" that immediately rocketed to the top of the political agenda in both the U.S. and the EU after the terrorist events of 9/11. A major characteristic of the resulting counterterrorist strategies has been the focus on maximum surveillance, especially in relation to immigration and the movement of people. As a result, immigration and crime—and especially serious crimes such as terrorism—are more explicitly framed as one single problematic issue. Although most of the concerns seem to be focused around third-country nationals and irregular migrants, the securitization of migration also seems to affect certain EU citizens themselves. Thus, for example, in December 2013, the German delegation at the EU interior ministers' meeting in Brussels outlined that it continues to oppose any inclusion of Romania and Bulgaria in the passport-free Schengen Area. In a similar vein, at the same meeting, the delegation of the United Kingdom—which is notably not a signatory to the Schengen Acquis—proposed the imposition of limits on free movement for migrants within the EU. Against the background of a Europe in which crime and immigration are increasingly being seen as coherent in the social and political discourse and in which there are growing concerns about the alleged lack of sufficient protection of the EU's external borders, it seems understandable that the Arab Spring and the resulting influx of third-country nationals has caused considerable anxiety in the member states. This migration was the largest and most visible influx of third-country nationals since the Second World War. It quickly became clear that the numbers of immigrants that the European continent was facing, with over one million migrants and refugees arriving in Europe in 2015, had thrown the international community into disarray. On top of existing worries about transnational crime, terrorist threats, and the sustainability of national welfare state arrangements, the impact of this modern exodus has been acutely felt across Europe. Both mainstream media and European leaders have characterized the situation as a "crisis," a "state of emergency," and even "Europe's meltdown."[15] It has further exposed serious weaknesses in the EU's governance and institutions that echo experiences of the financial crisis. The current situation has highlighted the continued existence of "two Europes"—that is, a division between Northwestern and Southeastern Europe and a wide gap between European ideals and citizens' perceptions and fears. The culmination of these reactions to modern-day mass migration has been in stark contrast to the ideal of collaboration and harmonization to create a Europe without internal borders in which the principle of free movement rules widely. Growing concerns about who are seen to "belong" in Europe and who are not, who are seen to be "deserving" to be in Europe and who are not, are spurring nationalistic debates and exclusionary policies and practices along ethno-racial lines.

Migration and Border Concerns and Control in the United States

In contrast with crimmigration in Europe, which was in part a response to mass migration and other tactile realities, crimmigration in the U.S. constructed unsubstantiated problems where none actually existed. No mass migration to the U.S.-Mexico border and no egregious securitization threats existed even after the 9/11 tragedy. Crimmigration in the U.S. is a product of neoliberal approaches to mass incarceration and the War on Drugs that overlay drug laws with immigration.

To understand the current debate about crimmigration and migration penology in the United States, it is necessary to go back to two pieces of legislation, the Antiterrorism and Effective Death Penalty Act (AEDPA)[16] and the Illegal Immigration Reform and Immigrant Responsibility Act (IIRIRA),[17] which arguably have been most responsible for framing the debate on crimmigration.[18] The legislation legitimized mass immigration detention for criminal convictions and popularized the legal provision for "aggravated felonies" that had been introduced in the Anti-Drug Abuse Act of 1988. More relevant to the development of border penology, however, is the addition of the AEDPA provision for the "mandatory detention" of persons charged with or convicted of aggravated felonies. Mandatory detention ensured that immigrants would be detained regardless of risk or dangerousness because the IIRIRA packed the aggravated felony category with misdemeanors under state law, including a variety of nonviolent offenses such as gambling and passport fraud. By mandating detention for nonviolent offenses, the legislation confused the justification for detention based on risk with punitive punishment and deterrence. It also opened the door for private prison firms to become political and financial players on the side of mass incarceration. Additionally, the legislation rationalized mass incarceration for migrants of color and helped establish the framework upon which the immigration enforcement patchwork would transform in relatively short order into the huge control regime that has dominated the political narrative since 2016. The 1996 act also added what amounts to force multipliers, adding state and local law enforcement to the existing federal migrant control force, which Marie Doris Provine et al. write about in this volume.[19]

This legislative framework facilitated the rapid growth of an administrative behemoth that included noticeable advances in technology and enhancements in the construction of detention facilities and enforcement staffing. The 9/11 tragedy served as catalyst for the Patriot Act,[20] which unleashed appropriations and executive power and gave rise to a variety of executive actions. The NSEERS Program sanctioned monitoring of Muslim communities,[21] and SBI-net, a financial boondoggle and policy failure, nonetheless introduced virtual border walls into the narrative. These efforts were successful in shifting the trajectory of crimmigration and border penologies to include border securitization while enlisting racist anti-terrorism tropes against Muslims.[22] To prepare the border to serve as a front line domestically in the war on terror, the government also increased enforcement staff and doubled and tripled detention capacity.

Migration control was intensely punitive under the Obama administration, with enforcement and detention policies guiding the use of prosecutorial discretion. In part the regime was initially the result of a political miscalculation within the administration that appeasing Republicans with punitive border control measures would in turn produce comprehensive immigration reform. Instead of progressive reform, Congress established bed mandates that maximized detention capacity, and Obama's presidency ended up responsible for 400,000 detentions annually, 34,000 per day, at a cost to the taxpayer of $3 billion. Additionally, Obama earned the moniker "deporter-in-chief" as he oversaw the patchwork of border controls that coalesced into "a formidable (enforcement) machinery."[23]

Trump has transformed Obama's punitive regime into a new moment of exceptional cruelty. This moment exists in part because of a long-standing administrative infrastructure that includes exceptional executive power and judicial impotence. The present is distinguished from the past by policies of extreme debasement of human rights values and indifference to human suffering. The term "exception" is used intentionally to assert government actions beyond the rule of law that are excused by the court and, hence, the rule of law.

The narrative has shifted under Trump from a discussion of detention facilities to concentration camps and from criminalization to obliteration. Trump's tweet on July 3, 2019, is, "If illegal immigrants are unhappy with the conditions . . . just tell them not to come. All problems solved!" As Trump would have it there would be no government responsibility for abuse and no accountability under law. Enter at your own risk. His practices have animalized migrants and transferred all risk for what transpires after migrants cross the border onto the migrants themselves. This constitutes a grave exception to constitutional norms and the rule of law. It is a deliberate strategy that Giorgio Agamben has observed is the starting point for discussions about the power of sovereignty.[24]

The sovereign narrative includes a new component that has migrants assuming the risk for government-sponsored degradation, misery, and death. Gone is the sense of institutional self-policing and government accountability that accompanies the rule of law. Salvadoran refugees Oscar Martinez and his daughter Valeria bore that risk. There was no official investigation into their all too preventable demise, which was caused by Trump's "Remain in Mexico" initiative. Quite the opposite; Trump's comments imply that Oscar Martinez was at fault. He has also sadistically called for harsher conditions with a reminder for Congress to authorize funding for his border wall. Trump has ignored his own Office of Inspector General, which issued a report condemning "dangerous overcrowding" at the border camps. Although the infrastructure for Trump's cruelty precedes him, Trump has transformed migration control into a fascist reality show about "killable bodies" of color that appeal to the president's white nationalist base. By banking on sovereign authority, Trump has loaded authoritarian nationalism onto the backs of migrants and refugees, creating a situation at the border in which migrants having killable bodies has become the new norm.[25]

Central Concepts and Questions of *Crimmigrant Nations*

Now that we have mapped out why and how migration is seen as a problem to both the United States and the European Union and how this over time has resulted in different measures being taken to curb migration and to exclude immigrants, we will turn to a discussion of the central concepts of the book: crimmigration, nationalism, and populism. In so doing, we will discuss recent scholarship without claiming to provide a state-of-the-art overview and define how, given the rich scholarship on some of the concepts, the central concepts are to be understood in the context of this edited collection and what questions we aim to address for each concept.

Crimmigration: The *How* of Immigration and Border Control

There is a growing literature that addresses, describes, and criticizes expressions of state penal power in the field of migration and border control as a great concern. For over a decade now, scholars have analyzed migration and border control in terms of risk, penalty, governmentality, sovereignty, privatization, and securitization.[26] They have observed how the penal power of the state is expressed through coercive tools including deportation, detention, and criminalization[27] and have discussed the increasingly porous boundaries between the civil, administrative, and criminal fields generally and the particular pertinence of this to the study of migration, borders, and "preventive" interventions.

A vital aspect of the exclusionary policies toward migrants has been a growing reliance on the use of penal power and criminal justice measures. Criminal justice practices, particularly as they intersect with migration and border control, play a central structuring role in generating inhospitalities and hostilities. The interlacing of crime control with border control subjects people on the move to the full range of criminalization processes. The processes of entwining and interlacing immigration law and criminal law are a two-way street, as each legal domain exerts a gravitational pull on the other so that both substance and procedure might be transferred in either direction.[28] It is important to note that the two-way street serves a single purpose: to accentuate state power as it denigrates migrants. Crimmigration law criminalizes immigration offenses, emphasizes the immigration consequences of criminal acts, and super-sizes enforcement regimes. It securitizes borders, enhances enforcement, and "force multiplies" with local police. Central to the crimmigration thesis is the observation that while the immigration procedure is turning more into a criminal procedure and the powers of immigration and criminal law enforcement agencies are becoming interchangeable, this has not resulted in an equal transfer of due-process protections that individuals have under criminal law but not in immigration proceedings. Or, as Legomsky put it, "Immigration law has been absorbing theories, methods, perceptions, and priorities associated with criminal enforcement while explicitly rejecting the procedural ingredients of criminal adjudication."[29] As Aas argues,[30] these new forms of "bordered penality" follow a different logic: rather than subject migrants to over-enforcement, a parallel system is emerging that separates, segregates, and ultimately banishes nonmembers from society.[31] This total exclusion is an extreme form that follows yet another and different logic than deportability arguments, popularized in the 1980s, that see the criminalization of migration as a tool to discipline, but include vulnerable migrants for ongoing exploitation in the labor market.[32] This is where crimmigration ties in with neoliberalism, as this has spurred the punitive turn in many penal policies in Western nations.[33]

As noted by Weber and McCulloch, scholars have used the crimmigration thesis to analyze legal and institutional convergences in law, policing, security, legal process, and incarceration.[34] It has also stimulated a substantial secondary literature, including empirical research into its applicability in other jurisdictions, critique of its narrow legal scope, and suggestions for the expansion of the concept to include discursive and sociolegal dimensions. The concept of crimmigration has thus shown itself to be a powerful and systematic framework for the examination of punitive practices such as criminal deportation, immigration detention, and migration policing and is particularly useful in framing analyses of how immigration controls are enforced. Moreover, the thesis has continued to be expanded and reinterpreted as it has been applied in different settings to describe the mechanism or technologies of internal immigration control, addressing primarily the *how* of immigration border control. Perhaps, too, it is important to recognize the limits of crimmigration because of the limits of law to fully explain some of the more draconian abuses at the border.

In order to get a better understanding of the *why* of immigration and border control—and the *why* of the development of a "crimmigration control" system—we need to introduce nationalism and populism as important concepts that will provide important insights into what Bosworth and Guild have called "governing through migration control"—in other words, the power of politicians to frame a variety of social problems through the lens of migration and borders.[35] By opening the field to a debate about the role of nationalism and populism in migration control, we intend for the discussion to consider the use of migration control as a catalyst into darker realities.

Nationalism and Populism: The *Why* of Immigration and Border Control

Nationalism is one of the most powerful social forces sweeping across affluent societies in response to globalization and mass mobility. Resurgent nationalism has the power to cut across established alliances to place national interests, national sovereignty, national resources, and national identity above all else. In the literature on the relationship between globalization and nationalism it has been acknowledged "that the various forces of globalization have the effect of stimulating a new attachment to local areas, issues and problems."[36] As noted by Mendelsohn, who analyzes the concept of nationalism in relation to migration policies in Austria and Hungary, the paradoxes inherent to processes of globalization, including the emergence of transnational communities, on the one hand, and the proliferation of small-scale ethnic movements, on the other, have been exposed.[37] This might lead to a normalization of nationalism despite continued trends of globalization and postmodernity.

The examination and analysis of the politics of nationalism therefore remain an important and urgent project. While synthesizing the work of Gellner, Smith, and Barth, Hou describes the doctrine of nationalism as pulling together "national autonomy, national unity, and national identity."[38] Nations and nationalism, therefore, propagate a sense of shared identity, solidifying a distinctive cultural heritage and personality for a given named population. This is achieved through normalizing histories and establishing a legitimized set of customs, traditions, and habits. Nationalism is a crisis of identity,[39] the response to the irregularities of modernity by taking pride in one's own nation. Threats to a country's national identity are thus seen as threats to the nation itself and therefore presented, and often accepted, as a justification for restrictive and harsh measures that are aimed at protecting the economic or security interests of "native" inhabitants against those of immigrants, the potentially dangerous other. This is where nationalism intersects with populism.

Populism is a political response from the political right or left that expresses animosity toward governing elites. Right populism also targets immigrants as an enemy of the people, while "the people" are defined in white nationalist terms. In 1989, few imagined that that the fall of the Soviet Union would trigger a dramatic increase in xenophobia demarcating "in-groups" from "out-groups" on the basis of immigration status, but that is exactly what happened starting in the 1990s. Nationalist movements replaced the Cold War's East-West ideological divide with a "we"-"they" demarcation designed around sovereign boundaries. "We" came to indicate a nationalist "we" with "they" comprising foreigners. As it turned out, right-populist movements cohered around and ginned up strong right-wing anti-immigrant politics. Populist movements were further energized after the tragedy of 9/11 as Muslims came to embody the other in both Western Europe and the United States.[40] Right-wing populism aligns the governing apparatus run by outsiders and in tension to governing elites. The populist critique says that, since corrupt government elites betray the expression of the people, the people instead turn to a charismatic leader who speaks on their behalf.[41] This charismatic leader can wield authoritarian power against governing elites and immigrants. Since the beginning of the 1990s, the notion of populism has been used by criminologists to make sense of the ongoing public support for repressive and zero-tolerance political agendas.[42] In so doing, they introduced the concept of *punitive* populism: "the notion of politicians tapping into, and using for their own purposes, what they believe to be the public's generally punitive stance."[43] Over time, the concept changed into *penal* populism,[44] but continued to refer to the situation in which politicians allowed the electoral advantage of a policy to take precedence over its penal effectiveness. When it concerned matters of crime and criminal justice, several scholars observed not only that this trend—despite some differences—was visible in many Western liberal democracies,[45] but also that populism was not a strategy or a practice that was only applied by right-wing parties. Everybody and every party, whether on the left or the right side of the political spectrum, seemed to tap into the lingering public insecurities and fears around crime.

As some of the chapters of this book will show, it was only a matter of time before concerns and fears around migration and borders would be used in a similar matter. It is on that note that Bosworth and Guild[46] use Simon's "governing through crime" theory to illustrate what they call the process of "governing through migration control" with which they refer to the development that they witness in several countries,[47] the UK being their prime case study, where the politics of national identity that aspires to solidarity and shared values are based on the forcible exclusion of growing numbers of people. Recent scholarship has also tied populism to neoliberalism. The agonist is less the state and more state regulation of the market. The enemy is less the state per se and more the welfare state, or at least the practice of providing social benefits for immigrants. Alt-Right leaders in the United States, for example, seek to exclude immigrants and reverse social policies in place since the New Deal. All the while, policing powers increase, along with the criminalization of immigrants. The argument in parts of Western Europe is "welfare chauvinism": to limit the welfare state to citizens, and in the United States to reverse it altogether.[48]

Nationalist Sentiments in Europe

The so-called European refugee crisis has caused far-right politics to gain momentum all throughout Europe and refugees to be dubbed a threat to the project of nationalism. As a result, a moral imperative to help others in need has been replaced by a patriotic duty to defend the nation-state.[49] We can see evidence of nationalism reshaping the electoral landscape and political order in Europe. For example, in 2016, voters in the UK decided to break from the European Union out of nostalgia for national identity and national interests. While still grappling with the implications of Brexit, the EU is now confronting a country at the heart of the continent making an exit from the EU's liberal values. Hungary in 2018 reelected Prime Minister Orbán, and he and his Fidesz party have chipped away at Hungary's democratic checks and balances, curbed judicial independence, and clamped down on the independent media. Hungary's democratic backsliding has been accompanied by a drumbeat of xenophobic rhetoric, directed against refugees and "Brussels," the *de facto* capital of the Union. Lynne Haney was one of the first sociologists to identify this political development in Hungary as central European governments resisted pressures and assumptions about European integration and mobilized their criminal justice systems to reaffirm national sovereignty.[50] It is in this context that she introduces the concept of penal nationalism. While looking into the case of Sweden, Barker further builds upon Haney's concept of penal nationalism to capture the different pieces of the increasingly complex puzzle that aims to make sense of the anti-immigrant policies and practices that we are witnessing across the globe. Barker further complicates that picture by also showing how growing concerns about the welfare state—and hence welfare nationalism[51]—are an important factor in explaining exclusionary anti-immigrant policies.

Other than what is sometimes thought by non-Europeans, and other than what Europe likes to present itself to be—one unified Europe—Europe has always struggled with conflicting visions of its identity, of a unifying idea that will erase national particularities. As Hazard rightfully observes, this is a generous, but extremely difficult wish with such irreducible values.[52] We are witnessing now, after a long process of integration, a return to instinctive nationalist sentiments. In the face of fear, people want to feel safe; hence a leader who can promise security and protection is gathering the popular support. At the same time, the incapacity of the European leaders to prove solidarity by voluntarily taking in refugees generated a huge amount of pressure on the few countries that had no other choice. Greece and Italy are some of the main entry points in the EU and were put in the position of facing the influx of refugees alone. As a result, large numbers of people went unregistered across Europe, which gave rise to criticism and anti-immigration phobias. The discourse is simple: appealing to national values, national identity, national borders, and national interest, politicians convince citizens that they all have a palpable enemy: the refugee. Although the 2019 European elections did not see the anticipated overwhelming victory of nationalist right-wing parties throughout Europe, the rise of these parties on the national level is disconcerting.

Above All: America First!

Nationalism and populism are concepts seldom applied to scholarship on American politics. That is because nationalism generally correlates to ethnicity,[53] and, as a "nation of immigrants,"[54] the country sees anti-immigrant movements as contradicting the dominant sense of national identity. Civic nationalism, not ethnic nationalism, comprises the dominant strain of nationalism.[55] By definition civic nationalism is procedural, abstract, and somewhat lifeless. It fails to quench the emotional fulfillment that people expect of nationalism. Emotional fulfillment in America is an individual quest. America's procedural nationalism is based on shared principles, liberty, and equality, embedded in the founding documents. Thomas Jefferson told us we are to find happiness of our own device—not by identifying with the nation. People clamoring to sate passion through identity must look to the individual,[56] or associations with other people,[57] not the nation-state. For Alexis de Tocqueville, bonds that tie Americans are to be found in shared interests. Lipset observes that this makes it difficult for citizens to imagine sharing commitments to the nation as a whole.[58] Similarly, until recently, the government was never seen as the enemy of the people, and the people rarely saw immigrants as the enemy.

At least that is what the dominant narrative would have us believe about American nationalism. A subtextual narrative has also been present throughout American history. It exposes a critical right- and white-nationalist turn. It is about America's racist and exclusionary roots. People on the left condemn it, while white nationalists embrace it. This turn focuses on exclusionary provisions in founding texts that limit the franchise to white propertied males and legitimize slavery. It excludes people of color and ties Americans together by common white European ancestry and the Protestant religion. Jefferson was a slaveholder, and his words conveyed the belief that blacks were inferior side by side with having inalienable rights. The constitution considered slaves less than human.

While slavery constituted the racist roots for America's immigrant experience, Ben Franklin's hatred of Germans helped introduce the concept of American nativism. John Higham refers to the exclusion of people within the country in terms of nativism and those outside in terms of nationalism.[59] In the immigration context, we shall refer to broad racist exclusions of people of color in terms of white nationalism.

Until recently, white nationalism has been little more than an irritant to American politics and an outright danger to minorities, but generally occupied little beyond fringe group status in society. White nationalism was financed by a small set of right-wing philanthropists such as John Tanton in the '80s and '90s and the Koch and Mercer families in the 2010s. And they preyed on white sympathizers mostly in dying industrial centers or in die-hard white-separate suburbs whose "American dreams" seem to have passed by. By the early twenty-first century, the Koch brothers and the Mercer family joined Tanton to fund a variety of extreme right-wing organizations and support racist policy ideas that, through their exorbitantly financed lobbying organizations, began to enter the mainstream polity.[60]

By the 2010s, the "Alt-Right" Richard Spencer and Jared Taylor added a well-dressed metrosexual glean of self-awareness and irony to American fascism. Suddenly the movement seemed to some less scary. With Mercer money, policy papers, and advice coming from FAIR and CIS, the Alt Right, under the leadership of Spencer and Taylor, helped Trump assuage concern in Conservative elite circles and manipulate enough white, disillusioned voters to bring Trump to power. The Trump card for these wealthy few was their anti-elite cred within white nationalist circles.[61]

With Trump's election, the white nationalist margins had assumed the mainstream by entering the White House. The margins had converged with the state. White nationalists Stephen Miller, Attorney General Jeff Sessions, and other Tanton veterans were now driving immigration policy, leading by late spring 2018 to the forced separation and internment of children at the U.S.-Mexico border and the travel ban of Muslims who hoped to visit and attend schools in the U.S. The court upheld the travel ban, pretty much removing the perception of constraint on presidential power over immigration exclusions.[62] American fascism is now a state brand espoused by President Trump, and the consequences are dangerous, particularly on the immigration front. Immigration law provides a cover for authoritarian and racist movements.

The rise of nationalist sentiments and populist rhetoric intended to either reassure or threaten different social groups and shine light on the governmental role of boundary reinforcement during insecure times. An in-depth analysis of these processes and dynamics can illustrate, following Bosworth and Guild,[63] how migration control is being used as a site of governance in which citizenship and belonging, rather than criminalization and control, are the primary considerations of government, and how these considerations play into the potential reasoning behind (cr)immigration control measures. By considering the rise of nationalism, we intend to spark consideration of post-criminologies and post-crimmigration frames for understanding border control. This brings us naturally to the consideration of a third aspect that will play a central role throughout this edited collection: the sorting of individuals along ethno-racial lines.

The *Who* of Immigration and Border Control

Immigration law has always allowed for racism. Because of its highly discretionary nature, immigration law is prone to discriminatory practices on a variety of fronts. Additionally, scholarship on immigration law has underemphasized the role of race. This is caused for the most part by the focus of crimmigration scholarship on doctrinal issues, and immigration law is ostensibly neutral in terms of how doctrine has developed.

Much of crimmigration scholarship has underplayed the social fact that most of the migrants being discussed are of color and that enhanced policing powers are racist in their impact on immigrants of color.[64] Additionally, because of the unusual circumstances surrounding the origins of immigration law in sovereignty, the government has had plenary power to engage in intentional discrimination against immigrants subject to the most cursory standard for review.

Governments in general can discriminate in border controls, police stops, detention, and removals and can engage in racial profiling. Immigration law's acceptance of discrimination is remarkable and must be compared with the criminal justice system and its corollary constitutional constraints and with countries in Europe that use different standards for othering migrants. The criminal justice system may be rife with racism, but at least the discrimination is *de facto*, covert, and implicit by law. The difference between criminal law and immigration law for our purposes is that immigration law can treat immigrants in ways they cannot treat individuals in the criminal justice system.[65] Similarly, they can treat immigrants in ways they cannot treat citizens. Beyond that, however, it is difficult to deny the disparate impact that border enforcement has on migrants of color.

Crimmigration, nationalism, and populism all touch upon the *who* of intensified immigration and border control: in the context of crimmigration, this is discussed along the lines of membership and the creation of legal categories; in the context of nationalism and populism, an "us versus them" rhetoric is being deployed to highlight the differences and dangers against which the nation-state needs to be protected. Once again, the racial dynamic involved in nationalist-based exclusions must be discussed. This protection goes beyond the protection against criminal behavior, against jobs being taken by cheap labor, or against the abuse of the welfare state: protection is deemed necessary to protect the national identity and cultural fabric of countries against the influences of "others."[66] In that sense, while discussing crimmigration and nationalism, it is impossible to not also delve into the matter of *who* bears the brunt of the increased, harsh, and exclusive migration and border control measures—in other words, the question of to what extent and how these measures are racialized.

Kevin Johnson contends that "the day will come when the consensus will be that race is central, not peripheral, to a full understanding of modern immigration and nationality law and policy."[67] The founding of the Immigration and Customs Enforcement (ICE) in 2003 institutionalized the centrality of race in immigration control.[68] Crimmigration scholars agree with this consensus. There are growing intersections between crimmigration and border control scholarship, Latinx critical legal theory (Latcrit), and critical race scholarship in the United States. Border criminologies scholarship has delved into Derek Bell's dictate to tell one's own stories, and Fathi[69] has applied Kimberlé Crenshaw's initial applications of intersectionality and immigration to examine race, gender, and immigration status.[70] Ian Haney Lopez's LatCrit investigation into whiteness has also been applied to questions of membership, citizenship, and migration control. This interest in combining these two frameworks is well placed.

Crimmigration scholars in Europe have not engaged with the terminology of race as explicitly and directly as critical race scholars would have liked. Without downplaying the exclusionary effects and social sorting of immigration and border control, European scholars tend to see and discuss these processes along the lines of nationality and ethnicity while acknowledging that discriminatory and racist motives will underpin these dynamics and practices. In their recently published edited volume, Bosworth, Palmer, and Vasquez "start the response . . . to this lacuna [of race] in the [crimmigration] literature."[71] Their book critically examines the relation between migration, migration control, and social constructions of race from a variety of disciplines and perspectives. Interestingly enough, race is a more subtle concept in European contributions to the volume. The chapters on Europe generally combine race and nationalism and race and class.[72] Thus, whereas race is a first-order principle for U.S. scholars, it is co-first with nationality and ethnicity as clear proxies for race in Europe. The implication is that literature on nationalism is more comprehensive in its narratives about the European experience with crimmigration.

Existing crimmigration and race scholarship focuses on concepts surrounding the racist effects of crimmigration case law and enforcement practices along with empirical research that examines attitudes toward crimmigration and ethnographies of local policing practices that enforce crimmigration. The literature recognizes that Latinos bear the brunt of excessive crimmigration enforcement in the U.S.,[73] and that crimmigration is a tool for the racial subordination of Latinos, including the expansion of racial profiling.[74] Although none of these laws and policies explicitly mention race, they are an example of racialism in crimmigration because they criminalize unauthorized Latino immigrants and produce their deportation.[75] As Steve Garner suggests, for the most part the crimmigration literature amounts to not much more than a case study in the literature about the racist criminal justice system.[76] Pickett,[77] for example, outlines how local police enforcement emerged as an important means for transmitting anti-Latino sentiments. Johnson laments that critical race theory remains an underutilized resource in crimmigration scholarship.[78]

Crimmigration exists in a context of explicit anti-immigrant racism. There is nothing implicit about the Muslim travel ban, referring to Mexicans as rapists, or hailing the military to the border to deter caravans of Central American refugees from exercising their right to apply for asylum. As critical race theory delivers new approaches to a shifting landscape of social change outpacing law, immigration law anxiously awaits its *Brown v. Board of Education* moment, which rejects Jim Crow exclusion. Crimmigration scholars are armed for battle in this regard. By interlacing concepts with critical race theory and LatCrit scholarship and combining them with growing border control literature, the authors in this volume use this opportunity to continue connecting the dots between legal systems and racist social controls. The research in this volume has documented and subjected to critique the categorical displacement of people on account of race and national origin and forms of discrimination, not on the basis of holding individuals responsible for something they may have done as much as on account of who they are and where they are from. This kind of racism is more comprehensively addressed through a critical analysis of nationalist and populist ideologies and practices on the rise in Europe and in the United States.

While we concede that critical race work in this field is incomplete and remains overdue, we follow Bosworth and Aas as they link crimmigration in Europe to a lack of citizenship rather than racism. Bosworth's observation helps distinguish chapters in this volume about the United States and Europe, but should also inform the discussion on both sides of the Atlantic. Whereas we now have a clearer grasp on the extent to which the process of crimmigration is visible and how it manifests itself in different countries worldwide, the timing seems to be right to further flesh out and theorize its underlying membership theory by bringing in the notion of nationalism.

Crimmigrant Nations: Analyzing Trump, Brexit, and Fortress Europe

This book highlights a disturbing national trend that has legitimized debate over violence against immigrants. Recent events highlight the fact that white nationalist perspectives countenance the use of violence against immigrants. These chapters are presented to lend social critique to this disturbing trend, relying on empirical data, and theoretical concepts designed to be part of the debate in the months and years ahead.

The book provides ample proof that penal populism is a shared concept in the U.S., the UK, and the European continent. The authors show how political leaders on both sides of the Atlantic tap into public insecurities and fears about crime and security. They apply the concept of penal populism to migration under the thematic concepts introduced by Stumpf, Bosworth and Guild, and Krasmann. Increasingly since the "migration crisis" of 2015–16, the authors show, national leaders have tapped into right-wing politics to exploit fear about migrants and asylum seekers. Increasingly governance is perceived through the lens of migration control, using strategies of criminalizing and securitizing migrants and migration. Race is embedded within the increasingly fascist mission of right-wing governance strategies, with people of color comprising the *who* of draconian migration control. Finally, it is important to note that it is unclear from the following chapters the extent to which states are using nationalism or nationalist organizations are using states to promote their agenda. Wendy Brown has inquired about the demise of state sovereignty and whether forms of penal populism have become part of a response to this eventuality.[79] This goes to the question of reevaluating the agonist and the relationship among the state, the market, and nationalist desires for migration control. Perhaps the march toward fascism will triangulate the three elements through racist migration control.

In Part I, we introduce migration and asylum controls in Trump's America, the UK's Brexit, and Fortress Europe, with chapters by Tony Platt, Dario Melossi, and Ana Aliverti. These chapters are intended to introduce the reader to the blending of border control, criminalization, and securitization strategies in the United States, Europe, and Britain that provoke fear and anxiety while exercising oppressive state powers in furtherance of right-wing populist strategies. As similar as they sound, the control scenarios play out much differently in these three spaces, with different politics, institutions, culture, and social norms of control.

Platt states early in Chapter 1 that "we live in dangerous and uncertain times, the 'interregnum' that Antonio Gramsci predicted would unleash a 'great variety of morbid symptoms,' and face enormous political, intellectual, and strategic challenges." The morbid symptoms Platt refers to consist of the "crackdown on undocumented and documented immigrants accused of petty crimes. . . ." Platt ushers the reader into a critical examination of institutions of the carceral state—criminal and juvenile courts, prisons and jails, private police and national security operations. His objective is to show that the crackdown in immigrants is symptomatic of "an erosion of social democracy . . . and a whiff of fascism."

In Chapter 2, Dario Melossi introduces the reader to Fortress Europe and an in-depth glimpse of criminalization, securitization, and migration control in the Italian region. Melossi argues that a strengthened Fortress Europe in the twenty-first century has been a result the European Union's failure to advance mass democratic society, highlighted with the failure to deal humanely with the refugee crisis of 2014. Melossi states that this is because of limited cultural development "exemplified by the lack of a common language." The EU's failure to land on a united response to the refugee crisis in 2014 has thus fed the reactionary backlash that has hardened the walls of Fortress Europe. Whereas Platt documents fissures in the carceral state that would allow for resistance and alternative futures, Melossi envisions a strengthened public sphere in a united Europe that could provide space for the dialogue that is needed to address the current populist and racist backlash.

In Chapter 3 Ana Aliverti introduces Brexit and the role that crimmigration, border criminologies, and punitive penology have played in separating the UK from the European continent. Aliverti shows that the "electoral purchase of nationalism and populism" in the UK exists because of "imperial melancholia and nostalgia, which were unhinged during the referendum campaign." Her argument is reinforced by empirical research that shows how immigration law has contributed to "producing this cultural milieu and legitimizing extreme forms of exclusion."

Part II introduces the *how*, *why*, and *who* methodology in Trump's white nationalist approach to immigration control. Juliet Stumpf starts off in Chapter 4 by revisiting the concept of crimmigration that she coined in 2006 to grapple with the triangulation of exclusionary concepts in the context of neo-nationalism. Stumpf reviews the intersection of immigration law and criminal law that spawned a new direction for critical immigration studies. She then zeroes in on the development of crimmigration scholarship through the *who*, *where*, and *how* of migration control in the context of neo-nationalism. Crimmigration under Trump exposes a widening gap between reasoned purposes and actual deployments of government power. Increasingly, rationales are based on empty neo-nationalist rhetoric and populist rhetoric and feint to nil substantive grounds for generating securitization powers. Stumpf narrates the growing intersection among crimmigration, border criminologies, and enemy penology under the guise of a "meta-conversation about whether to turn inward and shut the world out, or eject or intern those determined not to belong."

In Chapter 5, Sappho Xenakis and Leonidas Cheliotis carry the meta-conversation in the direction of social economy. They examine the immigration penal system through the lens of whatever has become of neo-liberalism under Trump. The authors examine a binary relationship between those who are optimistic and those who are pessimistic about penal reform. Their discussion of Trump stretches these categories beyond the constraints of neoliberal logic to envision a new post-neoliberal frame that holds economic isolationism and what they refer to as "nationalist authoritarianism."

Robert Koulish examines the limits of U.S. immigration law to provide justice for migrants and refugees as he examines immigration law through the lens of sovereignty in Chapter 6. He provides an analysis of the case *U.S. v. Trump* as an example of how the court engages legal formalism for the purpose of abdicating judicial review authority, which gives the executive the license to indulge imperial whims over immigration and immigrants. Like Stumpf, Koulish shows how the court securitizes empty rhetoric with appeals to nationalism and securitization, with the case outcome rationalizing excessive state action, in the absence of real crises.

In Chapter 7, Doris Marie Provine extends the volume's theme to focus on immigration enforcement, which she terms "low-hanging political fruit." Specifically, Provine inquires into the institutional shift from increasingly passive congressional power to imperial executive authority. The shift drives politically expedient demonization of undocumented immigrants and asylum seekers as "enemies of the state," a phrase coined by Susanne Krasmann.[80] Like Koulish, Provine shows how constitutional institutions abdicate authority to the executive, this time through congressional passivity. "Enforcement, by default, becomes the currency of reform." The punitive shift that Provine documents coincides with the shift from neo-liberalism to nationalist authoritarianism discussed by Xenakis and Cheliotis. Provine's focus on enforcement is in contrast to Xenakis and Cheliotis on imprisonment.

The American scenario concludes in Chapter 8 with a different approach to Trump's governing strategies. Rashawn Ray and Simone Durham conduct empirical research on Twitter, Trump's preferred means of communicating his thoughts to the public. These tweets reveal unmitigated anti-immigrant animosities that enhance understandings of crimmigration and border criminologies, as Koulish refers to in chapter 6.

Chapter 9 gives Trump's America a final look that uses Russia as a comparison. Agnieszka Kubal and Alejandro Olayo-Mendez compare the migrant experience of immigration processes in Russia to U.S. Operation Streamline. The authors are reminded of the shared humanity of immigrants in trouble in countries as disparate as the U.S. and Russia to emphasize the *how* in terms of the troubles that bureaucratic efficiency may spell for an administrative system, no matter where it is located.

In Part III Maartje van der Woude introduces two recent "crises" in Europe: the "euro crisis" of 2008 and the so-called migration crisis of 2015–16. Whereas the EU boasted a coordinated response to the monetary crisis of 2008, the migration crisis of 2014 has ignited what van der Woude refers to as "renationalization" of EU member states. Van der Woude implies that the failure of the EU is in part because of the failure of the Schengen *Aquis*, which had embedded intra-EU border controls within the principle of free movement. Chapter 10 provides another reason for the failure of European public space to handle the so-called migrant crisis that Melossi says has contributed to resurgent nationalism. Van der Woude describes member state's reneging on the Schengen Agreement and turning to national decision-making to enforce national borders against migration and asylum-seeking within the EU. Using the Netherlands, a traditionally international and tolerant country, as a case study, van der Woude documents how Geert Wilders, the "Dutch Trump," has advanced renationalization using securitization and politicization techniques of control to help secure new racism in Europe's anti-migrant controls.

Helene Gundhus's Chapter 11 depicts Norway as a "Janus faced" humane and "inclusive society" that has the highest deportation rate among European countries. Gundhus documents diminishing inclusions for "young strangers" having "uncertain civil rights status." Penal borders for Gundhus are really about the welfare state's populist-oriented policing strategies. Such strategies include the panoptic logic of policing "young strangers" by making their life situation worse without necessarily prosecuting them. The idea is to expel "dangerous immigrants" as part of "changing the traditional system of prevention within the national state towards a more punitive state."

In Chapter 12, De Pelecijn and De Ridder convey the story of Brussels, perhaps the most international European city, converted by propaganda into the "capital of European Jihadism." The authors explain the acceleration of the country's anti-terror laws in the context of rising nationalist fears, which in turn have generated a "terro-turn" in Belgian migration control.

As much as van der Woude analyzes intra-Schengen border controls, the Schengen concept is inclusive of hard borders at the outside edges of the Schengen zone. As Witold Klaus demonstrates in Chapter 13, Poland is situated on the Schengen Zone's eastern edge. Klaus applies the crimmigration, new penology, and enemy penology concepts to Poland's post-"migration crisis" of 2015. Unlike the other countries in Fortress Europe, Poland had experienced greater emigration than immigration until 2016, when Ukranian refugees fled to Poland. Klaus observes that Poland's external border was constructed, as a prerequisite for entering the zone, as a civilizing, velvet curtain in the East. Poland's civilizing welcome was selectively deployed: a soft welcome for Ukrainians, harder for Muslim Chechens, a population of refugees, Klaus says, who experienced closed borders after 2015 and were left in precarious conditions and in danger outside the EU borders.

Agreed to in March 2016, the EU-Turkey deal is a statement of cooperation between European states and the Turkish government. It seeks to control the crossing of refugees and migrants from Turkey to the Greek islands and was initially intended to curb the large numbers of refugees arriving in Europe—or losing their lives on the way—in 2015. In Chapter 14, Kasli and Yanasmayan describe life outside the Schengen Zone to document asylum seekers in Kumkapi Deportation Center in Istanbul setting fire to their beds and escaping into the unknown, therewith shining an important light on the status of Turkey as a so-called safe country for refugees and asylum seekers. The authors illustrate how migrants are depicted as oppositional figures to authoritarian ruling power populism of the Adalet ve Kalkınma Partisi (the Justice and Development Party, AKP). Since 2002, the AKP has solidified its rule through elections on the backs of "so-called" enemies of the Turkish state. Even with a republican ideal and civic identity rooted in ethnicity, enemies of Turkey are diverse and plentiful: "Seculars, Alevi, Kurds, Westerners, LGBTQs, feminists and even anti-capitalist Muslims." These groups have ostensibly defied the "so- called unity" of the "new Turkey" without engaging in criminal behavior. The anti-immigrant discourse is part of the larger exclusion and is identified by appeals to foreign policy and citizenship. Harsh anti-migrant policies are explained through long-standing ethno-religious divisions that "polarize and dominate Turkish politics."

A penultimate observation: crimmigration itself is a controversial concept and has been bandied about in different ways among this volume's authors, with several taking issue with the term itself and its applicability to the countries they discuss. While we as critical immigration scholars subject the term to critical inquiry, we recognize that rightwing scholars have boastfully used the term. Part of our critical approach to crimmigration is to deconstruct the term and reterritorialize it for critical analysis.

Finally, the chapters in this volume are a response to the growing crisis of white nationalism in the U.S., UK, and Europe. White nationalism is responsible for mass shootings around the globe, but rather than receiving universal condemnation, it has forged its way into mainstream politics. This volume forces us to recognize the mainstreaming of white nationalism through immigration policy and law with particular emphasis on migrants and refugees of color who have become the victims and resistors to this state violence.

In the following chapters, the authors convey their own versions of state-sponsored exclusions with unique empirical cases and with reference to country-specific laws and policies. Shared in the diversity of cases is a recognition that society has entered into an increasingly dangerous phase of immigration politics. It is a phase that criminalizes migration through state narratives animalizing migrants and refugees and devaluing their lives. It must not be lost that how the EU, UK, and U.S. treat their migrants and refugees has consequences for the legitimacy of these political entities in the years to follow.

Notes

This edited collection is one of the outputs of the five-year research project "Getting to the Core of Crimmigration" (project number 452-16-003), which is financed through the VIDI research scheme by the Netherlands Organisation for Scientific Research (NWO). We would like to thank NWO for its support. We would also like to acknowledge the support of the Joel and Kim Feller Foundation. For their critical and constructive comments, we would like to express our appreciation to our readers and research assistants, including Jennifer Chacon, Jamie Longazel, Kelsey Drotning, James Cooke, Dena Robinson, immigration law students at the UMD Carey School of Law, and participants at the 2018 Law and Society Meetings Roundtable, the Populism and Nationalism of Immigration Law and Policy in the Age of Trump, Brexit, and Fortress. A special shout-out goes to the Koulish family, Stephanie, Valen, Olivia, and Julian, for love, patience, and support. We would like to extend our appreciation to Justine Stefanelli, Ph.D., for her expert editorial assistance.

1. Helene Gundhus and Katja Franko, "Global Policing and Mobility: Identity, Territory, Sovereignty," in *The SAGE Handbook of Global Policing*, ed. Ben Bradford, Beatrice Jauregui, and Ian Loader (London: SAGE, 2016), 497–514.

2. Claudia Postelnicescu, "Europe's New Identity: The Refugee Crisis and the Rise of Nationalism," *Europe's Journal of Psychology* 12, no. 2 (2016): 203–9, http://doi.org/10.5964/ejop.v12i2.1191.

3. Juliet Stumpf, "The Crimmigration Crisis: Immigrants, Crime, and Sovereign Power," *International Organizations Law Review* 56 (2006): 356–420.

4. Daniel Kanstroom, "Deportation, Control, and Punishment: Some Thoughts About Why Hard Laws Make Bad Cases," *Boston College Law School Journal* 113 (2000): 1890–1935; Kanstroom, "Criminalizing the Undocumented: Ironic Boundaries of the Post-September 11th 'Pale of Law,'" *Boston College Law School Journal* 29 (2004): 639–70.

5. Maartje A. H. van der Woude, Joanne P. van der Leun, and Jo-Anne A. Nijland, "Crimmigration in the Netherlands," *Law and Social Inquiry* 39, no. 3 (2014): 560–79.

6. Leanne Weber and Jude McCulloch, "Penal Power and Border Control: Which Thesis? Sovereignty, Governmentality, or the Pre-emptive State?" *Punishment & Society* 21, no. 4 (2019): 496–514.

7. Such a multiscalar approach has also been advocated by Nancy Wonders, "Just-in-Time Justice: Globalization and the Changing Character of Law, Order, and Power," *Critical Criminology* 24, no. 2 (2016): 201–16; Monica W. Varsanyi, Paul G. Lewis, Doris Marie Provine, et al. "A Multilayered Jurisdictional Patchwork: Immigration Federalism in the United States," *Law and Policy* 34, no. 1–2 (2012): 138–58; David Moffette, "The Jurisdictional Games of Immigration Policing: Barcelona's Fight against Unauthorized Street Vending," *Theoretical Criminology* (2018), https://doi.org/10.1177/1362480618811693.

8. The Area of Freedom, Security and Justice is a collection of home affairs and justice policies designed to ensure security, rights, and free movement within the European Union (EU). European member states agreed to the harmonization of private international law, extradition arrangements between member states, policies on internal and external border controls, common travel visa, immigration, and asylum policies and police and judicial cooperation.

9. Hans-Jorg Albrecht, "Fortress Europe—Controlling Illegal Immigration," *European Journal of Criminal Law and Criminal Justice* 10, no. 1 (2002): 1–22.

10. Annalisa Lendaro, "A 'European Migrant Crisis'? Some Thoughts on Mediterranean Borders," *Studies in Ethnicity and Nationalism* 16 (2016): 148–57, https://doi/10.1111/sena.12169.

11. Van der Woude and Patrick van Berlo, "Crimmigration at the Internal Borders of Europe? Examining the Schengen Governance Package," *Utrecht Law Review* 11, no. 1 (2015): 61–79.

12. Tim J. M. Dekkers, van der Woude, and van der Leun, "Exercising Discretion in Border Areas: On the Changing Social Surround and Decision Field of Internal Border Control in the Netherlands," *International Journal of Migration and Border Studies* 2, no. 4 (2016): 382–402; Vanessa Barker, "Penal Power at the Border: Realigning State and Nation, *Theoretical Criminology* 21 (2017): 441–57; Barker, *Nordic Nationalism and Penal Order: Walling the Welfare State* (London: Routledge, 2017).

13. Valsamis Mitsilegas, "Border Security in the European Union: Towards Centralized Controls and Maximum Surveillance," in *Whose Freedom, Security and Justice?*, ed. Anneliese Baldaccini et al. (Oxford: Hart, 2007), 361–62.

14. Mitsilegas, *The Criminalization of Migration in Europe: Challenges for Human Rights and the Rule of Law* (London: Springer, 2015).

15. Janet Daley, "Without Borders in Europe, There Is No Hope of Ending This Migrant Crisis," *Telegraph*, Sept. 5, 2015, http://www.telegraph.co.uk/news/worldnews/europe/11846760/; Peter Foster, "Migrants' Great Escape to the 'Other' Europe Reveals Stark Divide," *Telegraph*, Sept. 5, 2015, https://www.telegraph. co.uk news/worldnews/europe/eu/11846703/Migrants-great-escape-to-the-other-Europe-reveals-stark-divide.html; Emma Graham-Harrison et al., "Cheering German Crowds Greet Refugees after Long Trek from Budapest to Munich," *Guardian*, Sept. 5, 2015, https://www.theguardian.com/world/2015/sep/05/refugee-crisis-warm-welcome-for-people-bussed-from-budapest; Ian Traynor, "Refugee Crisis: East and

West Split as Leaders Resent Germany for Waiving Rules," *Guardian*, Sept. 5, 2015, https://www.theguardian.com/world/2015/sep/05/migration-crisis-europe-leaders-blame-brussels-hungary-germany.

16. Antiterrorism and Effective Death Penalty Act of 1996, Pub L. No. 104-132, 440, 110 Stat, 1276–77.

17. Illegal Immigration Reform and Immigrant Responsibility Act of 1996, Pub. L. No. 104-208, 321, 110 Stat. 3009, 3009-627 [amending INA 101(a)(43), 8, U.S.C. 1101(a (43)].

18. Stumpf, "Crimmigration Crisis," 367–419; César Cuauhtémoc Garcia Hernandez. "Creating Crimmigration," *Brigham Young University Law Review* 6, (2013): 1457–1516; Kevin R. Johnson, "Race Matters: Immigration Law and Policy Scholarship, Law in the Ivory Tower, and the Legal Indifference of the Race Critique," *University of Illinois Law Review* 3 (2000): 525–58.

19. Doris Marie Provine, Monica W. Varsanyi, Paul G. Lewis, and Scott H. Decker, *Policing Immigrants: Local Law Enforcement on the Frontlines* (Chicago: University of Chicago Press, 2018).

20. USA PATRIOT Act (U.S.H.R. 3262, Public Law 107-56).

21. Robert Koulish, *Immigration and American Democracy: Subverting the Rule of Law* (London: Routledge, 2010); Cole 2003.

22. Ibid.

23. Doris Meissner, Donald M. Kerwin, Muzaffar Chishti, and Claire Bergeron, "Immigration Enforcement in the United States," *Migration Policy Institute* (2013), https://www.migrationpolicy.org/research/immigration-enforcement-united-states-rise-formidable-machinery.

24. Veena Das and Deborah Poole, *Anthropology in the Margins of the State* (Sante Fe: School of American Research Press, 2004); Giorgio Agamben, *Homo Sacer: Sovereign Power and Bare Life* (Bloomington, Calif.: Stanford University Press, 1998); Peter Fitzpatrick. "Bare Sovereignty: Homo Sacer and the Insistence of Law," *Theory & Event* 5, no. 2 (2001).

25. A. C. Thompson. "Inside the Secret Border Patrol Facebook Group Where Agents Joke about Migrant Deaths and Post Sexist Memes," *Propublica*, July 1, 2019.

26. Katja Franko Aas and Mary Bosworth, *The Borders of Punishment: Migration, Citizenship and Social Exclusion* (Oxford: Oxford University Press, 2013; Ana Aliverti, "Making People Criminal: The Role of the Criminal Law in Immigration Enforcement," *Theoretical Criminology* 16, no. 4 (2012): 417–34; Bosworth, Franko, and Sharon Pickering, "Punishment, Globalization and Migration Control: 'Get Them the Hell out of Here,'" *Punishment & Society* 20, no. 1 (2017): 34–53; van der Woude, Barker, and van Der Leun, "Crimmigration in Europe," *European Journal of Criminology* 14, no. 1 (2017): 3–6; Dean Wilson and Weber, "Surveillance, Risk and Pre-emption on the Australian Border," *Surveillance & Society* 5 (2002): 124–41; Mark Noferi and Koulish, "The Immigration Detention Risk Assessment," *Georgetown Immigration Law Review* 29, no. 45 (2014); Aas, "Bordered Penality: Precarious Membership and Abnormal Justice," *Punishment & Society* 16 (2014):

520–41; Barker, "Penal Power at the Border," 441–57; Didier Bigo, "Security and Immigration: Toward a Critique of the Governmentality of Unease," *Alternatives: Global, Local, Political* 27 (2002): 63–92; Aliverti, "Making People Criminal," 417–34; Weber and Pickering, *Globalization and Borders: Death at the Frontier* (London: Palgrave, 2011); Koulish, "Blackwater and the Privatization of Immigration Control," *Saint Thomas Law Review* (2008); Bigo, "Security, Exception, Ban, and Surveillance," in *Theorizing Surveillance: The Panopticon and Beyond*, ed. D. Lyon (Devon, UK: Uffculme Willan, 2011; Bigo, "Security and Immigration," 63–92.

27. Barker, "Global Mobility and Penal Order: Criminalizing Migration, A View from Europe," *Sociology Compass* 6 (2012): 113–21; Barker, "Democracy and Deportation: Why Membership Matters Most," in *The Borders of Punishment: Migration, Citizenship and Social Exclusion*, ed. Aas and Bosworth (Oxford: Oxford University Press, 2013): 237–54; Bosworth, *Inside Immigration Detention* (Oxford: Oxford University Press, 2014).

28. Stumpf, "Crimmigration Crisis," 367–419.

29. Stephen H. Legomsky, "The New Path of Immigration Law: Asymmetric Incorporation of Criminal Justice Norms," *Washington & Lee Law Review* 64 (2007): 469.

30. Aas, "Bordered Penality," 520–41.

31. Also see Leanne Weber and Benjamin Bowling, "Valiant Beggars and Global Vagabonds: Select, Eject, Immobilize." *Theoretical Criminology* 12, no. 3 (2008): 355–75; Synnøve Ugelvik and Thomas Ugelvik, "Immigration Control in Ultima Thule: Detention and Exclusion, Norwegian Style," *European Journal of Criminology* 10, no. 6 (2013): 709–24.

32. Alessandro De Giorgi, "Immigration Control, Post-Fordism, and Less Eligibility: A Materialist Critique of the Criminalization of Immigration across Europe," *Punishment & Society* 12, no. 2 (2010): 147–67; Nicholas de Genova, "The Deportation Regime: Sovereignty, Space, and the Freedom of Movement," in *The Deportation Regime: Sovereignty Space and the Freedom of Movement*, ed. Nicholas de Genova and Nathalie Peutz (Durham, N.C.: Duke University Press, 2010); Kitty Calavita, *Immigration at the Margins: Law, Race, and Exclusion in Southern Europe* (New York: Cambridge University Press, 2005).

33. David Garland, *The Culture of Control: Crime and Social Order in Contemporary Society* (Chicago: Chicago University Press, 2001); Emma Bell, *Criminal Justice and Neoliberalism* (Basingstoke: Palgrave Macmillan, 2011).

34. Weber and McCulloch, "Penal Power and Border Control," 4–5; Mary Fan, "The Case for Crimmigration Reform," *North Carolina Law Review* 92, no. 1 (2013): 74–148; Weber, *Policing Non-Citizens* (Abingdon: Routledge, 2013); Aas, "'Crimmigrant' Bodies and Bona Fide Travellers: Surveillance, Citizenship and Global Governance," *Theoretical Criminology* 15, no. 3 (2011): 331–46; Alvierti, "Making People Criminal," 417–34; Katherine Beckett and Heather Evans, "Crimmigration at the Local Level: Criminal Case Processing in the Shadow of Deportation," *Law and Society Review* 49, no. 1 (2015): 241–77.

35. Bosworth and Mhairi Guild, "Governing through Migration Control: Security and Citizenship in Britain," *British Journal of Criminology* 48, no. 6 (2008): 703–19, https://doi.org/10.1093/bjc/azn059.

36. Anthony D. Smith, *Nationalism: Theory, Ideology, History* (John Wiley & Sons, 2013), 147.

37. Rebecca Mendelsohn, "The European Refugee Crisis: Nationalist Backlashes within the European Union," *MJUR* 7 (2017): 150–76.

38. Ernest Gellner and John Breuilly, *Nations and Nationalism* (Ithaca, N.Y.: Cornell University Press, 2008); Kuang-Hao Hou, "Synthesising Gellner, Smith, and Barth: Building a Preliminary Analytical Framework for Exploring the Relationships between Ethnic Groups, Nations, and Nationalism," *Asian Ethnicity* 14, no. 4 (2013): 471.

39. Smith, *Nationalism and Modernism* (London: Routledge, 2003).

40. Thomas Greven, "The Rise of Right-Wing Populism in Europe and the United States," *Friedrich Ebert Foundation* (2016): 1–11, https://www.fesdc.org/fileadmin/user_upload/publications/RightwingPopulism.pdf.

41. Jens Rydgren, "France: The Front National, Ethnonationalism, and Populism," in *Twenty-First Century Populism*, ed. Daniele Albertazzi and Duncan McDonnell (London: Palgrave MacMillan, 2008); Cas Mudde, *The Populist Zeitgeist: Government and Opposition* (London: Cambridge University Press, 2004).

42. Anthony Bottoms, "Philosophy and Politics of Punishment and Sentencing," in *Politics of Sentencing Reform*, ed. Chris Clarkson and Rod Morgan (Oxford: Oxford University Press, 1995).

43. Ibid., 40.

44. John Pratt, *Penal Populism* (London: Routledge, 2007).

45. J. V. Roberts, L. J. Stalans, D. Indermaur, and M. Hough, *Penal Populism and Public Opinion: Lessons from Five Countries* (New York: Oxford University Press, 2003); Jonathan Simon, *Governing through Crime: How the War on Crime Transformed American Democracy and Created a Culture of Fear* (London: Oxford University Press, 2006); John Pratt, "When Penal Populism Stops: Legitimacy, Scandal and the Power to Punish in New Zealand, Australian and New Zealand," *Journal of Criminology* (2008), http://www.highbeam.com/doc/1G1-190794149.html; van der Woude, "Dutch Counterterrorism: An Exceptional Body of Legislation or Just an Inevitable Product of the Culture of Control?," in *The State of Exception and Militant Democracy in a Time of Terror*, ed. Afshin Ellian and Gelijn Molier (Dordrecht: Republic of Letters Publishing, 2012), 69–95.

46. Bosworth and Guild, "Governing through Migration Control: Security and Citizenship in Britain," 703–19, https://doi.org/10.1093/bjc/azn059.

47. Simon, *Governing through Crime.*

48. Tim Reeskens and Wim van Oorschot, "Disentangling the 'New Liberal Dilemma': On the Relation between General Welfare Redistribution Preferences and Welfare Chauvinism," *International Journal of Comparative Sociology* 53, no. 2 (2012): 120–39; Willem de Koster, Peter Achterberg, and Jeroen van der Waal, "The

New Right and the Welfare State: The Electoral Relevance of Welfare Chauvinism and Welfare Populism in the Netherlands," *International Political Science Review* 34, no. 1 (2013): 3–20, https://doi.org/10.1177/0192512112455443.

49. Mendelsohn, "European Refugee Crisis," 150–76.

50. Lynne Haney, "Prisons of the Past: Penal Nationalism and the Politics of Punishment in Central Europe," *Punishment & Society* 18, no. 3 (2016): 346–68, https://doi.org/10.1177/ 1462474516645686.

51. Barker, *Nordic Nationalism and Penal Order.*

52. Paul Hazard, *La crise de la conscience européenne, 1680–1715* (Paris: Fayard, 1989).

53. Ernest Gellner and John Breuilly. *Nations and Nationalism* (London: Taylor & Francis 1993); Craig Calhoun, *Nationalism and Cultures of Democracy* (Durham, N.C.: Duke University Press, 2007).

54. John F. Kennedy, *Nation of Immigrants* (New York: Harper Collins, 1964).

55. Rogers Brubaker, "The Manichean Myth: Rethinking the Distinction between 'Civic' and 'Ethnic' Nationalism," in *Nation and National Identity*, ed. Hanspeter Kriesel, Klaus Armingeon, Hannes Slegrist, and Andreas Wimmer (Zürich: Verlag Rüegger, 1999); Noah Pickus, *True Faith and Allegiance: Immigration and American Civic Nationalism* (Princeton, N.J.: Princeton University Press, 2009).

56. Alexis De Tocqueville, *Democracy in America*, ed. Eduardo Nolla (Chicago: University of Chicago Press, 2012).

57. De Tocqueville, *The Old Regime and the Revolution* (New York: Harper & Brothers, 1983); Robert D. Putnam, *Bowling Alone: The Collapse and Revival of American Community* (New York: Simon & Schuster, 2000).

58. Seymour Martin Lipset, *Political Man: The Social Bases of Politics* (Baltimore: Johns Hopkins University Press, 1981).

59. John Higham, *Strangers in the Land: Patterns of American Nativism 1860–1925* (New Brunswick, N.J.: Rutgers University Press, 2002).

60. Christine Harrison, *Combatting Nativism: Protecting the Rights of Immigrants* (Montgomery, Ala.: Southern Poverty Law Center, 2019).

61. Ibid.

62. *Trump v. Hawaii*, No. 17-965, 585 U.S._(2018).

63. Bosworth and Guild, "Governing through Migration Control," 703–19.

64. Johnson, "Race Matters," 525–58.

65. Johnson, "Immigration and Latino Identity," *Chicano-Latino Law Review* 19, no. 1 (1998): 197–212; Jennifer M. Chacón and S. B. Coutin, "Racialization through Enforcement," in *Race, Criminal Justice and Migration Control*, ed. Mary Bosworth, Alpa Parmar, and Yolanda Vazquez (Oxford: Oxford University Press, 2018).

66. Francis Pakes, "The Politics of Discontent: The Emergence of a New Criminal Justice Discourse in the Netherlands," *Howard Journal of Criminal Justice* 43, no. 3 (2007): 284–98; Pakes, "The Ebb and Flow of Criminal Justice in the Netherlands," *International Journal of the Sociology of Law* 34 (2009): 141–56.

67. Johnson, "Race Matters," 556.

68. David Perry, "Why Critics Say It's Time to abolish ICE," *Pacific Standard* (2018).

69. Mastoureh Fathi, *Intersectionality, Class and Migration: Narratives of Iranian Women Migrants in the UK* (London: Palgrave Macmillan, 2017).

70. Kimberlé Crenshaw, "Mapping the Margins: Intersectionality, Identity Politics, and Violence against Women of Color," *Stanford Law Review* (1990); Tanja Bastia, "Intersectionality, Migration and Development," *Progress in Development Studies* 14, no. 3 (2014): 237–48; Fathi, *Intersectionality, Class and Migration.*

71. Bosworth, Parmar, and Vasquez, *Race, Criminal Justice, and Migration Control.*

72. Ibid.

73. Amada Armenta, *Protect, Serve, and Deport* (Oakland: University of California Press, 2017); Yolanda Vásquez, "Constructing Crimmigration: Latino Subordination in a 'Post-Racial' World, *Ohio State Law Journal* 76, no. 3 (2015): 600–657.

74. Ibid.

75. Armenta. *Protect, Serve, and Deport.*

76. Steve Garner, "Crimmigration: When Criminology (Nearly) Met the Sociology of Race and Ethnicity," *Sociology of Race and Ethnicity* 1, no. 1 (2015): 198–203.

77. Justin T. Pickett, "On the Social Foundations for Crimmigration: Latino Threat and Support for Expanded Police Powers," *Journal of Quantitative Criminology* 32, no.1 (2016): 103–32.

78. Kevin R. Johnson, "Roll Over Beethoven: "A Critical Examination of Recent Writing About Race," *Texas Law Review* 82, no. 3 (2003): 717–34.

79. Wendy Brown, *Walled States, Waning Sovereignty* (New York: Zone, 2010).

80. Susanne Krasmann, "The Enemy on the Border: Critique of a Programme in Favour of a Preventative State," *Punishment & Society* 9, no. 9 (2007): 301–18.

I

Border Criminologies

1

Insecurity Syndrome

The Challenges of Trump's Carceral State

Tony Platt

> The illegality that is supposedly to be eradicated becomes the *raison d'etre* of the security apparatus and enters into the "insecurity syndrome" that affects the entire state.
>
> —ÉTIENNE BALIBAR, 2004

By April 2018, the Trump administration had managed to accomplish a difficult task: be tougher on immigration policy than the Obama administration.

In the first quarter of 2017, arrests in the United States by Immigration and Customs Enforcement (ICE) agents working for the Department of Homeland Security (DHS) increased by 37 percent over the previous year. Given the fear of surprise raids and reluctance to trust public officials, the families of undocumented immigrants became much more hesitant to report crime, especially sexual assaults and domestic violence, and to attend public events since the election of Donald Trump. There are reports of immigrants getting rounded up while dropping off children at school. Church attendance has dropped. "People leave their loved ones in the emergency room and run away," said the chief executive of a hospital in New York. In Atlanta, where immigration-related arrests increased by 40 percent in 2017, many immigrants have stopped driving their cars for fear of being stopped for petty infractions. In California, where 80 percent of agricultural workers are undocumented Mexicans, paranoia is a requisite for survival: people live in "a cordon terror," on constant alert for paramilitary squads of ICE agents. "If you're in this country illegally," says the director of Atlanta's DHS office, "you should be scared."[1]

The crackdown on undocumented and documented immigrants accused of petty crimes and infractions in the United States represents a larger trend throughout the West: erosion of social democracy, consolidation of neoliberalism, tightening of borders, and a whiff of fascism. We live in dangerous and uncertain times—the "interregnum" that Antonio Gramsci predicted would unleash a "great variety of morbid symptoms"—and face enormous political, intellectual, and strategic challenges.[2]

Under the auspices of the Cabinet-level Department of Homeland Security, created in 2002 in the wake of September 11 and expanded the following year, American immigration control looks and acts much like a criminal justice operation, but one that is better coordinated and funded, and provides even fewer rights than criminal courts. Incarceration, surveillance, and deportation are now significant components of immigration enforcement. Detention of immigrants increased from about 20,000 in 1961 to an average of 450,000 during the Obama presidency. The number of noncitizens, mostly Mexicans, formally removed from the United States increased sixteen-fold from 1986 to 2012, and there was an unprecedented increase in immigration-related prosecutions.[3]

The annual appropriation by Congress for immigration custody operations grew from $49.3 million in 1982 to more than $2 billion in 2013, mainly to the benefit of private corporations that contract with government agencies to build and run detention centers.[4] In addition, the DHS sends billions of dollars to regional and local governments for "terrorism prevention." The Senate's vote in June 2013 to "secure the border" included an allocation of $30 billion to double the number of Border Patrol agents, a "staggering figure," notes political scientist Marie Gottschalk, "roughly equal to what all fifty states together spend on corrections each year, or approximately seven times the annual budget of the federal Bureau of Prisons."[5]

The presidential campaign of 2016 was the occasion for a nasty and rancorous argument about immigration, crime, and race. Trump successfully mobilized a coalition of old guard conservatives, evangelical organizations, neo-nationalists, and government functionaries working as police, guards, and immigration enforcers to fight back against an imagined enemy of terrorists, black anarchists, and violent Mexicans in the same way that Richard Nixon in 1969 had framed the Sixties as an assault on traditional American values. In one of many reckless speeches, Donald Trump implied to a crowd in Wilmington, North Carolina, that gun owners might need to take matters into their own trigger fingers if Hillary Clinton became president and appointed judges opposed to the Second Amendment.[6] "Stop and frisk worked very well in New

York. It brought the crime rate way down," claimed Trump without a shred of evidence at the first presidential debate. "We have gangs roaming the street. And in many cases, they're illegal immigrants. And they have guns. And they shoot people"[7] The Obama administration had been responsible for allowing "border deaths, narco-terrorists, and waves of violent illegal criminals into America," said Trump with, as usual, no facts to back up the claim. In fact, the rate of violent crime is lower than it was in the 1980s, and New York's murder rate is the lowest it has been in decades.[8]

Trump made no effort during his campaign to incorporate liberal motifs into his rhetoric or make nuanced concessions to the complexity of policy. Those who wanted to curb police lawlessness and racism were promoting "a war on our police," he said. "The attacks on our police, and the terrorism in our cities, threaten our very way of life. Any politician who does not grasp this danger is not fit to lead this country."[9]

The Trump platform openly adopted rhetoric and imagery that smacked of classical fascism and an apocalyptic vision of the United States facing "the possibility of economic and social upheaval" caused by "an economic crash like we've seen before" or a terroristic attack that "would turn Manhattan into Hiroshima II." He articulated a politics of anti-politics that called for draining Washington, D.C., of "career politicians" and a hyperbolic characterization of the United States as "the world's whipping boy," treated like a "punching bag" by China. His call to revive the grandeur of a mythic past emphasized that American borders and patriotism were under attack and that a masculinist revolt against American "spinelessness" and emasculation was required. Trump flayed the "established media" while exploiting its fascination with the candidate's flamboyant style, creatively using visual culture and spectacles to evoke *the people* and make his political supporters feel as though they were insiders participating in their own governance.[10]

During the campaign, Trump regularly characterized the police as beleaguered and "afraid for their jobs, they're afraid of the mistreatment they get," and terrorists as indulged by the Obama administration's weak policies. "I would leave Guantanamo just the way it is, and I would probably fill it up with more people that are looking to kill us."[11]

In November 2016, with Donald Trump elected as president, Republican domination of Congress and state legislatures, appointment of a hardline attorney general who had opposed the most modest prison reforms during the Obama presidency, and a decisive shift to the right in the U.S. Supreme Court, the politics of law and order was back in fashion, not as a regression to the Nixon era, but as a forward-looking shift to a much more explicitly authoritarian use of power. "The problem in our poorest communities," warned

Trump ominously, "is not that there are too many police, the problem is that there are not enough police."[12]

For all that has been said about Trump's mercurial and narcissistic temperament, his impetuosity and grandstanding, and his tendency to opportunistically scavenge a political philosophy from discarded ideologies, his views about immigration, criminal justice, welfare, and race are long-standing and quite consistent.

In his 2011 book *Time to Get Tough*, which was geared toward a political campaign—"A great leader can bring America together"—Trump made immigrants, particularly Mexican immigrants, synonymous with a propensity for criminality, again the evidence be damned. There was nothing subtle about the argument. Why, he asked, "have we suddenly become an annex of Mexico's prison system?" He called for a crackdown on undocumented immigrants during the Obama administration's unprecedented crackdown on immigrants, which broke all records for rounding up people whose visas had expired and deporting those with criminal records. "We should not let ourselves become the dumping ground for other countries' undesirables," proclaimed Trump while the Obama administration set up special courts to speed up the process of detaining and criminalizing people who tried to enter the country illegally. Desperate to find a tiny difference with Obama's immigration policies, Trump objected to the "resort-like accommodations" in detention centers where people awaiting a deportation hearing were offered health and welfare classes, movie nights, and bingo. Such soft, sentimental liberalism was making the United States into a "laughingstock."[13]

Under the Trump administration, ICE agents became emboldened to round up folks who had committed minor criminal infractions or violated immigration laws. "Before, we used to be told, 'You can't arrest those people,' said a ten-year veteran. "Now those people are priorities again. And there are a lot of them here."[14] The administrative machinery, thanks to the previous government, was in place and ready to. Obama had given the go-ahead to more than three million deportations in the hope that this concession to the Right would prompt Congress to pass comprehensive immigration reform and create a path to citizenship for many undocumented immigrants. When this failed, "he worked," notes Julia Preston of the Marshall Project, "to restrain the deportations machine his administration had created." Obama directed ICE to give priority to persons accused of serious crimes and those involved in border violations. All that the Trump administration needed to do was shift ICE's priorities, with noncriminal cases getting the same attention as criminal cases. Trump's orders, as the *New York Times* noted, "expanded prosecutorial priorities so broadly that, as a practical matter, there no longer exist any priorities at all."[15]

Workers snared in immigration enforcement have almost no legal recourse because the government is not obligated to provide attorneys. Nonprofit organizations are overwhelmed by massive caseloads. Immigrants rounded up in the San Joaquin Valley, for example, end up in the privately owned Mesa Verde prison, where they receive a perfunctory video hearing in a Sacramento court before being deported.[16]

One of Trump's first decisions was to sign an executive order that banned immigration for ninety days from seven majority-Muslim countries: Iran, Iraq, Libya, Somalia, Sudan, Syria, and Yemen. It suspended the admission of Syrian refugees indefinitely and all other refugees for 120 days. The purpose of this order was supposedly to evaluate and strengthen vetting procedures against potential terrorists. It potentially involved revocation of between 60,000 and 100,000 visas, depending on estimates by different government officials.

In June 2017, the U.S. Supreme Court ruled partially in favor of the government and reversed a decision issued by a lower court, though it restricted the policy to "foreign nationals who lack any bona fide relationship with a person or entity in the United States." The court's decision led to months of administrative and legal squabbling about who was and was not eligible for entry into the United States. By early 2018, the Trump administration received judicial approval to ban entry to the United States of most individuals from Chad, Iran, Libya, North Korea, and Syria and to increase the level of vetting of applicants from Somalia and Venezuela, but several state governments and civil liberties organizations continued to challenge specific elements of the ban. Moreover, many federal judges intervened to slow down the implementation of executive orders. Beneficiaries included Indonesian Christians in New Jersey, Somalis in Florida, and some 700,000 "dreamers"—immigrants originally protected by Obama's Deferred Action for Childhood Arrivals (DACA) executive order that Trump rescinded in September 2017.[17]

The long-term threat to civil liberties emanates from changes taking place throughout the carceral state, not only in the nation's immigration policies. While a great deal of attention was being paid to Trump's possible impeachment or removal and to his unvarnished bigotry and bombastic rhetoric, his administration was quickly transforming the appellate levels of the federal judiciary, as well as stimulating a significant shift to the right in legislative policies at the state level. Whether it is a President Trump or President Pence in the White House, everyday criminal justice policies irretrievably hardened, posing an enormous challenge to the progressive movement for the next decade.

Vice President Mike Pence, who was responsible for turning Trump's dystopian vision into mundane policies, rose to national prominence as a congressman (2002–11) and then governor of Indiana. He helped to build the right-wing evangelical Christian base of the Republican Party by campaigning for the restriction of birth control to married women and for criminalization of abortion. In Congress, he made a case for teaching "intelligent design" alongside evolution and became a leader of the far-right caucus. As governor he was an ardent advocate of the Religious Freedom Restoration Act that would have legalized discrimination by businesses against gays and lesbians. A leading proponent of unregulated capitalism, he has close ties to the right-wing Koch brothers, who bankrolled his political career and envisioned him as presidential material. In return, Pence helped to bring into the Trump administration sixteen high-ranking officials with ties to the Kochs.[18]

With Trump's help, the government's strategy regarding the judiciary was to appoint extremists to lifelong positions as federal appellate judges. Mostly conservative white men recommended by the Federalist Society and Heritage Foundation, they included nominees who were rated "not qualified" by the American Bar Association, supported "conversion therapy" for gay youth, described transgender children as part of Satan's plan, and compared *Roe v. Wade* to the *Dredd Scott* decision. For a position on the Eastern District of North Carolina court that has never had an African American judge, the Trump administration nominated Thomas Alvin Farr, who, as a protégé of the notoriously racist senator Jesse Helms, had been active in efforts to suppress black voting rights, in the words of a federal court, with "almost surgical precision." While the publicity generated by these nominations forced several candidates to withdraw from consideration, Trump's appointments represented the most effective stacking of the federal judiciary since the Nixon presidency, potentially shaping legal doctrines for a generation: the twelve regional, federal appeal courts decide some 60,000 cases annually, compared to about eighty heard by the Supreme Court.[19]

At the state level, where the Republican Party in 2017 controlled the governorship in thirty-three states and the governorship and legislatures in twenty-five states, conservative activists moved quickly to pass right-wing policies.[20] The attack on reproductive rights was as widespread as were efforts to expand the right to own guns. State governments also adopted a range of policies that increase punishments for protest and civil disobedience and whittle away what is left of undocumented immigrant rights. Texas passed a ban on sanctuary cities that makes it a crime for police officers to refuse to comply with ICE regulations. Georgia required its Bureau of Investigations to publish a list of all immigrants with criminal records who are released from ICE custody in Georgia. Mississippi passed legislation prohibiting cities or public universities from adopting sanctuary policies that would impede cooperation with federal immigration officials. Tennessee added longer sentences for criminal convictions in cases where the defendant was illegally in the country at the time of the offense and had been previously deported for a criminal offense.[21]

A particularly important trend in state-level carceral politics is the wave of "back the badge" bills that increase penalties for assaulting cops, penalties that include petty assault enhancements that are likely to be used as tools to punish activists. Encouraged by the Heritage Foundation and nationally known right-wing ideologues such as Edwin Meese and Bernard Kerik to go after Black Lives Matter groups, many states passed "blue lives matter" legislation: designating attacks on police as hate crimes in Kentucky; imposing a life sentence without parole for the murder of an officer in Mississippi; trying juveniles aged thirteen or older as adults for assaults on police in Georgia; and extending prison sentences for crimes against police in Arkansas, Utah, Nevada, Kansas, North Dakota, and South Dakota. Similarly, Oklahoma, in response to the Dakota Access Pipeline protests, significantly increased penalties for trespass or vandalism against refineries, pipelines, and oil- and gas-processing plants.[22]

These laws provide county and state prosecutors with additional tools to coerce protestors into accepting plea deals and to increase the punishment of those who unsuccessfully try to fight charges. The message of this swath of legislation is clear: don't organize, don't protest, and don't cause trouble.

Democratic Party gains in the 2018 mid-term elections may slow down, but not reverse, the consolidation of hardline criminal justice and immigration policies, many of which were created or endorsed by Democrats, from Johnson to Obama. Moreover, the First Step Act, widely celebrated as a bipartisan reform of the federal prison system, will benefit only a fraction of prisoners nationwide and excludes 11,000 prisoners convicted of violating immigration laws, overwhelmingly for nonviolent crimes.[23]

The challenges we face are extensive and go far beyond racialized immigration policies and unregulated police power. We need a broad understanding of what constitutes the carceral state and a deep historical framework.

What is called the *criminal justice system* is inextricably linked to a much more expansive set of institutions that incorporates a complex network of agencies and operations, public and private, and incorporates unregulated, transnational homeland security operations and brutalist maximum-security prisons, punitive public welfare regulations, and social engineering campaigns carried out in the name of nation-building.

Today, private police perform exactly the same functions as public police, either as subcontracted by government agencies or as the direct employees of industries, businesses, malls, and middle-class communities. Security workers outnumber public police by more than 25 percent, and security companies are the recipients of government contracts that far exceed the amount of public money spent on criminal justice operations nationally.

The line between agencies of social control and service institutions is often blurred. Public schools, for example, now incorporate security measures into their routine functioning, while prisons and jails increasingly incorporate medical and psychological techniques into the work of guarding. American public welfare puts millions of women and children into a limbo between desperate poverty and a criminalized status and condemns millions of former prisoners to civil death.[24]

Criminal justice institutions, whether narrowly or expansively defined, do not monopolize the job of social control. The millions of people who come under their purview do not stay put in police cells, criminal courts, reformatories, jails, and prisons. They also are subject to discipline in schools and punishment on welfare; stopped and frisked, entered into data banks, corralled on the streets, and herded out of malls and city centers; deported across borders, and locked away in military prisons, black sites, and refugee camps; and engaged in resistance, from hunger strikes in prison to street protests urgently demanding that *Black Lives Matter*.

Punishment is not a single, decisive act with clear parameters and time limits. The arrestee, the incarcerated, the suspect, the welfare recipient, and the deportee are subject to an unfolding process in which they become a category of person to be followed, tracked, documented, and constantly made visible, as if they had a blazon attached to their clothes or a tattoo permanently imprinted on their body.[25]

The carceral state is not only a mopping-up operation, limited to managing social outcasts and a specific population of law-breakers at the margins of society. It also plays a critically important role in legitimating and preserving inequality, criminalizing opposition movements, and backing up democratic institutions with fiercely repressive power as needed during regular periods of exceptional emergencies. State violence is a routine and regular phenomenon of governance. It is not by accident that social groups defined as politically dangerous or economically expendable are also perceived as hotbeds of criminality and overrepresented in arrest, conviction, incarceration, and deportation statistics.[26]

The routine processing of individuals through the criminal justice system and extraordinary actions against a whole group of people on the basis of their collective dangerousness, foreignness, or expendability are mutually reinforcing: populations targeted for collective punishment are invariably demonized as dangerous and contaminated. Take, for example, the case of Mexicans and Mexican Americans who today are the primary target of deportations and immigrant detention. In 2010, Mexicans accounted for nearly three-quarters of all deportations, with nationals from Guatemala, Honduras, and El Salvador accounting for another 15 percent.[27] The majority of almost 420,000 deportees in 2012 had either no criminal record or had committed traffic and minor drug offenses. "When you have more than a thousand people deported every day," observes sociologist Tanya Maria Golash-Boza, "that's a policy of mass deportation."[28]

Latinos in the United States have always been disproportionately arrested and incarcerated in local jails and state prisons and disproportionately detained and prosecuted for violations of immigration law. In addition to previous, large-scale importations and deportations of Mexicans and Central Americans—the so-called *repatriation* campaign of the 1930s, *Operation Wetback* in 1954, and millions swept up by the Department of Homeland Security since September 11—Mexicans were routinely targeted by mob violence from the Gold Rush through the 1920s, especially in the wake of a war against Mexico (1846–48) that made Mexicans strangers in their own land. During this period, 547 cases of lynching have been documented, a *per capita* rate comparable to the lynching of African Americans.[29] In the early twentieth century, federal and state authorities regularly linked crime and marijuana use with the "Mexican problem."[30]

From 1950 to 1960, under a contract ratified by the Mexican and U.S. governments, almost 3.5 million *braceros* were recruited to work temporarily as a migrant labor force in Texas, California, New Mexico, Arizona, and Arkansas. Integrated into the economy, they were socially isolated and politically marginalized and subjected to carceral living conditions: barns, stables, warehouses, garages, and mosquito-infested bogs were turned into fetid camps; contractors price-gouged workers for food and other services; travel outside camps and workplaces was restricted; and those who complained were likely to be labeled communists and sent home. "The picture of the ideal worker drawn by managers of migration," noted Ernesto Galarza in his groundbreaking investigation, "was that of the man of the barracks, the man in a camp who spent all of his time under supervision if not under surveillance. . . . Outside the barracks the limits of freedom were prescribed, and they were also the limits of the job."[31]

There are efforts under way in Congress to revive the *bracero* program and import a pool of some two million "guest workers" from Mexico. They would not be allowed to bring family members with them; if fired, they would be deported at their own expense without legal recourse. If legislation sponsored by Representative Bob Goodlatte (Virginia) passes, it will facilitate an accelerated campaign against undocumented immigrants, most of whom have lived in the United States for decades, as well as institutionalize the exploitation of second-class agricultural workers.

Today, Latinos are over-represented in the state prisons of Arizona, California, Colorado, Mississippi, Nebraska, New Jersey, New Mexico, Oregon, Pennsylvania, Utah, and Washington. They are jailed at five times the rate of white defendants in New York, and are about 35 percent of all federal prisoners and almost 50 percent of all federal defendants. In 2012, Latino men were about 88 percent of all immigrants sentenced for immigration-related crimes.[32] When you add the millions of Mexicans who have been subjected to deportation without due process and victimized by mob violence, detention, and incarceration, it is a massive number, comparable in rate and proportion to the experiences of African Americans.

The use of extraordinary legislation and emergency laws to target problematic and potentially dangerous populations long preceded the post–September 11 counter-terrorism measures. The liberal rule of law has always coexisted with selective authoritarianism. Now it is normal practice.[33]

The shift to the right under the Trump administration is real, the construction of authoritarian measures in the works. But we are not yet under the gaze of an omniscient panopticon administered by a centralized system of command and control. We certainly live in ominous and messy times, but the carceral state is rife with political and legal fissures and is by no means a closed system. While it is indeed extensive, multifaceted, and resourceful, it is also full of tensions and internal conflicts, more like Kafka's self-imploding penal colony than Orwell's Big Brother.

As of January 2019, the president is in a battle with the FBI, has fired his own handpicked attorney general, and is under investigation by the Justice Department. The federal judiciary is by no means united in support of Trump's immigration policies. Libertarian Republicans and liberal Democrats continue to advocate a reduction in mass imprisonment, despite the Department of Justice's calls for longer prison sentences in response to an imagined surging crime rate and "rise in vicious gangs."[34]

Some police chiefs resisted Trump's order to crack down on undocumented immigrants and refugees protected by sanctuary cities. "We are not going to work in conjunction with Homeland Security on deportation efforts," said Los Angeles police chief Charlie Beck shortly after Trump was elected president. "That is not our job, nor will I make it our job." When the mayor of Oakland, California, warned community-based organizations that an immigrant raid was impending, ICE's acting director called it a "reckless decision" and likened Libby Schaaf to a "gang lookout yelling 'Police!'"[35]

Clearly, the Trump victory represented a right-wing politics in ascendancy and an ideology confirming Paul Gilroy's insight that "the heritage of fascist rule survives inside democracy as well as outside it," but we must be careful not to see "fascism everywhere" or conflate Trump's right-wing populism with a consolidated authoritarian state. Trump has more in common with George Patton, the right-wing American general who was considering a plunge into politics at the time of his death in 1945, than with Hitler; and with Jesse Ventura, the former wrestler and entertainer who made a successful run on the Reform Party ticket for governor of Minnesota in 1993, than with Mussolini. It was Ventura who prompted Trump to first aspire to political office. "Nonpoliticians like Ventura are the wave of the future," he wrote in 2000.[36]

Persistent inequality, a right-wing government in ascendancy, tensions within ruling and economic elites, and widespread malaise and resistance will again give us many opportunities to express a vision of social justice and organize opposition. And when there are political openings, we need to be ready with a strategy and concrete ideas.

In this chaotic moment, dystopian ideas flourish. "Not since Watergate," observes Mike Davis, "has so much uncertainty and potential disorder infected every institution, network, and power relationship." Though our era is reminiscent of previous defeats and setbacks, what historian Leon Litwack described as the "terrifying sense of personal betrayal and anguish" that accompanies the crashing of great hopes, the past does not precisely reproduce itself, and regression is not inevitable.[37]

In 1967, Noam Chomsky urged intellectuals to ask, "What have I done . . . to create, or mouth, or tolerate the deceptions that will be used to justify the next defense of freedom."[38] Chomsky's context was what the Vietnamese call the American War, but the question is equally applicable to our moment in history. Many leading intellectuals have played key roles in beefing up state power and modernizing policing and security. There was the University of Chicago's Morris Janowitz calling for police to undergo "realistic training in sharpshooting and precision firing"; a group of "realists," led by James Q. Wilson, Donald Trump's favorite criminologist, making it possible for urban police to penetrate the everyday lives of impoverished communities through "broken windows" policies; and neo-liberals who helped presidents from Johnson to Reagan to transform a "war on poverty" into a "a war on crime."[39]

Too many of our colleagues were not only complicit in the carceral state, but also were among its architects and propagandists: they came up with rationales for police killings, designed stackable bunks and windowless cells for prisons, debated whether drugs or the electric chair or firing squads are the most humane way to kill people on death row, and devised techniques to identify potential terrorists by separating, as a right-wing think tank puts it, "the trustworthy cooperators from the non-cooperators."[40]

Recent events suggest that social activism and organized opposition can have far-ranging impact on carceral institutions that always bend to the arc of power, but are vulnerable to movements from below.[41] It was, for example, collectively planned hunger strikes by isolated, degraded, and demonized prisoners, held in solitary confinement for decades in a remote hellhole of a prison in northern California, that forced prison officials in 2015 to negotiate a reduction in cruel and usual punishments.[42] It was widespread opposition to police killings of African Americans (*not* the killings themselves that have happened regularly and routinely for more than a hundred years) that forced federal and local governments to hold hearings and issue reports on how to make the police more accountable during the Obama administration. It was highly localized, often spontaneous street protests that quickly segued into a Black Lives Matter movement that could command a meeting with a president and issue a manifesto of political demands.[43]

For academics in the United States who think of ourselves as activists and public intellectuals, this is the moment we need to seize. But we have a great deal to do in terms of repairing our relationships with progressive organizations and movements. It will not be easy to recover trust. Intellectuals routinely operate as public intellectuals—as talking heads in the media, op-ed writers, expert witnesses, and government consultants—but rarely as participants in or collaborators with activist social movements and left political parties. There are too few intellectuals such as Edward Said who made the case that "the proper attitude of the intellectual outside the academy is some sort of defiance."[44]

In order to rebuild a relationship with new movements for social justice, we need to excavate our own institutional history and understand the role played by academics and professionals in promoting the *fear of crime* and constructing a carceral state that stretches from interrogation techniques used in Iraq to ICE raids on undocumented immigrants.

Doing work that is historically grounded and interdisciplinary and that illuminates the less-than-obvious will go a long way to restoring trust. It is up to us to demonstrate that we can be socially useful in our work and that we can be cooperative both within academia and with communities and organizations fighting for social justice. We need to be alert to the unequal relationships of power between intellectual and subject; give as much attention to the social contexts of our work as we do to our disciplinary skills; and make sure that the products of our work are used in politically and ethically responsible ways. And let's not forget cultivating an attitude of defiance.

Notes

Epigraph: Étienne Balibar, *We, the People of Europe! Reflections on Transnational Citizenship* (Princeton: Princeton University Press, 2004), 62.

1. "Feature: 100 Days of ICE," Immigration and Customs Enforcement, United States Department of Homeland Security, 2017, https://www.ice.gov/features/100-days?ex_cid=trumpbeat; Michael Greenberg, "In the Valley of Fear," *New York Review of Books* (December 20, 2018); Caitlin Dickerson, "Immigration Arrests Rise Sharply as Trump Mandate Is Carried Out," *New York Times* (May 17, 2017).

2. Antonio Gramsci, *Selections from the Prison Notebooks*, ed. Quintin Hoare and Geoffrey Nowell Smith (New York: International Publishers, 1971), 276; Zygmunt Bauman, "Times of Interregnum," *Ethics and Global Politics* 5, no. 1 (2012): 49–56.

3. Anil Kalhan, "Immigration Surveillance," *Maryland Law Review* 74, no. 1 (2014): 1–86; Juliet Stumpf, "The Crimmigration Crisis: Immigrants, Crime, and Sovereign Power," *American University Law Review* 56, no. 2 (2006): 367–419; Marie Gottschalk, *Caught: The Prison State and the Lockdown of American Politics* (Princeton: Princeton University Press, 2015), chapter 10; Kalhan, "Rethinking Immigration Detention," *Columbia Law Review Sidebar* 110 (July 21, 2010): 42–58.

4. "DHS Announces Grant Allocations for Fiscal Year (FY) 2015 Preparedness Grants," Department of Homeland Security Press Office, July 28, 2015; Torrie Hester, "Deportability and the Carceral State," *Journal of American History* 102, no. 1 (2015): 150.

5. Gottschalk, *Caught*, 237.

6. Nick Corasaniti and Maggie Haberman, "Trump Suggests Gun Owners Act against Clinton," *New York Times* (August 10, 2016).

7. Lucy McBath, speech at National Democratic Convention, July 26, 2016, http://time.com/4424704/dnc-mothers-movement-transcript-speech-video/; Aaron Blake, "The First Trump-Clinton Presidential Debate Transcript, Annotated," *Washington Post* (September 26, 2016), https://www.washingtonpost.com/news/the-fix/wp/2016/09/26/the-first-trump-clinton-presidential-debate-transcript-annotated/?utm_term=.6cba763651bf.

8. Donald J. Trump, *Time to Get Tough: Making America #1 Again* (Washington, D.C.: Regnery, 2011), 143; Ashley Southall, "New York Crime Plunges to Level Unseen Since '50s," *New York Times* (December 28, 2017).

9. Donald Trump's speech to the Republican National Convention (July 21, 2016), http://www.politico.com/story/2016/07/full-transcript-donald-trump-nomination-acceptance-speech-at-rnc-225974; Donald Trump, "Full Text: Donald Trump Campaign Speech in Wisconsin" (August 17, 2016), http://www.politico.com/story/2016/08/full-text-donald-trumps-speech-on-227095.

10. Trump, *Time to Get Tough*, 2, 3, 7; Trump, *The America We Deserve* (Los Angeles: Renaissance, 2000), 19, 25, 26; Paul Gilroy, *Against Race: Imagining Political Culture Beyond the Color Line* (Cambridge, Mass.: Harvard University Press, 2000), 156.

11. Trump, *Time to Get Tough*, 137; Trump, *America We Deserve*, 110, 242, 260; "Transcript of the New Hampshire GOP Debate, Annotated," *Washington Post* (February 6, 2016), https://www.washingtonpost.com/news/the-fix/wp/2016/02/06/transcript-of-the-feb-6-gop-debate-annotated/; Alexander Bolton, "Trump Calls for More Prisoners in Gitmo," *The Hill* (December 19, 2015), http://thehill.com/blogs/ballot-box/gop-primaries/263809-trump-calls-for-more-prisoners-in-gitmo.

12. Trump, "Full Text: Donald Trump Campaign Speech in Wisconsin" (August 17, 2016), http://www.politico.com/story/2016/08/full-text-donald-trumps-speech-on-227095.

13. Trump, *Time to Get Tough*, 136, 137, 174, 149–51.

14. Nicholas Kulish, Caitlin Dickerson, and Ron Nixon, "Agents Discover a New Freedom on Deportations," *New York Times* (February 26, 2017); Maria Sacchetti, "Immigration Arrests Soar Under Trump; Sharpest Spike Seen for Noncriminals," *Washington Post* (May 17, 2017).

15. Julia Preston, "Trump: The New Deportation Threat," *New York Review of Books* (May 25–2017): 8–12; Vivian Yee, "As Arrests Surge, Immigrants Fear Even Driving," *New York Times* (November 26, 2017).

16. Greenberg, "In the Valley of Fear."

17. *Per Curiam* opinion of U.S. Supreme Court, *International Refugee Assistance Project v. Trump* and *Hawaii v. Trump* (June 26, 2017); Michael D. Shear and Adam Liptak, "Supreme Court Takes Up Travel Ban Case, and Allows Parts to Go Ahead," *New York Times* (June 26, 2017); White House, *Executive Order Protecting the Nation from Foreign Terrorist Entry Into the United States* (January 27, 2017), https://www.whitehouse.gov/presidential-actions/executive-order-protecting-nation-foreign-terrorist-entry-united-states/; The White House, *Executive Order Protecting the Nation from Foreign Terrorist Entry into the United States*, March 6, 2017, https://www.whitehouse.gov/presidential-actions/executive-order-protecting-nation-foreign-terrorist-entry-united-states-2/; Amy Howe, "Justice to Review Travel Ban Challenge," *SCOTUSblog* (January 19, 2018), http://www.scotusblog.com/2018/01/justices-review-travel-ban-challenge/; Liz Robbins, "Judges Nationwide Are Digging in Their Heels and Delaying Deportations," *New York Times* (February 10, 2018); Adam Liptak and Michael D. Shear, "Justices Refuse White House Bid in 'Dreamer' Case," *New York Times* (February 27, 2018).

18. Jane Meyer, "The President Pence Delusion," *New Yorker* (October 23, 2017).

19. Shira A. Scheindlin, "Trump's Most Troubling Legacy? His Judges," *New York Times* (November 10, 2017); Charlie Savage, "Courts Reshaped at Fastest Pace in Five Decades," *New York Times* (November 12, 2017); Savage, "Poor Vetting Sinks Nominees for Federal Judge," *New York Times* (December 19, 2017); William Barber II, "A Terrible Choice for Judge," *New York Times* (December 27, 2017).

20. Alexander Burns and Mitch Smith, "G.O.P.-Led States Race to Cement Their Priorities," *New York Times* (February 12, 2017).

21. Jenny Jarvie, "Texas' New Ban on 'Sanctuary Cities' Could Put Police in Jail if They Fail to Enforce Immigration Holds," *Los Angeles Times* (May 4, 2017); H.B. 452, Sess. of 2017, GA 2017; S.B. 2710, Sess. of 2017, MS 2017; H.B. 1041, Sess. of 2017, TN 2017; "Mid-Year Overview of 2017 State Immigration Legislation," Catholic Legal Immigration Network, August 2017, https://cliniclegal.org/resources/mid-year-overview-2017-state-immigration-legislation.

22. H.B. 14, Sess. of 2017 (Ky. 2017); H.B. 645, Sess. of 2017 (Mi. 2017); S.B. 160, Sess. of 2017 (Ga. 2017); H.B. 112, Sess. of 2017 (Ark. 2017); H.B. 443, Sess. of 2017 (Ut. 2017); S.B. 541, Sess. of 2017 (NV. 2017); S.B. 112, Sess. of 2017 (Ks. 2017); H.B. 1123, Sess. of 2017 (Ok. 2017).

23. Tony Platt, "Criminal Justice Reform in the U.S. Has a Long History of Repressive Outcomes," *Salon*, December 27, 2018, https://www.salon.com/2018/12/27/criminal-justice-reform-in-the-u-s-has-a-long-history-of-repressive-outcomes/.

24. Stanley Cohen, "The Punitive City: Notes on the Dispersal of Social Control," *Contemporary Crises* 3 (1979): 360.

25. Michel Foucault, *The Punitive Society: Lectures at the College de France, 1972–1973*, ed. Bernard E. Harcourt (New York: Palgrave Macmillan, 2015), 7–9.

26. Robin D. G. Kelley, "Beyond Black Lives Matter," *Kalfou* 2, no. 2 (Fall 2015): 330–37.

27. Gottschalk, *Caught*, 220.

28. Tanya Maria Golash-Boza, *Deported: Immigrant Policing, Disposable Labor, and Global Capitalism* (New York: New York University Press, 2015), 7–11.

29. Hester, "Deportability and the Carceral State," 141–51; William D. Carrigan and Clive Webb, *Forgotten Dead: Mob Violence against Mexicans in the United States, 1848–1928* (New York: Oxford University Press, 2013).

30. John Helmer, *Drugs and Minority Oppression* (New York: Seabury, 1975), 54–79.

31. Ernesto Galarza, *Merchants of Labor: The Mexican Bracero Story* (Charlotte, N.C: McNally & Loftin, 1964), 258.

32. Leah Sakala, "Breaking Down Mass Incarceration in the 2010 Census: State-by-State Rates of Race/Ethnicity," *Prison Policy Initiative* (May 28 2010), http://www.prisonpolicy.org/reports/rates.html; Ram Subramanian et al., *Incarceration's Front Door: The Misuse of Jails in America* (New York: Vera Institute of Justice, February 2015); Gottschalk, *Caught*, 215; Hester, "Deportability and the Carceral State," 147;

Ashley Nellis, "The Color of Justice: Racial and Ethnic Disparity in State Prisons," Sentencing Project (2016), http://www.sentencingproject.org/wp-content/uploads/2016/06/The-Color-of-Justice-Racial-and-Ethnic-Disparity-in-State-Prisons.pdf.

33. Didier Bigo, "Globalized (In)security: The Field and the Ban-opticon," in *Terror, Insecurity and Liberty: Illiberal Practices of Liberal Regimes after 9/11*, ed. Didier Bigo and Anastasia Tsoukala (London: Routledge, 2008): 10–48.

34. "Attorney General Sessions Delivers Remarks at the 63rd Biennial Conference of the National Fraternal Order of Police," U.S. Department of Justice press release (August 28, 2017).

35. Julie Hirschfeld Davis and Julia Preston, "Trump's Deportation Pledge Could Require Raids and Huge Federal Force," *New York Times* (November 15, 2016); Thomas Fuller, "Chief of Immigration Agency Compares Oakland's Mayor to 'Gang Lookout,'" *New York Times* (March 1, 2018).

36. Gilroy, *Against Race*, 152, 153; Platt, "The Strange and Shocking Similarities Between Donald Trump and 'Old Blood and Guts' Patton," *History News Network* (March 11, 2016), http://historynewsnetwork.org/article/162220; Trump, *America We Deserve*, 19.

37. Mike Davis, "The Great God Trump and the White Working Class," *Jacobin* (February 7, 2017), https://www.jacobinmag.com/2017/02/the-great-god-trump-and-the-white-working-class/; Leon Litwack, "Hellhound On My Trail: Race Relations in the South from Reconstruction to the Civil Rights Movement," in *Opening Doors: Perspectives on Race Relations in Contemporary America*, ed. Harry J. Knopke et al. (Tuscaloosa: University of Alabama Press, 1991), 25.

38. Noam Chomsky, "The Responsibility of Intellectuals," *New York Review of Books* (February 23, 1967).

39. Morris Janowitz, "Social Control of Escalated Riots," University of Chicago Center for Policy Study, 1968; Elizabeth Hinton, *From the War on Poverty to the War on Crime: The Making of Mass Incarceration in America* (Cambridge, Mass.: Harvard University Press, 2016).

40. Gerald D. Robin, "Justifiable Homicide by Police Officers," *Journal of Criminal Law, Criminology, and Police Science* 54, no. 2 (June 1963): 225–31; Lynn Arrington, "Better Design Means Better Management," *Corrections Today* 49, no. 2 (April 1987): 86; Lorna A. Rhodes, *Total Confinement: Madness and Reason in the Maximum Security Prison* (Berkeley: University of California Press, 2004), 41; David Segal, "Prison Vendors See Continued Signs of a Captive Market," *New York Times* (August 29, 2015); Manny Fernandez, "Delays as Death-Penalty States Scramble for Execution Drugs," *New York Times* (October 9, 2015); Adam Nagourney, "Aloha, and Welcome, Unless You're Homeless," *New York Times* (June 4, 2016); Peter W. Huber and Mark P. Mills, "How Technology Will Defeat Terrorism," *City Journal* (Winter 2002): 24–33.

41. Stuart Hall and Phil Scraton, "Law, Class and Control," in *Crime and Society: Readings in History and Theory*, ed. Mike Fitzgerald, Gregor McLennan, and Jennie Pawson (London: Routledge & Kegan Paul, 1981), 460–97.

42. Keramet Reiter, "(Un)Settling Solitary Confinement in California's Prisons," Social Justice Blog, September 28, 2015, http://www.socialjusticejournal.org/?p=3214; Ian Lovett, "California Agrees to Overhaul Use of Solitary Confinement," *New York Times* (September 2, 2015).

43. "A Vision for Black Lives: Policy Demands for Black Power, Freedom & Justice," *The Movement for Black Lives* (July 2016), https://policy.m4bl.org/.

44. Edward W. Said, "On Defiance and Taking Positions," in *Beyond the Academy: A Scholar's Obligations*, ed. George R. Garrison et al. (New York: American Council of Learned Societies, Occasional Paper # 31, 1995).

2

Migration, Populism, Racism

Between "Old" Italy and "New" Europe

Dario Melossi

The questions of migration, the construction (or defense?) of a European Union, and the rising tide of populism have all been at the center of the European political scene for a while. They are intimately related to each other. In this essay, I will try to disentangle some of the connections among these dimensions, starting from an analysis that I offered many years ago in a volume called *The State of Social Control*.[1] There, I tried to show that the concept of social control, as this had developed within American social sciences in the first half of the twentieth century, was inextricably linked to the overcoming of the traditional European concept of the state and to the inexorable advancement of a mass democratic society of which the U.S. has been the primary example. I now try to apply some of those ideas to the current conditions of the European Union. I then analyze more specifically the case of a region of Europe, the Italian region. I come to the conclusion that the very limited social and cultural development of a united Europe—best exemplified by the lack of a common language—makes it basically impossible for the EU to decide on issues as challenging of its traditions as the question of migration. The failure of the EU on such matters feeds a reactionary backlash on which populism has been thriving.

The increasingly frantic pace of capitalist development was famously described by Karl Marx and Frederick Engels in the *Manifesto*:

> Constant revolutionizing of production, uninterrupted disturbance of all social conditions, everlasting uncertainty and agitation distinguish the bourgeois epoch from all earlier ones. All fixed, fast-frozen relations, with their train of ancient and venerable prejudices and opinions

> are swept away, all new-formed ones become antiquated before they can ossify. All that is solid melts into air, all that is holy is profaned, and man is at last compelled to face with sober senses his real conditions of life, and his relations with his kind.[2]

Marx and Engels's apology for the bourgeoisie and *ante litteram* globalization can be expressed no better than in migratory movements to appreciate the peculiar state of affairs that is an intimate feature of capitalism. About eighty years later, in a striking essay on "Human Migration and the Marginal Man," the doyen of the Chicago School, Robert E. Park, opposed theories basing cultural differences on "physical environment" or "race" in what he called a "catastrophic theory of progress," according to which "the forces which have been decisive in the history of mankind are those which have brought men together in fruitful competition, conflict, and co-operation."[3] And, he goes on, "among the most important of these influences have been migration and the incidental collisions, conflicts, and fusions of people and cultures which they have occasioned."[4]

Indeed, the idea of social control developed first in Chicago in the context of emigration from Europe to the U.S. more than a century ago. In the "Babel of languages" that was Chicago at the time, social control was seen as based in communication and language. This was the view developed particularly by George Herbert Mead.[5] In Chicago and in the U.S. generally, the issue of social order could no longer be tackled simply through the political legal and philosophical idea of the state, on the example of "old" Europe, but needed to be constructed through the social scientific concept of social control.[6] In other words, whereas the concept of order embedded in the idea of the state is a normative presupposition that is then supposed to be enforced by organizations that we usually call "state organizations" (the police, the judiciary, the army), the idea of order expressed in the concept of social control is the idea of an order that needs to be constructed in everyday life. No wonder the former belongs in the disciplines of law and political science and the latter is simultaneous with the invention of the new discipline of sociology. Of course, the fact that the basic order of society is an order that is daily constructed in interaction (and is enormously more solid and important than any legal-political construction) is not something that starts in the twentieth-century United States. It goes back to the very beginning of any social formation. What was new, however, in 1910 or 1920 Chicago—as the locale epitomizing this process—was that society's self-reflection, through its social scientists (and even its legal theorists),[7] somehow became aware of the process, which was no longer hidden in quotidianity but was conceptualized and problematized not as an obvious aspect of society but as an issue that needed reflection and concerted social action. The reason for such realization, I claimed in *The State of Social Control*, was the tumultuous social change that was not only represented by migration but that in migration processes found its most obvious point of emergence.

European Democracy, Elites, and Language

Could some of the ideas explored in the previous paragraph, referring to early twentieth-century America, have some purchase on today's Europe? The political centrality of debate on migration is probably one of the elements that the two situations have in common. Starting in the mid-1990s, in Europe, everybody appeared extremely concerned with the issue of migration, an issue that seemed to run parallel to that of the construction of Europe (those were the heady times of the Maastricht treaty and the hope in the drafting of a true "European Constitution"). What is "social control" in Europe today? An echo of such a question can be found in the German Federal Constitutional Court's famed 1993 decision about the constitutionality of the Maastricht treaty,[8] where the court declared "admissible" but not "well-founded" the complaint about the "diminution of democracy" that the transformation envisioned in the Maastricht treaty would have brought about (for the citizens of the German Federal Republic). The argument centered on the concept of "living democracy"—the idea, that is, that democracy cannot be conceived only as a formal requirement but that it has to be lived and legitimated by ongoing citizen participation. According to the argument of the court as developed by the German legal theorist Dieter Grimm—who was a member of the court—the very substance of democracy, if not its form, is based in the existence of certain minimal conditions that we could summarize, using a Habermasian concept, as the existence of a living European "public sphere" or, in other words, of a *demos*. This is a concept that is taken for granted at the national level, but what about the European level? Would such a "European public sphere" exist? For instance, do properly European political parties or mass media of communication actually exist?[9] Of course, in Europe today, as in 1993, there is nothing that could remotely be defined as a European public sphere; therefore, no "European democracy," no European *demos*, would then appear to be possible. Grimm then goes on to trace the root cause of such a situation to the absence of a common European language, because even the only language that could aspire to play such a role, the English language, is functionally spoken by a very small group of citizens (and even more so today, after Brexit).

The question pointed out by Grimm here is the lack of a collective identity constituted through a "capacity for transnational discourse."[10] This is a *structural* weakness of the EU. That does not mean—as has been unfortunately misunderstood[11]—that such a weakness would be caused by the absence of some kind of traditional foundation, a *Volksgemeinschaft* to be found in the past. Judge Grimm was not, in spite of his name, a Romantic. On the contrary, I believe a "capacity for transnational discourse" would imply a vision of Europe grounded in the future, in a project, in a "new Europe" created in the same way in which European colonists created a "New World" in America. Such a vision could only ground itself in the existence of a vibrant and effective European public sphere. In fact, the construction of unified and central standpoints, able to overcome the tendency to fragmentation and drift, was the way in which the problem of social control was framed in North America at the beginning of the twentieth century—in the very concept of social control by Mead and others, as we have seen. In this sense, a few years before, Durkheim also had written memorably on the democratic state as a "strong" state, better able than any other political form to warrant an efficacious communication channel between political elites and the masses.[12]

The role of the elites seems to be to help establish those channels, those communication processes, that are able to organize and coordinate "the public." In other words, what happens today within the sundry national publics—that is, constituted within *one* (or one *dominant*) language—shall—might?—happen tomorrow within a transnational European conversation. The problem, of course, is that today the EU seems to be strong enough to contribute to destructurate national public spheres but not really strong enough to help constitute the creation of transnational discourses and publics. Unfortunately, the spectacle performed by "elites" recently, especially in connection with Brexit and the issue of migration, has been one of abysmal failure.

The Italian Case: Migration and Racism since the Economic Crisis

The situation of migration in Europe as this had developed between the 1990s and the economic crisis that started in 2007–8 was well analyzed by Kitty Calavita for Southern Europe (Italy and Spain), and by Joanne van der Leun for the Netherlands (representing however more generally the situation of Central and Northern Europe). During the "globalization" years of the 1980s and 1990s the situation of immigration in each country seemed to be the result of large-scale migratory movements on a global scale, together with governments' attempts at somehow *controlling* immigration,[13] creating thereby an extensive area of so-called irregular or undocumented migrants.[14] The main difference between countries of Southern Europe and more established countries of immigration in Western Europe was essentially that, whereas in Southern Europe most migrants were so-called economic migrants who, when they could not migrate regularly (that is, most of the time) had to go through periods of straightforward undocumentation, in the Netherlands and the UK most migrants, especially unskilled and from the so-called Third World, were asylum-seekers. This situation was essentially a product of the freezing up of borders that all throughout Europe had accompanied the aftermath of the oil crisis of 1973 that had put an end to the age of relatively easy mass migration during the European "economic miracle," when millions of poor people from Southern and Eastern Europe, Asia, and the Caribbean had been able to look for better fortune in the industrial centers of Europe. As Kitty Calavita in fact has shown, immigration laws would "welcome" immigrants only as workers, their legal status relying on temporary work permits very difficult to get because of very complicated procedures.[15] These laws did not allow immigrants to settle. They were seen as useful "others" willing to work under conditions and for wages that locals largely rejected and that were part of a substantially "post-Fordist" economic environment—where migrants would take the most problematic and marginal jobs, from seasonal harvesting to construction work, from home care for the old and the disabled to precarious health industry jobs, from the lower end of sex work to downright criminal occupations in the illegal economy. Such marginalization on the job market would produce concomitant processes of racialization and criminalization. Not so dissimilar would be the fate of aspiring asylum-seekers in central and northern Europe. As we will see, the main change in Italy after 2008 would be that here too, now, the marginality of migrants would no longer present itself in the guise of the "undocumented" economic migrant but in that of the asylum-seeker.

The emergence of an issue of racialization (and racism) appeared quite clearly in Italy subsequent to the economic crisis and the so-called Arab Spring. A rather steady flow of refugees started crossing the Mediterranean Sea, escaping the turmoil in a number of North African and Middle Eastern countries. Things were much worsened by the war in Libya and the death of Muammar Gaddafi in 2011, which made what was until then a relatively prosperous country fall into the deep turmoil of civil war and become an insecure place, especially for African people who went through Libya or, as had happened until 2011, worked there. Both the steady flow of migrants and internal political pressure in European countries, for instance in Italy, for recognition of the possibility of asylum (until then abstractly included in the Italian Constitution but never translated into practice) made it so that people crossing the Mediterranean began to be recognized at least as potential asylum-seeking refugees who could gain a tentative and uncertain status that was "less illegal" than had been the case previously for undocumented economic migrants. The numbers of refugees began to increase at the time when Italy was slowly and laboriously recovering from the worst economic crisis in its modern history. The continual shipwrecks and mass drownings taking place in the tract of sea between Libya and Sicily pushed the center-left government of the time to launch an important sea operation, based in the Italian navy, named "Mare Nostrum" that, in 2014, rescued about 170,000 refugees. Even though the government at the end of 2014 decided to discontinue the costly and increasingly debated operation, in 2015 and 2016—in concomitance with the "refugee crisis" that was taking place in Europe and that brought almost 900,000 migrants to Germany alone—the number of refugees hovered around the same quantity every year. However, starting with the agreement between the EU and Turkey in March 2016 and then between Italy and Libya in 2017, Europe started closing its borders. First the center-left government of Renzi, then, after the elections of March 4, 2018, the new Italian government created by an alliance of the hard-to-define "five-star" movement and the right-wing and xenophobic (former Northern) League, increasingly closed the borders and made it harder and harder for refugees to reach Italy. At the same time, an increasing number of freshly arrived migrants found themselves at some point in the process of acquiring refugee status and enjoying (rather limited) rights, among which was the right to work (which did not mean, of course, the right to work according to norms and rights of Italian workers). Such a process was aptly dubbed the "refugeeization of the workforce."[16] Because whoever arrived in Italy routinely applied for asylum—even if only a few, mainly those arriving from Syria and a few other countries, had the prospect of attaining full refugee status—and because Italian legislation had a lesser form of international status called "humanitarian protection" that allowed for a piecemeal insertion of migrants into Italian society,[17] the condition of asylum seekers became the new "normal" condition of freshly arrived migrants in Italy.[18] The leader of the League, Matteo Salvini, the new "strong man" of Italian politics, took over the political right-wing from Silvio Berlusconi, shifting hegemony from a right-wing conservative slant with a strong neo-liberal flavor to a social-nationalistic direction that had contact points with similar political alignments emerging in this period in a number of countries, European and non-European, from Hungary's Orbán to Brexiters in the UK and Le Pen in France—not to mention, of course, Trump in the U.S. and leaders in countries including Turkey, the Philippines, Russia, India, China, and Brazil. The Northern League was characterized from its very beginning by a racist component toward Southern Italians and had centered for a while on claims of autonomy or even secession from Italy. Increasingly, under Salvini's leadership, the party has veered toward nationalism, and the racist slant has turned toward strangers and immigrants, particularly African migrants and refugees.

Italians were obliged to face the reality of a phenomenon of "racism" or—better said—would have been obliged to face such a phenomenon had not the League done its best to deny its existence (for instance, one of its leaders could publicly insult an elected Democratic Party member of parliament of African origins, comparing her features to those of "an orangutan," and at the same time claim that such an epithet had been pronounced in the heat of political debate and had no racist content whatsoever).[19]

Such dramatic denial of racism had roots in Italian society. Growing up in postwar Italy, in the 1950s and 1960s, I can recall that, even among left-wing rank-and-file members, there was not much recognition of the historical reality of racism. Of course, there was talk about anti-Semitism and what the Germans and, more specifically the Nazis, had done to the Jews. Very little of the talk, however, was about how Italians had participated in the persecution of the Jews or, even less, of Italians' racism toward people of color during the colonial wars of the first half of the twentieth century in Africa—in Libya, Ethiopia, Somalia, Eritrea. "Racism" was a word generally reserved for stories that would come from the Southern states of the United States, perhaps in a not coincidental conjunction with Cold War propaganda.

Of course, for a long time in Italy there were no people of color around. In a city such as Bologna, for instance, where I lived, and where jazz and the game of basketball were big popular passions, black people were usually Americans who visited for the occasional game or for the wonderful Bologna jazz festivals that took place in the late 1950s and 1960s. Issues of migration went basically unnoticed. In an area that had only partially contributed to Italian emigration and that, if anything, in the 1950s and 1960s had seen immigration from Southern Italy, an immigration that had in the 1970s exhausted itself, migration was not an issue at all. No one could have predicted what would start happening in about ten or fifteen years.

Actually, a long tradition of racist thinking not only had been present for a long time in Italian society but more specifically had been indigenous to the most famous criminological current that Italian culture had nourished, the so-called Positive School of criminal anthropology. However, the racism of the Positive School, even if it did not spare the "colored races"—as Cesare Lombroso writes in his *Criminal Man* (1896)—was directed first of all toward the Southern Italian "race," which was seen as "tainted" by African infiltrations. In 1926, Antonio Gramsci had noted, in a famous essay on *la questione meridionale* ("the Southern question"):

> It is well known what kind of ideology has been disseminated in myriad ways among the masses in the North, by the propagandists of the bourgeoisie: the South is the ball and chain which prevents the social development of Italy from progressing more rapidly; the Southerners are biologically inferior beings, semi-barbarians or total barbarians, by natural destiny; if the South is backward, the fault does not lie with the capitalist system or with any other historical cause, but with Nature, which has made the Southerners lazy, incapable, criminal and barbaric — only tempering this harsh fate with the purely individual explosion of a few great geniuses, like isolated palm-trees in an arid and barren desert. The Socialist party was to a great extent the vehicle for this bourgeois ideology within the Northern proletariat.[20] The Socialist party gave its blessing to all the "Southernist" literature of the clique of writers who made up the so-called positive school: the Ferri's, Sergi's, Niceforo's, Orano's and their lesser followers, who in articles, tales, short stories, novels, impressions and memoirs, in a variety of forms, reiterated one single refrain. Once again, "science" was used to crush the wretched and exploited; but this time it was dressed in socialist colors, and claimed to be the science of the proletariat.[21]

Actually, Gramsci's article followed by many years the lively debate about "the Southern question" or *meridionalismo* that had been raging at the turn of the century, especially between 1898 and 1906, and that saw in the initiative of the journal *Il pensiero contemporaneo* its center.[22] Indeed, Gramsci had not been the first to note the connection between positivistic theories and the stereotyping of Southerners — Napoleone Colajanni's work being probably the most critical of the positivists from a sociological perspective.[23] Colajanni had especially criticized, defining it as racist, the work by Alfredo Niceforo, who had written of the "two Italies," the Northern and the Southern, where the "Mediterranean lineage" was unavoidably and unfortunately marked by African influence (to the point that these analyses of the Positive School became ground for which, at Ellis Island, officers were uncertain whether Southern Italians should be classified as "whites").[24] Such flawed bloodlines meant "barbarism": Southerners were "inferior beings" according to parameters set by the urban, bourgeois, industrial, "rational" culture of Northern Italy.

It seems that, generally speaking, the ready-made racist's handbook is rather repetitive, no matter the object of its insults. In such a handbook, the human being stigmatized as "inferior" is generally described as poor, lazy, indolent, dirty, smelly, unintelligent, sexually promiscuous, violent, criminal, unreliable, given to intoxicating substances, and so on. These images repeat themselves unendingly, never linked to the same skin color, or language, or religion, or ancestry, or nationality, but invariably applicable, according to the same script, to ever-changing characters. For instance, in *Heimat Babylon*, Daniel Cohn-Bendit and Thomas Schmid's well-deserving book, one of the first works to appear in Europe to discuss the increasing, pervasive European fear about the new wave of international migration, the authors remind us that Benjamin Franklin, in 1751, worried about the increase in non-English colonists in his beloved Pennsylvania because the excessive number of *German* peasants flowing in would have endangered the lily-white character of the colony.[25] Already in the 1990s, also in Italy, the "great fear" of migrants and refugees had started, taking over newspapers and newscasts and giving birth to the new shameful exploitation of such fear for electoral gains and more generally for political power games. As a Dutch scholar, Teun A. van Dijk, had claimed in a text entitled *Elite Discourse and Racism* (1993), every social grouping has resources in itself of xenophobic and/or racist discourse, but what is really important for that to emerge is that *official* discourse, by political, cultural, or media elites, makes it acceptable and legitimate.[26]

This idea, by van Dijk and Ter Wal, crossed my mind when, in the same period, I happened to visit an exhibit in Bologna about the sources and history of racism in Italy entitled *La menzogna della razza* (The falsehood of race). It was a sort of play on words about a journal called *La difesa della razza* (The defense of the race) that had been published at the peak of Fascist power in Italy, between 1938 and 1943. The foundation of the journal marked the start of a true and proper *state racism* in Italy a few months before the passing of the "race laws" that would mark the official start of anti-Semitic persecution.[27] What I found particularly interesting in the exhibit was the mixture, in the journal, of pretensions to "scientific" discourse, with anthropological motifs akin to those of the Positive School mentioned earlier and an array of cartoons, images, and "jokes" (which it is probably still possible to hear around Italy). Two groups were the targets of the journal: people of African descent, who had already been the victims of Italian colonialism for decades—where the goal was that of legitimating it by reaffirming the superiority of the white man, and specifically of the Italian white man (a kind of "white man's burden" rhetoric)—and, as mentioned, Jewish people, in industrious and fruitful cooperation with our German ally.[28]

The viewing of the exhibit reminded me of van Dijk's theory. Italy's colonial past, upheld and articulated by "cultural products" such as the journal *La difesa della razza*, had somehow constituted, within Italy's cultural heritage, a backdrop of racist discourse, a "resource" of racism ready to be unearthed when the right conjuncture would present itself. This happened with the migration process that started between the 1980s and 1990s. An unending succession of racism-laced statements by (some) political leaders, mass-media characters, and now, crucially, "social media" have somehow contributed to rediscovering and once again making legitimate a racist discourse that, after the political elections of March 4, 2018, seems to have found its climax. A few months before the elections, in Macerata, a usually very quiet small town in the Marche Region in the central part of Italy, the body of an eighteen-year old drug addict, Pamela Mastropietro, was discovered, horrendously mutilated, after having left a recovery community center and purchased a small quantity of heroin from some Nigerian men. (At the time of this writing, the details of her death, supposedly at the hands of those very men, still appear quite uncertain.) On February 3, 2018, a young distraught man, unrelated to the victim and who had shown sympathy for the Northern League and neo-Fascist political formations, went on a "vendetta" rampage within the city of Macerata, shooting with a gun from his car at all the African-looking men he encountered, wounding six of them. This chain of events took place one month before the political elections of March 4, 2018, while there was a crescendo of official statements against immigrants and refugees, and caused enormous sensation all over the country (the young man had a copy of *Mein Kampf* in his room that was shown on TV; a few days later Amazon had sold thousands of copies of the book).[29] The elections of March 4 saw a strong affirmation of the Five Star political movement and the League, which went on to create a coalition for government. In the year after the elections, the League in particular seems to have almost doubled its favor among the voters according to various polls, a favor that seems to be connected to its stance on issues of migration.[30]

In Conclusion: Migration and Conflict in the Constitution of New Europe

On the one hand, the Italian case could be seen as a textbook failure of those European elites that we discussed at the beginning. On the other hand, the issue is much more complex than the fact that no European elites were able to articulate a progressive European policy alternative to the social-nationalistic—in short neo-Fascistic—agenda that ended up temporarily prevailing, at least in Italy. Perhaps European-minded Italian elites were too weak—something of a recurrent curse of Italian politics, it would seem. The question is rather that, without a true European *demos*, the only democratic discussion can take place at the national level, but is by its nature confined to a parochialism that is unable to measure up to the real issues of European construction and to dealing with migration. The construction of a European *demos* is the real issue, it seems to me, because only at that level will it be possible to build the kind of "social control" necessary to govern migration processes toward an enlightened vision. Typical of this has been the discussion about so-called Dublin rules, which are the sum of rules and procedures established in treaties signed in Dublin, for the enforcement of the principle by which an individual applying for asylum can only do so in one EU member state; that member state is usually the one of "first entry." This rule, of course, places an uneven burden on countries at the borders of Europe, such as Italy. Italy complained several times that this amounted to leaving the country alone to deal with the "emergency" situation about the refugees crossing the Mediterranean by boat. The accrued legitimation of League policies owed much to a propaganda that was able to exploit this fact. The League politicians were certainly in bad faith in this, because they did nothing to support a solution worked out—and approved!—by the European Parliament[31] that would have changed the Dublin rules in a reasonable direction quite favorable to Italy, but that was never approved by the European governments.[32] They would rather exploit the anti-European propaganda made possible for them and in which they found company in those Eastern European governments—such as Hungary and Poland—that were most adamant in rejecting any revision of the Dublin rules but that shared with Salvini's positions a rabid right-wing anti-immigrant and anti-European populism.

A similar marker of the irrational public discussion about immigration is given by the total absence of the demographic argument. There is consensus among demographers that with the current level of birth rates in most European countries—notably in Italy and Germany around 1.3 births per woman—in the course of a couple generations these countries will need millions and millions of migrants to simply refurbish their workforce. It is noticeable, for instance, in the case of Italy that, with more than five million migrants regularly registered on Italian soil,[33] the general Italian population has been stable for years. Obviously, those migrants have replaced Italians and in most cases have replaced unproductive, retired Italians by much younger and more productive workers. But this obvious argument in favor of migration is not even considered by European nationalistic elites, who would rather call for Italians and Europeans generally to make more children with a rhetoric that once again is reminiscent of some of the most classic among Mussolini's speeches. Furthermore, behind the suspicion for what is called a "replacement" agenda by "liberal cosmopolitan and plutocratic" elites lurks an essentially racist attitude: replacement is wrong because it would entail replacing whites with blacks — even if, in Italy, the number of African migrants are only about 20 percent of the total; the debate about migration centers mostly on its most visible aspect, the refugees coming by boat from Africa.

Perhaps we should turn our hopes from the action of elites to that of social movements — *European* social movements. After all, if one looks at the way in which national states, especially Italy and Germany, were created in the nineteenth century, then we realize that the development of a national consciousness was the result of the emergence of social and cultural movements within which a new oppositional and transformative language was being created. These communities had to be "imagined"[34] within a language that created history, poetry, novels, music, instantiating the new reality-to-be. All of this happened in a continuous exchange with political organizations that were striving to give voice to common interests, values, and hopes — the substance of social movements. In other words, the "constitution" of a new political and legal subject, such as the EU, may acquire life only insofar as it represents the instrument, the tool, for the affirmation of a certain constellation of values and interests,[35] which may, of course, find themselves in opposition to other, alternative constellations of values and interests. It would be a great victory for Europe indeed if it could become the arena for such confrontations — not, as it is now, a confrontation in which the opposition is simply between Europe and its negation. The fundamental issue, in order to tackle head-on the conundrum of the creation of a European "public sphere," seems to turn into the question of a *constituent process*, a process that goes together with the formation of a common language and a common sphere of public interaction. We could even state, in Durkheimian fashion, that the coming into being of such a common language may be taken to be an indicator of the real, social, "thick" existence of a European Constitution.

Europeans cannot really converse among themselves about the question of immigration and refugees without building a common house of language and culture able to sustain the public debate that would be needed. The question of a more rational and humane approach to the issue of immigration and refugees in Europe is strictly intertwined with the process of creating the EU itself, because the relationship between Europe and the reality of international migration is not simply a relation framed by good values and sentiments. Only a truly united Europe would have the political strength to fashion a real migration policy — and to welcome migrants in its midst. A Europe that, as it is now, is a patchwork of miserable statelets can never achieve the strength of a common policy. The divisions and differences between such statelets in terms of different interests, access dates to the EU, level of development, vicinity of external borders, and so on are too many. A truly united Europe could come to existence only if it were supported by an adequate "social control"—that is, by a capacity of creation of a common mind, a consensus able to carry and support political decision.

There is much similarity with the issue of the abolition of slavery in America in the second half of the nineteenth century. Abolition of slavery was intimately connected with the question of the construction of a federal Union (as opposed to a Confederacy) because it reflected the values and the interests of a certain constellation of powers, those of the industrial North as opposed to the rural South. In other words, it reflected a project of what the new American polity would be that was a radical alternative to the Southern one. What is at stake today in Europe is something comparable: how to tackle the issue of immigration, especially immigration from Asia and Africa, is a matter intimately connected with the project of building one European structure and not another.

In the 2014 documentary film *Io sto con la sposa* (On the side of the bride), by director Gabriele del Grande, we see a Palestinian poet and an Italian journalist meet a group of refugees in Milan who crossed the Mediterranean Sea by boat to flee the war in Syria. The two decide to help the refugees complete their journey to Sweden and hopefully avoid getting themselves arrested. They invent a ruse, to fake a wedding, because who would ever arrest a bride and her guests? So the bride and a dozen or so Italian and Syrian friends as wedding guests cross the whole of Europe on a four-day journey from Milan to Sweden. The film and the events told in the film are one and the same thing. The story of the film reminds us—once again thinking of the American struggle for the abolition of slavery—of the so-called Underground Railroad, a network of secret routes and safe houses established during the first half of the nineteenth century, used by African American slaves to escape north into free U.S. states and Canada with the aid of abolitionists—such as the Quakers—who were sympathetic to their cause. Likewise, recently the mayors of Palermo and Naples have offered the support of their harbors to receive the boats of the nongovernmental organizations that are still saving migrants in spite of the strong campaign of the Italian government against them and the "closing up" of Italian harbors to their boats, or even, paradoxically, to the boats of the Italian Coast Guard itself (a court in Catania, Sicily, had requested authorization to proceed against Deputy Premier and Interior Minister Matteo Salvini for kidnapping because in August 2018 he refused to allow over one hundred migrants saved by the Italian Coast Guard to get off the Diciotti ship during a ten-day-long stand-off; the Italian Senate denied the authorization).

Immigrants and refugees are those who have not only the highest stakes but also the greatest ability to be part of the process of construction of a real European democracy and the debate necessary to make it unfold.[36] The two processes of integration, of Europe and of immigrants and refugees, are one and the same. But can Europe be its own promised land? Can we, as Europeans, be, at the same time, the place we want to escape from (like the refugees) and the place where we want to go (like the refugees)? These questions would seem to be in the mind of those who, in the 1990s, took to drawing on the walls of French cities the writing *Étrangers, ne nous laissez pas seuls avec les Français!* Today there are many Italians who are indeed tempted to write the same on their walls: *Stranieri, non lasciateci soli con gli italiani!*[37]

The picture previously drawn about the rising vocabulary of racism in Italy today will only be overcome by the rise of anti-racist social movements throughout Europe in pursuit of a European project of development that sees anti-racism as an essential aspect of its platform. A crucial element for such a movement will have to rely on youth. All throughout Europe youth social organizations, often made up of young people belonging to different countries, work on the migrants' cause, often in some connection with what has been without doubt the most successful EU policy, the so-called Erasmus program of student exchange among European universities. It is not by chance that all studies about fear of migration come to the conclusion that openness toward migrants and favor for the process of European construction are strongly linked.[38] And both attitudes are linked to that part of the population that is younger, better educated, left-leaning, and with social capital. Indeed, one of the most interesting results of a study we did years ago in Emilia-Romagna was that the very fact of interacting with migrants in everyday life lowered the fear and preoccupation about them.[39] In every European country member of the EU, pro-globalization forces and "souverainist" forces face each other with very different leanings about European and migration processes. The same developments happened at different times in different countries.[40] The political strength of the souverainist/populist positions has been increasing especially in the Eastern and Southern regions of Europe. Particularly damaging to the progressives has been the process of "Brexit," given that the more cosmopolitan and pro-globalization currents were particularly tied to the UK and to the role of London as the *de facto* moral and cultural capital of Europe (ask members of the so-called Erasmus generation). In this view, Brexit is an ominous disaster first of all for Europe (but it will also be one for the UK) and is quite unbelievable how little, on the Southern side of the Channel, we asked the UK to remain! Whether cosmopolitan elites and social movements will in the end be able to prevail is crucial for the future of migrants in Europe but is crucial at the same time for us (old) Europeans. That the unity of Europe and the hospitality for migrants will have to be reached through a long and extended process of European internecine conflict there is no doubt. Also, there is no doubt that the constitution of a new democratic European social order will be one and the same with a "New Europe" that will be open and hospitable to migrants. Going back to our Chicagoan starting point, such a New Europe will have to speak a new language, a Babelic pidgin English poetically prefigured, perhaps in the language spoken by Salvatore in Umberto Eco's *The Name of the Rose*,[41] the heretic Dolcinian monk[42] escaped from persecution, who speaks a pidgin Latin, a pastiche of all European languages. As about the eve of modern Europe, likewise today a new European society and a new European language to tell the new society will emerge together, made up of a Babel of European and non-European languages, to mirror the peoples that will have come together to constitute New Europe.[43]

Notes

This contribution develops ideas first sketched in an essay presented at the 16th Annual Conference of the "European Society of Criminology," Münster, Germany (September 2016).

1. Dario Melossi, *The State of Social Control: A Sociological Study of Concepts of State and Social Control in the Making of Democracy* (Cambridge: Polity; New York: St. Martin's, 1990).

2. Karl Marx and Frederick Engels, *The Communist Manifesto* (London: Penguin, 1848), 83. About this, see Marshall Berman's beautiful book *All That Is Solid Melts into Air* (1982; New York: Penguin, 1988).

3. Robert E. Park, "*Human Migration and the Marginal Man*," in *On Social Control and Collective Behaviour* (Chicago: University of Chicago Press, 1928).

4. Ibid.

5. George H. Mead, "The Genesis of the Self and Social Control," in *Selected Writings* (1925; repr. Indianapolis: Bobbs–Merrill, 1964), 267–93.

6. Melossi, *State of Social Control*.

7. Such as in "sociological jurisprudence" and later in "legal realism."

8. Gerhard Wegen and Christopher Kuner, "Germany: Federal Constitutional Court Decision Concerning the Maastricht Treaty," *International Legal Materials* 33 (1994): 388–444.

9. Dieter Grimm, "Does Europe Need a Constitution?," *European Law Journal* 1 (1995): 282–302; Melossi, "Security, Social Control, Democracy and Migration within the 'Constitution' of the EU," *European Law Journal* 11 (2005): 5–21.

10. Grimm, "Does Europe Need a Constitution?," 297.

11. Jürgen Habermas, "Comment on the Paper by Dieter Grimm: 'Does Europe Need a Constitution?,'" *European Law Journal* 1 (1995):303–7; Habermas, "On the

Relation between the Nation, Rule of Law, and Democracy" (1996), in Habermas, *The Inclusion of the Other* (Cambridge, Mass.: MIT Press, 1998), 129–54.

12. Émile Durkheim, *Professional Ethics and Civic Morals* (1898–1900) (Glencoe, Ill.: Free Press, 1958), 86–96.

13. Kitty Calavita, *Immigrants at the Margins: Law, Race, and Exclusion in Southern Europe* (New York: Cambridge University Press, 2005); Joanne Van der Leun, *Looking for Loopholes: Processes of Incorporation of Illegal Immigrants in the Netherlands* (Amsterdam: Amsterdam University Press, 2003); Melossi, *Crime, Punishment and Migration*. London: SAGE, 2015.

14. Currently, estimates of undocumented migrants hover around 11–12 million in the United States and "only" 2–3 millions in the EU.

15. Calavita, *Immigrants at the Margins*.

16. Nick Dines and Enrica Rigo, "Postcolonial Citizenships and the 'Refugeeization' of the Workforce: Migrant Agricultural Labor in the Italian Mezzogiorno," in *Transitions in Europe: Contexts, Practices and Politics*, ed. Sandra Ponzanesi and Gianmaria Colpani (Lanham, Md.: Rowman and Littlefield International, 2015), 151–72.

17. This "humanitarian protection" would then be canceled in the first act of the new government about immigration, the so-called Salvini decree.

18. In ways not too dissimilar from what had previously happened in Northern and Central European countries after the closing up of borders following the so-called oil energy crisis of 1973.

19. In January 2019 the League politician in question, Senator Calderoli, was criminally convicted for having compared black former minister Kyenge to an "orangutan."

20. At the time, Gramsci was the leader of the Communist Party, which he had just helped create in 1921. One of the objectives of the party was from the very beginning to organize the poor peasants of the South whom the Socialist Party—the Communists charged—had substantially forgotten, paying attention only to the Northern working class.

21. Antonio Gramsci, "Some Aspects of the Southern Question," in *Selections from Political Writings (1921–1926)* (1926; repr. London: Lawrence and Wishart, 1978), 441–62.

22. In 1993 there appeared a very useful anthology of the contributions to this debate edited by Vito Teti: *La razza maledetta: Origini del pregiudizio antimeridionale* (Rome: manifestolibri).

23. Napoleone Colajanni, "Per la razza maledetta," in Teti, *La razza maledetta*, 89–101.

24. Sandro Mezzadra, "Il nuovo regime migratorio europeo e le metamorfosi contemporanee del razzismo," *Studi sulla questione criminale* 2, no. 1 (2007): 13–29.

25. Daniel Cohn-Bendit and Thomas Schmid, *Heimat Babylon: Das Wagnis der multikulturellen Demokratie* (Hamburg: Hoffman und Campe, 1992).

26. Jessika Ter Wal, ed., *Racism and Cultural Diversity in the Mass Media* (Vienna: Ercomer, 2002).

27. A classic statement on such a concept may of course be found in Michel Foucault, *Society Must Be Defended* (1976; repr. New York: Picador, 2003).

28. See the Catalogue of the Exhibit, edited by Centro Furio Jesi (1994).

29. A number of news articles and comments about these events were published in the *Guardian* in those very days. About the general situation at the time of writing (January 2019), see the essay by Caitlin L. Chandler, "Rome: Where Migrants Face Eviction as Fascists Find a Home," *New York Review of Books, Daily*, https://www.nybooks.com/daily/2019/01/28/rome-where-migrants-face-eviction-while-fascists-find-a-home/.

30. In the summer of 2019, a new sudden political turnaround developed when Mr. Salvini, taken by some kind of political hubris, undermined his own political chances by breaking the alliance with the Five Star Movement and calling for new elections. As a result of such an abrupt request, the Five Star Movement decided to ally themselves with the Democratic Party, an alliance that has a majority in Parliament, but probably not in the electorate. It is still to be seen what the new government resulting from such change will do about the issues here discussed.

31. Cecilia Wickström, "Report (A8–0345/2017) on the Proposal for a Regulation of the European Parliament and the Council Establishing the Criteria and Mechanisms for Determining the Member State Responsible for Examining an Application for International Protection Lodged in one of the Member States by a Third-Country National or a Stateless Person," European Parliament (2017).

32. Please remember that the European Union is definitely not a "democracy": European laws are adopted jointly by the European Parliament *and* the Council (the representatives of the twenty-eight governments).

33. IDOS, *Dossier Statistico Immigrazione* (Rome: Idos, 2918).

34. Benedict R. Anderson, *Imagined Communities: Reflections on the Origin and Spread of Nationalism* (London: Verso, 1991).

35. A paradigmatic model for this type of analysis, again for the U.S. is Charles Beard's classic text *An Economic Interpretation of the Constitution of the United States* (New York: Macmillan, 1913).

36. In the *European* of January 28–31, 1993, one could read the following letter written (in English) by a Filipino worker from Milan, Italy: "It is important for English to be understood and spoken throughout Europe. I am a Filipino and have studied English since I was eight. English has been the language of learning in schools and colleges in the Philippines for more than 50 years. I am now in Italy working as a domestic helper and find it very difficult to communicate with Europeans who do not speak English. I agree . . . that English is an enriching influence in Europe."

37. A literal translation into the "American" language would be, "Foreigners, don't leave us alone with the Americans!," even if it seems to me that the irony of the request is especially apparent in societies where the status of outsider and the status

of foreigner almost completely coincide, such as in France or, especially, Italy. Not so in the United States.

38. Melossi, ed., *Multiculturalismo e sicurezza in Emilia-Romagna: Prima parte*, Quaderno n. 15 Città Sicure Project (Bologna: Regione Emilia-Romagna, 1999); Alin M. Ceobanu, "Usual Suspects? Public Views about Immigrants' Impact on Crime in European Countries," *International Journal of Comparative Sociology* 52 (2011): 114–31.

39. Melossi, *Multiculturalismo e sicurezza in Emilia-Romagna.*

40. For instance, the current turn of events in Italy reminds one of what happened in the UK between the 1970s and the 1980s, when the moral panic about "mugging" was the object of the crucial *Policing the Crisis: Mugging, the State, and Law and Order,* by author Stuart Hall and his collaborators (London: Macmillan, 1978). A few years later Paul Gilroy would write *There Ain't No Black in the Union Jack* (1987; repr. London: Routledge, 2002).

41. Umberto Eco, *The Name of the Rose* (Boston: Harcourt, 1983).

42. Brother Dolcinus was the founder of a radical Franciscan movement in Northern Italy in the second half of the thirteenth century who preached the end of the church and the feudal system and called for the creation of an egalitarian and libertarian society with no distinction of wealth or gender. He and his lover Margherita were burned at the stake as heretics in 1307.

43. This, of the constitution of some Utopia, some project of social change, is the attitude of all social innovators, who walked in very large numbers the lands of Europe! Nowhere is this clearer than in Münster (see the unnumbered note at the beginning of this chapter's endnotes), the story of which, in the sixteenth century, I learned in a novel written in 1999 by four writers from Bologna who assumed the collective name of Luther Blisset (a "collective" later to be known as Wu Ming) in a novel entitled *Q*—which you can find now translated in all European languages. Hopefully, we shall avoid the cages, like those on the walls of the St. Lambert's Church in Münster, that held the remains of the leaders of the Anabaptist revolt.

3

The Promise of the Border

Immigration Control and Belonging in Contemporary Britain

Ana Aliverti

Criminologists have long been concerned with the relationship between crime and social order. Following Durkheim, they suggest that crime and punishment have a structuring and normative function.[1] Through the language and imagery of crime, we make sense of the social world and our position within it. In a context of profound social changes, the language of crime offers neat categories and quick fixes. Crime has become "a lingua franca . . . to debate, dissect, and diagnose the condition of 'the' social order itself'"[2] and to delimit the boundaries of a civilized society. Such a boundary-making function has often relied upon and fueled racialized ideas of lawlessness. In the UK, for example, "black criminality" has been historically constructed as particularly threatening and un-British.[3] Even on the face of falling crime rates across many Western countries since the 1990s, these publics remained convinced that criminality was on the up. So too politicians vehemently reacted against this criminological finding and refused to revise their policies and discourse on crime.[4] This disconnect between the "empirical reality of crime" and the public attitudes and responses to it reveals the cultural salience of crime to articulate deep public desires and fears.[5] It also highlights the importance of crime for maintaining the myth of the sovereign state.[6]

The meanings and imageries attached to lawlessness and crime are being reconfigured in a postcolonial globalized world. Global interconnectedness and interdependence produced by new forms of political and economic imperialism have resulted in growing exposure and vulnerability to risk and a heightened perception of insecurity.[7] Societies in the prosperous West are no longer shielded from the consequences of distant wars, extreme poverty, failing states, or despotic autocracies. Global inequalities are vividly brought home not just by the media, but by the most routine interactions in the schoolyard, the doctor's office, a police station. In this disorienting and perplexing scenario, these publics have reverted to the state in search of soothing certainty and a longed sense of order. The national space has been resurrected as the site of certainties and order.

In the UK as elsewhere, these demands and the political responses to them have been articulated through the language of immigration and the border offered as a tool to restore a sense of discernible order and legible world.[8] A two-decades-long national obsession with immigration in Britain culminated with the electoral campaign to pull out from the European Union. The success of the referendum to exit the EU in June 2016 relied on the promise of regaining territorial sovereignty allegedly relinquished through EU membership. The British exit from the EU signaled not only a worrying trend in the rise of nationalisms in mainstream politics, it also laid bare the increasing symbolic purchase of the language of immigration and immigration controls to articulate ideas and ideals about social order.

In this chapter, I explore how immigration has shifted the cultural salience of crime for articulating and diagnosing the conditions of social order. The traditional criminological focus on crime, as border criminologists have argued,[9] falls short in capturing this new cultural milieu where border controls acquire a distinctive meaning to understand and act upon the social world. In the first section, I review the criminological literature on the symbolic power of crime and draw on its findings to analyze the contemporary salience of immigration. I show how the new policy and discursive emphasis on migration controls mark a shift in the social and cultural understanding of order and disorder and on the operation of state power (including penal power) for shoring up the boundaries of belonging. The electoral purchase of nationalisms and populisms across the West capitalized on fears and anxieties brought about by globalization and mass migration and the hopes and desires of a less chaotic and more stable and ordered social world. Their success rests on the wielding of mighty sovereignty in the service of the nation's survival. In the UK, as I show in the second section, those desires are shaped by imperial melancholia and nostalgia that were unhinged during the referendum campaign. In the last section, I turn to the place of immigration law and policies for producing this cultural milieu and legitimizing extreme forms of exclusion. I draw on observations in police custody and informal conversations with law enforcement officers to understand their own appraisals of the promises that the border bears. From their accounts, it evidences a more skeptical, ambivalent, and even cynical view of their role and capacity to deliver on the promises of the imagined community. Moments of self-doubt, confessions of emotional stress, and ambivalence about their role cast doubts on the assumptions on which the border control apparatus rests and foreshadow promising avenues for disruption and resistance.

The empirical data relied upon in this chapter is part of a project examining police and immigration cooperation in England. The project aims at evaluating arrangements in British policing to systematically identify foreign nationals in police custody and consider whether they are eligible for removal or deportation from the country. The project involved observations of custody processes during September and December 2017 (approximately 340 hours of observations) in two main "hub" police custody suites in one of Britain's largest police forces. During this time, I shadowed immigration officers embedded in custody and observed their daily interactions with police staff and individuals arrested. I also conducted semi-structured interviews with immigration and police staff at various ranks, including custody officers, sergeants, inspectors, and police constables, and immigration officers, chief immigration officers, and managers. In total, I conducted twenty-six in-depth interviews of approximately forty-five minutes each. The analysis of findings presented here is brief and limited, but offers an insight into themes that will be developed in future work.

Immigration, Crime, and Social Order

In the early 2000s, David Garland diagnosed an emergent culture of crime control in the U.S. and the UK.[10] Increased crime rates in the 1970s and onward coupled with a changed class distribution in victimization and the ubiquity of crime in the media contributed to a remarkable shift in crime control policies and politics. Crime not only became more salient as a social phenomenon, it also acquired a new role as a vehicle to diagnose the condition of social and moral order and the place of the state as guarantor of security. As Ian Loader and colleagues documented when interviewing residents in an English rural district in the 1990s, "crime-talks" and the vocabulary and imagery evoked by them help to constitute people's sense of place and belonging. Through the lenses of crime and disorder, people give shape to their "imagined community."[11] The crime policies, discourses, and practices born out of the late twentieth century shaped that social order by institutionalizing responses to social problems that in turn had profound social impacts, like mass incarceration.[12] Similarly, Jonathan Simon detected an emerging form of governance through crime that he associated with the growing punitiveness in the turn-of-the-century United States.[13] Crime, he argued, has become a "model problem" through which other social problems, from school truancy to drugs and poverty, are framed, conceptualized, and acted upon. Crime, in short, is a form of governance. It is a tool to legitimize the exercise of penal power that, as sociologists of punishment documented, falls disproportionately on socially disadvantaged minorities.

In a recent book, anthropologists Jean Comaroff and John Comaroff observed that global capitalism has triggered a "tectonic shift in the relationship between governance, capital, and the state."[14] Economic deregulation and the deterritorialization of capital have created liminal spaces where the lines between the licit and the illicit, civility and chaos, are difficult to draw, and in turn a perception of rising lawlessness has spread. Focusing on post-apartheid South Africa, they argued that crime has been increasingly mobilized to yield new truths and normative knowledge about a changing world and to redefine the boundaries of civil and uncivil society along the axes of race and class. Criminal justice actors, and the police in particular, have been tasked with restoring a semblance of order through law. Yet, as the Comaroffs provocatively posed, the efforts and desires to reestablish a sense of discernible order continuously stumble with its impossibility. Not only has state sovereignty been fractured or lamed through privatization and globalization, crime has become undecipherable, impossible to measure and to solve. In this inchoate and edgy world, they argued, authority is facing a difficult time in asserting itself.[15]

Yet, state sovereignty, or at least the specter of it, is far from waning. As crime has lost some of its symbolic allure and power for defining and framing the boundaries of social order, new frames of references have emerged to produce truth and to constitute problems of security and civility. Mass migration triggered and facilitated by globalization has posed profound questions about the viability of the nation-state, from the distribution of public wealth to the limits and content of citizenship, and has driven home the ethical, legal, social, and political implications of living in a growing, interconnected world. In this context, global human movement has been constructed as a threat and securitized through discourse, laws, and practices.[16]

At the discursive level, "immigration," with its attendant racial and class connotations, has become a powerful symbol and an important reference point to apprehend the world, diagnose the condition of social order, make judgments about how it ought to be, and prescribe solutions. As Bourdieu explains, "Symbols are the instruments *par excellence* of 'social integration': as instruments of knowledge and communication . . . , they make it possible for there to be a consensus on the meaning of the social world, a consensus which contributes fundamentally to the reproduction of the social order."[17] He also notes that relations of communication are intrinsically political. They depend on the material or symbolic power of the agent to impose a particular form of seeing the world, a frame of reference, a system of classification. Symbolic power is "a power of constituting the given through utterances, of making people see and believe . . . , an almost magical power which enables one to obtain the equivalent of what is obtained through force."[18] Immigration has come to symbolize the threats and insecurities produced by a boundless world and its securitization a dominant framework through which to conceptualize it.

As border criminology scholars have documented, immigration is being managed in punitive ways through criminal justice or criminal justice-like institutions, laws, and practices in countries across the world.[19] Borders, in the form of old-fashioned fences and walls or more modern technologies, have become the ultimate way to perform sovereignty.[20] The resort to force—including military force—to stop unwanted migrants evokes a masculine, patriarchal protector of the nation soothing social anxieties and fears.[21] In doing so, as Vanessa Barker argues,[22] the state deploys its material and symbolic power to reset a national frame of reference affirming its authority and the boundaries of national membership. In what she calls "penal nationalism," Barker identifies an emergent and hybrid form of state power whereby penal power is instrumentalized for nationalistic purposes: to shore up national identity and sovereignty.[23] In the same way that nation-state formation was pursued through violence, conquest, and subjugation, the attempts to resurrect the national frame through penal power have enormous costs. Penal nationalism, Barker explains, relies on the brutalization and dehumanization of those perceived as not fitting into the national picture and legitimizes the infliction of legally sanctioned violence against them in ways that are not permissible in other circumstances in modern democracies. As such, penal nationalism distorts justice and intoxicates democracy.

Penal powers, in particular the police, as the most visible embodiment of them, have a remarkable capacity for imposing classifications because they can back them up with coercion.[24] As others have shown, policing is constitutive of social relations and hierarchies and productive of social bonds and solidarity.[25] The everyday exercise of coercion by the police—who is stopped on the streets, why some individuals are singled out for further checks, and how people are treated in custody—is profoundly consequential for shaping assumptions of "suspicious populations" and for making them appear "common-sense."[26] In the remainder of the chapter I explore how this new common sense on immigration has been pandered to for electoral gains, exalting deep-seated sensibilities about the limit and character of the nation and propping up social fragmentation and exclusions.

The State of the British Nation: Brexit, Imperial Melancholia, and the Last Bastion of Sovereignty

The promise of the border to produce a semblance of safety and ease social anxieties has been seized by political parties and leaders from all sides of the political spectrum across the world during recent major electoral contests. Pandering to racialized fears in the United States, Donald Trump, in his successful presidential bid, relied heavily on promises to seal off the Southern border with Mexico and to pursue mass deportations of unwanted foreigners. During his first days in office, Trump announced a travel ban on citizens from certain Muslim-majority countries. While his campaign and first year of presidency have been plagued by scandals and criticized by the lack of a serious program of government, immigration remained the backbone of his mandate and of his puzzling ascendance to power. At the other side of the Atlantic, electoral gains if not downright victories were made in several European countries (including France, Austria, Italy, Germany, Greece, and the Netherlands) by parties running on anti-immigration manifestos and against EU ruling. The worrying rise in the influence of populisms and nationalisms in mainstream politics catalyzed social and economic anxieties, which were accentuated during the so-called refugee crisis in 2015 and 2016 and the terrorist attacks in Paris in 2015. The upsurge in the number of people escaping poverty and fleeing bloody wars in Syria, Afghanistan, and Iraq was seized by the tabloid media and the political right to extol fears of "cultural" contamination and terrorist threats and to call into question the capacity of the European Union to control the continent's external borders.

In the UK, the electoral campaign and debates in the run-up to the UK referendum to exit the EU were in tune with and fed into the new nationalisms emerging elsewhere. While then–prime minister David Cameron's decision to hold a referendum vote in June 2016 on the UK's future relationship with the European Union was primarily conceived as a way to put an end to long-lasting divisions at the heart of the Conservative Party between Eurocentric and Euroskeptic factions, the process rapidly spiraled out to resurrect debates about Britain's national identity. Despite the vague and piecemeal details of what post-Brexit Britain would look like and accusations of false and deceiving statements by critics, Brexit supporters successfully framed the vote in terms of national sovereignty through the slogan of "bring back controls" to the British Parliament.[27] It scorned the international elites in Brussels and New York and claimed to give an unhinged voice to "ordinary, decent British people" whose concerns about job security, multiculturalism, and basic living conditions have been for too long dismissed as exaggerated and racist.[28] Unsurprisingly, debates around sovereignty were conflated with national survival. Political sovereignty was conceptualized as an indispensable aspect of the protection and integrity of the nation. Orchestrated by opportunist politicians and unscrupulous media empires, the message of the campaign touched a delicate nerve in British national consciousness. The Brexit vote galvanized and gave political voice to deep-seated sensibilities among sectors in society who cleaved to social memories about Britain's past and entertained hopes for resurrecting it.[29]

The formation and reproduction of the nation are psychosocial and political processes, and the linkage between people is "imagined," invented, and arbitrary.[30] In modern times, political authority played a key role in delimiting and reproducing the boundaries of national belonging and creating the nation-state as a natural political unit. Territorial integrity, popular sovereignty, and ethnically homogeneous population united into the classic single definition of the modern European nation-state and had enduring implications for shaping the global order and national identities. The formation of the European nation-state depended on territorial expansion and the global hierarchies that ensued. As historians of the British Empire explained, the formation of Great Britain as a nation in the late nineteenth century relied upon its global conquests and, at the same time, required a strict dissociation from its imperial dominions geographically, morally, and ethnically.[31] The self-identities of empires as civilized and white were produced through their contrast to the backwardness and blackness of the distant colonies.[32] As we will see, the legacies of colonial ordering of nations and populations endure as former colonial powers act out their sovereignty to protect the nation.

Postwar Great Britain is imagined as stable, cohesive, and disciplined, globally omnipresent and dominant, and self-contained within the shores of the British Isles. As Paul Gilroy has argued, British national identity has been profoundly shaped by its imperial past and its ambivalent stance toward it.[33] Cultural disorientation and mixed feelings of postcolonial guilt, pride, melancholia, and anxiety led to a pathological response of denial of colonial ties and responsibilities toward postcolonial subjects and a reaffirmation of national identity along racial lines. The central place of race in British national identity has had an enduring effect in the country's chronic hostility toward strangers, outsiders, racialized groups.[34] The ascription of the label of "migrant" to non-white people and the country's troubled relationship with its "internal others" evidence the stubborn legacy of colonialism in the contemporary national portrait.[35] For some time in the UK, "immigration talks" had a key symbolic role for articulating narratives of moral and "cultural" decline and fantasies of invasion, contamination, overcrowding, and insolvency.[36] Conflated with race, discourses around immigration produce national spaces as "natural" and uncontaminated and create "ecologies of belonging."[37]

Brexit took stock of this "imperial melancholia" and the longings for resurrecting a prouder, less complicated, and whiter Britain. It fleshed out a bold, soothing, and easy fix to the existential insecurities and anxieties engendered by globalization. It avowed and reaffirmed the emotional, physical, and social identification of part of the British society with that "imagined community." Emotional attachments to the nation are not primal; rather, they are constructed and require daily cultivation and reinforcement.[38] The referendum campaign offered a platform for social catharsis and an opportunity to unearth and extol British nationalism. According to the British Election Study,[39] Leave and Remain voters were starkly divided by the motivations for voting in the referendum. While the key concerns of the former were "immigration" and "sovereignty," the latter mentioned the economy. As the authors of the study concluded, the referendum was not about the position each side took in relation to a single issue but the priority of different issues for voters. Immigration dominated the campaign and ultimately decided the vote. The Brexit vote capitalized on a three-decades-long obsession with net migration figures and refugee intakes and more recent concerns about free movement within Europe. European enlargement since the early 2000s that lifted immigration controls on citizens of various European countries propped up fears of being swamped by the "lumpen proletariat" next door.[40] Eastern Europeans are engrossed by the list of racialized minorities, and some national groups became the main targets of public despise. Stories about Polish swan eaters, drunken Latvian lorry drivers, Romanian shoplifters, Estonian benefit swindlers, and Bulgarian queue-jumpers abounded and contributed to sediment assumptions and ideas of Eastern European cultural otherness.

As the referendum results revealed, these sensibilities and anxieties among a large section of the British public are a powerful force. Brexit blew out traditional divisions along party lines and evidenced stark geographical and national differences. While the Leave vote concentrated in England and Wales (except for London, Manchester, and other metropolitan areas), the Remain vote won in Scotland and Northern Ireland. Brexit appealed to both Conservative and Labour voters, including in Labour strongholds in the Midlands and Northern England. The analysis of results by ward showed significant fragmentation within constituencies. Areas that voted for Remain had pockets of Leave voters and vice-versa. For example, Oxford voted Remain, but an analysis of wards revealed stark differences between, on the one hand, deprived areas where Leave dominated and the central areas near colleges where students reside that largely voted for Remain, on the other.[41]

The demographic makeup of the Brexit voter was sharp and clear: it was the older generation with no or lower educational attainment who turned up to the polls and tilted the balance. Education was the strongest predictor of voting preferences: 68 percent of voters with university degrees voted to Remain, whereas 70 percent of voters with only a secondary school diploma or no degree voted to Leave. The Remain vote won among the under-twenty-five by an astonishing 71 percent, while Leave sized the vote of the over-sixty-five (by 64 percent).[42] Ethnicity played a key role as well in predicting voting preferences. Nationally, white voters were generally pro-Leave, while nonwhite voters supported Remain — except in some London wards. Ethnicity disrupted the association between the Leave vote and education in some wards in the Birmingham area where the pro-EU vote won among ethnic minority groups with low levels of educational qualifications.[43] As sociologist Gurminder Bhambra argued, despite the public portrayal of Brexit as the victory of the have-nots, those left behind by economic globalization, Leave supporters were disproportionately concentrated within the "propertied, pensioned, well-off, white *middle* class based in Southern England."[44] The portrayal of Brexit as a white, working-class arousal is not only statistically incorrect, she argued, it is also disingenuous, because it conceals the fact that class inequalities are overwhelmingly borne by ethnic minorities and downplays the significance of racism in the opposition to immigration.

Referendum debates and campaigning brought to the surface tensions in multicultural conviviality and licensed blatant expressions of xenophobia and racism. In a widely condemned poster by the UK Independent Party (UKIP), voters were urged to "break free from the EU and take back control" by a photograph featuring a long queue of people trying to cross the Croatia-Slovenia border at the peak of the refugee crisis in 2015.[45] The pro-Brexit ad was compared to pro-Nazi propaganda and accused of pandering to racialized fears of nonwhite migration. Unsurprisingly, the referendum campaign and results unleashed an abrupt rise in "hate crimes." Police statistics showed an increase of 29 percent in recorded hate crimes between 2015/6 and 2016/7,[46] the largest increase since hate crimes have been recorded as a crime category. "Race hate crime" accounted for 78 percent of the overall hate crime count. A Home Office report on hate crime trends states that the sharp increase in recorded hate crimes reflects a "clear spike" in the occurrence of these crimes, particularly during the referendum campaign and vote (between April and June 2016) and cannot be explained merely by better police recording practices.

As mass human mobility is increasingly conceptualized as a problem of governance and a threat to the character of the nation, the reassertion of the border has become the standard political response to the challenges of globalization in many Western democracies. Electoral manifestos have exploited and reinforced lingering reservoirs of nationalism among powerful nations, with worrying societal consequences. Recent electoral contests laid bare the increasing symbolic purchase of the language of immigration and immigration controls to articulate ideas and ideals about social order and brought to the surface deep-seated, "common-sense" assumptions and emotions about national belonging in the social epidermis. In the next section, I turn to an examination of the productive function of immigration law and its enforcement for forging this cultural milieu and explore possible avenues for disrupting it.

Producing and Disrupting Borders through Immigration Law and Its Enforcement

The electoral gains of nationalisms and populisms in many Western democracies call for a pause to understand the underlying assumptions, fears, and desires driving these outcomes. Cultural studies have documented the powerful role of media and political and legal discourses for ascribing meaning, constructing reality, and creating a normative order.[47] The symbolic order and the power relations that it sustains rely on their naturalization, their taken-for-grantedness nature. Despite evidence pointing to the contrary,[48] immigration common sense stubbornly clings to immigration myths: that "immigrants" drive up crime rates, drain the welfare estate, and are a financial burden. As with crime, public perception of net migration rates is consistently higher than official statistics and is impermeable to "hard facts."[49]

In the UK, immigration common sense has been solidified through daily doses of tabloid and mainstream media reporting and increasingly restrictive immigration laws and policies. Raids in restaurants and houses, and traffic operations in central areas to find "immigration offenders," contribute to the public humiliation and racialization of people and spaces and to the reinforcement of the boundaries of belonging. Vans commissioned by the Home Office in 2013 threatening passersby to "go home or face arrest" paraded through London boroughs with high concentrations of minority ethnic communities and formed part of a broader government program to make the country a "hostile environment" for illegal immigrants.[50] Public authorities and charities have been required to share data on suspected immigration offenders within schools, doctor's offices, and homeless shelters.[51] The Immigration Acts of 2014 and 2016 expanded law enforcement powers and created new restrictions and liabilities on banks, landlords, the driving licensing authority, employers, and health care staff. In deploying its symbolic power, the government has not merely responded to the public concerns about "immigration" but has helped constitute it.

As scholars have argued, immigration laws naturalize differential treatment and precarity.[52] Through their enforcement, the boundaries of national belonging are further racialized and those targeted are reminded of their non-belonging.[53] Racialization through immigration law enforcement has broader implications for citizens. Recent stop-and-search figures showed that one in five individuals stopped by immigration officers between 2012 and 2017 were British,[54] while a survey on the use of powers to stop drivers without reasonable suspicion or reason fell disproportionately on ethnic minorities.[55] Traffic checks are a key strategy in immigration law enforcement.[56] The criminalization of "driving while undocumented" in sections 43 and 44 of the Immigration Act of 2016 is feared to further legitimize the use of racial clues in traffic stops.

Immigration laws, through illegalization and criminalization, are important instruments of social ordering.[57] They turn complex societal issues into matters of individual responsibility and make coercion a natural response to unauthorized mobility. As frontline staff, immigration officers play an important role in rationalizing and legitimizing state coercion against "immigration offenders." Their accounts shed light on how they perceive and rationalize their jobs in terms of harm prevention and law enforcement, while at the same time uncovering doubts and ambivalences about the promises of safety and boundedness that they are supposed to fulfill.

Ted, an immigration officer in charge of investigating "sham marriages," explains that immigration lawbreaking is a form of cheating and a matter of individual choice. By law, registrars are obliged to report to the Home Office any notice of marriage between a British or EEA (European Economic Area) national and a "third-country national." He routinely monitors the list of notices and "invites" couples to assess their authenticity. Leaving aside the gendered and racialized assumptions in asserting "marriage authenticity," he notes that "sham marriages" interviews are not only meant to identify "dodgy" couples for removal; even "happily married couples with kids" can be removed through these interviews. He admits that his job is sometimes stressful: "Removing families is stressful, but then I think they put themselves in that situation for overstaying their visas. They could have gone back and come in with a visa." When I pressed him to elaborate on why he thought that these families do not regularize their status, he reckoned it is "because they fear they won't be given a visa" (field notes October 2017). By appealing to the language of lawbreaking, Ted's account turns illegalization into a matter of individual blame while oozing a subtle ethical discomfort and helping rationalize his job. For him and for some of his colleagues, conceptualizing their work as removing people who break immigration rules helps with that detachment and depoliticizes their role. On his way back from an "enforcement visit" in a house where he and his team arrested three men for overstaying their visas, Ajay commented to me without much prompting that "this job isn't for anyone. It requires a neutral mind, no judgment. Immigration is a sensitive issue and [we] can't believe what people say to us, it requires neutrality, not getting too involved, keeping distance" (field notes November 2017).

Others refer to the social harms of illegality and the role of immigration enforcement for tackling abuse and welfare drain,[58] and ultimately for sustaining the UK's state solvency. Maria, an immigration inspector who leads a unit dealing with serious immigration crimes, talks about the economy of illegalities created by those who flout immigration rules: "People are so desperate and will do whatever to get a document," including paying large sums to fake an employment sponsorship. Her job, she explains, is to curtail those illegal networks created to bypass immigration controls and ultimately to prevent a range of social harms produced by immigration illegalities: "When people are hired and live illegally, they harm the community, they take places in schools, in the NHS, and get jobs that others can't get" (field notes November 2017). For her, the border is a protective device to prevent exploitation and harm.

Sam, an immigration officer, confessed to me that "personally I would remove everybody." He talks about his frustration about not being able to do enough: "It is never enough, people slip through the net." In custody, he is dealing with a man from Vietnam who had been arrested by the police on a raid at a nail bar where he was working. "If you go to his address, you will probably find twenty more Vietnamese," he mutters with impotence and alludes to the limited role of enforcement for disrupting the rife economy of illegality. Applying his professional instinct, he confidently gauges the chances of removal for this man: Vietnamese don't get visas very frequently, so he is likely to have come on a back of a lorry, he will need to fill an application for an EDT [emergency travel document] in English and in Vietnamese, but "they won't tell the truth either way." "Vietnamese are not easy to remove," he sighs, resigned, plus he has an eight-months' pregnant girlfriend. "That's what happens. They come here and have kids. Then you can't remove them." In his view, "free movement" has compounded matters. "Free movement was designed for people like you, or business people, not for the people who come without a job, without knowing the language, vulnerable to all sorts of exploitation." When he is out on visits, he is often disgusted and shocked by the conditions where people live. As he goes on, Sam lets out a less assertive, even compassionate stance and a more troubled and complex picture of his role. "Our job is very negative. There are no good results: either they go back or are released into poverty" (field notes October 2017).

"Getting rid of people," as it turns out, is not only difficult but painful. As Jackie suggests, empathy and compassion for the suffering of others can disrupt essentialized identities and differences and unsettle the very premises through which power operates.[59] Motherhood, in her case, impels her to question the ethical limits of her job: "I went to a removal center"—she comments fleetingly—"and met a Ghanaian who came here at four. I have a five-years-old. It's cruel. Why do we do that?" (field notes November 2017). Other immigration officers born to immigrant parents relay the emotional stress and anxiety that their job sometimes generates. Monique, whose parents emigrated from India decades ago, tells me that her job made her aware of how desperate people are to stay in this country and how emotionally draining it was when she first started. She recalls people touching her feet and begging her not to remove them. Her job opened her eyes to the "global distribution of unequal life chances"[60] and to her accident of birth: "They are human beings at the end of the day. It's just that they've not been born in this country. . . ." And she continues, "I'm very fortunate that I go home to my family every day" and admits her fortune is down to pure luck: "This is a great country. I love this country. People tell me 'you are lucky to have been born here'" (field notes September 2017). As she conjectures, shared immigration pathways and ancestry can lead to identification and recognition and to inadvertently cast doubts on migration controls.

Conclusion

The contemporary political purchase of border control and impulses to seal the border are, as Weber and McCulloch explained, an attempt to reinscribe the state and redraw the boundaries of belonging at a time "when the processes of globalization . . . are challenging the meaning and significance of borders."[61] Brexit brought to the fore the significance and productivity of migration and border controls for contemporary governance. Yet, as voters came to realize in the morning of June 24, 2016, far from the virile, confident imagined nation that Brexit would deliver, the post-referendum UK appears depleted, disoriented, and more socially fragmented and debilitated, unable to heal the wounds laid bare by the contest. Resurrecting the myth of sovereignty comes at a great price. While the fantasies of reviving British global influence by revitalizing former colonial ties have not yet materialized, turning its back to Europe exposed the fragilities of the UK's island status and the dangers and trade-offs that come with political and economic dominance.

The impulse to seal the border posed a number of paradoxes. As a report by the House of Lords' European Union Committee indicated, the exit from the EU will terminate the UK's privileged access to police and criminal justice measures—including ECRIS, EAW, SIS II, Eurojust, and Europol.[62] These measures were regarded as vital by the then home secretary Theresa May, to "stop foreign criminals from coming to Britain, deal with European fighters coming back from Syria, stop British criminals evading justice abroad, prevent foreign criminals evading justice by hiding here, and get foreign criminals out of our prisons."[63] Losing that access and diminishing cooperation with its European partners, Lord Kirkhope warned, will jeopardize public security and will turn the UK into "a little island off the continent."[64]

The promise of the border fades away not only because of its ineffectiveness as a security device. People just keep trying to enter no matter the risks involved, as police and immigration staff frustratingly complain. "We are losing the fight," one immigration officer concluded abashedly. His belligerent choice of words conveys his sense of impotence and of being outnumbered. The very premise on which bordering is sustained shakes in times of globalization as the borders of belonging are increasingly difficult to draw. Enforcing borders in an unequal world is ethically and emotionally taxing, as border enforcement officers attest. In its attempts to racialize citizenship, the border control apparatus meets its own limit, as Tara found out. Her authority to wield power is constantly put into question by her skin color. As she rummages around police custody searching for "visible" foreigners, she is yelled at by a "a drunk British man" telling her, "You shouldn't be here in this country." She laughs.

As immigration common sense is undisturbed by facts, doubts and questions cast by the women and men tasked with enforcing the border are powerful reminders of its pitfalls. These pockets of compassion in a sea of dehumanizing otherness may hold the key for the undoing of the border.[65] As this chapter has argued, finding the cracks in the solidified immigration common sense that sustains and legitimizes power is a promising step to disrupt the toxic and damaging effect of the border control apparatus.

Notes

This chapter benefited from discussions and comments from colleagues and friends. I would like to thank Alpa Parmar and the editors of this volume for their feedback, as well as attendees at the Law and Society Association Annual Conference (Toronto,

June 2018) and at the American Society of Criminology Annual Conference (San Francisco, November 2019).

1. D. Garland, *Culture of Control: Crime and Social Order in Contemporary Society* (Oxford: Oxford University Press, 2001); I. Loader, "Policing, Recognition, and Belonging," *Annals of the American Academy of Political and Social Science* 605 (2006): 201–21; J. Simon, *Governing through Crime: How the War on Crime Transformed American Democracy and Created a Culture of Fear* (Oxford: Oxford University Press, 2007).

2. Jean Comaroff and John Comaroff, *The Truth about Crime: Sovereignty, Knowledge, Social Order* (Chicago: Chicago University Press, 2017).

3. S. Hall, C. Critcher, T. Jefferson, J. Clarke, and B. Roberts, *Policing the Crisis: Mugging, the State, and Law and Order* (London: Macmillan, 1978); P. Gilroy, *There Ain't No Black in the Union Jack* (Abingdon: Routledge, 2002).

4. M. Hough and J. Roberts, "Public Opinion, Crime, and Criminal Justice," in *The Oxford Handbook of Criminology*, ed. A. Liebling, S. Maruna, and L. McAra (Oxford: Oxford University Press, 2017).

5. T. Caldeira, *City of Walls: Crime, Segregation, and Citizenship in Sao Paulo* (Berkeley and Los Angeles: University of California Press, 2000).

6. Garland, "The Limits of the Sovereign State: Strategies of Crime Control in Contemporary Society," *British Journal of Criminology* 36 (1996): 445–71.

7. K. Franko, *Globalization and Crime* (London: Sage, 2003); Franko, "Criminology, Punishment, and the State in a Globalized Society," in *The Oxford Handbook of Criminology*, ed. Liebling, Maruna, and L. McAra (Oxford: Oxford University Press, 2017).

8. M. Bosworth, Franko, and S. Pickering, "Punishment, Globalization and Migration Control: 'Get Them the Hell Out of Here,'" *Punishment & Society* 20 (2018): 34–53.

9. Bosworth and M. Guild, "Governing through Migration Control: Security and Citizenship in Britain," *British Journal of Criminology* 48 (2008): 703–19; K. F. Aas and Bosworth, eds., *The Borders of Punishment: Criminal Justice, Citizenship and Social Exclusion* (Oxford: Oxford University Press, 2013); V. Barker, *Nordic Nationalism and Penal Order: Walling the Welfare State* (Abingdon: Routledge, 2017); L. Weber and J. McCulloch, "Penal Power and Border Vontrol: Which Thesis? Sovereignty, Governmentality, or the Pre-emptive State?," *Punishment & Society* (2016): 1–19.

10. Garland, *Culture of Control.*

11. Loader, E. Girling, and R. Sparks, "Narratives of Decline: Youth, Dis/order and Community in an English 'Middletown,'" *British Journal of Criminology* 38 (1998): 389.

12. Garland, *Culture of Control.*

13. Simon, *Governing through Crime.*

14. Comaroff and Comaroff, *Truth about Crime.*

15. Ibid., 141.

16. Bosworth, "Border Control and the Limits of the Sovereign State," *Social & Legal Studies* 17 (2008): 199–215; Bosworth and Guild, "Governing through Migration Control," 703–19.

17. P. Bordieu, *Language & Symbolic Power* (Cambridge: Polity, 1992), 166.

18. Ibid., 170.

19. A. Aliverti, "Policing, Migration and National Identity," Introduction to the special issue of *Theoretical Criminology* 23 (2019); K. F. Aas and Bosworth, *Borders of Punishment* (Oxford: Oxford University Press, 2013); Bosworth, "Border Criminologies: How Migration Is Changing Criminal Justice," in *Changing Contours of Criminal Justice*, ed. Bosworth, C. Hoyle, and L. Zedner (Oxford: Oxford University Press, 2016).

20. W. Brown, *Walled States, Waning Sovereignty* (New York: Zone, 2010).

21. I. Young, "The Logic of Masculinist Protection: Reflections on the Current Security State," in *Women and Citizenship*, ed. M. Friedman (New York: Oxford University Press, 2005).

22. Barker, *Nordic Nationalism and Penal Order: Walling the Welfare State* (Abingdon: Routledge, 2017).

23. Ibid., 79.

24. Barker, "Policing Difference," in *SAGE Handbook of Global Policing*, ed. Loader, B. Bradford, B. Jauregui, and J. Steinberg (Abingdon: Routledge, 2006), 216; Barker, *Nordic Nationalism and Penal Order*.

25. Loader and A. Mulcahy, *Policing and the Condition of England: Memory, Politics and Culture* (Oxford: Oxford University Press, 2003); Loader, "Policing, Recognition, and Belonging," 201–21; D. Harkin, "The Police and Punishment: Understanding the Pains of Policing," *Theoretical Criminology* 19 (2015): 43–58.

26. S. Ahmed, *Strange Encounters: Embodied Others in Post-Coloniality* (Abingdon: Routledge, 2000).

27. See Leave official website: http://www.voteleavetakecontrol.org/briefing_control.html (accessed February 28, 2019).

28. M. Muñiz, "Brexit and the Anti-Elite Era," *Oxford University Politics Blog* [online], 2016, https://blog.politics.ox.ac.uk/brexit-anti-elite-era/.

29. A. Gardner, "Brexit, Boundaries and Imperial Identities: A Comparative View," *Journal of Social Archaeology* 17 (2017): 3–26.

30. B. Anderson, *Imagined Communities: Reflections on the Origin and Spread of Nationalism* (London: Verso, 2016).

31. D. Armitage, *The Ideological Origins of the British Empire* (Cambridge: Cambridge University Press, 2000); C. Hall and S. Rose, "Introduction," in *At Home with the Empire: Metropolitan Culture and the Imperial World*, ed. C. Hall and S. Rose (Cambridge: Cambridge University Press, 2006).

32. E. Said, *Orientalism* (London: Penguin, 2003); F. Fanon, *Black Skin, White Masks* (1986; repr. London: Pluto, 2017).

33. Gilroy, *After Empire: Melancholia or Convivial Culture* (Abingdon: Routledge, 2004).

34. Gilroy, *There Ain't No Black in the Union Jack*; Gilroy, "'My Britain Is Fuck All': Zombie Multiculturalism and the Race Politics of Citizenship," *Identities* 19 (2012): 380–97.

35. R. Cohen, *Frontiers of Identity: The British and the Others* (Harlow, Essex: Longman, 1994); D. Rabin, *Britain and Its Internal Others, 1750–1800: Under Rule of Law* (Manchester: Manchester University Press, 2017).

36. Gilroy, "'My Britain Is Fuck All': Zombie Multiculturalism and the Race Politics of Citizenship," *Identities* 19 (2012): 380–97.

37. D. Moore, J. Kosek, and A. Pandian, *Race, Nature, and the Politics of Difference* (Durham, N.C.: Duke University Press, 2003).

38. M. Billig, *Banal Nationalism* (London: Sage, 2014).

39. C. Proser, J. Mellon, and J. Green, *What Mattered Most to You When Deciding How to Vote in the EU Referendum?* (London: British Election Study, 2016), https://www.britishelectionstudy.com/bes-findings/what-mattered-most-to-you-when-deciding-how-to-vote-in-the-eu-referendum/#.XHkLRNHLeuX.

40. While the political limits of the European Union have expanded several times, the most recent process of enlargement toward the East, incorporating the Czech Republic, Estonia, Hungary, Latvia, Lithuania, Poland, Slovakia, and Slovenia in 2004, followed by Bulgaria and Romania in 2007, were particularly controversial across many Western European countries.

41. P. Waugh, "Revealed: Britain's Deep Divisions in the Brexit Vote, with Education, Race and Age Key Factors," *Huffington Post*, 2016, https://www.huffingtonpost.co.uk/entry/brexit-new-eur-referendum-bbc-analysis-age-race-educational-qualification_uk_58986ffce4b0a1dcbd02faf7?guccounter=1.

42. Moore, "How Britain Voted," *YouGov*, 2016, https://yougov.co.uk/topics/politics/articles-reports/2016/06/27/how-britain-voted.

43. M. Rosenbaum, "Ethnic Dimension to Birmingham's vote," *BBC News*, 2016, https://www.bbc.co.uk/news/uk-politics-36703570.

44. G. K. Bhambra, "Brexit, Trump, and 'Methodological Whiteness': On the Misrecognition of Race and Class," *British Journal of Sociology* 68 (2017): 215.

45. H. Stewart and R. Mason, "Nigel Farage's Anti-Migrant Poster Reported to Police," *Guardian*, 2016, https://www.theguardian.com/politics/2016/jun/16/nigel-farage-defends-ukip-breaking-point-poster-queue-of-migrants.

46. Home Office, *Hate Crime, England and Wales, 2016/17* (London: Home Office, 2017).

47. Hall, Critcher, Jefferson, Clarke, and Roberts, *Policing the Crisis*; Ahmed, *Strange Encounters: Embodied Others in Post-Coloniality* (Abingdon: Routledge, 2000).

48. C. Dustmann and T. Frattini, "The Fiscal Effects of Immigration to the UK," *Economic Journal* 124 (2014): 593–643.

49. S. Blinder and L. Richards, *UK Public Opinion toward Immigration: Overall Attitudes and Level of Concern* (Oxford: University of Oxford, the Migration Observatory, 2018), available at https://migrationobservatory.ox.ac.uk/resources

/briefings/uk-public-opinion-toward-immigration-overall-attitudes-and-level-of-concern/.

50. H. Jones, Y. Gunaratnam, G. Bhattacharyya, et al., *Go Home?: The Politics of Immigration Controversies* (Manchester: Manchester University Press, 2017); B. Bowling and S. Westerna, "'A Really Hostile Environment': Adiaphorization, Global Policing and the Crimmigration Control System," *Theoretical Criminology* (2018), https://doi.org/10.1177/1362480618774034.

51. See, for example, the following media coverage: "Pupil Data Shared with Home Office to 'Create Hostile Environment' for Illegal Migrants," *Guardian*, December 15, 2016, https://www.theguardian.com/uk-news/2016/dec/15/pupil-data-shared-with-home-office-to-identify-illegal-migrants; "NHS Hands over Patient Records to Home Office for Immigration Crackdown," *Guardian*, January 24, 2017, https://www.theguardian.com/uk-news/2017/jan/24/nhs-hands-over-patient-records-to-home-office-for-immigration-crackdown; "Don't Blame The Immigrants: We Want to See Patients Not Passports," *Huffington Post*, September 29, 2017, http://www.huffingtonpost.co.uk/dr-louise-tomkow/dont-blame-the-immigrants_b_18136476.html; "Charities Referring Rough Sleepers to Immigration Enforcement Teams," *Guardian*, March 7, 2017, https://www.theguardian.com/society/2017/mar/07/charities-giving-home-office-details-of-rough-sleepers-says-report.

52. J. Chacón and S. B. Coutin, "Racialization through Enforcement," in *Race, Criminal Justice and Migration Control*, ed. Bosworth, A. Parmar, and Y. Vazquez (Oxford: Oxford University Press, 2018).

53. Parmar, "Policing Belonging: Race and Nation in the UK," in Bosworth, Parmar, and Vazquez, *Race, Criminal Justice and Migration Control*.

54. C. Boutaud, A. Cantwell-Corn, and D. Mancini, "Thousands of British Citizens Swept Up in Immigration Spot Checks," Bureau of Investigative Journalism, 2017, https://www.thebureauinvestigates.com/stories/2017–10–09/review-homeoffice-immigration-checks.

55. "'Driving while Black': Liberty and StopWatch's Briefing on the Discriminatory Effect of Stop and Search Powers on Our Roads," Liberty, 2017, https://www.libertyhumanrights.org.uk/sites/default/files/Liberty%20Driving%20While%20Black.pdf.

56. A. Armenta, "Between Public Service and Social Control: Policing Dilemmas in the Era of Immigration Enforcement," *Social Problems* 63 (2016): 111–26.

57. C. Dauvergne, *Making People Illegal: What Globalization Means for Migration and Law* (New York: Cambridge University Press, 2008); Alvierti, "Making People Criminal: The Role of the Criminal Law in Immigration Enforcement," *Theoretical Criminology* 16 (2012): 417–34.

58. Aliverti, "The Wrongs of Unlawful Immigration," *Criminal Law and Philosophy* (2015): 1–17.

59. Bosworth and G. Slade, "In Search of Recognition: Gender and Staff–Detainee Relations in a British Immigration Removal Centre," *Punishment & Society* 16 (2014): 169–86.

60. J. Heyman, "U.S. Immigration Officers of Mexican Americans, Citizens, and Immigration Police," *Current Anthropology* 43 (2002): 480.

61. Weber, and McCulloch, "Penal Power and Border Control: Which Thesis? Sovereignty, Governmentality, or the Pre-emptive State?" *Punishment & Society* (2016): 8.

62. These are some of the criminal justice institutions, measures, and instruments the UK has currently access to through EU membership: the European Criminal Records Information System, the European Arrest Warrant, SIS II (the Schengen Information System II), Eurojust (the EU's judicial cooperation unit), and Europol (the EU's law enforcement agency).

63. Quoted in House of Lords, *Brexit: Future UK-EU Security and Police Cooperation*; 7th Report of Session 2016–17 (London: House of Lords, 2017), 9.

64. Ibid., 26.

65. A. Mcleod, "The U.S. Criminal-Immigration Convergence and Its Possible Undoing," *American Criminal Law Review* 49 (2012).

II

Crimmigration under Trump

4
The Terrorism of Everyday Crime

Juliet P. Stumpf

Two Tales

An asphalt path runs through a grassy swath alongside a quiet waterway in the Netherlands. The day is cloudy, softening the angles of the houses and trees across the water. A dark-haired teenage boy dressed in white approaches a blond boy in blue, who leans on crutches. The dark-haired boy attacks the boy with crutches, hitting and kicking him until he falls to the ground. The violence shocks; it shatters the scene.

What is the state's role in responding to this incident? Which institutional system, aside from medical services, should deploy to address this violent interaction? Perhaps social services are appropriate: social workers trained in bullying or school officials experienced in violence among school-aged youth. What about the criminal justice system? After all, assault is a crime.

Other government institutions that harness state authority include immigration control agencies and national security forces like the military and antiterrorism units. These last, however, seem inapposite to a teenage assault.

Now affix a label to the scene: "Muslim migrant beats up Dutch boy on crutches."[1] Does that label bring the other institutions closer to the scenario? Does it make it a difference if the scene appears in a video stacked with two other anti-Muslim videos and disseminated via Twitter by Britain First, widely held to be an extremist neo-nationalist group.[2]

There is no reason to believe that immigration agents or national security forces would respond to this scenario. With the introduction, however, of the keywords "Muslim" and "migrant," these authorities appear in the mind's eye. They enter the frame.

In fact, the Netherland's criminal justice system and social services network, but not its immigration or national security forces, responded to the encounter between the youths. Police arrested the attacker and the videographer, and the juvenile justice system took over. Despite the label affixed to the video, the police report never identified the first boy as either Muslim or an immigrant. According to media reports, both the assailant and victim were Dutch, and the Dutch authorities criminally prosecuted and convicted the assailant.[3]

That trio of anti-Muslim videos might have suffered the instant obscurity of most old tweets, the incident they depicted constituting a small part of a day's work for the responsible Dutch institutions. However, on November 26, 2017, U.S. president Donald Trump retweeted the videos to his 44 million Twitter followers, provoking a national and international outcry protesting his elevation of anti-Muslim propaganda. Britain First's characterizations of the videos and its motives in tweeting them became front-page news. News media described the little-known organization as a fringe group that "insists that white Christian civilization is under threat from Muslims."[4]

Prime Minister Theresa May turned to Twitter to rebuke the American president. Politicians across the international and ideological spectrum joined her condemnation.[5] In January 2018, President Trump canceled a planned visit to England, and in March 2018 the leaders of Britain First were convicted of hate crimes for harassing Muslims.[6]

The second story has a similar theme despite its different facts:

Interstate 10 runs straight as an arrow through the flatlands of Texas. When it reaches Van Horn it is about fifty kilometers (or thirty miles) north of the border, not far from Big Bend National Park. There, a deep culvert butts up against the highway. Looking down from the edge of the interstate, the cement bottom of the culvert is a steep nine-foot drop.

On the evening of November 19, 2017, two men lay at the bottom of the culvert. They had sustained severe gashes and multiple broken bones. One man did not survive the night. The other awoke with no memory of what had happened. Both were U.S. Customs and Border Patrol agents.[7]

Which governmental authority is appropriate for addressing this incident? As before, the criminal justice system took this on. Are there, though, other government institutions that could be viewed as playing a role?

Culberson County sheriff Oscar Carrillo investigated, coordinating with the FBI and other law enforcement agencies. Their first task was to determine whether this was an accident or an attack. The investigators soon confirmed that no shots had been fired. The injuries were the result of some kind of blunt trauma.[8]

But between the start and end of the investigation, this criminal matter became something else. The day after the incident, the National Border Patrol Council, a nongovernmental organization, decried the "ambush" by "undocumented immigrants" who "likely used rocks to bash the agents."[9] National leaders added their voices. The same afternoon, Texas senator Ted Cruz called the "attack" a "stark reminder of the ongoing threat that an unsecure border poses to the safety of our communities and those charged with defending them."[10] Early in the evening, President Trump condemned the incident, describing the injured agent as "brutally beaten"[11] and tweeting out a promise to "seek out and bring to justice those responsible." He ended his tweet with the reminder that the United States "will, and must, build the Wall" on the U.S. southern border with Mexico.[12]

Two weeks of intense investigation followed. On Sunday, November 29, 2017, Sheriff Carrillo told the *Dallas Morning News* that the agents likely ended up in the culvert as a result of an accident, not an assault.[13] After 620 interviews, the FBI had found no evidence of an attack or scuffle.[14] The men's injuries, Carillo reported, were more consistent with a fall than an attack.[15]

Considered separately, these two tales — mysterious injuries in Texas, a retweet of anti-Muslim videos — have little in common. One took place in Texas, and the other half a continent and an ocean away. They occurred at different times, involved different conduct by different people, treated different kinds of harm.

What they share is the early and insistent mischaracterization of the facts and a narrative about national security threats rising inside national borders in the form of dangerous migrants. First, the interpretation of the events offered initially was wrong. The initial interpretations were based on assumptions, misunderstandings, and racial and religious bias. In Texas, the rush to judgment of undocumented immigrants beat out the necessarily slower process of investigating the truth. In England and Washington, D.C., Britain First's characterizations of the videos, retweeted without comment by President Trump, were both inaccurate and intended to inflame anti-Muslim sentiment.

Second, both incidents became platforms for inflaming popular concern about national security. The Texas incident did not occur at the border, but rather fifty kilometers north of it. It took place next to an interior U.S. highway, not a border checkpoint. Yet Senator Ted Cruz's comments about the Border Patrol incident emphasized that unsecured borders were a threat to American communities. President Trump directly tied the incident to the need for a physical international barrier — a wall — between the United States and Mexico.

Similarly, while President Trump did not comment on the anti-Muslim videos in his retweet, the White House soon clarified his message. Asked about the president's decision to share the videos with his 44 million followers, White House spokesperson Sarah Huckabee Sanders made a direct connection with national security. "The threat is real," she declared, "what the president is talking about, the need for national security and military spending, those are very real things, there's nothing fake about that."[16] Her statement drew an explicit connection between the anti-Muslim videos and the national security of the United States.

That there is a gap between the actual acts depicted in each incident and the way they were characterized is not unusual. What is significant is that the message cloaked common criminality as national security. Despite the characterization of these incidents by local, national, and international leaders as symbols and warning signs of threats to national security, there is no terrorist, no terrorist act, terrorist threat, border threat, or border breach in either incident. Although the incidents are draped with a penumbra of threat, none of the allegations and rhetoric surrounding the incidents points to an act of terrorism or intent to commit an act of terrorism or threaten national security.

Instead of terrorist activity or threats against the United States, both incidents appeared to involve actions that are criminal in nature. To be sure, some are serious crimes of violence. An assault on a Border Patrol agent, or a schoolchild, or a teenager, is a serious act with a potentially severe outcome. Each is a criminal act. None, however, are acts of terrorism.

In each incident, initial ambiguity about the facts was met with a narrative about national security. Between the report of the injuries to the Border Patrol agents and the conclusion of the investigation hung a moment of ambiguity and opportunity. That moment of ambiguity opened the opportunity for state and national leaders to make a claim about the character of the incident. Characterizing it as a national security issue, as testament to the need to build up the border, gave the incident political and ideological clout. Similarly, the intriguingly unannotated retweet of the videos, without context, manufactured a moment of ambiguity that the White House filled with the fear of a threat to national security.

These two tales illustrate an approach to regulation of migration that yokes everyday criminality to the pulse-quickening call of national security. This approach shifts the frame from the idea that terrorism arises beyond the border to the notion that national security resides terrifyingly within the everyday, domestic business of criminal justice. These examples of the recharacterization of domestic crime demonstrate the connections currently being forged between criminality and terrorism, national security, immigrants, and the border.

This chapter examines how everyday crime can be imbued with the exceptional areas of border control and securitization. It traces the braiding together of criminality, border control, and national security. The interweaving of these three themes paves the way for new legal frameworks of exclusion that draw on the extraordinary sovereign powers imbued in national security and immigration control institutions. These new legal frameworks are themselves ephemeral, but they leave behind lasting practices and apparatuses of government power.

The chapter begins by tracing the interplay between crime, border control, and securitization and explores the foundational theories that describe how they relate to one another. The second half draws from that foundation to assess the role of these intersections in light of the international growth of neo-nationalism, which holds as a core principle the restriction of immigration as a means of defining who belongs and who may govern. The chapter argues that this crosshatching of criminality, migration control, and national security creates a powerful tool for promoting the principles of neo-nationalism.

Intersections of Crimmigration, Border Penology, and Enemy Penology

How did criminality, border control, terrorism, and national security come to be interwoven? Here, the chapter outlines the development of crimmigration and analyzes how it draws lines of membership, delineating insiders from outsiders across lines of race and citizenship status. The challenge is to excavate how the crimmigration thesis intersects with the insights of the border penology and enemy penology theories to see how securitization and technologies of border control enlarge the impacts of crimmigration.

What Is Crimmigration?

Crimmigration, identified in 2006, is the intersection of immigration and criminal law. It is the merger of the two areas in both substance and procedure, making them merely nominally separate.[17] Crimmigration is a weedy concept, propagating across borders and academic disciplines. It has become an entire field of study, as scholars have brought context and meaning to it. The study of crimmigration is transnational, intercontinental, interdisciplinary.[18] It implicates racial, socioeconomic, and postcolonial critique.[19] It maps the historical, sociological, legal, and criminological characteristics of crimmigration.[20]

Historically, crime control and immigration law were considered conceptually discrete bodies of law and policy. Criminal law sought to address harm to individuals and society from violence or fraud or evil motives. Immigration law governed border crossing and managed decisions about who may visit or work or live in the nation and for how long. Criminal punishment looked backward to the punishable act; immigration law was oriented toward the present and future, considering whether the individual was desirable based on race, socioeconomics, health, family ties, or skills, among others.[21]

That distinction between immigration and criminal law held up in U.S. law for more than a century. In the nineteenth century, when the federal government decided to exclude and deport three Chinese residents of San Francisco and New York on the basis of their race, courts turned to foreign policy and international law, not crime control, to justify the government's action.[22] When, during the Red Scare of the 1950s, the United States marooned in New York Harbor a three-decade resident of New York returning from a trip to his native Hungary, the U.S. Supreme Court turned to foreign policy and the war power, not a connection between crime and securitization, to justify his prolonged detention.[23]

The late twentieth century witnessed a transformation as the separate spheres of immigration and criminal law converged.[24] Once the war on drugs in the 1980s channeled the use of crime control and policing to focus on communities of color, the way lay open to combining immigration control and crime control practices.[25] Illegal entry and illegal reentry arrests and prosecution rose steeply.[26] Enforcement capacity expanded, with a massive ramp-up in immigration enforcement personnel that rendered the then–Immigration and Naturalization Service the largest armed law enforcement agency in the federal government.[27] Capacity for immigration detention ballooned.[28]

The crimmigration merger has three facets. The first is an overlap between the substance of immigration law and criminal law, so that criminal convictions become almost inescapable grounds for mandatory deportation.[29] A plea in criminal court to driving under the influence or unlawful possession of a prescription drug may be grounds for deportation.[30]

On the other side of the coin, immigration-related conduct came to be defined as criminal.[31] Marrying a U.S. citizen solely for the purpose of obtaining lawful permanent residence became a crime in 1986.[32] Crossing the border without authorization had been on the books as a crime for a century, but because of the economic and historical interdependence between Mexican workers and American agriculture, that border-crossing conduct generally had been either overlooked or treated as an administrative violation.[33]

The late twentieth-century shift to mass deportation and detention changed this picture. Long before the election of Donald Trump, pipelines connected criminal arrest to deportation and immigration arrest to prosecution.[34] Crimmigration law now imposes both immigration and criminal sanctions for the same offense. When a noncitizen violates immigration law that has been defined as criminal or a crime that is a deportable offense, incarceration followed by deportation is the common result.[35]

The expansion of crimmigration did not go entirely unchecked. Courts stepped in occasionally to trim the edges of crimmigration. In 2010, the U.S. Supreme Court halted the deportation of lawful permanent resident Moones Mellouli when immigration authorities attempted to deport him on the basis of possession of a sock they argued constituted drug paraphernalia.[36] Had the Court agreed, Mellouli's status as a lawful permanent resident of the United States, his decades of residence, and his family ties in the United States would not have factored into the question of his deportation.[37] In *Mellouli*, the Supreme Court limited how criminal convictions could serve as grounds for deportation. The Court restricted the power of judges considering deportation to undertake a fresh adjudication of facts underlying a criminal conviction. This limitation on crime-based deportation was an important check given that the crime in question may have occurred years before and the conviction obtained in a different context: in the criminal justice system, with its different legal standards and burdens.

The second characteristic of crimmigration is the resemblance between immigration enforcement and criminal law enforcement, leading to blurring between the lines of administrative immigration and criminal justice authority. For example, immigration officials began self-identifying as police and testing the limits of their administrative authority to stop, arrest, and search.[38] On the crime control side, some state or local criminal justice officials implemented immigration enforcement policies, leading to disparate impacts on Latinos.[39]

Finally, the process of prosecuting immigration violations resembles criminal procedure. An important example is immigration detention. Previously scarcely used, pre-hearing administrative detention became routine. Functionally indistinguishable from pretrial criminal detention, it differed from the criminal system in offering drastically limited opportunities for release.[40]

Theories of Crimmigration, Border Penology, and Enemy Penology

Three theoretical strands — crimmigration, border penology, and enemy penology — triangulate the territory taken up by the exercise of penal power and securitization in border control. Each of these theories connects either border control with criminality or criminality with national security and then explains how the convergence of border control, criminality, and security creates a powerful rhetorical tool. Following these strands and discovering the points at which they cross reveal the imposition of border control and national security narratives onto scenarios that are traditionally seen through a criminal justice lens. In 2018, Leanne Weber and Jude McCulloch issued a provocative call to parse these intersections, to resist the tendency to view them as either unconnected issues or isolated pairings.[41]

Understanding the power of grafting together criminality and national security requires a map of the intersections among three theories of crimmigration, border penology, and enemy penology. Each theory explores manifestations of state penal power in the fields of migration, border control, and criminality. The theories intersect, but they bring different tools and different perspectives to bear on the crisscross of securitization, criminality, and migration. Each concerns itself with *where* government control strategies operate—inside or outside of real or conceptual bordered spaces—but each emphasizes different questions.[42]

Crimmigration, or the intersection of immigration and criminal law, describes *how* border control operates.[43] Immigration and criminal law exert a gravitational pull on one another, drawing the substance and process of criminal law into immigration law and vice versa, while leaving behind procedural protections. As a result, state sovereign power expands to draw excluding lines of membership by way of deportation, detention, criminal punishment, and the alienating narratives that accompany them.[44]

Border penology, which brings a new penology perspective to border control studies, addresses *why* migration control functions as it does.[45] Similarly to crimmigration, it describes the insertion of crime control discourses and technologies into border control strategies. These "criminalizing discourses" justify punitive and exclusionary policies. Border penology connects the three dots of criminality, migration control, and national security in the association of asylum seekers with terrorism. With this trident of governmentality, citizenship itself is defined not as a legal status or as a permanent membership, but in contrast to the noncitizen. Identified "as a source of potential risks in contemporary political discourse, his/her movements an intelligible object of policing, and his/her body a legitimate object of confinement," the noncitizen is a proper subject of preemptive governmental action through preventative infrastructures.[46]

Enemy penology, a scheme of legal regulation of exclusion of enemies that operates outside of criminal law, concerns itself with *when* governmental control operates on the excluded enemy.[47] In contrast to traditional criminal punishment, which looks backward in time to a punishable event, enemy penology seeks to preempt the possibility of an event, like a terrorist attack, by imposing state control to foreclose the possibility of the event.

Enemy penology also identifies a new *where* for governmental control strategies. In contrast to military strategies, where the enemy "appears from outside, belonging to the war-time order," or criminal law, where the criminal culprit "appear[s] within, and threaten[s] society," the political criminal is both inside and outside. This "enemy of the state" is both within and without, "a part of society" and "a figure that in threatening the constitution transgresses the border."[48]

The border in enemy penology becomes a boundary, as enemy penology "opens up a kind of a third space aiming at externalizing" individuals perceived as threats "through the invention of an additional, quasi-legal system."[49] This space is a paradigmatic border, a boundary between rule and exception, between inside and outside.

Crimmigration, border penology, and enemy penology manifest as a way of governing membership in U.S. society, enhancing differences between insiders and outsiders. Each of these theories explores who is in the zone of exclusion, which defines its targets by citizenship status, race, gender, and history of colonialism.[50] Membership theory, which examines the way that law patrols the boundaries of belonging, sheds light on how the criminal and immigration systems employ the same or similar tools to draw lines of exclusion.[51] In the current moment, criminal law and immigration law play a common role in social choices about who is a member of society and the nation-state and who is not. Criminal and immigration law both serve to separate the individual from the rest of society through physical exclusion and the creation of rules that establish lesser levels of citizenship status.[52] Immigration and criminal law employ state power to punish or otherwise publicly condemn the individual offender.

Border penology similarly emphasizes the role of membership in drawing attention to the construction of citizenship on the basis of exclusion. It is through formulating the rights and privileges denied to noncitizens that the content of citizenship emerges. Mary Bosworth and Mhairi Guild have noted that "in the process of identifying those who are denied certain rights, the form and basis of these rights have been simultaneously established and formalized." As a result, "this purportedly inclusive ideal [of citizenship]" is founded "on the exclusion of others."[53]

Enemy penology adds a third facet to the role of membership. Securitization takes exclusion to the extreme, transforming it from confinement and shutting out to an "eliminative ideal," in which the enemy, indeterminately defined to include the "alien other in our midst," is eliminated, even exterminated.[54]

The crime control, deportation, and securitization systems thus function similarly to determine who is a member of society and who should be excluded or even eliminated from it. Each is, therefore, a system of inclusion and exclusion, conferring insidership and imposing outsidership. These boundaries of belonging have a moral overlay, designating and distinguishing the innocent and the guilty, the admitted and the excluded, the threat and the threatened.

These three theories came into sharp focus with the criminalization of migration and securitization that occurred after the events of September 11, 2001. The securitization of migration after the terrorist attacks established a track record of legitimizing administrative and military detention and marginalizing disfavored groups. After September 11, securitization had fallen most heavily on Muslim and Arab noncitizens and their communities. The new U.S. Department of Homeland Security created dual programs, the Absconder Apprehension Initiative and the Special Registration provisions, that explicitly targeted young Arab Muslim men for interviews. These programs were the main means of securitizing this community. They worked, however, not through direct application of national security criminal or terrorism charges, but rather through arrest and deportation for immigration violations.[55]

These programs were controversial both because of the targeting of Muslims and because of questions about the effectiveness of the programs as antiterrorism tools. The programs forged a strong connection between immigration and securitization in a way that augmented government authority over both the border and the immigrant populace.

The next step in crimmigration would move the logic of border penology firmly into the interior and entrench securitization in crimmigration. In 2008, crimmigration reached a pinnacle when ICE launched an arrest and deportation program called Secure Communities.[56] Secure Communities reconstituted the governance of immigration as a means of crime control in the interior of the country, separate and apart from border control. It set the stage for the securitization of crimmigration.

Under Secure Communities, detention and deportation flourished once the immigration agencies had perfected the handoff to U.S. immigration authorities of any noncitizen who had a brush with law enforcement. These techniques played out without the slowing effect of discretionary prosecution decision-making and without assessment of whether the sanction of expulsion was proportional to the alleged criminal conduct.[57] Deportations topped 400,000 in 2014.[58]

After 2014, deportation levels dropped, for two main reasons.[59] First, most courts examining the enforcement methodology that sustained large-scale immigrant detention concluded that it failed to meet constitutional standards. State and federal courts around the country began to step in to stem a mass violation of the constitutional right to be free of unlawful search and seizure.[60]

Second, reaching these high levels of arrest and deportation required dipping deeply into established immigrant communities in the interior of the United States. At the time of this writing, about 11 million undocumented residents live in the United States. Under U.S. law, there are almost no statutes of limitations on deportation grounds for criminal violations, and a wide range of convictions constitute grounds to deport.[61] Under the Secure Communities program, an arrest was sufficient for undocumented immigrants to find themselves in danger of deportation.[62] Family and community ties are seldom recognized as mitigating factors in deportation decisions based on crimes. Lawful permanent residents with criminal conviction histories and long-term undocumented residents with lives and families in U.S. communities were detained and deported in large numbers.[63]

Responding both to the mounting body of judicial opinions finding elements of the program unconstitutional and to outcry from impacted communities, the Department of Homeland Security discontinued the Secure Communities program. Instead, it installed a priority-based system that emphasized prosecutorial discretion.[64] This was a move away from crimmigration and the securitization of migration.

In 2016, despite the troubled legal and political history of this full-on crimmigration strategy, the Trump Administration announced it would resurrect the Secure Communities program.[65] Something powerful and compelling was required to legitimize the return of this discredited crimmigration policing strategy. That powerful, legitimating ingredient was national security.

The Terrorism of Everyday Crime

National security is a compelling claim that enables governments to align support for a common goal, gather and deploy national resources like funds and personnel, and gain support for governance-enhancing legislation and rulemaking. Securitization instills a sense of urgency and threat that effectively rallies support for liberty-constraining government measures. A national security crisis is an optimal time to seek legitimacy for claims that the common defense requires subordination of the liberties of individuals and minority groups.[66] In her work on enemy penology, Susanne Krasmann has noted that just as the criminal is perceived "as a danger within society" in need of control in the name of social defense, "terrorist threats now are being considered as risks not only threatening society and the liberty of one and all, but also in the sense of their impelling the defence of the State as the guarantor of security."[67]

Crimmigration also augments state authority at the border and the interior. It reaches deeply into settled communities, sorts the desirable from the undesirable, and either segregates the undesirable within the border through incarceration or immigration detention, or expels them beyond the border on the basis of criminal or immigration violations.

Crimmigration is easy to access because it is already in place. Because crimmigration is the intersection of immigration and criminal law, it draws on existing, continuously operating institutions and systems. The enforcement infrastructure already exists to scale detention and deportation up or down. Thus, crimmigration is a more stable, consistent source of social control than securitization alone.

Crimmigration enables government officials to restrict noncitizen access to courts and lawyers, either directly by granting immigration officials the power to deport summarily based on a belief that the noncitizen committed an enumerated set of crimes,[68] or functionally through decisions to detain in places and under conditions that make representation all but impossible.[69]

Crimmigration also taps into what David Garland has described as the emergence of fear of crime as a prominent cultural theme.[70] Crimmigration constructs and dramatizes harm that immigrants and criminals perpetrate on society. It replaces the image of the hardworking immigrant crossing the border in search of a better life, whom society embraces or grudgingly tolerates, or the delinquent as a disadvantaged subject of rehabilitation, with the alien pinned on the border between what can and cannot be controlled, an object of fear.

Criminalizing and securitizing the border and those who cross it leads to two results. First, when the state identifies an immigration issue as a matter of public concern, when it galvanizes popular dismay, the subsequent public call for the state to act becomes much stronger. Linking migration to national security compels immediacy of state action. Linking it to criminality compels regularity of state action. Together, the quality of state action must be immediate and regular. An emergency that occurs with regularity requires exceptional exertions of state power, permitting regular exceptions to protections against deprivations of liberty and due process.[71]

Reframing criminal activity as a national security issue augments rhetorical and actual government power. The Texas story that begins this chapter illustrates how much it mattered that the death be a crime and a crime committed by undocumented immigrants. It was important that undocumented immigrants had assaulted the border patrol because it was important to a public understanding that unauthorized immigrants commit crimes, that in fact the border is the place where law enforcement's task is as much to regulate border crossings as to hold back the criminal element. The criminal alien is the smuggler, the drug dealer, the gang member, and people desperate enough for a better life in the United States that they are willing to turn to crime to reach it. It was critical that the public recognize that battle, that it affirm it and, most importantly, make the connection between the crime of assault and the necessity for massive policing resources at the border and in the interior.

Securitized crimmigration frees the state to act preemptively, to prevent crime or migration or both. When both criminality and migration become issues of national security, the state is entitled and expected to prevent them.[72] In combination, securitization and crimmigration create a crosshatching of authority to use the preemptive power of securitization, the punitive power of crime control, or the broad administrative authority of migration control.

The utility of this crosshatching for exercising broad executive exclusionary power becomes apparent in two situations involving noncitizens. First, in 2018, the Trump Administration separated close to 3,000 children from their noncitizen parents.[73] The justification for this policy connected national security with crimmigration. Then-U.S. Attorney General Jeff Sessions deemed the appearance at the border of large numbers of Central Americans, including families, to be a national security issue.[74] Declaring that "a crisis has erupted at our Southwest Border that necessitates an escalated effort to prosecute those who choose to illegally cross our border," Sessions characterized the crisis and its solution as enmeshed in national security. "To those who wish to challenge the Trump Administration's commitment to public safety, national security, and the rule of law," he stated, "I warn you: illegally entering this country will not be rewarded, but will instead be met with the full prosecutorial powers of the Department of Justice."[75] This securitization led to the assertion of a legal rule on a mass scale based in criminal law: the attorney general's decision to prosecute 100 percent of unauthorized border crossers for illegal entry.[76] These included parents accompanied by children.[77]

Second, the everyday nature of criminality justified a novel legal rule requiring separation of children from parents alleged to have crossed the border without permission. Secretary of Homeland Security Kirstjen Nielsen stated that "operationally what that means is we will have to separate your family."[78] Family separation was an everyday occurrence, she explained. "That's no different than what we do every day in every part of the United States when an adult of a family commits a crime. If you as a parent break into a house, you will be incarcerated by police and thereby separated from your family. We're doing the same thing at the border."[79] Separation as a means of border control and national security, in other words, is as common as common crime.

The three-point nexus among security, crimmigration, and border penology has also paved the way for mass temporary deportation of asylum seekers through the Remain in Mexico policy that instituted the removal of asylum seekers from the United States to Mexico to await hearings.[80] The Remain in Mexico policy arose in the context of groups of people leaving Central America, where intense violence had led thousands of people to flee. The trip from the northern triangle through Mexico to the United States had become dangerous, and the groups, which at times grew to 1,500–2,000 people, banded together for safety. Many of them planned to seek asylum in the United States upon arriving at a port of entry.[81]

President Trump tweeted that "big flows of people" were coming to take advantage of the United States and that the caravans were dangerous.[82] He called for deploying the National Guard, the reserve of military force maintained by the states and occasionally deployed for federal purposes. The next step was to expel the asylum seekers temporarily to Mexico.

By constituting the members of the caravan as dangerous flows of people and calling on the military to augment the border patrol, the administration framed the caravan as an invasive force needing a military response and a source of hypercriminality. President Trump declared, "Our issue is strong borders, no crime; [the Democrats'] issue is open borders, let MS-13 all over our country."[83] The asylum-seeker, standing in for the criminal and the alien, became a proper subject of new legal constraints drawn both from security and border control.

Unlike national security, crimmigration operates at the level of daily life. Terrorism is terrifying; it is panic-inducing. Compared to criminal acts, however, terrorist attacks are rare. Crime is ubiquitous, pervasive. Violent actions and destruction of property occur every day. The U.S. public is already sensitized to perceive Muslims as terrorists. To President Trump's vast Twitter following, the videos communicated that Muslims also represent the introduction of a criminal element into the Western world—one that their children could encounter on the way to the schoolyard.

Crime control and immigration violations give the state many more entry points for encounters with individuals on the periphery of membership. For example, immigration law prohibits undocumented immigrants from holding federally recognized driver's licenses.[84] Many nevertheless must drive to work or drive children to school. Driving without a license is a crime, and, in many places, the arrest alone channels the noncitizen into the deportation system.[85]

As another example, the Trump administration has focused on courthouse arrests in cities that resist his deportation policy preferences.[86] Immigration agents have entered courthouses in plain clothes, asked clerks for information about witnesses and parties, or discovered through their own surveillance databases the dates of probation check-ins. Agents have initiated conversations with those in the courthouse or attempted to make identity matches electronically.[87]

Immigration arrests in courthouses exact a closure of access to justice for those under the crimmigration microscope. ICE, the interior immigration enforcement agency, has targeted courthouses as a substitute for arresting noncitizens at jails and prisons in jurisdictions that prohibit transfer from state and local criminal custody to federal administrative custody.[88] These courthouse encounters have raised concerns about discouraging victims from accessing victim services, parties from pursuing their claims, and witnesses from testifying in criminal and civil cases. They have involved courthouse employees in immigration enforcement. They also send a message to courts and the public that immigration enforcement trumps the business of the judiciary.

The significance of these ICE actions for purposes of this chapter is that the arrests insert themselves into the everyday business of courthouses. Courthouses are where the business of law gets done. The everyday business of the courts is to make the multitude of large and small decisions that shape the rights and responsibilities of people, corporations, and government actors, to use the law to stitch the tattering in the fabric of society. ICE's determination to use courthouses as a crimmigration site illustrates how deeply crimmigration can reach into the infrastructure of society.

Crimmigration, Securitization, and Neo-Nationalism

What purpose might these entwined sources of authority and their accompanying technologies of control serve? Because each of them functions to draw and patrol lines of belonging and exclusion, they will serve political, social, and philosophical ends oriented toward policing membership. That describes the contemporary trend toward nationalism or neo-nationalism. A core principle of nationalism is the restriction of immigration. The reconstruction of criminality as a form of national security threat supports the central anti-immigration, racialized tenet of neo-nationalism.

What Is Neo-Nationalism?

Neo-nationalism, or new nationalism, has garnered attention as the ideology most heavily influencing U.S. executive branch policy, especially immigration policy, under the Trump administration. Neo-nationalism is a contemporary subcategory of nationalism, which is a set of political beliefs centered on the idea that the government should be in the hands of a people, usually a specific cultural group. Nationalism thrives on the building or enforcing of boundary markers that delineate group membership. These boundary markers are often highly visible, providing facile identification of group membership. They may consist of physical appearance, dress, or language ability or rely on race and religion to determine the bounds of membership.[89]

Neo-nationalism rests on the foundation of nationalism, but holds to specific policy preferences. Sociologists Maureen Eger and Sarah Valdez have described the policy preferences of neo-nationalism as displaying "a penchant for anti-establishment populism, disdain for supranational organizations, [and] a desire to limit access to the nation and its benefits to certain groups of ethnic minorities."[90] In line with many conservative systems of thought, it emphasizes traditional values and law and order. Neo-nationalism is associated with nativism, right-wing populism, anti-globalization, protectionism, and Euroskepticism.[91]

Neo-nationalism is widely acknowledged to have driven the election of Donald Trump, and continues to drive his administration's agenda.[92] Donald Trump as a candidate ran for president on an "America First" platform that promised to close the border, especially to Muslims and Mexicans.[93] His election was perceived as a powerful statement about immigration restriction.[94]

Immediately after taking power, the Trump administration began removing the United States from international agreements, compacts, and negotiations and otherwise sought to reduce the global presence of the United States.[95] A prime example of this closure and its manifestation in immigration policy was the December 2017 announcement of the U.S. ambassador to the United Nations Nikki Haley of the United States' withdrawal from the UN Global Compact on Migration. She stated:

> Our decisions on immigration policies must always be made by Americans and Americans alone. We will decide how best to control our borders and who will be allowed to enter our country. The global approach in the New York Declaration is simply not compatible with U.S. sovereignty.[96]

Ambassador Haley's statement exemplified the administration's emphasis on border control and exclusion. Her rejection of a global approach to managing migration is consistent with the isolationism that serves nationalist ends.

The Role of Crimmigration and Securitization in Neo-Nationalism

Long before the Texas events or Trump retweets occurred, crimmigration established the institutional logic for the securitization of migration and criminality. Crimmigration is an effective frame for executing neo-nationalism because it serves a number of neo-nationalist aims. First, it is in line with a primary neo-nationalist goal of restricting immigration.[97] Combining criminal and immigration enforcement enables rapid scaling of immigrant incarceration and deportation. Crimmigration generates massive and rapid expulsion,[98] facilitates mass detention,[99] and enables mass arrests.[100]

Second, crimmigration is fundamentally about membership and exclusion. And it permeates the nation working most effectively not at the border or in criminal court, but rather in the places, actions, and relationships that make up the daily lives of both immigrants and citizens.

Securitization, in turn, has played a powerful part in developing the neo-nationalist narrative. In the United States, the face of the national security threat has been the Arab Muslim, rattling the gates to the nation, probing for weakness in its defenses in order to enter and commit terrorist acts. The "Muslim ban" that Trump promised during his campaign and sought to enact through Executive Order after taking office is illustrative.[101] And as the White House made clear, retweeting the anti-Muslim videos was consistent with this theme. It is the theme to which Trump consistently returned, emphasizing the necessity of isolating America for its own protection, strengthening its own sovereignty, and returning to peculiarly American values. The incidents depicted in the videos occurred outside the United States. Those depicted in them are the people whom the U.S. president promised to keep out.

The securitization approach, however, has an Achilles heel. The legitimizing force of securitization lessens as time passes from the moment of the last national security crisis. As the crisis of the 2001 terrorist attack abated, the legitimacy of singling out groups on the basis of religion, Arab ethnicity, or nationality waned. The securitization provisions that targeted noncitizen Muslims and Arabs were softened and incorporated into routine immigration enforcement work. The NSEERS Special Registration program was put on hold and then shut down in 2016. Many of its innovations were folded into the surveillance technology and became a routine part of immigration enforcement.[102] By the time President Trump took office in 2017, the event that had shaken the nation and built the foundation for acceptance of modern securitization had lost its immediacy.

Justifying major limitations on immigration that involved restrictions of liberty would require something more. That was the introduction and integration of everyday criminality of immigrants into a national security narrative. Retooling the connection between crimmigration and national security provided a fresh and compelling reason to permit more authoritarian measures at the border, but also in the interior, where immigrant communities were settled.

National security rationales for government action usually call for control of a national crisis. Control of crime, on the other hand, requires no crisis. As a society, we accept as a matter of course that controlling crime is a social necessity, requiring an active police force in every state and county. The two stories at the beginning of this chapter illustrate how powerful the combination of national security and crime control can be. Both incidents were claimed to be national security issues; in reality each was handled as a crime.

Framed this way, crimmigration augmented by securitization became a critical tool for neo-nationalism. Trump administration rhetoric that combined indefinite threats to national security, a border crisis, and a crime surge perpetrated by immigrants of color helped to solidify those links. Securitized crimmigration frees the state to act preemptively to prevent crime or migration or both. When both criminality and migration become issues of national security, the state is expected to prevent them.[103] In combination, securitization and crimmigration create a crosshatching of authority to use the preemptive power of securitization, the punitive power of crime control, or the broad administrative authority of migration control.

New nationalism has played out through already well-established structures of crimmigration, the merging of immigration and criminal law.[104] Claims about national security, connected intimately and immediately with migration and crime control, have been an intensely powerful way to actualize the new nationalism. This is a globalized conflict between two projects: maintaining the sovereignty of nation-states and furthering the inclusion of racialized communities within those states. The international conversation about globalization, nationalism, sovereignty, and pluralism is similarly threaded through with the dialogue about migration, national security, and crime control.

National security, border control, and criminal law meet naturally in crimmigration. They form a potent medicine consisting of the urgency and power of national security, combined with the everyday, everywhere nature of common crime control.

Notes

I am grateful to Mary Bosworth, Elspeth Guild, Emily Harris, Stephen Manning, Valsamis Mitsilegas, Lucia Zedner, and anonymous peer reviewers for valuable feedback and insights. John MacMorris-Adix, Helen Lee, and Sarah Malik provided excellent research assistance.

1. Peter Baker and Eileen Sullivan, "Trump Shares Inflammatory Anti-Muslim Videos, and Britain's Leader Condemns Them," *New York Times*, November 29,

2017, https://www.nytimes.com/2017/11/29/us/politics/trump-anti-muslim-videos-jayda-fransen.html. The group labeled the second video, "Muslim destroys a statue of Virgin Mary!" In the third, a crowd of men enters a building in an unidentified city. Some make their way to the top. Rocks fly. A man pushes a youth off the roof. Britain First dubbed this video, "Islamist mob pushes teenage boy off roof and beats him to death!"

2. Dan Bilefsky and Stephen Castle, "British Far-Right Group Exults over Attention from Trump," *New York Times*, November 29, 2017, https://www.nytimes.com/2017/11/29/world/europe/britain-first-trump.html.

3. John Wagner and Ashley Parker, "Trump Retweets Inflammatory and Unverified Anti-Muslim Videos," *Washington Post*, November 29, 2017, https://www.washingtonpost.com/news/post-politics/wp/2017/11/29/trump-retweets-inflammatory-and-unverified-anti-muslim-videos. The rooftop incident turned out to have occurred four years earlier in Egypt in 2013, amid violence following the overthrow of Islamist president Mohamed Morsi. The perpetrators were criminally prosecuted and sentenced to death.

4. Bilefsky and Castle, "British Far-Right Group Exults."

5. Tim Hains, "UK PM Theresa May: Trump Retweeting Anti-Muslim Tweets Wrong Thing to Do," *RealClear Politics*, November 30, 2017, https://www.realclearpolitics.com/video/2017/11/30/uk_pm_theresa_may_retweeting_anti-muslim_tweets_wrong_with_to_do.html.

6. Richard Pérez-Peña, "Anti-Muslim Extremists Retweeted by Trump Are Convicted of Hate Crimes," *New York Times*, March 8, 2018, https://www.nytimes.com/2018/03/08/world/europe/britain-first-hate-crime-uk.html.

7. Press Release, Department of Homeland Security, "*Border Patrol Agent from Big Bend Sector Killed in Line of Duty*," November 19, 2017, https://www.cbp.gov/newsroom/local-media-release/border-patrol-agent-big-bend-sector-killed-line-duty.

8. Chris Quinn, "U.S. Border Patrol Agent Dies from Injuries Suffered while on Patrol Near Big Bend Sunday Morning," *My San Antonio*, November 19, 2017, http://www.mysanantonio.com/news/local/texas/article/U-S-Border-Patrol-agent-dies-from-injuries-12369731.php.

9. Katherine Lam, "Border Patrol Agent Appeared to Be Ambushed by Illegal Immigrants, Bashed with Rocks before Death," *Fox News*, November 21, 2017, https://www.foxnews.com/us/border-patrol-agent-appeared-to-be-ambushed-by-illegal-immigrants-bashed-with-rocks-before-death.

10. Press Release, U.S. Senator for Texas Ted Cruz, "*Sen. Cruz Issues Statement on Attack on Two Big Bend Sector Border Patrol Agents*," November 19, 2017, https://www.cruz.senate.gov/?p=press_release&id=3496.

11. President Donald Trump, *Remarks by President Trump before Cabinet Meeting*, November 20, 2017, https://www.whitehouse.gov/briefings-statements/remarks-president-trump-cabinet-meeting-2/.

12. Trump, Twitter Post, November 19, 2017, 5:29 p.m., https://twitter.com/realDonaldTrump/status/932420488642617344.

13. Alfredo Corchado, "Investigators Explore Possibility That Border Patrol Agent Died in Accident," *Dallas Morning News*, November 29, 2017, https://www.dallasnews.com/news/mexico/2017/11/29/investigators-explore-possibility-border-patrol-agent-died-accident.

14. Dave Alsup, Scott McLean, and Darran Simon, "The FBI Hasn't Found Any Evidence that Border Patrol Agent Was Murdered," *CNN*, February 8, 2018, https://www.cnn.com/2018/02/08/us/border-patrol-agent-death-investigation/index.html.

15. John Burnett, "A Border Patrol Agent Dies Mysteriously. The Sheriff Has A Simple Theory," *NPR*, April 2, 2018, https://www.npr.org/2018/04/02/598872658/a-border-patrol-agent-dies-mysteriously-the-sheriff-has-a-simple-theory.

16. Erica R. Hendry, "Trump's Anti-Muslim Retweets Make Americans Less Safe, Analysts Say. Here's How," *PBS*, November 30, 2017, https://www.pbs.org/newshour/world/trumps-anti-muslim-retweets-make-americans-less-safe-analysts-say-heres-how.

17. Juliet Stumpf, "The Crimmigration Crisis: Immigrants, Crime, and Sovereign Power," *American University Law Review* 56 (2006): 367.

18. See, e.g., Valsamis Mitsilegas, "Constitutional Principles of the European Community and European Criminal Law," *European Journal of Law Reform* 8 (2006): 301, 324; Mary Bosworth and Mhairi Guild, "Governing through Migration Control: Security Citizenship in Britain," *British Journal of Criminology* 48 (2008): 703; Ana Aliverti and Mary Bosworth, "Introduction: Criminal Justice Adjudication in an Age of Migration," *New Criminology Law Review* 20 (2017): 1; Aliverti, "Making People Criminal: The Role of the Criminal Law in Immigration Enforcement," *Theoretical Criminology* 16 (2012): 417. See also Mitsilegas and Niovi Vavoula, "The Evolving EU Anti-Money Laundering Regime: Challenges for Fundamental Rights and the Rule of Law," *Maastricht Journal of European and Comparative Law* 23 (2016): 261; Mitsilegas, "The Transformation of Privacy in an Era of Pre-Emptive Surveillance, *Tilburg Law Review* 20 (2015): 35; Justine Stefanelli, "Who's Rule of Law? An Analysis of the UK's Decision not to Opt-in to the EU Asylum Procedures and Reception Conditions Directives," *International and Comparative Law Quarterly* 60 (2011): 1055–64; Michael Fordham, Justine Stefanelli, and Sophie Eser, "Immigration Detention and the Rule of Law: Safeguarding Principles," *British Institute for International and Comparative Literature* (2013).

19. E.g., Bosworth, Alpa Parmar, and Yolanda Vázquez, *Race, Criminal Justice, and Migration Control: Enforcing the Boundaries of Belonging* (Oxford: Oxford University Press, 2018). See also César Cuauhtémoc García Hernández, "Creating Crimmigration," *BYU Law Review* (2013): 1485; Christopher N. Lasch, "Sanctuary Cities and Dog-Whistle Politics," *New England Journal on Criminal and Civil Confinement* 42 (2016): 159, 163–64; Vázquez, "Constructing Crimmigration: Latino Subordination in a 'Post-Racial' World," *Ohio State Law Journal* 76 (2015): 599, 650.

20. Aliverti, *Crimes of Mobility: Criminal Law and the Regulation of Immigration* (London: Routledge, 2015) (tracing the history of crimmigration law in the UK);

Parmar, "Intersectionality, British Criminology and Race: Are We There Yet?," *Theoretical Criminology* 21 (2017): 35, 40 (pulling together the threads of crime, migration, racialization, and security); Francis Pakes, "Global Forces and Local Effects in Youth Justice: The Case of Moroccan Youngsters in Netherland," *International Journal of Law, Crime and Justice* 38 (2010): 109 (examining crimmigration through the lens of globalization).

21. Jeffrey Fagan and Tracey L. Meares, "Punishment, Deterrence and Social Control: The Paradox of Punishment in Minority Communities," *Ohio State Journal of Criminal Law* 6 (2008): 173–229.

22. *Fong Yue Ting v. United States*, 149 U.S. 689 (1993).

23. *Shaughnessy v. Mezei*, 343 U.S. 206 (1953).

24. See Stumpf, "Crimmigration Crisis," 403; Cuauhtémoc García Hernández, *Crimmigration Law* (Chicago: American Bar Association, 2015); Jennifer M. Chacón, "Managing Migration through Crime," *Columbia Law Review* 109 (2009): Sidebar 135; Bosworth and Guild, "Governing through Migration Control," 707–8 ("Since 1998, the criminalising discourses surrounding migration, as well as attendant legislation and government reports, have only appeared to vindicate the restriction of transnational mobility" in the UK).

25. See Alina Das, "Inclusive Immigrant Justice: Racial Animus and the Origins of Crime-Based Deportation," *UC Davis Law Review* 52 (2018): 171, 185–89; Cuauhtémoc García Hernández, "Immigration Detention as Punishment," *UCLA Law Review* 61 (2014): 1346, 1360.

26. Bryan Baker, Department of Homeland Security, Office of Immigration Statistics, *Annual Report: Immigration Enforcement Actions: 2016* (2017): Figure 9, https://www.dhs.gov/sites/default/files/publications/Enforcement_Actions_2016.pdf; DHS Office of Immigration Statistics, *2016 Yearbook of Immigration Statistics* (2017): Table 39, https://www.dhs.gov/sites/default/files/publications/2016%20Yearbook%20of%20Immigration%20Statistics.pdf.

27. Doris Meissner *et al.*, "Immigration Enforcement in the United States: The Rise of a Formidable Machinery," *Migration Policy Institute* (January 2013), https://www.migrationpolicy.org/research/immigration-enforcement-united-states-rise-formidable-machinery.

28. See Vázquez, "Crimmigration: The Missing Piece of Criminal Justice Reform," *University of Richmond Law Review* 51 (2017): 1093, 1126.

29. Stumpf, "Doing Time: Crimmigration Law and the Perils of Haste," *UCLA Law Review* 58 (2011): 1705, 1710.

30. 8 U.S.C. § 1182(a)(2); 8 U.S.C. § 1227(a)(2) (defining the exclusionary ground of the "crime involving moral turpitude"). See also Rebecca Sharpless, "Toward a True Elements Test: Taylor and the Categorical Analysis of Crimes in Immigration Law," *University of Miami Law Review* 62 (2008): 979.

31. *Compare* 8 U.S.C. § 1325 (defining the crime of "improper entry by alien," colloquially known as "illegal entry") *with* 8 U.S.C. § 1227 (a)(1)(B) (defining the deportability ground of "present in violation of law").

32. Immigration Marriage Fraud Amendments of 1986, Pub. L. No. 99–639, 100 Stat. 3537 (codified as amended in scattered sections of 8 U.S.C.).

33. See Victor C. Romero, "Decriminalizing Border Crossings," *Fordham Urban Law Journal* 38 (2010): 273, 291–94.

34. See Cuauhtémoc García Hernández, "Naturalizing Immigration Imprisonment," *California Law Review* 103 (2014): 1449, 1478.

35. Hiroshi Motomura, "The Discretion That Matters: Federal Immigration Enforcement, State and Local Arrests, and the Civil-Criminal Line," *UCLA Law Review* 58 (2011): 1819, 1822.

36. *Mellouli v. Lynch*, 135 S. Ct. 1980 (2015). The government alleged that a sock found in Mellouli's possession was used to hold eight prescription pills and was therefore a form of drug paraphernalia. On counsel's advice, Mellouli had pled guilty to the paraphernalia charge to avoid certain deportation based on possession of the pills.

37. Ibid. See also Nancy Morawetz, "Understanding the Impact of the 1996 Deportation Laws and the Limited Scope of Proposed Reforms," *Harvard Law Review* 113 (2000): 1936, 1938–39 (describing how Congress expanded deportation consequences for drug crimes and aggravated felonies and restricted avenues for relief from deportation).

38. Stumpf, "Crimmigration Crisis," 367, 388.

39. See Bosworth, Parmar, and Vázquez, *Race, Criminal Justice, and Migration Control*, 230, 231. For example, in Arizona, law enforcement officials were ordered to desist from racial profiling and abuse of immigrant arrestees. See Adam Edelman, "Pardoned Former Arizona Sheriff Joe Arpaio Announces Senate Run," *NBC News*, January 9 2018, https://www.nbcnews.com/politics/politics-news/pardoned-former-arizona-sheriff-joe-arpaio-announces-senate-run-n836111.

40. Mark Noferi and Robert Koulish, "The Immigration Detention Risk Assessment," *Georgetown Immigration Law Journal* 29 (2014): 45, 94.

41. Leanne Weber and Jude McCulloch, "Penal Power and Border Control: Which Thesis? Sovereignty, Governmentality or the Preemptive State," *Punishment in Society* (2018): 1–19.

42. Ibid., 2. This mapping exercise relies heavily on Weber and McCulloch's insightful work.

43. Ibid., 3 (citing Stumpf, "Crimmigration Crisis," 367).

44. See Stumpf, "Crimmigration Crisis," 380, 405.

45. See Weber and McCulloch, "Which Thesis?," 3–8 (citing Bosworth and Guild, "Governing through Migration Control," 703).

46. Bosworth and Guild, "Governing through Migration Control," 711.

47. See Weber and McCulloch, "Which Thesis?," 3 (citing Susanne Krasmann, "The Enemy on the Border: Critique of a Programme in Favour of a Preventive State," *Punishment and Society* 9 (2007): 301).

48. Krasmann, "Enemy on the Border," 304, 305.

49. Ibid.

50. See Weber and McCulloch, "Which Thesis?," 3.

51. See Chacón, "Producing Liminal Legality," *Denver University Law Review* 92 (2015): 709.

52. See Stumpf, "Crimmigration Crisis," 381.

53. Bosworth and Guild, "Governing through Migration Control," 706.

54. See Krasmann, "Enemy on the Border," 311. *See also* Koulish, "Profit, Plenary Powers and Militarization: A 'Perfect Storm' Scenario for Immigration Control," *Journal of Migration and Refugee Issues* 3 (2007): 149. ("The securitization process refers to discursive practices designed to persuade the American public that foreigners pose an existential threat to the American way of life.")

55. Department of Justice, Office of the Deputy Attorney General, *Guidance for Absconder Apprehension Initiative* (2002); "Registration and Monitoring of Certain Nonimmigrants," *Federal Register* 67, August 12, 2002: 52,584; see also Shoba S. Wadhia, "Business as Usual: Immigration and the National Security Exception," *Pennsylvania State Law Review* 114 (2010): 1485, 1502.

56. U.S. Immigration and Customs Enforcement, "ICE Unveils Sweeping New Plan to Target Criminal Aliens in Jails Nationwide: Initiative Aims to Identify and Remove Criminal Aliens from All U.S. Jails and Prisons," March 28, 2008: Press Release.

57. See Motomura, *Immigration Outside the Law* (Oxford: Oxford University Press, 2017). See also Maartje van der Woude and Joanne van der Leun, "Crimmigration Checks in the Internal Border Areas of the EU: Finding the Discretion that Matters," *European Journal of Criminology* 14 (2017): 27.

58. Bryan Baker, Department of Homeland Security, Office of Immigration Statistics, *Annual Report: Immigration Enforcement Actions: 2016* (2017), https://www.dhs.gov/sites/default/files/publications/Enforcement_Actions_2016.pdf; U.S. Immigration and Customs Enforcement, *Fiscal Year 2017 ICE Enforcement and Removal Operations*, December 13, 2017, https://www.ice.gov/removal-statistics/2017#.

59. DHS Office of Immigration Statistics, *Annual Report: Immigration Enforcement Actions*: 2015 (2017), https://www.dhs.gov/sites/default/files/publications/Enforcement_Actions_2015.pdf.

60. *Miranda-Olivares v. Clackamas County*, No. 3:12–cv–02317–ST, 2014 WL 1414305 (D. Or. 2014); *Galarza v. Szalczyk*, 745 F.3d 634, 645 (3d Cir. 2014). See also *Morales v. Chadbourne*, 793 F.3d 208 (1st Cir. 2015); *Moreno v. Napolitano*, 213 F. Supp. 3d 999 (N.D. Ill. 2016); *U.S. v. Raya-Vaca*, 771 F.3d 1195 (9th Cir. 2014); *U.S. v. Melendez-Castro*, 671 F.3d 950 (9th Cir. 2012); see also Lasch, "Federal Immigration Detainers after Arizona v. United States," *Loyola Los Angeles Law Review* 46 (2013): 629.

61. 8 U.S.C. § 1227(a).

62. Motomura, "Discretion that Matters," 1819, 1822; Eisha Jain, "Arrests as Regulation," *Stanford Law Review* 67 (2015): 809, 829–30.

63. Alina Das, "Policing Immigration Symposium: Immigration Law and Institutional Design," *University Chicago Law Review* 80 (2013): 137, 157; Stumpf, "Doing Time," 1705, 1730.

64. Department of Homeland Security, *Policies for Apprehension, Detention, and Removal of Undocumented Immigrants* (2014), https://www.dhs.gov/sites/default/files/publications/14_1120_memo_prosecutorial_discretion.pdf.

65. Executive Order No. 13768, Federal Register 82, January 25, 2017: 8799.

66. William Rehnquist, *All the Laws But One: Civil Liberties in Wartime* (1998; repr. New York: Knopf, 2001). See also María Joao Guia, "Crimigración Securitización y la Criminalización de los Migrantes en el Sistema Penal, 16 Annuario de Faculdade Direito de Universidade," *Coruna* (2014): 591, 593–94; Didier Bigo, "Security and Immigration: Toward a Critique of the Governmentality of Unease," *Alternatives* 27 (2002): 75–76; Boldizsár Nagy, "Hungarian Asylum Law and Policy in 2015–2016: Securitization Instead of Loyal Cooperation," *German Law Journal* 17 (2016): 1033.

67. Krasmann, "Enemy on the Border," 8.

68. Jill E. Family, "A Broader View of the Immigration Adjudication Problem," *Georgetown Immigration Law Journal* 23 (2009): 595, 611–32 (describing deportation methods outside of immigration court adjudication); Jennifer Lee Koh, "Removal in the Shadows of Immigration Court," *Southern California Law Review* 90 (2017): 181 (noting that "the vast majority of persons ordered removed never step foot inside a courtroom"); Wadhia, "The Rise of Speed Deportation and the Role of Discretion," *Columbia Journal of Race and Law* 5, no. 1 (2014): 1 (observing that the majority of people deported never saw a courtroom or immigration judge).

69. See Stephen Manning, "The Artesia Report," 2016, last accessed July 6, 2019, https://innovationlawlab.org/the-artesia-report/the-artesia-report; Stumpf, "Civil Detention and Other Oxymorons," *Queen's Law Journal* 40 (2014–15): 55, 58.

70. David Garland, *The Culture of Control* (Chicago: University of Chicago Press, 2001).

71. See Krasmann, "Enemy on the Border," 305 (citing Giorgio Agamben, *Means without End: Notes on Politics* (Minneapolis: University of Minnesota Press, 2000).

72. See Krasmann, "Enemy on the Border," 301. See also Zedner, "Pre-Crime and Post-Criminology?," *Theoretical Criminology* 11, no. 2 (2007): 61–81; Zedner, *Security* (London and New York: Routledge, 2009).

73. Government Accountability Office, *Unaccompanied Children: Agency Efforts to Reunify Children Separated from Parents at the Border* (2018): GAO-19–163, https://www.gao.gov/products/GAO-19–163.

74. Department of Justice, Office of Public Affairs, "Attorney General Announces Zero-Tolerance Policy for Criminal Illegal Entry," April 6, 2008, https://www.justice.gov/opa/pr/attorney-general-announces-zero-tolerance-policy-criminal-illegal-entry.

75. Ibid.

76. Ibid.

77. Ibid.

78. John Burnett and Richard Gonzales, "Homeland Security Secretary Defends Separating Families Who Cross Border Illegally," *NPR*, May 10, 2018, updated June 18, 2018, https://www.npr.org/2018/05/10/609480137/homeland-security-secretary-defends-separating-families-of-illegal-border-crosse.

79. Ibid.

80. Richard Gonzales, "Trump Administration Begins 'Remain in Mexico' Policy, Sending Asylum-Seekers Back," *NPR*, January 29, 2019, https://www.npr.org/2019/01/29/689819928/trump-administration-begins-remain-in-mexico-policy-sending-asylum-seekers-back.

81. "Migrant Caravan: What Is It and Why Does It Matter?," *BBC News*, November 26, 2018, https://www.bbc.com/news/world-latin-america-45951782.

82. Alex Horton, "Why U.S.-Bound 'Caravans' of Central American Migrants Are Getting Trump's Attention," *Washington Post*, April 1, 2018, https://www.washingtonpost.com/news/worldviews/wp/2018/04/01/why-a-u-s-bound-caravan-of-central-american-migrants-is-getting-trumps-attention/.

83. David Jackson, "Trump Says He Likes the Immigration Issue in This Election," *USA Today*, June 23, 2018, https://www.usatoday.com/story/news/politics/2018/06/23/donald-trump-says-he-likes-immigration-issue-election/728054002/.

84. *Minimum Standards for Driver's Licenses and Identification Cards Acceptable by Federal Agencies for Official Purposes*, 6 C.F.R. § 37 (2017); Annie Lai, "Confronting Proxy Criminalization," *Denver University Law Review* 92 (2015): 872, 891.

85. Lai, "Confronting Proxy Criminalization," 872, 891.

86. Immigration and Customs Enforcement, *FAQ on Sensitive Locations and Courthouse Arrests*, January 31, 2018, https://www.ice.gov/ero/enforcement/sensitive-loc ("U.S. Immigration and Customs Enforcement has for some time had established practices in place related to civil immigration enforcement inside courthouses. However, the increasing unwillingness of some jurisdictions to cooperate with ICE in the safe and orderly transfer of targeted aliens inside their prisons and jails has necessitated additional at-large arrests"); Maya Rhodan, "Plainclothes Officers Arrested Immigrants at a Courthouse. Can They Do That?," *Time*, September 18, 2017, http://time.com/4946747/immigration-plainclothes-brooklyn-courthouse.

87. Jeff Gammage, "Report: ICE Arrests of Undocumented Immigrants at Pennsylvania Courthouses Scare Away Victims, Witnesses," *Philadelphia Inquirer*, January 30, 2019, https://www.inquirer.com/news/ice-immigration-arrest-undocumented-courts-temple-university-20190130.html.

88. Ibid.

89. Nicholas W. Barber, "Citizenship, Nationalism, and the European Union," *European Law Review* 27 (2002): 241–59 (citing Manning Nash, *The Cauldron of Ethnicity* [Chicago: University of Chicago Press, 1989]: 10–17).

90. Maureen A. Eger and Sarah Valdez, "Neo-Nationalism in Western Europe," *European Sociological Review* 31 (2015): 115–30 (describing neo-nationalism as

using nationalism as the lens through which policy preferences are determined, having "a penchant for anti-establishment populism, disdain for supranational organizations, a desire to limit access to the nation and its benefits to certain groups of ethnic minorities," emphasizing traditional values, law and order, and restriction of immigration as a central focus).

91. Ronald Inglehart and Pippa Norris, "Trump, Brexit, and the Rise of Populism: Economic Have-Nots and Cultural Backlash," 7 (July 29, 2016), https://ssrn.com/abstract=2818659 ("populist discourse typically emphasizes nativism or xenophobic nationalism, which assumes that the 'people' are a uniform whole, and that states should exclude people from other countries and cultures"); see also ibid. ("Populism favors mono-culturalism over multiculturalism, national self-interest over international cooperation and development aid, closed borders over the free flow of peoples, ideas, labor and capital, and traditionalism over progressive and liberal social values").

92. Ibid. ("Trump's rhetoric seeks to stir up a potent mix of racial resentment, intolerance of multiculturalism, nationalistic isolationism, nostalgia for past glories, mistrust of outsiders, traditional misogyny and sexism, the appeal of forceful strongman leadership, attack-dog politics, and racial and anti-Muslim animus.")

93. "The 45th President of the United States Donald J. Trump," https://www.donaldjtrump.com/about (accessed June 27, 2019).

94. Harry Enten and Perry Bacon Jr., "Trump's Hardline Immigration Stance Got Him to the White House," *FiveThirtyEight*, September 12, 2017, https://fivethirtyeight.com/features/why-polls-showing-daca-as-popular-even-among-republicans-dont-tell-the-whole-story/ (accessed June 27, 2019).

95. United States Department of State, *Communication Regarding Intent to Withdraw from Paris Agreement*, August 4, 2017: Press Release, https://www.state.gov/r/pa/prs/ps/2017/08/273050.htm; *Memorandum on Withdrawal of the United States from the Trans-Pacific Partnership Negotiations and Agreement*, Federal Register 82, January 23, 2017: 8, 497; United States Department of State, *The United States Withdraws from UNESCO*, October 12, 2017: Press Release, https://www.state.gov/r/pa/prs/ps/2017/10/274748.htm; United States Mission to the United Nations, *United States Ends Participation in Global Compact on Migration*, December 2, 2017: Press Release, https://usun.state.gov/remarks/8197; Randall Lane, "Inside Trump's Head: An Exclusive Interview with the President, and the Single Theory That Explains Everything," *Forbes*, October 10 2017, https://www.forbes.com/donald-trump/exclusive-interview/#58443c8dbdec ("Doesn't he feel a responsibility to honor agreements from previous administrations? President Trump has a quick response: 'No.'").

96. United States Mission to the United Nations, *United States Ends Participation*.

97. Eger and Valdez, "Neo-Nationalism," 118 (identifying "ardent opposition to immigrants [as] the common denominator" of neo-nationalist parties in Europe).

98. Doris Marie Provine, "The Criminalization of Immigrants as a Racial Project," *Journal of Contemporary Criminal Justice* 27 (2011): 261, 269.

99. See Cuauhtémoc García Hernández, "Naturalizing Immigration Imprisonment," 1483.

100. Jennifer Chacón, "Unsecured Borders: Immigration Restrictions, Crime Control and National Security," *Connecticut Law Review* 39 (2007): 1827, 1846–48.

101. *Protecting the Nation from Foreign Terrorist Entry into the United States,* Executive Order No. 13769, Federal Register 82 (2017): 8977.

102. Anil Kalhan, "Immigration Surveillance," *Maryland Law Review* 74 (2014): 47.

103. Zedner, "Pre-Crime and Post-Criminology?," 61–81.

104. Stumpf, "Crimmigration Crisis," 367, 381.

5

The Trumping of Neoliberal Penality?

Trump's Presidency and the Rise of Nationalist Authoritarianism in the United States

Sappho Xenakis and Leonidas K. Cheliotis

From the early 1970s, following fifty years of stability, the use of imprisonment in the U.S. set out on a long-sustained and rapid rise. Over the next four decades or so, the country's imprisonment rate more than quadrupled, reaching levels far above those found anywhere else in the world.[1] The rise to hegemony of neoliberal dogma and policy around the same period has prompted a wealth of scholarship identifying linkages between the advent of neoliberalism and intensified state punitiveness in the form of custodial punishment. The size of the prison population in the U.S. began to fall in 2010, however, and by 2015, had dropped by 8.4 percent to return to 2005 levels.[2] Whereas some have interpreted the reduction in imprisonment as possibly portending the rollback of punitive policies and practices, others have problematized the significance attributed to the fall in the prison population, arguing that penal excesses may have become more diffuse but not more diluted. The election of Donald Trump to the White House in 2016 has meanwhile raised questions not only about the likely direction of imprisonment trends in the country, but also about whether the concept of neoliberalism retains its purchase in explaining levels and patterns of state punitiveness.

To date, Trump's election has not substantively affected either of the divergent assessments of penal trends in the U.S. On one hand, optimistic outlooks have shown notable tenacity in the face of Trump's presidency, essentially suggesting that ongoing positive reforms to the penal system will not be impeded despite the new president having campaigned as a "law and order" candidate and pursued several punitive policies since assuming office. Pessimistic perspectives, on the other hand, have multiplied as well as intensified, warning that the prospects for progressive penal reform under the new administration are even dimmer than before, not least because of Trump's self-proclaimed allegiance to "law and order,"[3] or rather his preference for "order" above all.[4]

This chapter sets out, first, to outline the main arguments raised from each camp, including with regard to the likely effects of Trump's presidency, and second, to draw out the implications these arguments carry for the utility of neoliberalism as a key referent with which contemporary penal trends are interpreted. We argue that both camps have typically appeared to assume the persistence of neoliberal socioeconomic policy, optimists treating this as a push factor behind what they see as the reduced use of imprisonment and pessimists conversely approaching it as a propellant of punitive criminal justice policies and practices. Once, however, we stretch our analysis beyond the strictly penological scope characteristically adopted by optimists and pessimists alike, we are led to different conclusions both about the present and future role of neoliberalism in penal matters and about Trump's own part in the evolution of state punitiveness. More specifically, given Trump's embracing of economic isolationism in lieu of the norms, rules, policies, and practices that underpin neoliberal international order, neoliberalism can no longer be taken for granted as a socioeconomic reality in the U.S., let alone as a force determining penal trends in the country. While the U.S. may well be on the verge of an era of increased state punitiveness, the driver behind it is more likely to be Trump's proclivity toward what we term "nationalist authoritarianism." As we show, nationalist authoritarianism manifests itself most acutely in the intensified harshness of the treatment accorded to underprivileged ethno-racial minorities and irregular migrants in particular. Its reach, however, appears also increasingly to extend to middle-class segments that were previously unlikely to find themselves targeted by penal authorities.

Neoliberalism and Imprisonment: The Neoliberal Penality Thesis

In the development of a clear and cogent thesis concerning the relationship between neoliberalism and imprisonment, a key role has been played by Loïc Wacquant,[5] not only within his work as such, but also through the broad and sustained scholarly debate he has thereby helped to galvanize. Wacquant has insisted on the distinctiveness of punishment under neoliberalism from that under capitalism per se, arguing that state punitiveness has been and continues to be at its most acute within jurisdictions in which neoliberalism has advanced fastest and furthest.[6]

For Wacquant, neoliberalism entails the articulation of four specific logics: economic deregulation, welfare retrenchment, the cultural trope of individual responsibility, and an ever-more expansive penal apparatus. Rather than being tangential to or a deviation from neoliberalism, Wacquant argues that punishment serves an essential function within it: managing the social reverberations of "advanced social insecurity" that neoliberal policies generate among the lower and middle classes. At the bottom of the class structure, punishment works to contain the disorders stoked by the "objective" insecurity of the unemployed poor and a flexibilized and welfare-lite workforce and demonstrates a systematic social and ethno-racial bias as it punishes and warehouses the primarily Black "urban (sub)proletariat" (rather than disciplining it with a view to enhancing labor exploitability).[7] At the same time, "punishing the poor" creates a convenient outlet for the "subjective" insecurity experienced by the middle classes, "whose prospects for smooth reproduction or upward mobility have dimmed as competition for valued social positions has intensified and the state has reduced its provision of public goods."[8] Punishment of the lower socioeconomic classes thereby provides a means by which neoliberal political leaders can compensate for legitimacy lost in pursuit of other social and economic policy goals.[9]

Another key dimension of penality under neoliberalism to have been explored by Wacquant is its transnationalism; indeed, for Wacquant, neoliberalism should be understood as a transnational political project, carried out by a global elite comprised of the senior executives of multinational corporations, high-ranking politicians, top officials of international governmental organizations (e.g., the IMF and the World Bank), and their cultural-technical experts (e.g., legal and media professionals), with their goal being to "remake the nexus of market, state, and citizenship from above."[10] Moreover, according to Wacquant, it is actors within the United States that have been the progenitors and primary international disseminators of this neoliberal project of which the "new 'punitive common sense'" is a crucial component.[11]

The importance of transnationalism to neoliberal penality has also been elaborated by reference to international migration and the rise in punitive regulation toward it. It has been widely argued that since the 1970s, especially in Europe, undocumented migrants have been constituted as criminal subjects by prohibitionist immigration policies, and, whether through administrative detention or incarceration in conventional prisons, migrants' treatment has served to discipline low-wage and surplus labor at the same time as helping to divert and expend the anxieties of the region's middle classes.[12] It has also been contended that the punitive treatment of migrants is a dramatic performance of sovereignty by neoliberal states seeking to shore up the legitimacy they have risked in promoting the outward flow of jobs and inward flow of "job-destroying imports," from commodities to highly specialized or low-cost labor.[13]

Other scholarship on neoliberal penality has focused on privatization trends in the provision of imprisonment, focusing particularly, but not exclusively, on developments in the U.S. Neoliberal commitment to the privatization of public services, with the purported intention of reducing strains on the public purse, has fueled an expansion in private provision, even if—or, rather, because—public expenditure has in many cases increased in tandem with the burgeoning of corporate interests in this area.[14] Schlosser argues, for instance, that the U.S. has seen the rise of a "prison-industrial complex" in which a set of bureaucratic, political, and economic interests have collaborated to press for increased public spending on imprisonment, effectively fixing a need for a steady supply of prisoners entering the penal system, regardless of the legal and moral illegitimacy of such a compulsion.[15]

The notion of a "prison-industrial complex" has nevertheless been subject to criticism for exaggerating the significance of corporate interests in driving prison expansion in the U.S. and implying the existence of a conspiracy between business and political elites to subvert justice for profit. More nuanced accounts have pointed out that the country's prison-building boom has served politicians seeking to stimulate weak local economies in their constituencies (even if such economies have not always benefited to the extent expected)[16] as much as it has rewarded the diverse array of businesses involved in the provision of imprisonment in the U.S. Gilmore's account of the largest prison construction program in the history of the world—in California, between 1982 and 2000—shows how a concatenation of local, national, and international developments produced surpluses of capital, labor, and land, which local power blocs chose to invest in carceral expansion with a view to making financial and political gains.[17] Yet other writers have pointed to the fact that neoliberalism has driven privatization both by expanding the private prison estate and by promoting the hybridization of public prisons as they have contracted out the delivery of select services (e.g., catering, security, medical, and furniture supplies) to private firms, have themselves allowed private and state-owned firms to exploit their prisoners' labor for profit, and have increasingly charged prisoners for costs related to their containment, from room and board to medical expenses.[18]

Elsewhere we have taken stock of debates about the significance and validity of neoliberal penality as a concept. Its mileage, we conclude, has been extended by the very identification of its limitations insofar as this has helped to indicate ways in which the concept might be refined, whether in terms of the method required to test it (e.g., the need for comparative perspectives) or in terms of substantive insights (e.g., the role played by institutional forces in mediating between crime trends, public opinion, and penal policy).[19] In the remainder of this chapter, we proceed to consider the present utility of neoliberal penality as an organizing concept for penological analysis in light of new controversies that have emerged, both concerning the direction of recent and ongoing penal trends in the U.S. and—beyond the penological field—regarding the current prospects of neoliberalism itself. In so doing, we discuss the likely penal, political, and economic effects attributed more recently to Trump's presidency.

Perspectives on Recent Penal Trends and the Impact of the Trump Presidency

Evidence of a decrease in the U.S. prison population since 2010, combined with Trump's election to the White House in 2016, has triggered questions about the current and likely future trajectory of state punishment in the country. In this essay, drawing on scholarly, media, and civil society sources, we elaborate on the reasoning behind the main divergent approaches offered in response thus far.

Optimistic Outlooks

Optimists have reasoned that crime drops, in conjunction with what they perceive to be the fading of public memories of high-crime eras and, above all, the pressures of budget constraints that have made the ever-expanding use of confinement increasingly prohibitive, have been helping to embed the incipient pattern of declining imprisonment.[20] Positive prognoses along these lines have been reinforced by a series of developments.

Several states have introduced more lenient custodial sentences, and states traditionally regarded as punitive have shown a reduced reliance on solitary confinement. Indeed, in 2016, even at the same time as electing Trump, who campaigned on a ticket championing a "tough on crime" approach, the states of California, Massachusetts, and Nevada voted to decriminalize marijuana, California and Oklahoma passed initiatives to reduce prison sentences, New Mexico brought in a constitutional amendment to prevent the jailing of those unable to afford bail, and in several states—including some that voted for Trump, such as Florida and Texas—there were victories for candidates for state prosecutor who had campaigned on a reformist platform.[21]

In addition, it has been pointed out that budgetary pressures have encouraged a marked move away from commitment to "tough on crime" policies within conservative right circles, with the establishment and activities of the "Right on Crime" lobby group testifying to the significant support garnered for criminal justice reform from powerful special interest groups such as the Koch Institute and the Heritage Foundation, as well as an array of high-profile current and former politicians, elected officials, and advisors. Alongside his son-in-law, Jared Kushner, a number of prominent Republicans that have been close to President Trump, such as former House Speaker Newt Gingrich, have been among those advocating criminal justice reform.[22] During the 2016 election campaign, the then Republican candidate for vice president, Mike Pence, also voiced his support for criminal justice reform.[23] This growth in reformist conservative positions on imprisonment has allowed bipartisan initiatives to arise, such as the Sentencing Reform and Corrections Act and the Prison Reform and Redemption Act. Although the Trump administration appears to have effectively halted the cross-party momentum that had been building toward sentencing reform, the supportive steps it has taken toward bipartisan proposals for changes intended to reduce recidivism and assist reentry have been welcomed by at least some campaigners as facilitative of penal liberalization.[24] Divisions within the Trump administration itself have also given optimists sustenance, particularly in the case of the prosecutorial treatment of marijuana supply and use, with Trump's conciliatory stance on the right of states to determine legality providing succor where the Department of Justice's more strident position under Jeff Sessions has drawn alarm.[25]

Above all, optimistic observers point to evidence of a significant public appetite for liberal reforms; several opinion polls have indicated the presence of strong sympathy for more moderate sentencing and corrections policies.[26] Hopes and expectations have consequently been expressed that apparently emergent decarcerative trends in the U.S. will not only persist, but will lead to the replacement of mass incarceration with parole and probation, the return of a rehabilitative emphasis in penal practices, or liberal modification along the lines of the Justice Reinvestment Initiative.[27] These are prospects that have been portrayed as having the potential to bring about "one of the most equality-enhancing institutional shifts" of our times.[28]

For optimists, the developments outlined above, allied with long-established constitutional limits to federal intervention at state and local levels (whereby sovereignty is divided between the central federal government and state governments), mean that the impetus already garnered for penal reform is unlikely to be impeded, whatever the punitive intentions of the Trump administration.[29] That there remains a possibility that the administration's policies might inflate federal incarceration rates is taken to be of negligible import to broader penal trends, given the small size of the federal prison sector, its imprisoned population estimated at a mere 12 percent of the national total.[30] Even within the federal arena, moreover, decisions taken by courts since the arrival of the Trump administration have invigorated optimistic readings of the country's checks and balances on executive power. Attention has been drawn in this regard to the fact that numerous new policies have been successfully challenged and struck down as unconstitutional, including but not limited to the so-called Muslim ban, the ban on transgender military service, the removal of protection from deportation for "Dreamers" (undocumented migrants brought to the country as children by their parents), and the introduction of financial penalties for "sanctuary cities" (jurisdictions pursuing limited engagement with or involvement in federal immigration enforcement actions).[31]

Pessimistic Outlooks

By contrast, however, more pessimistic commentators have drawn attention to indications of continuing and growing state punitiveness in the U.S.

First, the decline in the prison population has not been uninterrupted: seemingly telling of the resilience of the trend in mass incarceration, the total prison population rose in 2013 and 2014.[32] Nor has the downward trend in prison populations been all-encompassing: half of the U.S. states still saw increases between 2009 and 2013. What is more, approximately 70 percent of the nationwide drop between 2009 and 2014 stemmed from the reduced use of imprisonment in California, which came about as the result of a policy change effectively forced on that particular state by the U.S. Supreme Court in 2011. Consequently, it has been argued that the reduction in the prison population over recent years ought to be interpreted as the outcome of a highly irregular development in an outlier state rather than as a general trend.[33]

The decline in the U.S. prison population has also been described as more an exercise in the decentralization of corrections and the diffusion of penal control than as evidence of decarceration per se.[34] Cate, for instance, points out that, notwithstanding fanfare given by NGOs, politicians, and media outlets to reductions in the number of juveniles sent to state-run correctional institutions, the size of the detained juvenile population across the country has not declined.[35] Rather, responsibility for juvenile corrections has merely devolved and been dispersed from the state level to local and private authorities. Conditions of incarceration for juveniles in state-run institutions have meanwhile worsened and have also been found to be poor in county-level facilities.

Beckett et al. (2016) suggest, furthermore, that the recent enactment of more lenient drug and parole reforms in the U.S. has actually subtly served to justify increasingly severe punishment for those who do not qualify for more lenient treatment under such legislative amendments.[36] Likewise, Cadora (2014) has pointed to the way in which Justice Reinvestment Initiative reforms can work paradoxically to reinforce high rates of incarceration by producing minor successes that may nonetheless be interpreted as fulfilling reform goals in this area, ultimately forestalling pressures for more extensive decarceration.[37] Chiming with such analyses, Martin (2016) notes not only that state correctional budgets have seen negligible reductions, but also, more importantly still, that state controls designed to monitor the poor and unruly have actually been expanding in the community through the use of surveillance technologies and new programs of supervision and psychosocial regulation (especially pharmacological interventions) rolled out in cooperation with nonprofit actors.[38]

A deeper note of pessimism has been struck by numerous commentators as they have anticipated and diagnosed various adverse penal effects of the election of Donald Trump to the presidency. The theme of punishment was abundant in Trump's public pronouncements during the election campaign of 2016, often — but not always — with reference to irregular migration. Trump pledged, for instance, that within the first 100 days of taking office he would establish "a two-year mandatory minimum federal prison sentence for illegally re-entering the U.S. after a previous deportation, and a five-year mandatory minimum federal prison sentence for illegally re-entering for those with felony convictions, multiple misdemeanour convictions or two or more prior deportations."[39] As part of his campaign, Trump also called for the reinstatement and expansion of programs that have ensured that violent felons who use a gun to commit a crime are sent to prison for five years without the opportunity for parole or early release.[40]

Alongside Trump's reactionary rhetoric on crime and crime control, his decision to include in his administration figures with punitive records on law and policing (nominating Jeff Sessions as attorney general, for example), and the support his candidacy marshaled from private prison companies, have each been invoked to suggest that an end to the country's penal excesses remains far out of reach. Trump was the only presidential nominee in 2016 to call for an expansion in private provision of imprisonment, and the Trump-affiliated super PAC Rebuilding America Now received significant financial backing from the private prison firm GEO. Stocks in the two largest private prison companies in the U.S. saw a sharp rise in their value during the week after election day, reflecting expectations that a Trump win would improve the prospects of such firms.[41] In due course, this expectation appeared validated by the Trump administration's withdrawal of previous Department of Justice guidance to the Federal Bureau of Prisons to reduce the use of private prisons, on the grounds that the bureau's ability to meet the future needs of the federal correctional system would otherwise be impaired.[42]

Several other decisions have been interpreted as signaling the Trump administration's intentions to put more people behind bars. The Department of Justice's instruction to federal prosecutors to "charge and pursue the most serious, most readily provable offense," for example, has been described by many observers as a move to reinvigorate a harsher sentencing ethos, particularly toward drug offenders, thereby raising the prospect of a rise in the federal prison population.[43] The new administration's focus on immigrant criminality, pessimists claim, has made this prospect all the more likely.[44] A number of facts point in this direction. On one hand, irregular entry and reentry into the country have in recent years come to account for roughly half of all federal criminal prosecutions, and the increase in foreign-born prisoner numbers appears to have made a disproportionately large contribution to the expansion of the federal prison population.[45] On the other hand, the Trump administration has sought to tighten immigration law enforcement further: an executive order issued in January 2017, for instance, introduced an array of measures to enhance the enforcement of federal immigration laws,[46] and a subsequent memo by the Department of Justice directed federal prosecutors to prioritize criminal immigration enforcement.[47] Thus, between January and April 2017, a 38 percent increase was reported in the number of immigrants arrested by U.S. Immigration and Customs Enforcement (ICE) as compared to the same time span in 2016, despite the fact that the volume of undocumented migrants caught crossing the U.S.-Mexico border saw an "unprecedented drop" of 40 percent over January and February.[48] As of late March 2017, moreover, 22 percent of federal prisoners were foreign-born, against the majority of whom ICE had issued or was pursuing a deportation order.[49]

Findings from local-level research are even more striking. According to a report published by the Office of the New York City Comptroller Scott M. Stringer, nearly all ICE field offices around the country recorded increases in their use of arrest (primarily targeting individuals for a civil violation of immigration law) and deportation (including for individuals with no criminal convictions) between the final year of the Obama administration and the first year of the Trump administration. In New York itself, the total number of deportations by ICE increased by 150 percent during the same timeframe, with deportations of individuals with no criminal convictions rising at an even faster pace, by 265 percent, amounting to the largest growth in "noncriminal deportations" recorded for any ICE field office in the country. Significant upward trends have also been recorded in New York for the use of administrative arrest, ICE detainer requests (i.e., requests made by ICE to law enforcement agencies to hold an immigrant in custody longer so that ICE can gain custody of them), and the number of deportation cases reaching immigration courts. Despite the positive contributions immigrants are known to have been making to local economy and culture, the report concludes, many of them "are today living on a knife edge, afraid to leave their homes and communities, worried that one day they will be detained by U.S. immigration enforcement officials and not make it home to their families."[50]

More broadly, Trump's apparent penchant for exploiting his privileged role in shaping public discourse so as to preempt, suppress, or otherwise undermine resistance to his agenda, combined with the considerable success his administration has already had in promoting punitive policies beyond the carceral field itself, have provoked concerns as to the fate of the momentum seemingly achieved toward liberal penal reform to date. Pessimists underscore not only that Trump has publicly denigrated and even issued threats against those placing checks on his administration, from members of the judiciary and the intelligence community to segments of the mainstream mass media and the citizenry.[51] With a steady stream of inflammatory rhetoric on crime and its control, he has also sought to whip up public pressure in order to bring or keep officials behind his criminal justice initiatives as such. The implication here is that public fear of criminal victimization may be raised by Trump's repeated gross overstatement of crime trends and his insistent call for harsher criminal justice measures in response, and this in turn could bring a halt to the reformist plans of liberal-minded elected officeholders hoping to retain popular support.[52]

Relatedly, pessimistic expectations regarding liberal reform in the use of imprisonment have been couched in accounts of an upturn in punitiveness already effected across other parts of the criminal justice system. Critical scrutiny has been directed most notably toward steps taken by the Trump administration to embolden the police and augment their powers, from the decision to limit the Department of Justice's pursuit of civil rights suits against police departments to the rescinding of restrictions on the federal forfeiture of assets seized by state or local police forces, to the lifting of limits on the transfer of surplus military equipment to local police agencies.[53]

Concerns have similarly been expressed regarding the intensification of zero-tolerance policing of underprivileged ethno-racial communities and the adoption of a more draconian approach to tackling civil disobedience on the streets. One example of the latter can be found in the official reaction to protest in Washington, D.C., on the day of Trump's inauguration, when D.C. police kettled a group of approximately 300 protestors (including clearly identifiable journalists and legal observers), using tear gas and "sting-ball" grenades to keep the crowd in check, and rather than go on to issue suspected offenders with a fine (as would have been consistent with prior standard practice for such situations in D.C.), charged 230 of them with a felony rioting offense, carrying a maximum penalty of ten years' imprisonment and a fine of $25,000. As suggested by the D.C. chapter head of the American Civil Liberties Union and the Committee to Protect Journalists, the indiscriminate pursuit of serious felony charges against a mass of protesters, even if the majority of cases were dropped over the ensuing days, sent a clear and foreboding message to journalists and would-be protesters alike.[54]

Will Neoliberal Penality Be Trumped?

Whatever the merits of the distinct optimistic and pessimistic perspectives discussed above, they have generally not reflected on the shifting politico-economic trends that underpin penal trends. A tacit acceptance of the continuing relevance of neoliberalism can nevertheless be extrapolated from both perspectives. In optimistic assessments, the foundational principle of the neoliberal penality thesis seems to be inverted, neoliberalism apparently intensifying while imprisonment declines. That is to say, optimistic outlooks often attribute an important role to neoliberal politico-economic dynamics in shaping penal trends, crediting meso-level fiscal pressures on policymakers of all political shades as a key factor behind the seeming reduction in imprisonment. From pessimistic perspectives, meanwhile, a modified version of the neoliberal penality thesis can be discerned, with a more diffused mode of neoliberal penality unfolding, if one no less dystopian than its predecessor. This is a version in which the state may be retreating following the logic of neoliberal budgetary pressures, but only in the sense that it devolves more of its authority and responsibility for the delivery of punishment to private actors, both commercial and third-sector (i.e., charities). In fact, insofar as any drops in imprisonment rates may be regarded as the outcome of an increasingly empowered neoliberal compulsion to curtail government spending and responsibility for managing the punishment of offenders, they have raised the prospect of a more thorough neoliberalization of the penal field, in a manner reminiscent of the fully marketized prison environments found in some Latin American jurisdictions.[55]

The version of neoliberal penality emerging from pessimistic perspectives is additionally one in which the authority of criminal justice institutions is subject to heightened challenge to the extent that there have been repeated efforts on the part of the Trump administration to subvert formal structures and processes, not least by stoking punitive public sentiment to put pressure on elected officials. At the same time, pessimistic observations of the subjects of punishment suggest the potential for a departure from the operations and functions of neoliberal penality as commonly conceptualized to date. Albeit with new vigor, the overt targets of central government's punitive imperatives continue to match the profile of those previously identified as the "preferred clients" of inflated prisons under neoliberalism[56]—underprivileged ethno-racial minorities and irregular migrants in particular—, regardless of actual crime trends. Insofar as stigmatizing invective in relation to issues of crime and punishment has been directed by the Trump administration against members of the judiciary, the intelligence agencies, journalists of the mainstream media, and protesting members of the public, it raises the prospect of an expanded target in the middle classes. Should this be pursued further—the broadening and emboldening of police powers signaling that it might—, the function of punishment would no longer be the general discharge of displaced middle-class insecurities and the containment of unruliness among the lower classes, as foreseen within most iterations of the neoliberal penality thesis. Punishment would displace the insecurities of some (e.g., relatively disadvantaged white conservative) members of the middle classes, while disciplining others (e.g., affluent educated urban-dwelling liberals) in terms of their participation in public life, whether in their capacity as professionals or as private citizens.

Beyond questions about the present and future trajectory of criminal justice policies and practices as such, however, lies a further crucial debate that has to date been unduly neglected by punishment and society scholarship, despite the importance it ought to have for assessing the continuing relevance of the concept of neoliberal penality: that concerning the status and future of neoliberalism itself. Neoliberalism's future has received heightened critical scrutiny over recent years, primarily as a result of the financial crisis that struck the U.S. and much of Europe between 2008 and 2009 and the reactions of governments to these crises. On one hand, the crisis is argued to have provided incontrovertible evidence of the ideological and institutional failure of neoliberalism, particularly with regard to neoliberal faith in the self-correcting mechanisms of the market. On the other hand, the depth and persistence of commitment by Western governments to neoliberal principles appeared undone by the speed with which such governments were willing to openly abandon key tenets of the doctrine to intervene, with massive bail-outs and stimulus packages, so as to avert the collapse of banking and financial institutions in their countries.[57]

Much commentary in the immediate aftermath of the crisis lamented that it was effectively "business as usual" for neoliberalism. More recently, however, it has been argued that ongoing economic strains should be interpreted as signs of a deep structural crisis and of an impending major institutional restructuring of capitalism in which key tenets of neoliberalism will be jettisoned.[58] Economic analysis uncovering a retreat of core elements of globalization since 2008 suggests that this restructuring may have already begun. Salient features of what has been identified by some experts as nascent processes of "deglobalization" include a decline in net international flows of goods, services, and finance relative to GDP and a rise in state interventionism and trade barriers,[59] with negative implications for neoliberalism, given the priority accorded by the latter to removing obstacles that encumber these flows.

The likelihood of the large-scale dismantling of global trade and, more broadly, the institutions, rules, and norms that underpin neoliberal international order, has been regarded as coming a step closer with the arrival into office of Trump, an avowedly isolationist anti-free-trade U.S. president, one reportedly as unconvinced about the benefits of the North Atlantic Treaty Organization as he has been about the North Atlantic Free Trade Agreement.[60] Trump's vow to "put America First" in U.S. trading relations has led the administration to the decidedly non-neoliberal position of rejecting the Trans-Pacific Partnership (TPP) trade pact, stalling negotiations on the Trans-Atlantic Trade and Investment Partnership (TTIP), announcing sweeping aluminum and steel tariffs in a severe blow to the norms established by the World Trade Organization,[61] and propounding the merits of trade wars (as Trump memorably tweeted, "trade wars are good, and are easy to win").[62]

To the extent that such steps portend the demise of neoliberalism, they also signal the end of neoliberal penality, both as a practical reality where it has emerged and as a useful theoretical framework for scholarship seeking to interpret penal trends from now on. Thus, in the case of the U.S., whether levels of imprisonment continue to rise or state punitiveness mutates to focus primarily on irregular migration or becomes even more diffused in its manifestation, neoliberalism would be irrelevant as an organizing concept for penological analysis of emerging trends. To put the point differently, it is quite conceivable that the U.S. may be on the cusp of a period of increased state punitiveness, yet one driven not by neoliberalism, but by a nationalist authoritarianism that combines economic protectionism abroad with divisive identity-based politics at home. Substantively, the law-and-order policies under the Trump administration may not necessarily represent rupture with the policies pursued by neoliberal administrations of the recent past; it has been pointed out, for example, that while the more punitive treatment of irregular migrants has been an avowed commitment of Trump's White House and has been a key focus of its expressive crackdown on crime, the Obama administration itself deported more people than its own predecessors.[63] The causal role neoliberalism has thus far played, however, is likely to be trumped.

Notes

1. Jeremy Travis, Bruce Western, and Steve Redburn, eds., *The Growth of Incarceration in the United States* (Washington, D.C.: National Academies Press, 2014).

2. Federal prisons joined this trend late; their rates of incarceration continued to grow until 2013, since which time they have undergone four successive years of reduction; U.S. Department of Justice, "Prisoners in 2016," *Bulletin* 251149, 2018.

3. "Standing Up for Our Law Enforcement Community," *White House*, Jan. 21, 2017.

4. "Trump's Vision of a Lawless Order," *Atlantic*, Jul. 28, 2017.

5. Loïc Wacquant, *Prisons of Poverty*, expanded ed. (Minneapolis and London: University of Minnesota Press, 2009); Wacquant, *Punishing the Poor* (Durham, N.C., and London: Duke University Press, 2009).

6. See also Michael Cavadino and James Dignan, *Penal Systems: A Comparative Approach* (London: Thousand Oaks and New Delhi: Sage, 2006).

7. Wacquant, *Punishing the Poor*; Alessandro De Giorgi, A. *Re-Thinking the Political Economy of Punishment* (Aldershot: Ashgate, 2006).

8. Waquant, *Punishing the Poor*.

9. See also Leonidas K. Cheliotis, "Neoliberal Capitalism and Middle-Class Punitiveness: Bringing Erich Fromm's 'Materialistic Psychoanalysis' to Penology," *Punishment & Society* 15, no. 3 (2013): 247–73.

10. Wacquant, *Punishing the Poor*, 306–7.

11. Wacquant, *Prisons of Poverty*; Jeffrey I. Ross, ed., *The Globalization of Supermax Prisons* (New Brunswick, N.J.: Rutgers University Press, 2013).

12. De Giorgi, *Re-Thinking the Political Economy of Punishment*; Alessandro De Giorgi, "Immigration Control, Post-Fordism, and Less Eligibility: A Materialist Critique of the Criminalization of Immigration across Europe," *Punishment & Society* 12, no. 2 (2010): 147–67; Wacquant, *Prisons of Poverty*; Dario Melossi, *Crime, Punishment and Migration* (London: Sage, 2015).

13. Raymond Michalowski, "Donald Trump and Immigration: A Few Predictions," *Social Justice*, Jan. 16, 2016.

14. Emma Bell, *Criminal Justice and Neoliberalism* (Basingstoke: Palgrave Macmillan, 2011); see, e.g., Ruth W. Gilmore, *Golden Gulag* (Berkeley: University of California Press, 2007).

15. Eric Schlosser, "The Prison-Industrial Complex," *Atlantic Monthly*, Dec. 1998.

16. See further Gilmore, *Golden Gulag*.

17. Ibid.

18. De Giorgi, "Five Theses on Mass Incarceration," *Social Justice* 42, no. 2 (2015):

5–30; Christian Parenti, *Lockdown America* (London: Verso, 1999); James Kilgore, "Confronting Prison Slave Labour Camps and Other Myths," *Social Justice Blog*, Aug. 28, 2013.

19. See further Sappho Xenakis and Leonidas K. Cheliotis, "Whither Neoliberal Penality? The Past, Present and Future of Imprisonment in the U.S.," *Punishment & Society* 21, no. 2 (2019): 187–206.

20. David Dagan and Steven Teles, "Locked in? Conservative Reform and the Future of Mass Incarceration," *Annals of the American Academy of Political and Social Science* 651, no. 1 (2014): 266–76.

21. German Lopez, "The Case for Optimism on Criminal Justice Reform, Even Under Trump," *Vox*, Nov. 10, 2017.

22. Julia Harte, "Trump Seen as More Moderate on Criminal Justice, Law Enforcement," *Reuters*, Nov. 11, 2016.

23. Emily Cadei, "Pence's Support Gives Criminal Justice Reform Supporters Hope," *Newsweek*, Oct. 7, 2016.

24. Charles Fain Lehman, "White House Sends Congress Framework for Prison Reform," *Washington Free Beacon*, Feb. 28, 2018; Van Jones, "Prison Reform Is Possible Even in the Trump Era," *CNN* Opinion, Apr. 18, 2018.

25. Paige Winfield Cunningham, "The Health 202: Trump Is Backing Off the Marijuana Fight. But His Attorney General Has Not," *Washington Post*, Apr. 17, 2018.

26. Mona Lynch and Anjuli Verma, "The Imprisonment Boom of the Late Twentieth Century: Past, Present, and Future," in *The Oxford Handbook on Prisons and Imprisonment*, ed. J. Wooldredge and P. Smith (Oxford: Oxford University Press, 2016), 1–34.

27. William G. Martin, "Decarceration and Justice Disinvestment: Evidence from New York State," *Punishment & Society* 18, no. 4 (2016): 479–504.

28. Michelle Phelps and Devah Pager, "Inequality and Punishment: A Turning Point for Mass Incarceration?," *Annals of the American Academy of Political and Social Science* 663, no. 1 (2016): 185–203.

29. Ames Grawert, "Donald Trump's AG Nominee Jeff Sessions Is a Threat to Justice," *Time*, Jan. 6, 2016; Phelps and Pager, "Inequality and Punishment," 185–203; Lopez, "Case for Optimism on Criminal Justice Reform"; Lynch and Verma, "Imprisonment Boom," 1–34.

30. See, e.g., Pfaff in *Newsweek*, "Will the Trump Administration Jail More Drug Felons?," Jul. 12, 2017.

31. David Cole, "How the Courts Have Stymied Trump," *Nation*, Jan. 30, 2018.

32. Martin, "Decarceration and Justice Disinvestment"; Lynch and Verma, "Imprisonment Boom," 1–34; De Giorgi, "Five Theses on Mass Incarceration," 5–30.

33. Charis Kubrin and Carroll Seron, "The Prospects and Perils of Ending Mass Incarceration in the United States," *Annals of the American Academy of Political and*

Social Science 664, no. 1 (2016): 16–24; Jonathan Simon, *Mass Incarceration on Trial* (New York: New Press, 2015); Lynch and Verma, "Imprisonment Boom."

34. Jody Sundt, Emily Salisbury, and Mark Harmon, "Is Downsizing Prisons Dangerous? The Effect of California's Realignment Act on Public Safety," *Criminology & Public Policy* 15, no. 2 (2016): 315–41.

35. Sarah Cate, "Devolution, Not Decarceration: The Limits of Juvenile Justice Reform in Texas," *Punishment & Society*, 18, no. 5 (2016): 1–32.

36. Katherine Beckett, Anna Reosti, and Emily Knaphus, "The End of an Era? Understanding the Contradictions of Criminal Justice Reform," *Annals of the American Academy of Political and Social Science* 664, no. 1 (2016): 238–59.

37. Eric Cadora, "Civic Lessons: How Certain Schemes to End Mass Incarceration Can Fail," *Annals of the American Academy of Political and Social Science* 651, no. 1 (2014): 277–85. See also Marie Gottschalk, *Caught: The Prison State and the Lockdown of American Politics* (Princeton and Oxford: Princeton University Press, 2015).

38. Martin, "Decarceration and Justice Disinvestment."

39. Donald Trump, "Donald Trump's Contract with the American Voter," Oct. 22, 2016, https://assets.donaldjtrump.com/_landings/contract/O-TRU-102316-Contractv02.pdf.

40. Donald Trump, "Second Amendment Rights," 2016, https://assets.donaldjtrump.com/Second_Amendment_Rights.pdf. See also Eli Hager, "The Obama Criminal Justice Reforms That Trump Could Undo," *Marshall Project*, Oct. 8, 2016. Complementing these commitments has been Trump's enduring enthusiasm for capital punishment; in 2015, he promised that, if elected, he would mandate the death penalty for convicted murderers of policemen (*Washington Post*, "Donald Trump Wants the Death Penalty for Those Who kill Police Officers," Dec. 10, 2015; see further Trump, *The America We Deserve* (Los Angeles: Renaissance, 2000).

41. According to a complaint submitted by the Campaign Legal Centre to the Federal Election Commission in December 2016, the private prison company GEO Group illegally contributed $225,000 to the Trump-affiliated super PAC Rebuilding America Now, in violation of the seventy-five-year-old ban on government contractors making political contributions (Campaign Legal Centre, "Trump Super PAC Received Illegal Donations from Private Prison Company," Dec. 20, 2016). In the week after Election Day, stocks of GEO and CoreCivic rose more than 20 and 40 percent, respectively (*NPR* [National Public Radio], "Will the Private Prison Business See a Trump Bump?," Jan. 4, 2017).

42. *NPR*, "Will the Private Prison Business See a Trump Bump?"

43. See further Lynch, interviewed in *Slate*, "The DOJ's Drug Warrior," May 15, 2017; Sentencing Project, "Federal Prison Population Will Expand under New DOJ Directive," May 12, 2017; *Wall Street Journal*, "Federal Prison Population Expected to Grow Under Trump," Jun. 8, 2017.

44. Ibid.; *CBS News*, "What Is the Future of US Prisons under Trump Administration?," Nov. 23, 2016.

45. Patrisia Macías-Rojas, *From Deportation to Prison* (New York: New York University Press, 2016).

46. White House, "Standing Up for Our Law Enforcement Community," Jan. 21, 2017.

47. Department of Justice, "*Attorney General Jeff Sessions Announces the Department of Justice's Renewed Commitment to Criminal Immigration Enforcement*," Washington, D.C.: Department of Justice, Apr. 11, 2017.

48. "Homeland Chief: Illegal Border Crossings Dip 40%," *USA Today*, Mar. 8, 2017.

49. Department of Justice, "*Pursuant to Executive Order on Public Safety, Department of Justice Releases Data on Incarcerated Aliens*," Washington, D.C.: Department of Justice, May 2, 2017.

50. "The Demographics of Detention: Immigration Enforcement in NYC Under Trump," *Office of the New York City Comptroller Scott M. Stringer*, 2019, https://comptroller.nyc.gov/wp-content/uploads/documents/Demographics_of_Detention_022019.pdf: 4.

51. See, e.g., R. Ben-Ghiat, "Trump Is Following the Authoritarian Playbook," *CNN*, Jan. 17, 2017.

52. Ames Grawert and Natasha Camhi, *Criminal Justice in President Trump's First 100 Days* (New York: Brennan Centre for Justice at New York University School of Law, 2017).

53. See further Ruth Ben-Ghiat, "Trump Is Following the Authoritarian Playbook," *CNN*, Jan. 17, 2017; Steven Levitsky and Daniel Ziblatt, "Is Donald Trump a Threat to Democracy?," *New York Times*, Dec. 16, 2017.

54. Alan Pyke, "Federal Prosecutors Slap Felony Charges on More than 200 Inauguration Protestors," *ThinkProgress*, Jan. 24, 2017; Jon Swaine, "Four More Journalists Get Felony Charges after Covering Inauguration Unrest," *Guardian*, Jan. 24, 2017. A remaining fifty-nine defendants await trial at the time of writing.

55. On which see further Joey Whitfield, "Other Neoliberal Penalities: *Marching Powder* and Prison Tourism in La Paz," *Theoretical Criminology* 20, no. 3 (2015): 358–75.

56. Wacquant, *Prisons of Poverty*.

57. Kean Birch and Vlad Mykhnenko, eds., *The Rise and Fall of Neoliberalism* (London: Zed, 2010).

58. David M. Kotz, *The Rise and Fall of Neoliberal Capitalism* (Cambridge, Mass.: Harvard University Press, 2015).

59. See further, BMI Research, "Three Scenarios for Globalization: 2017–2030," Nov. 19, 2016.

60. E.g., Anne Applebaum, "Is This the End of the West As We Know It?," *Washington Post*, Mar. 4, 2016; Benjamin Kentish, "Donald Trump's Immigrant Crimes List Labelled 'Shocking in the Extreme' by Human Rights Groups,"

Independent, Jan. 26, 2017; Sam Fleming, "Trump Threatens NAFTA in Immigration Spat with Mexico," *Financial Times*, Apr. 2, 2018.

61. "Trump, China, and Steel Tariffs: The Day the WTO Died," *Council on Foreign Relations*, Mar 9, 2018.

62. Thomas Franck, "Trump Doubles Down: 'Trade Wars Are Good, and Easy to Win,'" *CNBC*, Mar. 2, 2018.

63. Michalowski, "Donald Trump and Immigration"; Marie Gottschalk, "Conservatives Against Incarceration?," *Jacobin*, Dec. 23, 2016.

6

Trump v. Hawaii

Trumpeting Authoritarianism with Formalist Analysis and Sovereign Norms

Robert Koulish

In an act of sovereign power, Abraham Lincoln suspended the right to habeas corpus during the Civil War. Some legal and political scholars argue that in doing so, Lincoln reasserted state sovereignty by exercising its right to suspend the rule of law. Drawing on this perspective, I argue that Trump's immigration-related executive orders have reinscribed nation-state sovereignty at the same time that they consolidate his own power in ways that mirror authoritarian rule. By taking this position, this essay advances a perspective of immigration law as the "canary in the coal mine" in Trump's onward march toward American fascism. Just as Trump's advance toward authoritarianism is brought to light through excessive cruelty at the U.S.-Mexico border, the immigration control regime shows what American fascism might look like as the Court legitimizes and defers to inordinate exclusionary power wielded against the most vulnerable human beings. If you want to see what could happen in Boise or Sheboygan, take a gander at the government-sponsored violence at the border.[1] The combination of legislative impotence and judicial acquiescence may have been responsible for the events preceding Trump, but the excessive power being wielded by Trump is truly exceptional.

How Did We Get Here?

The immigration control regime is comprised of many parts that mutually reinforce punitive bias against immigrants. Through a system of control embedded in the first series of federal immigration cases, sovereign exclusions receive special deference from the Court. This plenary deference allows the executive to abuse government power in violation of much-revered constitutional principle. In recent years, that power has been embraced by the political right and underestimated by liberals, who have tried to convince Americans that this power has dissolved into constitutional principles. In 2017, among Trump's first executive actions as president was to unleash executive power against Muslim immigrants. Since then he has ushered in a new narrative of migration control. That narrative has dehumanized migrants and refugees, giving license to Trump, acting as sovereign, to exceed the framework of constitutional norms that has been generally accepted as placing constraints. on government power. Additionally, the framework raises questions about the potential limits of crimmigration and border criminologies scholarship.

The Court's Complicity

The Supreme Court's recent decision in *Trump v. Hawaii*,[2] the immigration travel ban case, has shed light on the exemplary role that the Court has played in the use of exceptional executive power over immigrants. The case can be interpreted on many levels. Doctrinally the Court adopted a view of broad deference to the executive branch that allows the president to categorically ban immigrants from entering the country. This has made it easier for the executive branch to wield broad power to discriminate against immigrants, implicitly extending exclusions to include religion.[3] As an outcome, the case has helped augment executive power and reinforced the idea that the executive branch enjoys near plenary authority over entry decisions.

From a broader perspective, the Court's decision in *Trump v. Hawaii* can be read at the level of institutional norms and symbols. The case accommodated already existing punitive norms from two sources, the exclusionary mission of the immigration bureaucracy and precedent, which recognizes plenary power. Along the way, the Court has advanced the president's populist and white nationalist discourse that immigrants of color are the scourges of native-born whites and threats to white national identity.

The Court's reasoning has borne the hard shell of legal formalism, which has evolved through the decades but also helped immigration law remain an outlier in the public law field more generally. A version of new legal formalism (failure to verify facts or consider context) has helped legitimize Trump's assertions of executive power, as the case in its entirety has reinvigorated an old debate in immigration law about the role of sovereign power as an extra-constitutional rationale for excessive executive authority.

In this chapter I explain the *how* of punitive bias, defined as the power to exclude low-risk or no-risk individuals per whim, through exclusionary techniques legitimized by the Court that allow the administrative state to deploy techniques that are coercive to constitutional norms. I am particularly interested in the Court's role for a variety of reasons: with very few exceptions, the Court has consistently showed extreme deference to political branches, allowing behavior that exceeds constitutional principle. These anomalies begin with federal origins of immigration law created through the lens of sovereignty and plenary powers. In the heyday of the formalist era during the late nineteenth century, the Court turned a blind eye to constitutional prohibitions against excessive executive power and explicit discrimination. Because these early decisions have never been overturned, the precedent, along with formalist analysis, remained as a lethal arrow in the Court's immigration quiver. The conservative Court, encouraged by nativist immigration think tanks, used plenary norms to gloss over Trump's explicitly racist travel ban and to legitimize the exclusion of people because of their religion, without ever having to address the reasons behind the travel ban exclusion.

This essay examines the Court's role in legitimizing authoritarian executive power through extreme forms of deference to executive discretion. It examines the Travel Ban case with deliberate consideration of sovereignty and plenary powers and the punitive norms that have derived from these concepts. The analysis borrows from the theoretical frameworks that coauthors Mary Bosworth and Mhairi Guild[4] and Juliet Stumpf[5] have introduced respectively about migration control and crimmigration. Additionally, it suggests that migration control perhaps is most comprehensively understood through the lens of sovereign control, rather than through penology.

The first section introduces the theoretical framework for understanding crimmigration and border criminologies, and the second section introduces the lens of sovereignty as perhaps a more useful lens. In the third section, the chapter establishes relevant historical background to introduce legal formalism and plenary norms that legitimize the immigration exception. Then, it briefly introduces the Trump Travel Bans as a case study for Trump's path to authoritarianism using immigration law in *Trump v. Hawaii*. Finally, the chapter discusses the rise of punitive authoritarianism in the Trump administration through the lens of immigration law.

Crimmigration and Criminologies—The Framework

Crimmigration refers to the role of law in othering migrants and refugees. Specifically, it captures the intersection of criminal law and immigration law to cover immigration consequences of criminal acts, and criminal consequences to immigration offenses. Stumpf's contribution lays out a theoretical framework that critically analyzes crimmigration law doctrine and procedure through membership theory.[6] It infers that nonmembers are subordinated by law. Since Stumpf's original essay, other scholars have used this framework to critically examine the role of privatization, securitization, and risk in the detention, deportation, and exclusion of noncitizens.[7] For the most part, however, the work under the banner of crimmigration has been doctrinal. The blurring of criminal law and immigration law has created dangerous obstacles for migrants.

Bosworth and Guild's contribution adapts sociology and criminological theories of critical penology to migration control.[8] Their essay borrows from David Garland's "culture of control" and Jonathan Simon's "governing through crime" to frame the concepts of migration control and "border criminologies."[9]

The migration control frame has become a dystopian nightmare for immigrants of color. Bosworth and Guild further distinguish the term "migration control" from the term "crime control" by distinguishing the administrative characteristics of the latter. Migration administration borrows law enforcement resources and penal norms but distinguishes administration by pointing to the few procedural constraints that come with the administrative state.[10]

Moving Beyond Crimmigration and Crimminologies

In reality, however, migration control aggrandizes state power even beyond the power of the crime control and administration frames. Bosworth and Guild fail to contend with the sovereignty metaphor behind migration control that distinguishes immigration law from public law or administration generally from crime control. The metaphor recognizes state power that exceeds constitutional constraint.

The authors fail to consider characteristics of immigration administration that separate it from administrative apparatuses generally in the U.S. For example, federal rules of evidence do not apply to immigration court. Consequently, immigration court is not really an administrative law court, and immigration judges are not real administrative law judges. The immigration judge (IJ) lacks contempt power, which allows migration enforcement officers to ignore IJ decisions. The IJ is no neutral arbiter and can be bound by Department of Justice directives. In general, the immigration system enjoys an abundance of discretion but little autonomy; it provides few procedural safeguards[11] and little oversight and accountability, and it may appear to adhere more to policy directives than rule-of-law norms.

Migrants are denied the right to an attorney in immigration court and access to an independent magistrate, or even an immigration judge (in some cases), when faced with detain/release decisions. The administrative structure is exceedingly plastic in form; it bends to political whim and is hence particularly susceptible to criminalization and social control. With access to commanding federal enforcement resources that make immigration enforcement the federal government's largest law enforcement bureaucracy and a discourse that paints people of color as a potential risk as criminals, terrorists, or gang members, the migrant control system has the capacity to be uniquely punitive. In these and other ways, immigration law is distinguishable as much from the administrative apparatus as from criminal law.

Beyond that, however, the immigration exception has opened the door for executives to rule as tyrants. It is part of an exceptional control system that augments executive power and unleashes institutional bias against migrants that subverts the rule of law.

The Court is complicit in criminalization and securitization of migration. It has established an exceptional path for the development of immigration law that is almost unique in its non-law–like qualities. It has encouraged an authoritarian-intentioned executive to assert extraordinary power over migrants, so much so that its actions would likely be considered illegitimate if applied to any other legal field. That is not to say immigration law is not entirely outside the administrative law net. For example, federal courts are likely to defer to Immigration and Customs Enforcement (ICE) or Customs and Border Protection (CBP) with the much-criticized "*Chevron* deference"[12] as much as they defer to other administrative agencies under this deferential standard. It is clear that immigration agencies benefit from *Chevron* deference.

In addition to *Chevron*, however, immigration law dwells in the exceptional legal and cultural dead zone created over a century ago in the Chinese Exclusion Act cases. Under the plenary powers doctrine, originating in those cases in 1889 (discussed later), political branches enjoy near impunity in making immigration entry and exit decisions and are responsible for a culture of control and impunity over noncitizens at borders at ports of entry and internal.

As a creature of the executive branch reinforced by *Chevron*, immigration agencies enjoy discretionary powers that other agencies might envy. Additionally, until the immigration bureaucracy was recreated for the most part under the Department of Homeland Security (DHS) in 2003, it was among the bottom-feeding set of agencies within the federal bureaucracy. Enduring a legacy neglect and corruption and with little oversight, the bureaucracy served as a last-resort agency for wannabe federal employees. Since 2003 and in the post 9/11 era, as the new DHS enforcement force was established as ICE and CBP, migration enforcement has grown dramatically in size, but the racist impunity in its bones since immigration was first criminalized in 1929 has remained a substantial part of the control culture.

The Court's complicity in Trumpian tyranny at the border was revealed in *Trump v. Hawaii*,[13] which for Trump revitalized the salience of sovereignty and plenary norms. The Court has legitimized discrimination by cynically deploying a traditional type of legal reasoning referred to as "legal formalism."[14] The Court's method has been to apply formalist reasoning to plenary powers. Although legal formalism does not ensure the Court will be deferential to the executive, it does limit the scope of legal analysis to the text and generally forecloses consideration of social context or outcomes. Plenary power is a judicial construct that accommodates the government's sovereign authority. It excludes all but the most cursory of judicial review.

By applying formalism to plenary power the Court has legitimized government violence against vulnerable people. As an outcome in *Trump v. Hawaii*, the Court also legitimized cruelty and racist indifference to the impact of the ban on the lives of individual Muslim immigrants. That case helped propel Trump to continue his anti-immigrant agenda at the border. But take note: what the Court had achieved was to give license to the exclusionary mission of immigration enforcement and plenary power that was originally derived from the precedential *Chae Chan Ping* case, which first constituted the immigration exception of immigration law.

The Sovereign Exception Using Immigration Law: A Legal Framework

Donald Trump has come as close as any U.S. president to Carl Schmitt's vision of aggressive executive power,[15] with the possible exception of Abraham Lincoln in his suspension of habeas corpus during the Civil War. Schmitt introduces the "state of exception" as a government's political response to an imminent threat to its sovereign existence. As Schmitt says, "The sovereign is one who decides on the exception." This phrase refers to the sovereign suspending the rule of law in times of crisis or imminent threat. Immigration represents an instance in which the exception is limited to the narrow but permanent scope of immigration law. Thus, unlike Lincoln, Trump has normalized this subversion of law by using immigration law to drive his nationalist agenda. For observers who might doubt this claim, consider events in 2019 that shrugged off migrant deaths in immigration custody and along the banks of the Rio Grande, tore babies and small children from their mothers, and crowded migrants and refugees into privatized prison facilities, standing up.

Immigration law's path to authoritarianism begins in sovereignty, which has logic different from the rule of law, and holds the potential to apply to legal fields beyond immigration law.[16]

Schmitt defines the sovereign exception (to law) as "a case of extreme peril, a danger to the existence of the state, or the like. But it cannot be circumscribed factually and made to conform to a preformed law."[17] The concepts of new formalism and punitive bias are enlisted to help deconstruct Schmitt's notion of the sovereign exception in law. They comprise communicative elements that securitize actions made in the name of the sovereign exception. They regularize anti-immigrant responses that would be unlawful if adhered to citizens.

In practice, sovereignty has been the source of government power excluding people of color since 1889.[18] Since then, the system of sovereignty has been self-reproduced through exclusionary events. Exclusionary events are symbolized by securitization, a speech act that names national security threats or threats to sovereignty and actually constitutes threats through the power of language.[19] Through formalist review, the Court subsequently deferred to the political branch naming the risk.[20]

Sovereignty was self-reproduced through federal immigration policy for the first time when the Court deferred to Congress's plenary power to exclude Chinese laborers in *Chae Chan Ping* (1889).[21] Ever since, immigration procedures and outcomes were deployed that would be unconstitutional if applied to citizens.[22] For example, exclusions may occur on account of race, national origin, political opinion, and gender for government interest.

So what exactly is transgressed when the sovereign asserts the exception to the rule of law? The rule of law consists of basic principles meant to assure that no person, including the ruler, is above the law, and the law is not above the ordinary person (is accessible to the ordinary person).[23] It is a baseline assumption in public law that the courts will minimize discretion by interpreting statutes and individualizing justice through clear principles.[24] Statutes and regulations are promulgated and applied in a general and prospective manner, understood by the ordinary person, consistent in application, and possible to obey.[25] These components of due process are the basis for individualized justice, where decisions are roughly consistent and rules are proportionate and prospective.[26] With individualized justice, ambiguities are resolved in favor of the immigrant, like the criminal law rule of lenity suggests.[27]

The sovereign exception sacrifices individualized justice in the ceaseless bid for the nation-state's survival. Although it is not really at risk, survival is a ceaseless endeavor that in part is symbolized through discrete immigration exclusions. Ad hoc and arbitrary practices and racist exclusions are justified in the name of securitization.[28] Disregard for human rights and dignity are ostensibly a small cost to exact from the "alien other" in the name of sovereign self-preservation.

While the constitution functions as a constraint on government action, sovereign actions are unconstrained. Consider how the law treats discrimination in the anti-discrimination law and immigration law contexts. Anti-discrimination law represents society's concern for both fair treatment (liberty) and humanitarian norms under the Fifth and Fourteenth Amendments. For much of the twentieth century, courts have scrutinized government action for intentional discrimination and disparate treatment, which if found, shifts the burden of proof to the government to show it is not discriminating or that discrimination is narrowly tailored to a compelling state interest.[29]

It was requested of the Court that it find Trump's executive order (EO) in violation of the anti-discrimination provision of the INA. Unfortunately, the Court's formalist review helped it to avoid inquiring into the alleged discrimination. It did not matter if the executive order discriminated (yes, it did). It also did not matter if there was really a national security crisis (no, there was no evidence of crisis). Instead, the Court's inquiry was limited to whether the EO mentioned a national security purpose for issuing the travel ban (it did). Formalist review foreclosed upon follow-up inquiry into the veracity of Trump's rhetoric. As long as Trump's EO alluded to the four corners of the INA's national security provision, the Court's inquiry came to an alarming close.

Brief History of Immigration Law

In this section, I briefly describe the historical background depicting the development of immigration law with reference to plenary powers, punitive bias, and legal formalism. I define these terms as I go. Immigration law defies the evolving norms of public law generally because of the exceptional system of sovereignty that informs it.

The Court has located the source of immigration law inside the Constitution through an inherent executive branch power under Article 2,[30] or implied under Article I, Section 8 ("The Congress shall have power to . . . establish an uniform Rule of Naturalization")[31] and can be read into Article 2, Section 3 ("The President shall . . . take Care that the Laws be faithfully executed").[32] Whether or not the president derives his authority over immigration from an inherent power vested in the Constitution or through congressional legislation,[33] the Court emphasized that the judicial branch should give considerable deference to decisions and may only intervene when required by the "paramount law of the Constitution."[34]

In *Chae Chan Ping v. United States* the Supreme Court affirmed that Congress's "power of exclusion of foreigners" is "an incident of sovereignty belonging to the government of the United States."[35] Plenary powers were thus first rationalized in *Chae Chan Ping*:[36]

> Whether a proper consideration by our government of its previous laws, or a proper respect for the nation whose subjects are affected by its action, ought to have qualified its inhibition, and made it applicable only to person departing from the country after the passage of the act, are not questions for judicial determination.[37]

The cases that followed *Chae Chan Ping* solidified the plenary power doctrine.[38] Four years after *Chae* in *Fong Yue Ting*, the Court declared that the power to deport foreign nationals is "vested in the political departments of the National Government."[39] The Court stated that this power "is to be regulated by act of Congress and . . . executed by the executive authority."[40] In *Fong Yue Ting*, the Court declared that the power of "every sovereign nation" to deport noncitizens was "as absolute and unqualified as the right to prohibit and prevent their entrance into the country."[41]

Although the Chinese Exclusion Act was repealed in 1943, the case and its progeny have not been overruled.[42] Although no court has followed *Chae Chan Ping* itself since 1904,[43] immigration law cases have cited plenary power owing to the Chinese Exclusion Act cases as recently as 2016.[44]

Many factors are responsible for sustaining the Court's anachronistic use of plenary authority. First, the sovereign origins of federal immigration law provided disincentives to examine plenary power and thus also anti-immigration discrimination, chiefly because the Court has been uncomfortable with foreign policy.[45] Second, the Court in 1889 was engaged in legal formalist reasoning that helped secure substantive exclusions through legal formalism.

Third, immigration policy during the early nineteenth century emphasized anti-immigrant nativism responsible in 1924 with slowing immigration, and hence litigation, to a trickle for four decades after the Johnson-Reed Act of 1924 introduced national origins quotas. Johnson Reed was a racist policy that nostalgically tried to engineer a return to the country's comparative demographic homogeneity represented in the 1890 census, in a period just before immigration from Central and Southern Europe would diversify a country already mired in Jim Crow. Low levels of immigration understandably led to neglect at the country's two most celebrated immigrant landings and hastened the closing of Angel Island on the West Coast in 1940 and Ellis Island in 1954, which further discouraged immigration.[46]

It wasn't until the 1950s that the Supreme Court had the opportunity to critically reexamine the doctrine of plenary powers as they applied to constitutional requirements of due process. In 1950, the Supreme Court offered the clearest explanation of the plenary power doctrine. In *Knauff v. Shaughnessy*, the Court reiterated that the exclusion of aliens is "a fundamental act of sovereignty" that is "inherent in the executive power to control the foreign affairs of the nation."[47] The Court affirmed, "The decision to admit or to exclude an alien may be lawfully placed with the President."[48] In his opinion for the Court, Justice Sutherland declared:

> The action of the executive officer under such authority is final and conclusive. It is not within the province of any court . . . to review the determination of the political branch . . . to exclude a given alien.[49]

With such power, the Court inverts the rule of law concept of due process into a matter of political will: "Whatever the procedure authorized by Congress is, it is due process as far as an alien denied entry is concerned."[50]

Similarly, in *Shaughnessy v. United States ex rel. Mezei* (1953), the Court reaffirmed *Knauff*, resulting in the immigrant being held on Ellis Island for four years.[51] These two cases are still relied on by courts in regard to the plenary power doctrine.[52] The Court concluded that, under the plenary power doctrine, courts are not permitted to interfere with Executive Branch policies that regulate immigration or restrict admission of foreign nationals unless Congress expressly authorizes such judicial review.[53]

It is worth noting the sharp divergence between immigration law and other public law fields. As *Brown v. Board of Education* exemplified the legal realist turn in legal reasoning that recognized purpose, context, and consequence of legal decisions, immigration law missed this civil rights moment—except perhaps the Immigration Act of 1965 that removed national origins quotas—because it was stuck in formalist jurisprudence and as a consequence has remained stunted within a radical formalist framework.

By the 1970s, the Court established a modified formalism, inventing the Mandel test, to accommodate late Cold War exclusions. In *Kleindienst v. Mandel*,[54] the Court found that the U.S. Congress had granted the appellant the right to exclude aliens from the United States on any "facially legitimate and bona fide" basis, and judicial intervention with that policy was not appropriate. More recently, in *Kerry v. Din*,[55] the Court applied the same Mandel inquiry of whether the decision was made based on a "facially legitimate and bona fide reason." Since such inquiry requires little more than naming a "bona fide" statute or other sub-constitutional provision, the Court indeed found a facially legitimate and bona fide reason to exclude.

Immigration increased as a result of the 1965 Immigration Act. By the late

1970s and early 1980s, a new generation of immigration litigators brought innovative strategies to bear on the government's mistreatment of noncitizens of color from countries previously excluded or limited by national origins quotas. By the late 1970s and 1980s, a variety of new legal issues emerge, brought about by the following factors: the Cold War; undocumented immigration identified as a law enforcement issue; political asylum,[56] which introduced a new subfield of immigration law; and the mass detention of Cuban and Haitian refugees.[57] Additionally, by the late 1980s and 1990s, presidents H. W. Bush and Bill Clinton had begun to make sense of these factors in terms of the crimmigration regime.[58] It is important to note that crimmigration developed along the lines of the plenary power cases that allows government to treat immigrants in ways they could not treat citizens, hence criminalizing immigrants without providing criminal law procedures.

Applying Sovereignty to the Travel Ban

The *Trump v. Hawaii* case provides an opportunity to address racism embedded in punitive bias and legitimized through radical formalism in the immigration context. While a realist Court would have analyzed the travel ban within the context of Trump's statements and tweets, the Court continues to conceal discrimination against immigrants through radical formalism. It masks deference to the travel ban with new formalist reasoning that pairs securitization and punitive bias to legitimize hostile treatment of immigrants.

On January 27, 2017, the president issued an Executive Order entitled, "Protecting the Nation from Foreign Terrorist Entry into the United States."[59] The order announced that entry into the United States from Iran, Iraq, Libya, Somalia, Sudan, Syria, and Yemen would be "detrimental to the interests of the United States" and thus suspended entry of immigrants from these countries for ninety days.[60]

Three days after the Executive Order was signed, on January 30, 2017, the State of Washington filed suit in the U.S. District Court for the Western District of Washington, challenging sections 3(c), 5(a)-(c), and 5(e) of the Executive Order. The court issued a temporary restraining order (TRO). The Government filed a notice of appeal and sought an emergency opinion from the Ninth Circuit, including an immediate stay of the TRO. The Ninth Circuit denied the request for an immediate stay and requested responsive and reply briefs.[61] The Government took the position that the president's decision was unreviewable. The Ninth Circuit noted that this argument ran contrary to the fundamental structure of constitutional democracy.[62]

After the legal challenge to Trump's first Executive Order, a second Executive Order was issued.[63] The second Executive Order stated that nationals from the designated countries warranted "additional security" because "the conditions in these countries present heightened threats." It clarified that the suspension of entry applied to foreign nationals who (1) are outside the United States on its effective date of March 16, 2017, (2) do not have a valid visa on that date, and (3) did not have a valid visa on the effective date of EO-1—January 27, 2017.

Like its predecessor, Executive Order II was quickly challenged in federal court. On March 10, 2017, plaintiffs initiated suit along with a motion for a TRO. On March 16, the district court granted a motion for preliminary injunction.[64] In its response, the Fourth Circuit looked at the District of Columbia Circuit, which had stated that "a consular official's decision to issue or withhold a visa is not subject to judicial review, at least unless Congress says otherwise."[65] The court held that the doctrine of consular non-reviewability did not bar judicial review of constitutional claims, calling the Government's reliance on that doctrine "misplaced." The Fourth Circuit called out the Government for a dangerous proposition—that the federal circuit lacked the authority to review high-level government policy within the immigration context. They stated that the duty to say what the law is "will sometimes [involve] the 'resolution of litigation challenging the constitutional authority of one of the three branches,' but courts avoid [that] responsibility."[66]

The administration issued a third Executive Order to exclude foreign nationals from majority Muslim countries (Iran, Libya, Syria, Somalia, Yemen) and three countries that are not majority Muslim (Chad, Venezuela, and North Korea). The travel ban was announced by presidential proclamation on September 24, 2017. The president described the third iteration as a "more politically correct" version of the earlier travel bans. Still, here is a president who promised to ban Muslims by targeting territories and then put successive bans in place starting the first week of his presidency. At issue is whether the federal government can explicitly discriminate on the basis of religion and national origin. Even after stating that plaintiffs had not demonstrated a sufficient likelihood of success on the merits of the Establishment Clause claim, it seems the absence of an explicit response was tantamount to an inferred yes on the religion ban.

In the majority opinion, Justice Roberts rejected constitutional scrutiny for statutory interpretation. The Court then adhered punitive norms to the statute following formalist reasoning. First, the Court had the choice of pinning its decision on one of two relevant and contradictory provisions in the INA. Most recent is INA 1152(a), referred to as the nondiscrimination clause in the INA,[67] which was added to the INA in 1965 as part of Congress' reversal of the forty-year national origins quota. The nondiscrimination clause would have invited the Court to weigh in on the president's anti-Muslim discrimination. In the Court's estimation 1152(a) was not as germane as 1182(f), part of the INA since 1952; 1182(f) cabined the national security grounds that comprised the basis for the challenge to the president's proclamation.[68]

The Court deferred to the broad discretion that INA 1182(f) delegated to the executive to suspend the entry of aliens on national security grounds. The Court upheld the ban as long as it could conceive of a plausible national security justification, regardless of the actual justification, even if it were obvious that the president was motivated by animus toward Muslims.

As a safeguard, the Court named the proclamation's exemptions and waivers procedures as plausible national security justification. These procedures were added to Ban III. Justice Roberts insisted these procedures were a symbol of neutral principles. In dissent, Justice Breyer placed the exemptions and waivers in context and cited proof that the procedures were in fact not being relied on. Justice Sotomayor found the travel ban unconstitutional as a matter of law, emphasizing the plenary norms embedded in the president's public statements and tweets.

Radical Formalism, Punitive Bias, and the Travel Ban

In its substantive outcomes and line of reasoning, the Court has treated important immigration issues as if it were 1889, at least in broad terms, and with important exceptions.[69] In 1889 the Court adopted exclusionary norms that Chinese laborers are "vast hordes (of Chinese) . . . crowding in upon us."[70] History reveals that the Court's reference to "vast hordes" was nothing but a pejorative and racist reference to Chinese laborers.[71]

In 2017 and 2018, the Trump administration invoked similarly racist anti-Muslim rhetoric. In her dissenting opinion in *Trump v. Hawaii*,[72] Justice Sotomayor condemned the anti-Muslim messaging originating in Trump's public statements and tweets that constructed the national security risk.[73] The Travel Ban was "inexplicable by anything but animus."[74] Animus underlay the Court's formal application of statutory provision 1182(f). The Court's proclivity toward deference explains why the Court maneuvered around the equally compelling INA 1152(a)(1)(A), the anti-discrimination provision, which almost certainly would have produced a different result. The Court pretended 1152(a)(1)(A) held no sway because it applies to visas, not admissibility, a distinction without a difference, as scholars have observed. Such is the modus operandi of radical formalism, to remain within the four corners of a statute, guided by plenary norms that are at their heart exclusionary. Formalist review fails to analyze purpose and context and makes absolute certainties out of almost immaterial statutory distinctions. As Sotomayor stated, the majority was "ignoring the facts, misconstruing our legal precedent and turning a blind eye to the pain and suffering the proclamation inflicts upon countless families and individuals. . . ."

Of course, the Court's formal reasoning in 1889 must be distinguished from the new formalism of 2018. New formalism allows the Court to treat immigration agencies as if they held the same plenary power as Congress did a century before.[75] The Court accommodated the proclamation's new administrative waivers and exemptions within an already existing schema Congress introduced in 1952. The Court discerned categorical exclusions for national security purposes without fact-checking the president's rhetoric or placing his pejorative comments within political context. In dissent, Justice Stephen Breyer proposed a realist alternative that would have mustered relevant facts and outcomes. Additionally, since almost no waivers or exemptions had been issued in fact, Breyer noted that the waiver provisions were not meant seriously.[76] His reference to the exclusion of an eight-year-old girl with cerebral palsy was all the context that was really required to reject the Muslim ban.

Authoritarianism through Immigration Policy and Law

Following Breyer's cajoling to look behind the curtain, *Trump v. Hawaii* must be placed in a greater context of helping to unleash Trumpian authoritarianism. Rising authoritarianism under Trump has occurred through executive actions. From his first week in office Trump has brutalized immigrants in word and action. Almost immediately after his inauguration, battle plans through executive actions signaled the administration's strategy. On January 25, 2017, Trump signed two Executive Orders: *Border Security and Immigration Enforcement Improvements*[77] and *Enhancing Public Safety in the Interior of the United States*.[78] The Border Security Order notably ordered implementation of a border wall, but also mandated the DHS secretary to ensure the detention of undocumented foreign nationals pending the outcome of removal proceedings. The interior enforcement order notably threatened to end funding sanctuary jurisdictions, terminated the Priority Enforcement Program (PEP), and reinstated Secure Communities and the 287(g) Initiative.[79] The Order also labeled "aliens who illegally enter or who overstay" as a significant threat to public safety.[80]

On January 27, 2017, the administration issued the Travel Ban Executive Order that singled out individuals from several majority Muslim countries.[81] This was the first of three travel bans the president would issue. In the first days of the new administration, millions of people were prevented from entering the country. The exclusions wreaked havoc on thousands of arrivals and their families at international airports and provoked nationwide protest, which suggested a move too far.[82]

Indeed, it is both ironic and germane to the discussion about authoritarianism to see the Court limit executive authority in *U.S. v. Texas* but defer to executive actions when it comes to the travel ban. I distinguish the Court's decision in *Texas* from *Hawaii* by suggesting that *Texas* addresses inclusion, which has no bearing on sovereignty, while *Hawaii* addresses exclusionary events, which symbolize the reproduction of sovereignty.

As Trump warned during the campaign, a war on immigration would be particularly "proactive and nasty."[83] As part a of draconian, zero-tolerance[84] executive initiative,[85] in May and June 2018 (if not earlier), immigration enforcers bore down on women and children at the U.S.-Mexico border[86] and tore close to 3,000 Latino children from their parents' arms.[87] The children were then warehoused in animal-like cages and forcibly resettled with strangers in distant parts of the country. Many were subjected to harsh disciplinary measures, and some were sexually abused.[88] Despite many cases likely being credible asylum cases[89] under the 1980 Refugee Act,[90] CBP stopped individuals on the international bridge before they could even reach the U.S. side and unnecessarily detained and separated families who managed to cross the international marker. These encounters with law enforcement brought them into an administrative nightmare equipped with neither plans nor procedures to reunite the families upon resolution of the immigration case.[91] This strategy was deliberately[92] designed to deter families[93] from exercising their international and domestic right to apply for asylum.[94]

The Trump administration normalized this subversion of law through immigration law.[95] Each federal court injunction against the travel ban, for example, emboldened the administration to issue another.[96] Rather than accepting the court's decision or appealing it, the administration simply reworded parts of the ban that the court had previously found objectionable. And when a federal court ordered the administration to reunite children with their mothers, the administration delayed and subjected entire families to prolonged detention, ignoring judicial orders and family reunification deadlines.[97] The administration defied court orders, subverted the rule of law, and deliberately worsened situations for immigrants and accentuated Trump's drift toward authoritarianism. Regrettably, these horrifying examples of exclusion are merely highly visible instances of harsh exclusions that occur almost daily.

Adults are also torn from families through the administration's less visible recommitment to widely condemned 287(g) and Secure Communities programs, for example, along with ICE's deployment of a wider enforcement net to entice immigrants into expedited removal proceedings. Secure Communities and 287(g) precede the Trump administration, but they had been condemned and discontinued for racial profiling and other rights violations. As Trump's war on immigrants peaked in October 2018, the president ordered over 5,000 troops to the border as a first line of defense against a group of refugees seeking asylum heading north through Mexico from Central America's Northern Triangle. The military response was a securitizing cry: border security is national security, and facts don't matter.

Discussion and Conclusion

Embedded within the immigration system is license for racist exclusions. The Trump administration landed on immigration as a driving force of administration social policy because it embodies much of the wish list for this hate-filled administration—namely, broad assertions of executive power on the backs of migrants and refugees of color. Radical formalism has helped facilitate exclusionary messages through plenary authority that has existed in immigration law since its origins. Perhaps before the abuses at the border are corrected, the message must be taken seriously that the structure of immigration law is inherently racist, which explains that indeed immigrants can be subjected to inferior treatment within this legal field. The problems lie in the law and its limits to address abuse even more than in a hate-filled administrative apparatus.

The salient question is whether there is any stopping this seemingly runaway system in the age of Trump. The answer is, "I think so," but it's not so easy. First, the Court must foster the will to overturn the immigration exclusion precedent of *Chae Chan Ping*.[98] There is no need for the political branches to enjoy plenary power over immigration, particularly when justices place constraints on actions on other ostensible national security fields. Second, the Court must adopt a realist jurisprudence when examining immigration exclusions, which means earnest consideration of consequences, context, and purpose. A few justices willing to express empathy for the immigrant's plight would go a long way toward a realist critique.[99] Finally, the Court must bring the meat of constitutional scrutiny back into decisions that adversely affect people of color and other disempowered minorities.[100] The constitution may not be the end-all of securing justice in immigration law, but it sure matters in securing a modicum of consistent scrutiny over decisions in the immigration system. In terms of specifics, apply Fourth,[101] Fifth,[102] and Sixth Amendment[103] principles to immigration law.[104] In addition, Article I immigration courts would add important rule-of-law safeguards and hence greater predictability and consistency to the legal outcome of cases for individuals whose lives may be at stake. The rule of law should be a bottom-line expectation of justice for immigrants. In the meantime, Lincoln is spinning in his grave.

Notes

The author would like to thank the follow persons for research and editing assistance: Lindsay Bramble, Dena Robinson, James Cooke, Kelsey Drotning, and, for much appreciated comments during the authoring process, Jennifer Chacón, Jamie Longazel, and Maartje van der Woude.

1. Opheli Garcia Lawler, "The U.S. Government Is Caging Hundreds of Migrants under a Bridge," *Cut*, Mar. 29, 2019, https://www.thecut.com/2019/03/migrants-being-held-under-bridge-in-el-paso-what-we-know.html.

2. 585 U.S. __(2018).

3. It should be noted that the Court seemed to deny that the travel ban was a religious ban, although when government prefers one religion over another, there is a clear argument that immigrants are banned on the basis of religion.

4. Mary Bosworth and Mhairi Guild, "Governing through Migration Control," *British Journal of Criminology* 48, no. 6 (2008).

5. Juliet Stumpf, "The Crimmigration Crisis: Immigrants, Crime, and Sovereignty," *American University Law Review* 56, no. 2 (2006).

6. Ibid.

7. Ibid.

8. Bosworth and Guild, "Governing through Migration Control."

9. Ibid.

10. Katja Franko Aas and Bosworth. *The Borders of Punishment: Migration, Citizenship and Social Exclusion* (London: Oxford University Press, 2013).

11. *Hammad v. Holder*, 603 F.3d 536, 545 (9th Cir. 2010), explaining that rules of evidence are not applicable to immigration hearings.

12. *Chevron U.S.A., Inc. v. Natural Resources Defense Council, Inc.* 467 U.S. 837 (1984).

13. 585 U.S.__(2018). See also Hiroshi Motomura for discussion of sub constitutional norms that apply to statutes and regulations as a form of constitutional avoidance; Motomura, "Immigration Law After a Century of Plenary Power: Phantom Constitutional Norms and Statutory Interpretation," *Yale Law Journal* 100, no. 3 (1990).

14. See Goodwin Liu, "History Will Be Heard: An Appraisal of the Seattle/Louisville Decision," *Harvard Law and Policy Review* 2, no. 53 (2008).

15. See Carl Schmitt, *Political Theology: Four Chapters on the Concept of Sovereignty* (Chicago: University of Chicago Press, 2005), Chapter 1.

16. As in Lincoln's suspension of habeas corpus noted earlier.

17. Schmitt, *Political Theology*, 6.

18. See *Chae Chan Ping v. United States*, 130 U.S. 581(1889); *Fong Yue Ting v. United States*, 149 U.S. 698 (1893).

19. Barry Buzan, Ole Waever, and Jaap de Wilde, *Security: A New Framework for Analysis* (Boulder, Colo.: Lynne Rienner, 1998), 26.

20. Ibid.

21. *Chae Chan Ping*, 130 U.S. 581 (1889).

22. *Shaughnessy v. United States ex rel. Mezei*, 345 U.S. 206 (1953).

23. Brian Tamanaha, *On the Rule of Law* (Cambridge: Cambridge University Press, 2004). Lon Fuller provides a moral version of this foundational aspect of rule of law principles.

24. Ibid.

25. Ibid.

26. Ibid.

27. Cass R. Sunstein, "Testing Minimalism: A Reply," *Michigan Law Review* 104, no. 123 (2005).

28. Buzan, Waever, and de Wilde, *Security*, 26.

29. See Roy G. Spece Jr. and David Yokum, "Scrutinizing Strict Scrutiny," *Vermont Law Review* 40 (2015).

30. U.S. Const. art. I, § 1; see *Nishimura Ekiu v. United States*, 142 U.S. 651 (1892); see also U.S. v. Curtiss-Wright Export Corp., 299 U.S. 304 (1936).

31. U.S. Const. art. I, § 8.

32. U.S. Const. art. II, § 3.

33. In *East Bay Sanctuary v. Trump* before the 9th Circuit Court of Appeals, the federal government referenced 8 U.S.C. § 1182(f). *E. Bay Sanctuary Covenant v. Trump*, 909 F.3d 1219, 1236 (9th Cir. 2018).

34. Ibid.

35. *Chae Chan Ping v. United States*, 130 U.S. 581 at 608 (1889).

36. *Chae Chan Ping v. United States*, 130 U.S. 581 (1889).

37. Ibid., 609 (emphasis added). Although these cases have not been overruled, and thus are technically still "good law," it is also important to note that these cases are rooted in anti-Chinese sentiments from that time period.

38. See *Nishimura Ekiu v. United States*, 142 U.S. 651 (1892) (the Court sided with the United States government on the position that the final determination of facts of the case was to be made by the immigration authorities); *see also* Fong Yue Ting v. U.S., 149 U.S. 698 (1893) (the Court recognized that Congress had *almost unlimited discretion* to establish all aspects of the nation's immigration policy, including the rules and procedures for alien registration *and* deportation) (emphasis added).

39. *Fong Yue Ting v. United States*, 149 U.S. 698 (1893).

40. Ibid., at 713.

41. *Fong Yue Ting v. United States*, 149 U.S. 698 (1893).

42. See, e.g., *Castro v. United States Dep't of Homeland Sec.*, 163 F. Supp. 3d 157 (2016) (noting that "the Supreme Court reaffirmed Congress's power to vest

Executive officers with exclusive fact-finding authority respecting the admission of aliens," in Ekiu); *M.S.P.C. v. U.S. Customs & Border Prot.*, 60 F. Supp. 3d 1156 (2014) (noting that the final determination of right of admission lies in executive officers, "without judicial intervention"); *Phong Doan v. INS*, 78 F. Supp. 2d 1101, 2000 U.S. Dist. LEXIS 182 (2000) (finding that "the power to detain and expel either excludable or deportable aliens is a fundamental attribute of sovereignty").

43. *United States ex rel. Turner v. Williams*, 194 U.S. 279 (1904).

44. See, e.g., *Castro v. United States Dep't of Homeland Sec.*, 163 F. Supp. 3d 157 (2016) (noting that "the Supreme Court reaffirmed Congress's power to vest Executive officers with exclusive fact-finding authority respecting the admission of aliens," in *Ekiu*); *M.S.P.C. v. U.S. Customs and Border Prot.*, 60 F. Supp. 3d 1156 (2014) (noting that the final determination of right of admission lies in executive officers, "without judicial intervention"); *Phong Doan v. INS*, 78 F. Supp. 2d 1101, 2000 U.S. Dist. LEXIS 182 (2000) (finding that "the power to detain and expel either excludable or deportable aliens is a fundamental attribute of sovereignty").

45. Stephen Legomsky, "The New Path of Immigration Law: Asymmetric Incorporation of Criminal Justice Norms," *Washington and Lee Law Review* 64, no. 2 (2006): 469–528.

46. See César Cuauhtémoc García Hernández, "*Naturalizing Immigration Imprisonment*," 103 *Cal. L. Rev.* 1449, 1495 (2015) (immigration detention decreased), *History*, Angel Island Conservatory, http://angelisland.org/history/ (last visited Mar. 9, 2018) (Angel Island close date); *Ellis Island History*, Statute of Liberty-Ellis Island Found. Inc. (last visited Mar. 9, 2018), https://www.libertyellisfoundation.org/ellis-island-history#Laws. (Ellis Island close date).

47. *United States. ex rel. Knauff v. Shaughnessy*, 338 U.S. 537, 542 (1950).

48. Ibid., 543.

49. Ibid.

50. Ibid., 544.

51. *Shaughnessy v. United States ex rel. Mezei*, 345 U.S. 206 (1953).

52. See, e.g., *Gonzalez v. Ashcroft*, 278 F. Supp. 2d 402 (2003); *Mao Bing Mu v. Ashcroft*, 2004 U.S. Dist. LEXIS 30440 (2004); *Castro v. Cabrera*, 742 F.3d 595 (2014); *Castro v. United States Dep't of Homeland Sec.*, 835 F.3d 422 (2016); *Kiyemba v. Obama*, 555 F.3d 1022 (2009).

53. *Shaughnessy*, 345 U.S. at 215–16.

54. *Kleindienst v Mandel*, 408 U.S. 753 (1972).

55. *Kerry v Din*, 576 U.S. (2015).

56. See Refugee Act of 1980, Public Law, 96–212.

57. Following in part the Mariel Boatlift, wherein 125,000 Cubans arrived in South Florida in spring 1980.

58. Stumpf, "Crimmigration Crisis"; Cuahtemoc Cesar and Garcia Hernandez, *Crimmigration Law* (Washington D.C.: American Bar Association, 2015).

59. "Executive Order Protecting the Nation from Foreign Terrorist Entry into the

United States," January 27, 2017, https://www.whitehouse.gov/presidential-actions/executive-order-protecting-nation-foreign-terrorist-entry-united-states/.

60. 82 Fed. Reg. 8,977 (citing the Immigration and Nationality Act (INA) § 217(a)(12), codified at 8 U.S.C. § 1187(a)(12)), https://www.whitehouse.gov/the-press-office/2017/01/27/executive-order-protecting-nation-foreign-terrorist-entry-united-states.

61. *Trump v. Hawaii*, 859 F.3d 741 (9th Cir. 2017).

62. See *Boumediene v. Bush*, 553 U.S. 723, 765, 128 S. Ct. 2229, 171 L. Ed. 2d 41 (2008) (rejecting the idea that, even by congressional statute, Congress and the Executive could eliminate federal court habeas jurisdiction over enemy combatants, because the "political branches" lack "the power to switch the Constitution on or off at will").

63. "Executive Order Protecting the Nation from Foreign Terrorist Entry into the United States," March 6, 2017, https://www.whitehouse.gov/presidential-actions/executive-order-protecting-nation-foreign-terrorist-entry-united-states-2/.

64. *Int'l Refugee Assistance Project*, 2017 U.S. Dist. LEXIS 37645, 2017 WL 1018235, at 1.

65. *Saavedra Bruno v. Albright*, 197 F.3d 1153, 1159, 339 U.S. App. D.C. 78 (D.C. Cir. 1999).

66. *Zivotofsky ex rel. Zivotofsky v. Clinton*, 566 U.S. 189, 196, 132 S. Ct. 1421, 182 L. Ed. 2d 423 (2012) (quoting *INS v. Chadha*, 462 U.S. 919, 943, 103 S. Ct. 2764, 77 L. Ed. 2d 317 (1983)).

67. 8 U.S.C. § 1152(a)(1)(A) states: no person shall receive any preference or priority or be discriminated against in the issuance of an immigrant visa because of the person's race, sex, nationality, place of birth, or place of residence.

68. 8 U.S.C. § 1182(f) "Suspension of entry or imposition of restrictions by President as justification for this executive order" as justification for the executive order. That statute states, "*Whenever the President finds that the entry of any aliens or of any class of aliens into the United States would be detrimental to the interests of the United States, he may by proclamation, and for such period as he shall deem necessary, suspend the entry of all aliens or any class of aliens as immigrants or nonimmigrants, or impose on the entry of aliens any restrictions he may deem to be appropriate.*"

69. Michel Rosenfeld defines legal formalism as something internal to law, an internally unfolding practice that carves a domain of interaction that is separate from politics, in *Just Interpretations: Law between Ethics and Politics* (Berkeley: University of California Press, 1998), chapter 2. As I use the term "new formalism," it enables the social reproduction of sovereignty through acts of exclusion.

70. *Chae Chan Ping*, 130 U.S. 581 (1889).

71. Garrett Epps, "The Ghost of Chae Chan Ping," *Atlantic Monthly*, January 20, 2018.

72. *Trump v. Hawaii*, 585 U.S._ (2018), Sotomayor dissent.

73. "Trump asserted that 'we're having problems with the Muslims, and we're having problems with Muslims coming into the country . . . he opined that Muslims do not respect us at all" and "don't respect a lot of the things that are happening throughout not only our country, but they don't respect other things, . . ."; Sotomayor dissent at 6.

74. *Trump v. Hawaii*, 585 U.S._ (2018), Sotomayor dissent.

75. Daphne Renan documents the pooling of executive powers that did not exist during the heyday of late nineteenth-century legal formalism. The new formalism must contend with the Court's broad deference to this bundling of executive powers. See Renan, "Pooling Powers," *Columbia Law Review* (2015). 115, No. 2.

76. Yeganeh Torbarti and Mica Rosenberg, "Exclusive: Visa Waivers Rarely Granted under Trump's Latest U.S. Travel Ban: Data," *Reuters*, Mar. 6, 2018, https://www.reuters.com/article/us-usa-immigration-travelban-exclusive/exclusive-visa-waivers-rarely-granted-under-trumps-latest-u-s-travel-ban-data-idUSKCN1GI2DW.

77. Border Security and Immigration Enforcement Improvements, Exec. Order No. 13,767, 82 Fed. Reg. 8793 (Jan. 25, 2017), https://www.federalregister.gov/documents/2017/01/30/2017–02095/border-security-andimmigration-enforcement-improvements [hereinafter "EO 13767"].

78. Executive Order, January 25, 2017.

79. Section 287(g) of the INA 8 U.S.C. 1357(g)).

80. "Executive Order: Enhancing Public Safety in the Interior of the United States," January 25, 2017, https://www.whitehouse.gov/presidential-actions/executive-order-enhancing-public-safety-interior-united-states/.

81. Donald J. Trump, "Executive Order Protecting the Nation from Foreign Terrorist Entry into the United States," *White* House, Jan. 27, 2017, https://www.whitehouse.gov/presidential-actions/executive-order-protecting-nation-foreign-terrorist-entry-united-states/.

82. Eric Bradner, "Resistance to Trump's Travel Ban Mounts," *CNN*, Jan. 30, 2017, https://www.cnn.com/2017/01/29/politics/donald-trump-travel-ban-resistance/index.html.

83. @realDonaldTrump, Twitter (Sept. 9, 2015, 7:03 AM), https://twitter.com/realDonaldTrump/status/908646582807089152. Tweet by President Trump regarding immigration ("*We have made more progress in the last nine month against ISIS than the Obama Administration has made in 8 years. Must be proactive & nasty!*"). The tweet was part of a burst of tweets that intermingled terrorism and immigration. *See also*, @realDonaldTrump, Twitter (Sept. 9, 2015, 3:54 AM), https://twitter.com/realDonaldTrump/status/908645126146265090 ("*The travel ban into the United States should be far larger, tougher, and more specific but stupidly, that would not be politically correct*").

84. "Zero Tolerance Immigration Prosecution FAQ, U.S. Border Protection and Customs" (June 15, 2018), https://www.cbp.gov/newsroom/zero-tolerance-immigration-prosecutions.

85. Charlie Savage, "Explaining Trump's Executive Order on Family Separation," *New York Times*, Jun. 20, 2018, https://www.nytimes.com/2018/06/20/us/politics/family-separation-executive-order.html.

86. Maya Rhodan, "Here Are the Facts about Donald Trump's Family Separation Policy," Time, Jun. 18, 2018, http://time.com/5314769/family-separation-policy-donald-trump/.

87. Elise Foley, "As Many as 3,000 Migrant Families Separated at the Border Haven't Been Reunited," *Huffington Post*, Jul. 5, 2018, https://www.huffingtonpost.com/entry/separated-families-migrants_us_5b3e3fa9e4b09e4a8b2af139.

88. Jared Keller, "Trump's Child Separation Policy Will Scar Migrant Children Forever," *Pacific Standard*, Jun. 20, 2018, https://psmag.com/social-justice/trumps-child-separation-policy-will-scar-migrant-children-forever.

89. Neena Satija, "The Trump Administration Is Not Keeping Its Promises to Asylum Seekers Who Come to Ports of Entry," *Texas Tribune* (Austin, Tex.), Jul. 5, 2018, https://www.texastribune.org/2018/07/05/migrants-seeking-asylum-legally-ports-entry-turned-away-separated-fami/.

90. Refugee Act of 1980, Pub.L. 96–212, https://www.gpo.gov/fdsys/pkg/STATUTE-94/pdf/STATUTE-94-Pg102.pdf.

91. Priscilla Alvarez, "How Will Detained Children Find Their Parents?," *Atlantic*, Jun. 21, 2018, https://www.theatlantic.com/politics/archive/2018/06/how-will-kids-find-parents-trump-executive-order-family-separation/563264/.

92. The immigration system has often been referred to as byzantine. See George Radanovich, "Blame Congress for Immigration Inaction That Jeopardizes American Agriculture," *The Hill*, July 16, 2018, http://thehill.com/opinion/immigration/396265-blame-congress-for-immigration-inaction-that-jeopardizes-american-agriculture.

93. Dara Lind, "The Trump Administration Is Deliberately Starting a Legal Fight over Family Detention," *Vox*, Jun. 20, 2018, https://www.vox.com/2018/6/20/17485866/trump-executive-order-immigration-families-jail.

94. Tal Kopan, "Exclusive: Trump Admin Thought Family Separations Would Deter Immigrants. They Haven't," *CNN*, Jun. 18, 2018, https://www.cnn.com/2018/06/18/politics/family-separation-deterrence-dhs/index.html.

95. Laila Lalami, "How the Trump Administration Is Normalizing Immigrant Internment Camps," *Nation*, Jun. 20, 2018, https://www.thenation.com/article/trump-administration-normalizing-immigrant-internment-camps/.

96. Timeline of the Muslim Ban, ACLU Washington (last visited Aug. 16, 2018), https://www.aclu-wa.org/pages/timeline-muslim-ban.

97. Lind, "Trump's About to Miss Tuesday's Court-Ordered Deadline to Reunite Young Migrant Kids with Their Parents," *Vox*, Jul. 10, 2018, https://www.vox.com/policy-and-politics/2018/7/9/17549408/children-separate-order-together-violate-judge.

98. See, for example, the Brewer, Field, and Fuller dissents in *Fong Yue Ting*, 149, U.S. 698, 13 S. Ct. 1016, 37 L.Ed. 905.

99. Liu, "History Will be Heard."

100. See, for example, the Brewer, Field, and Fuller dissents in *Fong Yue Ting*, 149, U.S. 698, 13 S. Ct. 1016, 37 L.Ed. 905.

101. The right to privacy within 100 miles of the border. See *United States v. Martinez-Fuerte*, 428 U.S. 543 (1976).

102. The right to due process beyond what Congress says.

103. The right to counsel at government expense when one is too poor to hire an attorney.

104. Legomsky, "New Path of Immigration Law," 469–528.

7
A Path toward Nowhere
The Rise of Enforcement-Based Immigration Policy
Doris Marie Provine

> In 2001, if I talked about Dreamers, people thought it was a British rock group. And now, the word "Dreamers" turns up in the president's State of the Union address.
>
> — INTERVIEW WITH ARI SHAPIRO ON NATIONAL PUBLIC RADIO, "ALL THINGS CONSIDERED," FEBRUARY 6, 2018

In this February 2018 interview Senator Durbin went on to express his hope that Congress would debate legislation to protect young people brought into the country as children, something he did not see as a foregone conclusion: "That means the possibility that we could open the debate procedurally this week and engage in it next week. Let me quickly add — the United States Senate has not seen this kind of debate in over a year and a half. Many of the members have never seen it."[1] Durbin's remark is a reminder that Congress no longer provides a reliable platform for the airing and resolution of controversial issues like immigration and that immigration control has become a salient political issue worthy of presidential attention. How did we arrive at this juncture?

The brief Senate debate that Durbin hoped for did occur, but it yielded nothing. The issue has remained stalemated, with little prospect of a revival amid concerns about foreign wars, climate change, the economy, and electoral reform. Amid the chaos of the Trump-centered political universe, with its constant mean-spirited tweets and impulsivity, it is easy to miss this institutional withdrawal from meaningful engagement. Comprehensive immigration reform under Congressional leadership seems further away than ever. All eyes now are on President Trump, as they were on President Obama before him.

The current president, who has exacerbated long-standing tensions about newcomers, seems spectacularly unsuited to lead the effort to enact comprehensive immigration reform. The route to meaningful reform is blocked, however, not just by the president's angry rhetoric and questionable leadership skills, but also by the shift that has occurred in recent decades as the nation has moved toward a stronger, almost imperial executive branch and a weaker, more divided legislative branch. The decline of Congressional leadership in non-immigration contexts has been observed by others.[2] Particularly noteworthy has been the Congressional retreat from national defense, where the U.S. president has come to wield unprecedented power.[3] The groundwork for the kind of populist-style governance that the United States is now experiencing, in short, was laid before Trump took office.

Even under Obama, a strong advocate of comprehensive immigration reform and a master of conciliatory rhetoric, Congress proved inert. This pattern of congressional fecklessness represents a departure from what the founders intended in their constitutional design and a departure from how business used to be conducted in Washington. As Yuval Levin observed:

> Our Constitution puts Congress first, and its framers expected legislators to dominate the work of the national government. James Madison *took it for granted* (emphasis in original) that "in republican government, the legislative authority necessarily predominates" and expected the legislative branch to be always "extending the sphere of its activity, and drawing all power into its impetuous vortex." But things have not turned out that way. . . . Not wishing to take responsibility for making hard choices, members of Congress (particularly when the president is of their party) have long been happy to enact vague legislation at best and to leave big decisions to the executive and judicial branches. Over time, as this habit has hardened, they have lost the knack and the muscle memory for legislating.[4]

An indication of how poorly an executive-driven approach to immigration reform works was the January 2018 shutdown of the federal government because Congress and the president could not agree on how to respond to young people living in the country without legal status, the most sympathetic constituency in need of legal action. This crisis occurred not because the issue was particularly complex, but because members of Congress from the president's Republican Party *depended* on the president taking the initiative on immigration policy. In this case the president failed to deliver a consistent message about his expectations, and Congress was unable to negotiate its own proposal.

The drift toward executive-level activism and legislative passivity also changed the tenor of the immigration debate, moving it away from talk of comprehensive immigration reform and paths to citizenship and toward enforcement-based solutions under executive authority. This shift was evident as early as 1996, when Congress set the stage for increased executive authority to deport immigrants without secure legal status with two bills that increased executive authority to deport immigrants while reducing their due-process protections.[5] At the same it invited local police and sheriffs to become "force multipliers" in the federal enforcement effort. Comprehensive immigration reform was not under serious consideration.

The failure of Congress to be an active participant in resolving the nation's immigration dilemma, this chapter suggests, goes far to explain both President Obama's resort to executive orders to shape immigration policy and the wave of state and local immigration-related activism that began in the early 2000s. Politics abhors a vacuum. As hopes faded for a Congressional rewrite of federal immigration law, pressure for executive action increased, and states and local governments also felt pressure to "do something" about illegal immigration. In Arizona, for example, Governor Napolitano was facing increasing difficulty blocking restrictive state legislation by asserting that immigration was the federal government's responsibility.[6]

At the federal level President George W. Bush and President Obama responded with changes in recordkeeping that greatly increased their statistics on numbers of deportations.[7] Early in his second term, Obama began the now-familiar journey toward major executive immigration initiatives, perhaps hoping to stimulate Congress toward broader reform.[8] *Time* magazine noted this shift in a June 2012 news article describing the Obama administration's decision to end deportations of young undocumented immigrants, the Dreamers:

> It was also a harbinger of broader executive branch power, which has expanded under George W. Bush and Obama, in part as a response to historic levels of congressional recalcitrance. Instead of relying on Congress to institute the DREAM Act, Obama ordered his government to observe a near-approximation of its goals. Obama's brazenness in circumventing Congress will likely make the policy controversial and invite Republican criticism. It also makes the policy vulnerable: Implementation will be complicated and any future President could reverse the order.[9]

At the same time, Obama's executive orders and bureaucratic initiatives widened the scope and effectiveness of federal enforcement. His initiatives created a precedent and expectations of further executive action. With the federal government's support, states and municipalities have responded to the narrowing of the immigration debate with legislation and policy focused on enforcement. Lack of subnational authority to change legal status requirements, adjust immigration quotas, or create paths to citizenship makes enforcement, by default, the currency of reform at this level. Trump's innovation has been to put these tools to new uses and, in the process, to challenge certain received tenets associated with American federalism. More ominously, the Trump administration has subtly changed the terms of debate about immigrants, who have been increasingly cast as criminals and a national-security threat.

This shift away from deliberative democracy toward an outsized executive role and state and local immigration activism is likely to keep immigration policy indefinitely focused on the low-hanging political fruit: enforcement. Real reform requires the thoughtful discussion, quiet negotiation, and compromise that the national legislature, ideally, provides. Without the opportunity to fully air interests and concerns with a degree of privacy, immigration reform becomes a political third rail, too hot for most legislators to touch.

The Trump administration's determination to increase enforcement by any means possible has produced resistance and denunciation in some localities, stoking hopes that more immigrant-friendly policies will eventually prevail. There has been much discussion in the scholarly literature about citizenship at the local level, refusal to comply with detainer requests, and other aspects of the combative federalism that we are currently witnessing. The resistance to Trump and the scholarly work that is growing up around it may eventually help to shift public opinion toward strong demands for less draconian enforcement. The practical significance of resistance to the federal executive, however, is limited. On the ground, the federal enforcement power remains supreme and is being deployed, essentially without restraint. Courts are moving into the fray to impose some limits on how that power is exercised, but they cannot eliminate what federal law permits—an inhumane, dragnet approach to enforcement.

I begin by describing the shift from Congressional to executive authority to make immigration policy. There was little doubt at the nation's founding that policies regulating immigration were to be drafted and debated within Congress, not the executive branch. The brief provision in the U.S. Constitution related to immigration, as with other federal concerns, clearly puts Congress in the driver's seat. The remainder of the chapter explores the consequences of the rebalancing of powers that has occurred. I first show how the tools Obama developed to prioritize federal enforcement have been adopted by the Trump administration, but with innovations that have reshaped the image of immigrants, provoking increased controversy and pockets of resistance at the state and local levels. I conclude by considering the implications of the current moment, which may portend a long-term shift in the way newcomers to this nation are viewed in law and policy.

Federal Authority to Make and Enforce Immigration Law: A Slim, but Enduring Thread

The American Constitution has little to say about membership in the civic union, but what it does say has proven extremely important. Immigration, like slavery, is treated only briefly and indirectly. A few vague references in the 1787 document laid the groundwork for continuing African enslavement until a bloody civil war in the 1860s ended the practice and the Constitution was amended to guarantee the rights of the former slaves. Authority over immigration policy is similarly brief, indirect, and important.[10] The meagre relevant reference can be found in Article 1 of the Constitution, which sets forth the structure of the legislative power vested in the Senate and House of Representatives. Section 8 of that article provides a long list of specific powers, including, "To establish a uniform Rule of Naturalization, and uniform Laws on the subject of Bankruptcies throughout the United States." Section 8 concludes by vesting in Congress the power to make "all Laws which shall be necessary and proper for carrying into Execution the foregoing Powers." The founders clearly intended for law related to full civic membership in the new American nation to come from Congress, not the president, or the courts, or the states.

In its early years Congress did lay down some significant parameters, limiting naturalization to white persons in 1790 in keeping with the slavery policy, and providing for deportation of presumably disloyal individuals when a French invasion seemed possible (the Alien and Sedition laws in 1798–1801) In other respects, however, Congress was inactive, leaving states, cities, and towns free to enact their own laws restricting residence within their jurisdictions by the poor, criminals, and other undesired elements.[11] There was insufficient enforcement capacity at the federal level to administer effective restraints on immigration until late in the nineteenth century. Even then, if there was to be immigration control, it would have to occur at ports of entry, not along the vast borders the nation shared with Canada and Mexico, and certainly not in the nation's interior.

The practical limitations on the government's ability to carry out immigration-related policy came into play in 1849 through a series of Supreme Court cases that became known as the Passenger Cases.[12] The justices declared, as a matter of law, that Boston and New York could no longer collect head taxes on arriving immigrant ships. Major ports in these states had imposed these fees to help finance their extensive efforts to settle new immigrants. The Court reasoned that the head taxes were regulations of foreign commerce, a function held solely by the federal government. Implementation of this Court-declared policy, however, was impossible at first. There was no federal bureaucracy on hand to take over the work that port-city officials had been doing. For several years in New York City, state inspectors worked alongside their new federal counterparts to administer the new federal taxes and associated responsibilities. Only in 1921 did the quarantine operations finally move fully into federal hands.[13]

Not until 1882 did Congress actively seek to control the flow of foreigners into the United States. The issue was competition from Chinese immigrant labor. Under pressure from its West Coast members, Congress enacted the Chinese Exclusion Act, beginning what was to be a series of restrictions on entry by Chinese migrants. In this important legislation, Congress acted alone, without urging from then president Chester Arthur. President Arthur, in fact, vetoed the first version of the legislation on the grounds that certain provisions would endanger trade and good relations with China and would violate treaty obligations ("A nation is justified in repudiating its treaty obligations only when they are in conflict with great paramount interests").[14] His veto forced Congress to revise the law to obtain his signature.

The Chinese Exclusion Act and its progeny are mostly remembered for the racism and fear underlying their passage and for the Supreme Court's expansive response to the court challenges that followed. For purposes of our discussion, it should also be noted that in these cases the Court assumes that immigration policy will arise from the halls of Congress. Note, for example, how the Court couched its unanimous finding of the supremacy of federal authority in matters of immigration in *Chae Chan Ping v. U.S.*: "That the government of the United States, *through the action of the legislative department*, (emphasis added) can exclude liens from its territory is a proposition which we do not think open to controversy."[15] In a subsequent case, by a 6–3 majority, the Court embraced what became known as the plenary power doctrine, giving Congress virtually unfettered power in matters related to immigration and basically taking the courts out of the equation: "The judicial department cannot properly express an opinion upon the wisdom, the policy, or the justice of the measures enacted by Congress in the exercise of the powers confided to it by the constitution over this subject [alien entry and residence]."[16]

This series of cases also established that states and localities would be obliged to accept the immigrants in their jurisdiction without discrimination under the Fourteenth Amendment's equal protection clause, which forbids discrimination based on national origin. By implication, these subnational governments would not be engaged in enforcing federal immigration law or creating their own barriers to entry or assimilation within their jurisdictions. Such matters, the Supreme Court has repeatedly observed, implicate diplomatic relations with foreign states, the sole preserve of the federal government.[17]

This basic dividing line held until late in the twentieth century, with occasional challenges from states and cities attempting to prevent immigrants from receiving public benefits. Courts declared most of these laws in violation of the Fourteenth Amendment, or as interference with the federal prerogative in immigration enforcement. In *Plyler v. Doe*,[18] for example, a majority of the Supreme Court found Texas in violation of the Fourteenth Amendment equal-protection clause when it withheld state funds to educate children who had not been legally admitted to the United States and authorized school districts to deny them enrollment.

Federal supremacy in matters of immigration, of course, includes federal authority *not* to enforce its own laws. Within the American interior, toleration of the presence of unauthorized immigrants continued to be the rule until the 1990s, though there were two important exceptions, a massive deportation during the Great Depression in the 1930s and Operation Wetback in 1952. These short-term, but highly intrusive immigration sweeps could not have been conducted by the federal government acting alone. They required cooperation between local law enforcement and federal immigration agents, with local law enforcement assigned the role of junior partner in the endeavor. There were also occasional joint efforts to remove mobsters and other persons presumed to threaten public safety, but such arrangements were traditionally mission-specific and voluntary. Only a handful of federal agents were available for work in the heartland, and they were highly selective in the cases they chose to pursue.

On the border, enforcement efforts were for a long time only marginally more serious. Congress, which did not establish the Border Patrol until 1924, kept funding levels low under pressure from agricultural interests in Texas and further west. As Hernández notes, "The Border Patrol's beginnings were inauspicious."[19] The result was a relatively porous border and a thriving market for Mexican labor. Throughout the 1960s–80s, Massey, Durand, and Malone found in their massive study of over 12,000 households that there was a stable, mostly migratory pattern of seasonal employment that worked to the advantage of both countries. The size of the Border Patrol was increasing after 1965, but there was no clear trend in the odds of getting caught while attempting to cross the border.[20] Massey et al. estimate that, into the 1980s, "the odds of being apprehended on any given attempt at clandestine border crossing were about one in three, and nearly everyone got in after a few tries."[21]

Congress was more preoccupied in the 1960s with its formal admissions system than with upsetting the thriving immigrant labor market. In 1965 Congress amended the Immigration and Nationality Act to create a new visa allocation system responsive to civil-rights concerns of the era about racial discrimination in admissions. By 1986, however, the public mood had turned more hostile and more fearful of immigrants. The basic outlines of the 1986 Immigration Reform and Control Act, with its two-fisted approach—a path toward citizenship for millions of resident immigrants and employer sanctions designed to staunch further illegal immigration—are relatively well-known. The significance of this law for our purposes is in the manner of its adoption. Massey et al. describe a process filled with pitfalls, but driven by the determination of some members of Congress to respond to the public mood of anti-immigrant hysteria. Charles Kamasaki titled his book on the struggle to pass this legislation "the corpse that will not die."[22] Senator Alan Simpson and Representative Peter Rodino led this effort: "Through a series of backroom deals, historic compromises, and a delicate balancing of interests, they succeeded in crafting legislation that gave something to everyone and permitted Congress to go on record as taking visible and forceful action to stop illegal immigration."[23] The failure of this legislation to achieve meaningful enforcement through employer sanctions, however, led to pressure for tighter controls. In 1988 and again in 1990 and 1994 Congress acted to increase the resources of the Border Patrol and to tighten requirements. Historian Mae Ngai describes "a stunning militarization of the US-Mexico border" during the 1990s.[24]

The steady movement toward more enforcement-oriented legislation culminated in 1996 with the two major laws mentioned earlier, the Illegal Immigration Reform and Immigrant Responsibility Act and the Antiterrorism and Effective Death Penalty Act. These laws, in focusing narrowly on enforcement, left immigration policy in the hands of the executive branch. Congress was opting out of responsibility to design a comprehensive approach to immigration.

Toward an Enforcement-Only Immigration Regime

An early sign of the willingness of federal law enforcement to take up a policymaking role occurred early in the Clinton administration in the form of a new border strategy that became known as "prevention through deterrence." This policy, which involved deploying many officers and other resources at the most commonly used crossing points, was the brainchild of El Paso Border Patrol chief Silvestre Reyes. His innovation, initially named "Operation Blockade," became immediately popular in El Paso and was soon adopted elsewhere. Later that year, immigration officials used the approach in San Diego, the most popular crossing point from Mexico.[25] This new approach, which soon spread to other points of entry, was effective in shutting down convenient crossing points, but not in ending illegal entry. Migrants shifted their passage to the much more dangerous and isolated stretches of the border in desert and mountainous areas. The result of Reyes's fateful innovation and its rapid adoption elsewhere has been tragedy for thousands of immigrants who have died, and continue to die, of exposure, dehydration, and drowning.[26]

The rise of enforcement-only policymaking was made possible, in part, by the breakdown in this period of an old, elite-driven consensus favorable to immigration, including tolerance for illegal immigration to assist in the unpleasant jobs associated with crop harvesting, meat packing, and construction. As Daniel Tichenor notes, "The new Republican Congress that came to power in 1995 was unmistakably caught up by the popular wave of anti-immigrant policies that seemed to wash over the country between 1994 and 1996."[27] One telling indication of this anti-immigrant sentiment was the 1994 adoption in California of Proposition 187, a referendum supported by 59 percent of California voters. Proposition 187 cut off most government benefits to persons who could not prove legal status and called on local law enforcement to assist federal authorities in immigration arrests. Though a federal court almost immediately declared California's new law an unconstitutional interference with federal plenary power over immigration policy, Prop. 187 sent a strong signal to Washington, facilitating adoption of the Illegal Immigration Reform and Immigrant Responsibility Act (IIRIRA), which, among other provisions, declared unauthorized aliens to be ineligible to receive Social Security and other benefits.[28]

The major thrust of the 1996 legislative changes that Congress adopted, however, was to enhance the federal government's capacity to remove immigrants. This effort included, for the first time, detailed provisions for sharing federal enforcement power with local law-enforcement agencies. IIRIRA was especially generous in attempting to diffuse enforcement authority to the local level. Through what came to be known as the 287(g) program, Congress offered local law enforcement agencies the opportunity to take federally sponsored training to assist immigration agents in identifying and reporting immigrants without legal status. The training would prepare local police and sheriffs to act as immigration agents, with power to stop and detain suspected unauthorized immigrants or to assist in the booking process at local jails. No local law enforcement agents accepted this invitation until after the September 11, 2001, terrorist attacks, and even then, relatively few undertook training to enforce immigration law or assist in the booking process.[29] The groundwork was nevertheless being laid for increased local/federal cooperation. Through administrative action and voluntary agreements, federal immigration agents were being embedded in local law-enforcement agencies to fight gang violence and deal with other problems of mutual concern. Information sharing across levels was on the increase.

Congress was reconfiguring immigration policy in ways that would have profound effects on immigrants and public perceptions about immigrants. The invitation to local police and sheriffs to add immigration enforcement to their public safety mission exemplified the new framing of immigrants as criminogenic. Ignored were the increased risks of pretextual stops and racial profiling of suspected immigrants that would inevitably accompany the dispersal of enforcement authority. Instead, Congress did what it could to reduce accountability within the system. Despite its increasing severity, the immigration adjudication system remained in the civil sphere, which meant that it lacked the basic due-process protections required for adjudicating crimes.[30] The fiction that one's deportation is simply a readjustment of civil status, not a form of punishment, would continue to insulate federal agents from responsibility.

Most significantly, Congress was reshaping and building upon an immigration-enforcement regime that had in the past functioned only sporadically in the American heartland. The legal consequences of building a punitive system on a civil-law foundation and criminalizing immigrants have been capably explored by others, leading to the invention of a new term for this process: crimmigration.[31] Here it is important to note the power transfer that occurred when Congress opened the door to increased law enforcement, but with eviscerated protections from the excesses of that power. The enormous level of discretion that had always characterized immigration enforcement was now to be shared with local police departments and sheriffs and insulated further from critical scrutiny.

The Rise of Contentious Federalism

Growing public concern about the presence of approximately 11 million residents without legal status and the federal government's interest in local "force multipliers" encouraged states and some municipalities to get involved. Their legislative efforts have tended to reinforce federal government's enforcement-oriented agenda. Local immigration policymaking occurs mostly by the "back door," through licensing and benefits standards requiring legal status, through penalties designed to criminalize unauthorized immigrant workers, and through encouragement of cooperation between local law-enforcement agencies and federal immigration authorities.[32]

The entrance of states and some cities into the realm of immigration policymaking raised new dilemmas for the federal executive, and specifically for the U.S. president. While the federal government retains authority to determine how aggressively the nation would attempt to enforce immigration law, activism at the subnational level makes exercising this power more complex. President Obama and President Trump both confronted this issue, and both proved ready to take up this challenge. Their willingness to grasp the opportunity to engage local police and sheriffs in immigration enforcement is striking, not just as a major departure from how immigration law has been enforced in the past, but also because of the lack of accountability in this arrangement.

Under President Obama, the federal government continued to refine its efforts to get more immigration information into local hands and to seek local assistance in detaining suspected violators of immigration laws. Many of these efforts were rebuffed. For example, in 2008 the Obama administration began to roll out the Secure Communities program, which virtually mandated information-sharing by local jails with federal immigration databases. However, resistance to this program was pronounced in localities across the United States, particularly in major cities with large immigrant populations. Though the Obama administration insisted that it was only "going after the bad guys," data collected by the Transactional Records Access Clearinghouse (TRAC) consistently demonstrated that a significant proportion of immigrants detained and turned over to federal authorities as a result of Secure Communities were nonviolent offenders, and often were simply individuals who had been swept up in other law enforcement actions.

Despite objections voiced shortly after the program got underway in 2008, it was not until 2014, after a series of lawsuits and many refusals to participate, that the Department of Homeland Security finally acknowledged the need to change course. Justice Department lawyers also began to investigate overly zealous approaches to enforcement. As Chacón observes, "The Obama administration did begin to exercise its own enforcement effort more selectively over time in an effort to keep more immigrant communities intact pending broader immigration reform." By 2014, she concludes, "the Administration had set new and narrower enforcement priorities."[33]

The way the federal executive promoted its enforcement agenda is notable. It bypassed the states, the traditional partners in federalism, and offered formal contracts for immigration enforcement at the local municipal and county levels. Sheriffs and police departments were immediately drawn into the immigration-enforcement drama. Whether or not the Obama administration anticipated the resistance it was to encounter, it was undoubtedly aware of the traditional limits that federalism implied for imposing its will on local law-enforcement agencies.

Meanwhile, state and local legislators created an avalanche of immigration-related bills and resolutions. This activity was sometimes mostly symbolic, designed to send a message to constituents and, sometimes, to the federal government. Such was the goal of the Arizona legislature in 2010 when it adopted SB1070, whose stated goal was "attrition through enforcement." The key element in this omnibus law was the requirement that the state's law-enforcement officers assist in enforcing federal immigration law in the course of their work. The Supreme Court rejected most of this law in a 2012 decision that reaffirmed the federal government's plenary power in matters of immigration, but by then SB1070 had achieved its main purpose: to strongly assert local dissatisfaction with the pace of federal enforcement of immigration law.[34]

Probing the Limits of Executive Power

President Trump, with the help of the departments of Justice and Homeland Security, has maintained and deepened an executive-driven immigration agenda based on enforcement. His administration has engaged in relentless efforts to achieve funding for a wall on the southern border, to the point of ordering a partial shutdown of the government in December 2018 and threatening to use executive authority to achieve his goal. In his frequent tweets directed to the American public, President Trump has attempted to reframe immigrants as a dangerous, alien "other" to a degree not seen since the World War II wartime propaganda campaign against foreign enemies. While this full-press propaganda campaign is a new element in executive leadership, the enforcement-based agenda should by now be familiar to most Americans.

The Trump administration has embraced all the tools at the chief executive's disposal, tools developed and refined under President Obama's leadership. The differences between the two administrations lie in the details, thrust, and publicity accorded to the executive actions pursued, not in the tendency to govern through enforcement. Obama relied on prosecutorial discretion to justify executive orders exempting appealing classes of immigrants from deportation and attempted to prioritize enforcement to focus on the least attractive segments of the immigrant population. At the same time, however, he vastly increased the pace of enforcement on the border and in the nation's interior. President Trump has taken a similarly forceful approach, but with different ends in mind.

The extent to which President Trump has relied on Obama-era tools is striking. Like Obama, President Trump has relied upon his executive authority to attempt to reshape immigration priorities. Like Obama, he has attempted to engage state and local law enforcement officers in immigration control. President Trump has even attempted to rekindle the unsuccessful and abandoned 287(g) program and Operation Secure Communities, relying on the eagerness of a few states like Arizona to help enforce federal immigration law and attempting to force others into participation. The downsides of these programs — pretextual stops and racial profiling — are the same as in the past, and, as in the past, they have been largely unacknowledged.

Unlike its predecessor, however, the Trump administration has dispensed with any reluctance to engage local law enforcement in immigration enforcement. The Justice Department regularly threatens to withdraw federal funds from the nation's approximately 200 "sanctuary cities" that do not require city employees to report immigration status. The Department of Homeland Security uses negative publicity in an attempt to shame cities, counties, and states into compliance. Resistant municipalities and states also run the risk of retaliation by federal immigration agents who are at liberty to initiate enforcement where they see fit.

What is really at stake is the refusal of many jurisdictions to honor federal detainer requests. "Immigration detainers" are essentially requests, not legal orders, asking that local jailers hold people suspected of being unauthorized immigrants without a formal arrest warrant. Complying with these federal requests opens municipalities that maintain jails to suits by detained individuals for false imprisonment and violations of the Fourth Amendment's ban on unreasonable searches and seizures. Several courts have sided with the detained individual and have awarded monetary damages to immigrant plaintiffs. Sheriffs, who maintain county jails, have reason to be concerned about such lawsuits.

The Trump initiatives differ from those previous administrations, not just in the attempt to mandate, rather than invite, local cooperation, but also in the message that enforcement is to be done without restraint. Federal immigration agents no longer avoid arrests at court houses or other "sensitive" locations that had been identified by the Obama administration. Long-standing agreements between established, but unauthorized, immigrants and federal authorities are being ignored. In a February 2018 speech, President Trump went so far as to threaten to withdraw all federal immigration and border patrol officials from California in order to create a crime wave that would force California into compliance with his orders.[35]

At the local level, there are significant downsides to a no-holds-barred approach to immigration enforcement. The research that three colleagues and

I conducted on the response of local law enforcement agencies to federal calls to participate in immigration enforcement has an important bearing on this question.[36] With support from the National Science Foundation, we conducted national surveys of mid-sized and small-city chiefs and sheriffs in counties with significant immigrant populations. We supplemented this quantitative information with seven carefully selected site visits, where research teams conducted in-depth interviews with community activists, local officials, and immigrant-rights organizations. The picture that emerged from this research was of a multi-jurisdictional patchwork of responses to escalating federal collaboration requests, with a surprising lack of concrete policies at the local level. Over half of respondents to our surveys had no written policy to guide officers in their encounters with immigrants.

Police officers and sheriff's deputies encounter immigrants in routine daily activities—taking kids to school, driving to work, etc.[37] Searching for unauthorized immigrants in this context is a new frontier, one the Obama administration made some effort to keep within constitutional bounds. What the Obama administration did not consider, however, was the alienation from law enforcement that immigrants, documented and undocumented, were bound to experience, and the consequent risks to public safety that would result from the merging of policing and immigration enforcement. Treating local police and sheriffs as "force multipliers" in the effort to ferret out immigrants with problematic legal status also risks discrimination against all minorities who might appear to be immigrants. As Jennifer Chacón observes, "Past experience suggests that in localities where law enforcement is eager to engage in immigration enforcement, the arrest-to-deportation pipeline will not only place law-abiding people in the removal system, but will also expose a broader population of citizens and foreign nationals to racial profiling as agents without training in immigration law seek to contribute to immigration enforcement efforts."[38]

The key concept here is discretion. Law enforcement requires significant discretion on the front lines to be effective. Consider enforcement of traffic laws. Almost any car on the road is in violation of some rule, either because of defective equipment or improper handling, so enforcement is inherently selective and potentially biased. The same is true for local ordinance violations and many minor crimes, where the exercise of discretion is essential so that police and sheriffs can concentrate on more serious criminal activity. The problem is that legitimate discretion can be exercised to achieve illegitimate ends. Discretion is also important in processing minor offenses when an officer must frequently decide whether to issue a citation and release the individual or to arrest the person for booking or identification purposes. Booking involves transport to jail, communication with federal immigration agents, and the potential for deportation. Officers who are sympathetic to the president's position are more likely to book people they suspect are unauthorized immigrants.

Other encounters are similarly problematical. Unauthorized immigrants are sometimes victims of crimes, which necessarily complicates enforcement issues. Difficult questions arise about whether to arrest possible victims of human trafficking, how to deal with undocumented children and their parents, whether to detain undocumented witnesses of crime, how to identify and respond to victims of sex trafficking, and how to manage a host of heretofore unanticipated decisions. Neither government nor law enforcement leaders have provided a playbook to guide officers as they face these real-life situations.[39] This provides an opening that the Trump administration, with its embrace of aggressive, no-questions-asked enforcement, is prepared to exploit.

For immigrants, the only reasonable course is to distance themselves as much as possible from police and sheriff's deputies. Within the first three months of the Trump presidency, there was evidence that immigrant fears were having an impact. The Los Angeles police department reported a 10 percent drop in crime reporting from Hispanic communities. Police in New Jersey saw a 6 percent decrease in the first three months of the Trump administration.[40]

In the complex politics of immigration enforcement that is emerging, many police chiefs and sheriffs are destined to play a lonely role. The prevailing wisdom at this professional level embraces community policing, a perspective that is distinctly at odds with the Trump administration's enforcement-first approach.[41] National police organizations like the Major Chiefs Association of the International Association of Chiefs of Police and the President's Task Force on 21st Century Policing adopted the concept, and have applied it, to reject immigration enforcement at the local level. The President's Task Force stated, "Law enforcement agencies should build relationships based on trust with immigrant communities. This is central to overall public safety." One of its action items is to "decouple federal immigration enforcement from routine local policing for civil enforcement and non-serious crime."[42] The chiefs and sheriffs whom we interviewed during our site visits uniformly embraced community policing as a key to public safety and gaining the trust of resident immigrants as a priority. They emphasized the necessity for keeping roles separate. One police chief we interviewed put it this way:

> I thought, you know, if we're breaking down doors looking for immigrants, how in the world are we going to get information on the bad guys? You know? A lot [of immigrants] don't trust us to begin with, and

> then if we're starting to kick doors down and looking for green cards, you know, it makes it even harder. So, my thought process was, "Wait a minute, this is a federal issue. We'll continue to do our job and let the federal government do their job."[43]

Chiefs and sheriffs who continue to adhere to this point of view are being singled out for criticism by the Trump administration and sometimes by state and municipal leaders. In May 2017, Governor Greg Abbott of Texas signed Senate Bill 4, which prohibits chiefs and sheriffs and other authorities from interfering with a front-line officer's decision to contact immigration authorities, effectively doing an end run around any departments that attempt to place restraints on their officers. Law-enforcement leaders and municipal authorities who defy this law are subject to criminal penalties. The law takes aim at more liberal Austin and its surrounding Travis County, both of which opposed the bill, and both of which the state's attorney general named as defendants in a suit filed within hours of the bill's signing.[44] Recently adopted "anti-sanctuary" laws in Florida and Iowa require police to honor all requests by federal enforcement authorities to hold unauthorized immigrants.[45]

A few states, including Maryland, Washington, and California, are pushing back against this narrative. In April 2017, the California Senate passed a sanctuary state bill (SB 54) that restricts local law enforcement from using their resources to help federal immigration enforcement. The following month, Maryland's attorney general issued a twenty-seven-page memorandum describing in detail the limits on federal authority to coerce local participation in immigration enforcement. Washington State revised its driver's licenses in an effort to prevent ICE officials from relying on state databases to facilitate their enforcement actions.[46] Some cities and counties are also finding ways to resist the Trump administration's initiatives. San Francisco and Santa Clara County sued in federal court to prevent implementation of President Trump's executive order on sanctuary cities. Pressure from cities and counties also forced the Trump administration to apologize for mistakes it made in listing places failing to cooperate with its requests and to temporarily suspend its "Name and Shame" list.

From a broader perspective, however, one must ask how effectively states and municipalities can resist the federal executive's drive to find and deport unauthorized immigrants. The ability of federal immigration agents to roam freely across state and local jurisdictions and to conduct operations in sensitive areas like schools and courthouses tends to undermine any confidence immigrants might feel in local policies. States and municipalities that resist the Trump administration's harsh initiatives are signaling their support for more humane system, but their practical capacity to create such a system is severely limited. Federal authority to enforce a harsh policy with little nuance or empathy remains in place and enjoys considerable public support.

The impact of the Trump administration's policies will be felt regardless of how the courts rule on various executive orders. The harsh rhetoric and promises of beefed-up enforcement have empowered some front-line workers who agree with this approach, including members of the union representing the border patrol, which endorsed Trump for president. Federal agents are deporting long-standing residents with families whom they had previously allowed to stay as long as they registered with the local immigration office. Immigration and Customs Enforcement (ICE) reports that in the first 100 days after President Trump signed executive orders regarding the administration's enforcement priorities, it arrested more than 41,000 individuals, a 38 percent increase over the same period in 2016. Although the agency claims to be focusing, as the Obama administration did before it, on "bad hombres," the data actually show, once again, that this is not happening.

Within the ranks of many local law-enforcement agencies, the Trump initiative has exacerbated long-standing tensions between the rank and file versus the chiefs and sheriffs who supervise them over how deeply to become engaged in immigration enforcement. Chiefs and sheriffs who are more sympathetic to immigrants are being pressured to toe a federal line drawn without regard for their commitment to community policing. Municipal leaders are no longer in a position to quietly defer to their law-enforcement professionals in matters of policy. State legislatures are also being encouraged to get involved, as Texas has, with its heavy-handed restrictions on law-enforcement leadership in this matter. The Trump administration is effectively bypassing all lines of authority to appeal directly to individual police officers and sheriffs' deputies to assist the federal enforcement effort within the nation's interior.

At the same time, the administration is using the rhetoric of immigrant crime and insecure borders to ramp up public anxieties about illegal entry. Security concerns about immigrants, which had focused on Muslims after the 9/11 attack, now focus on Central Americans asking for asylum. The November 2018 deployment of federal troops at the southern border was a dramatic effort to communicate this message of migrants as a security threat.[47]

Conclusion

The shrinking globe has had the ironic result of reinforcing public interest in maintaining national boundaries and ensuring security, concerns that encourage enforcement-based policy and executive action. Political leaders are playing on a pervasive sense of overwhelming, uncontrollable change brought about by globalization and other causes, but interpreted as an "invasion" of foreigners. The solution, in this framing, becomes an impregnable wall and other harsh measures that will keep unwanted foreigners at bay. The danger is that fear of foreigners, with its built-in racial biases, will become a serious threat to democratic institutions, which require a degree of public trust and confidence to operate effectively. For scholars, this suggests the need for further reflection on the implications of what Weber and McCulloch describe as the "securitization agenda," with its "pre-crime" and prevention strategies, all of which tend to bypass traditional criminal procedures and open the door to broad administrative discretion to "externalize" perceived threats.[48]

The path toward a better outcome is difficult to see. The nation has grown accustomed to an executive-driven, enforcement-based immigration agenda. While court decisions are likely to put some limits on the Trump approach as a matter of law, the president retains the proverbial bully pulpit and the power to push for aggressive means of enforcing the harsh rules Congress has put in place. States and municipalities resistant to this approach can take only limited action, perhaps most valuable for its symbolism of solidarity with immigrants. Congress appears too weak and divided to take meaningful action, even against an unpopular president and even with ample constitutional authority to act. I fear that we are entering an era of populist politics promoting securitization themes that cast the federal executive in the dominant role in many areas, not just as enforcer in chief, but as policymaker in chief.

Notes

Senator Richard Durbin, during a February 2018 interview describing his seventeen-year battle to engage Congress with the need to protect from deportation the young people illegally brought into the United States as children. (Interview with Ari Shapiro on National Public Radio, "All Things Considered," February 6, 2018, transcript: "Sen. Dick Durbin on Finding a Bipartisan Deal to Protect Dreamers," http://: https://www.npr.org/2018/02/06/583778354/sen-dick-durbin-on-finding-a-bipartisan-deal-to-protect-dreamers.)

1. Ibid.

2. Examples include Charlie Savage, *Takeover: The Return of the Imperial Presidency and the Subversion of American Democracy* (New York: Back Bay Books/Little, Brown, 2007); and by the same author, *Power Wars: The Relentless Rise of Presidential Authority and Secrecy* (New York: Little, Brown, 2015); Arthur M. Schlesinger Jr., *The Imperial Presidency* (Boston: Houghton Mifflin, 1973); Donald R. Wolfensberger, "The Return of the Imperial Presidency?" *Wilson Quarterly* (Spring 2002): 36–41.

3. Richard S. Conley, ed., *Presidential Leadership and National Security* (New York: Routledge, 2018); Chris Edelson, *Power without Constraint: The Post-9/11 Presidency and National Security* (Madison: University of Wisconsin Press, 2016); Louis Fisher, *In the Name of National Security: Unchecked Presidential Power and the Reynolds Case* (Lawrence: University of Kansas, 2006); David Rothkopf, *Running the World: The Inside Story of the National Security Council* (New York: Public Affairs, 2005); Garry Wills, *Bomb Power: The Modern Presidency and the National Security State* (New York: Penguin, 2010).

4. Yuval Levin, "Yes, Trump Is Weak. So Is Congress," *New York Times*, Jan. 22, 2018, https://www.nytimes.com/2018/01/22/opinion/trump-congress-dysfunction.html.

5. The Illegal Immigration Reform and Responsibility Act of 1996 (IRIRA) and the Antiterrorism and Effective Death Penalty Act (AEDPA).

6. Kyrsten Sinema, Chapter 4, "No Surprises: The Evolution of Anti-Immigration Legislation in Arizona," in *Punishing Immigrants: Policy, Politics, and Injustice*, ed. Charis Kubrin, Marjorie Zatz, and Ramiro Martinez (New York: NYU Press, 2012), 62–88.

7. As *Los Angeles Times* reporter Brian Bennett explained, "Until recent years, most people caught illegally crossing the southern border were simply bused back into Mexico in what officials called 'voluntary returns,' but which critics derisively termed 'catch and release.' Those removals, which during the 1990s reached more 1 million a year, were not counted in Immigration and Customs Enforcement's deportation statistics. Now, the vast majority of border crossers who are apprehended get fingerprinted and formally deported. The change began during the George W. Bush administration and accelerated under Obama"; Brian Bennett, "High deportation figures are misleading," Los Angeles Times, Apr. 1, 2014, http://www.latimes.com/nation/la-na-obama-deportations-20140402-story.html.

8. Megan Slack, "President Obama's Four Part Plan for Comprehensive Immigration Reform," Jan. 29, 2013, *White House*, https://obamawhitehouse.archives.gov/blog/2013/01/29/president-obamas-four-part-plan-comprehensive-immigration-reform.

9. Adam Sorensen, "No Deportation for Young 'Illegals': Obama's End Run on Immigration Reform," *Time*, Jun. 15, 2012, http://swampland.time.com/2012/06/15/no-deportation-for-young-illegals-obamas-end-run-on-immigration-reform/.

10. As Daniel J. Tichenor notes, "The Constitution is all but silent about immigration." At the same time, he finds, the Founders were worried that immigrants, inexperienced in democracy, might undermine the stability of the new republic, a concern that helps explain the adoption of the Alien and Sedition Acts a few years later; Tichenor, *Dividing Lines: The Politics of Immigration Control in America* (Princeton, N.J.: Princeton University Press, 2002), 51.

11. Gerald Neuman, "The Lost Century of American Immigration Law (1776–1875)," *Columbia Law Review* 93, no. 8 (1993): 1833–1901; Benjamin J. Klebaner, "State and Local Immigration Regulation in the United States before 1882,"

International Review of Social History 3 (1958): 269–95; Anna Law, "Lunatics, Idiots, Paupers, and Negro Seamen: Immigration Federalism and the Early American Republic," *Studies in American Political Development* 28 (October 2014): 107–28.

12. Passenger Cases, 48 U.S. 283 (1849).

13. Neuman, *Strangers to the Constitution: Immigrants, Borders, and Fundamental Law* (Princeton, N.J.: Princeton University Press, 1996).

14. Chester Arthur, "Veto of the Chinese Exclusion Act," UVA Miller Center, Presidential Speeches (1882), https://millercenter.org/the-presidency/presidential-speeches/april-4–1882-veto-chinese-exclusion-act.

15. *Chae Chan Ping v. United States*, 130 U.S. 581 (1889) at 603.

16. *Fong Yue Ting v. United States*, 149 U.S. 698 at 731.

17. This sense of separation is reinforced by the Tenth Amendment: "The powers not delegated to the United States by the Constitution, nor prohibited by it to the States, are reserved to the States respectively, or to the people."

18. *Plyler v. Doe*, 457 U.S. 202 (1982).

19. Kelly Lytle Hernández, *Migra! A History of the U.S. Border Patrol* (Berkeley: University of California Press, 2010), 32; and see S. Deborah Kang, *The INS on the Line: Making Immigration Law on the US-Mexico Border, 1917–1954* (New York: Oxford, 2017).

20. Douglas E. Massey, Jorge Durand, and Nolan J. Malone, *Beyond Smoke and Mirrors: Mexican Immigration in an Era of Economic Integration* (New York: Russell Sage, 2002), 57.

21. Ibid., 70.

22. Charles Kamasaki, *Immigration Reform: The Corpse That Will Not Die* (Simsbury, Conn.: Mandel Vilar, 2019).

23. Ibid., 89–90.

24. Mae M. Ngai, *Impossible Subjects: Illegal Aliens and the Making of Modern America* (Princeton, N.J.: Princeton University Press, 2004), 266.

25. Massey, Durand, and, Malone, *Beyond Smoke and Mirrors*.

26. See, e.g., Joseph Nevins, *Operation Gatekeeper and Beyond: The War on "Illegals" and the Remaking of the U.S.-Mexican Boundary* (New York: Routledge, 2002); Raquel Rubio-Goldsmith, Celestina Fernandez, Jessie Finch, and Araceli Masterson-Algar. *Migrant Deaths in the Arizona Desert: La Vida no Vale Nada* (Tucson: University of Arizona Press, 2016).

27. Tichenor, *Dividing Lines*, 284.

28. (IIRIRA) Pub. L. 104-208, 110 Stat. 3009-546. The main focus of this 1996 law, however, was on enforcement, with more funds for border security, tougher penalties for illegal border crossing, and a new program to encourage local police and sheriffs to be trained as immigration agents and assist in booking immigrants in local jails. IIRIRA was supplemented by another immigration-related welfare law passed in 1996, the Personal Responsibility and Work Opportunity Reconciliation Act of 1996 (PRWORA), Pub. L. No. 104-193, 110 Stat. 2105. The Antiterrorism and Effective

Death Penalty Act (AEDPA), also adopted in 1996, authorized local police to arrest previously deported immigrants and to assist federal agents in emergency situations; AEDPA Pub. L. No. 104-132, 110 Stat. 1214.

29. Doris Marie Provine, Monica W. Varsanyi, Paul G. Lewis, and Scott Decker, *Policing Immigrants: Local Law Enforcement on the Front Lines* (Chicago: University of Chicago Press, 2017).

30. Stephen Legomsky, "The New Path of Immigration Law: Asymmetric Incorporation of Criminal Justice Norms," *Washington and Lee Law Review* 64, no. 2 (2007): 469–528.

31. Juliet Stumpf, "The Crimmigration Crisis: Immigrants, Crime, and Sovereign Power," *American University Law Review* 56 (2006): 367–419; Jennifer Chacón, "Border Exceptionalism in the Era of Moving Borders," *Fordham Urban Law Journal* 38, no. 1 (2010): 129–53.

32. Monica W. Varsanyi, "Immigration Policing through the Backdoor: City Ordinances, the 'Right to the City' and the Exclusion of Undocumented Day Laborers," *Urban Geography* 29, no. 1 (2013): 29–52.

33. Chacón, "Immigration and the Bully Pulpit," *Harvard Law Review Forum* 130, no. 7 (2017): 249–50.

34. *Arizona v. United States*, 567 U.S. 387 (2012).

35. Dan Mangan, "Trump Threatens to Yank Immigration Enforcement from California, Warns Crime Would Explode," *CNBC*, Feb. 23, 2018, https://www.cnbc.com/2018/02/22/trump-threatens-to-withdraw-immigration-enforcement-from-california.html.

36. Doris Marie Provine, Monica W. Varsanyi, Paul G. Lewis, and Scott Decker, *Policing Immigrants: Local Law Enforcement on the Front Lines* (Chicago: University of Chicago Press, 2017).

37. See, e.g., Amada Armenta, *Protect, Serve, and Deport* (Oakland, Calif.: University of California Press, 2017).

38. Chacón, "Immigration and the Bully Pulpit," 243–68.

39. Provine, Varsanyi, Lewis, and Decker, *Policing Immigrants*.

40. Lindsey Bever, "Hispanics 'Are Going Further into the Shadows' Amid Chilling Immigration Debate, Police Say," *Washington Post*, May 12, 2017, https://www.washingtonpost.com/news/post-nation/wp/2017/05/12/immigration-debate-might-be-having-a-chilling-effect-on-crime-reporting-in-hispanic-communities-police-say/?utm_term=.69f5ac74b564.

41. Community policing became the dominant approach to local law enforcement after urban riots in the 1970s and 1980s revealed a wide gap between urban communities and their police departments. Law-enforcement agencies—especially police chiefs in cities with diverse populations—began to adopt the idea as they became convinced that effective policing requires the active cooperation and assistance of all local residents, who are asked to offer their eyes and ears in the fight against crime.

42. Final Report of the President's Taskforce on 21st Century Policing, Recommendation 1.9 and Action item 1.9.1, May 2015, https://ric-zai-inc.com/Publications/cops-p311-pub.pdf.

43. Interview with Chief Roger MacLean, Allentown, Pennsylvania, Police Department, August 2009.

44. Kat Greene, "Texas Sues Local Pols to Enforce Sanctuary Cities Ban," *Law 360*, May 9, 2017, http://:https://www.law360.com/articles/921751/texas-sues-local-pols-to-enforce-sanctuary-cities-ban.

45. Florida's SB168 requires local governments to "use their best efforts to support the enforcement of federal immigration law"; Xander Peters, "Florida's New Anti-Sanctuary Cities Law Goes into Effect Today," *Orlando Weekly*, Monday, July 1, 2019, https://www.orlandoweekly.com/Blogs/archives/2019/07/01/floridas-new-anti-sanctuary-cities-law-goes-into-effect-today). Iowa's SF481requires local police to honor ICE detainer requests and to work closely with federal immigration authorities; Brianne Pfannenstiel, "Iowa 'Sanctuary' City Ban Signed into Law," *Des Moines Register*, https://www.desmoinesregister.com/story/news/politics/2018/04/10/iowa-sanctuary-city-ban-becomes-law-sf-481-reynolds-signs/504176002/.

46. Mary Papenfuss, "Washington State Changes Driver's License Requirements to Foil ICE," *Huffpost*, Jan. 26, 2018, https://www.huffingtonpost.com/entry/washington-drivers-license-immigration_us_5a6bdb43e4b06e253267b4da.

47. Susanne Krasmann, "The Enemy on the Border: Critique of a Programme in Favour of a Preventive State," *Punishment and Society* 9 (2007): 201–318; and see Leanne Weber and Jude McCulloch, "Penal Power and Border Control: Which Thesis? Sovereignty, Governmentality, or the Pre-Emptive State?," *Punishment and Society* 21 (2018): 1–19.

48. Leanne Weber and Jude McCullioch, "Penal Power and Border Control: Which Thesis? Sovereignty, Governmentality, or the Pre-Emptive State?," *Punishment and Society* 21 (2018): 1–19.

8

Trump Doesn't Tweet Dog Whistles, He Barks with the Dogs

Crimmigration as a Racial Project through the Lens of Trump's Twitter

Rashawn Ray and Simone Durham

"That is such a racist question." This was President Donald Trump's response to an important and relevant question asked by Yamiche Alcindor, black female journalist.[1] Alcindor asked whether Trump felt describing himself as a "nationalist" at a political rally in Houston, Texas, emboldened white nationalists and racist behavior.[2] Labeling oneself as a nationalist is a risky move, particularly given the word's long history of association with racist ideologies and discriminatory and heinous acts like genocide throughout world history. In addition to apparently supporting nationalism as a general ideology, Trump's position on immigration exhibits a nationalist perspective by characterizing immigrants in derogatory ways. In many regards, Trump's rhetoric and decision-making about immigration aligns directly with crimmigration by aiming to further normalize the criminalization of immigrants, particularly immigrants classified as Hispanic/Latino.

Trump's rhetoric over the past three years has been insidious to some and galvanizing and inspiring for others. Trump is critiqued for language that many say "goes too far," even for politics. In addition to speeches and interviews, Trump mostly shares his thoughts on Twitter, the use of which is important because it circumvents traditional modes of communication and allows for a person like the president or a high schooler to directly interact with the general public.[3] Twitter is so popular that mainstream and local news programs regularly use tweets as data sources. The issue, however, is that tweets in mainstream media are rarely analyzed by topic or over time. Social movement, digital humanities, and race scholars are starting to fill these important gaps. To contribute to this line of inquiry, we examine Trump's tweets for emergent themes about immigration and immigrants.

Drawing upon critical race theory, our chapter first summarizes theoretical accounts of the American racial hierarchy and highlights the role of racial projects in constituting this structure. We then discuss the racialization of Latinos as a group, then describe the rise of crimmigration as a racial project. Empirically, we examine how Donald Trump's rhetoric on Twitter supports crimmigration as a racial project and highlight how controlling images, dog whistle messages, and group threat orientations act as mechanisms to do so.

The American Racial Hierarchy and Racial Projects

The U.S. racial hierarchy has consistently rested on the marginalization of minority populations. These groups were consistently dehumanized and discriminated against socially and through American immigration policies.[4] Critical race theorists have long posited about the problematic and strategic workings of the American racial hierarchy. Some scholars discussed the ways that the U.S. was founded upon whiteness being defined in opposition to and elevated above nonwhite status.[5] Over time, the racial hierarchy subtly shifted in response to changes in racial composition. Who was included as white versus nonwhite changed based on the country of origin. While most white immigrant groups were able to assimilate into the privileged rank of Anglo-Saxon whites, black and brown immigrants were often relegated to a second-class citizenship.[6] As a result, descendants of enslaved Africans and indigenous people were continuously viewed as inferior to whites, while groups such as Italians and Irish were able eventually to assimilate with full rights of Anglo-Saxon citizenship.

The shifts in the racial hierarchy have led some scholars to posit that the contemporary hierarchy is shifting from a biracial to a triracial order.[7] This new structure is a three-category system including whites, honorary whites, and a group of collective blacks at the bottom. Some immigrants, based on phenotype, origins, and economic status, may be able to assimilate into either the white or honorary white groups. However, darker and poorer groups of immigrants may remain at the bottom of the hierarchy in the collective black group and continue to experience marginalization and discrimination.[8]

Regardless of the debate about the exact arrangement of the racial structure, racial and ethnic status play a consistent role in all aspects of social experience and interaction. Structural theories of race and racism such as the racialized social system approach[9] and the racial formation perspective[10] acknowledge the various ways race operates on a structural level to shape social outcomes for different groups. These theoretical perspectives also acknowledge the role of a pervasive racial ideology and racial hegemony that influence normative understandings of citizens about racial issues. Post–civil rights America was largely characterized by color-blind racism, in which mechanisms that reproduce racism and race manifest outcomes that seem to appear as nonracial without closer examination. The Barack Obama era ushered in rhetoric about a post-racial America. The Trump era, however, has all but debunked any semiotic acknowledgment about America being post-racial, color-blind or, even laissez-faire about race.[11] Rather, scholars and journalists assert that America may be again returning to an era in which overt forms of racism are privileged, accepted, and celebrated.

While color-blind ideology is still purported as a dominant racial ideology in the U.S., there has been a clear resurgence of explicit racism, xenophobia, and white nationalism since the political rise of Donald Trump.[12] The concept of racial projects provides a theoretical lens by which to make sense of America's ebb-and-flow relationship with racism. Racial projects are the interpretations, representations, and explanations of racial phenomena and meaning undertaken by individuals, groups, and institutions to create, support, challenge, or dismantle a particular racial structure and influence the distribution of resources across racialized groups.[13] This concept provides a framework to examine rising efforts toward crimmigration that may appear in both color-blind and more explicit forms in contemporary America. In the following text we discuss how the concept of racial projects becomes useful for making sense of the experiences of Latinos and South and Central American immigrants in the U.S.

Racialization of Latinos in the U.S.

Collectively, Latinos are the largest nonwhite racial group in the United States. The majority of Latinos in America are of Mexican origin (over 60 percent), although this group is becoming increasingly diverse as those from other Latin American countries migrate to the U.S. at higher rates.[14] Political debates about immigration in the Trump era center mostly on the southern border of the United States and the associated influx of Mexican immigrants and those fleeing dangerous and impoverished conditions in Central America.[15]

Despite a great deal of heterogeneity in their cultures and national origins, Latinos are frequently lumped together and racialized as a collective group. In fact, the often-used label of "Hispanic" was instituted by the U.S. government through the U.S. Census in 1970, encouraging Latinos of various nationalities to identify as one ethnic group. While the labels of "Latino" and particularly "Hispanic" are generally associated with ethnicity and culture rather than race, this group is still racialized as a collective marginalized minority group similar to other racial groups in the U.S. Consequently, Latinos are forced to navigate their placement in the American racial hierarchy in relation to whites, blacks, and other groups.[16] Dark-skinned Latinos, including Mexicans, are often categorized in the collective black category at the bottom of the triracial hierarchy.[17] Navigating this racialization has many implications, including the creation of disparities in health outcomes among Latinos.[18] Some Latinos experience racialization as a form of exclusion that they must develop navigation strategies to overcome. Latinos who are lighter-skinned and perceived as white are often able to better permeate social barriers better than those who are darker-skinned.[19]

Racialization processes associate specific groups with particular ideas about their statuses and roles in a given society. Because Latino immigrant populations largely remain at the bottom of the economic hierarchy in the U.S., as many work as agricultural and domestic workers, their racialization often has to do with their status as workers. This racialization also varies by a myriad of factors, including generation, skin tone, and gender.[20] Legal status and time since immigration are also influential in the racialized understanding of Latinos as dangerous or criminal, similarly to characterizations of African Americans.[21] Even more than their status as workers, this criminal image is often deployed in arguments against immigrants, including in Trump's rhetoric on Twitter.

Crimmigration as a Racial Project

The criminalization of Latinos is supported by processes of racialization, increasingly harsh federal immigration enforcement, and views of this group as a threat.[22] Crimmigration has emerged as a racial project meant to control immigrant populations viewed as a threat to the economic, political, and social hierarchies in the U.S. This phenomenon can be thought of as the convergence of the criminal justice and immigration enforcement systems to police and control particular group(s) in a given society. Crimmigration is supported by controlling images of groups deemed necessary to be overly policed and to be under authoritarian rule. It is also reinforced through political rhetoric, which may be spread through covert or overt messages. In twenty-first-century America, social media are a main platform by which to spread messages and control images aligned with crimmigration.

Crimmigration as a Social Phenomenon

The phenomenon of crimmigration developed in response to national security concerns after the September 11, 2001, plane hijackings and crashes.

Spreading from the United States, crimmigration has now taken root in Canada and countries across Europe. This racial project operates through the expansion of both consequences for immigration and criminal law and procedural tools to regulate migration, especially when it is unauthorized. Although a great deal of crimmigration efforts focus on regulating the movement of immigrants, the power of this project goes beyond immigrant populations and exerts influence over all who interact with and support immigrants in society.[23] In this regard, individuals who are perceived as immigrants are often criminalized and socially isolated. Because immigrants are seen as a threat, but also as a necessary tool in supporting the economy, countries engage in preventative securitization to prepare to deal with these threats if immigrants step out of needed roles.[24]

The Trump administration has put immigration policy and border security high on its federal agenda. As a result, immigration is a hot topic in all forms of media, highlighting the need for scholarly examination in how rhetoric and behavior around this phenomenon are changing. Despite empirical evidence showing there to be a weak relationship between immigration and crime, this supposed link is featured prominently in the immigration debate. An explanation for this conundrum may be in a theory about the "discourses of fear" that supports this myth and influences perceptions of immigrants.[25] Media coverage and political discussions of immigration on social media may be appealing to these exaggerated fears in order to create support for crimmigration policies. While the fears that uphold crimmigration structures may not be valid, their effects create very real and justified fears in immigrant populations of all documentation statuses that result in refusal to access public services and spaces as well as enduring exploitation and social exclusion.[26]

Racialization of Latinos creates particular controlling images of Latinos that support crimmigration. Controlling images are stereotypes that normalize inequality in the daily lives of people with particular social identities by associating them with particular, and usually negative, characteristics.[27] These images are often used, especially in the media, to bolster stereotypical claims and disseminate them widely so that they become a part of racial hegemony.[28] Controlling images of Latinos that support crimmigration rely on associating them with both physical and criminal characteristics.

Images regarding Latino workers characterize them as ideal subjects for grueling labor in order to justify their economic exploitation, particularly in agriculture.[29] Stereotypes of Latinos in film come in various forms, one of which is the villainous and violent "bandido,"[30] which creates an image of Latinos as criminal and deserving of punishment. This stereotype has been extended over time to associate Latinos with gang activity.[31] Latino immigrants are also generally stereotyped as illegal and therefore worthy of suspicion in relation to national security and terrorism.[32] Those on the conservative end of the immigration debate in America support an image of immigrants as "symbolic assailants,"[33] against whom use of force can be deployed in order to prevent crime. All of these images symbolically support the need for crimmigration in order to supposedly protect American citizens from Latino immigrants.

While technically only federal immigration officers have the legal standing to arrest undocumented immigrants, local and state police regularly detain suspected illegal immigrants and support crimmigration efforts. Similar to racial profiling of African Americans, profiling by police in areas highly concentrated with immigrant populations is more likely to result in discrimination against those immigrants in myriad ways.[34] Crimmigration is also supported by actors outside the government system, as immigration control and detention have become an increasingly privatized industry.[35] Political officials who support big business, such as Trump, may be even more likely to espouse rhetoric that supports crimmigration for this additional reason. Dog whistles are a common tactic for politicians to signal to supporters, while at times seeming benign to others.

Dog Whistles and Group Threat as Mechanisms of Crimmigration

Politicians aim to rally and inspire their supporters, as well as potential supporters, to action.[36] Throughout history, both dog whistle politics and more explicit racial sentiments have been used to do so. Dog whistle politics are when politicians engage in political messaging that means one thing to the general public and a different, and often more direct, meaning to a specific subgroup.[37] Dog whistle politics may very well be on full display on social media, particularly Twitter, where messaging has to be truncated to a particular length. Similar to an actual dog whistle, only the intended group can really interpret the coded messaging. Haney-Lopez discussed how President Reagan engaged in dog whistle politics when discussing "Cadillac driving welfare queens" in Chicago.[38] This dog whistle was meant to speak directly to conservatives who believe that poor people, particularly blacks who live in urban areas, are manipulating the government to receive more resources such as food stamps and payouts without properly earning or needing them. A more recent dog whistle is the strategy of some Republicans who use President Obama's middle name of Hussein to allegedly link him with terrorism and being un-American. Both of these dog whistles are ubiquitously untrue, but they still had powerful influence over the opinions of those in the groups they were directed to — namely, conservative white Americans.

Some scholars, however, go beyond the logic of dog whistle politics. Instead, they formally link the rhetoric of some politicians to racial resentment and group threat theory.[39] Over time, research has continuously showed an association between racial resentment and whites' opposition to race-based programs.[40] Part of racial resentment is fueled by concerns about immigrants taking jobs, acquiring unearned educational opportunities for children, increasing crime, and making neighborhoods less safe.[41] Rather than seeing the pot as having the ability to grow, some whites view the pot as potentially shrinking, with them being left on the outside looking in as a future potential numerical minority group relative to all nonwhites.[42] Moreover, whites view resources as zero-one sums.[43] Consequently, they view outgroups (in this case immigrants) as threats and start to form resentment of them that is racially motivated based on citizenship, ethnicity, skin tone, and language.

Trump may readily understand these theoretical frames. In turn, he may consciously work to not only engage in dog whistle politics, but also more directly galvanize a base of whites who feel they are being pushed to the side in favor of minorities "unfairly cutting the line ahead of whites."[44] News coverage of Trump's tweets provides evidence that this may be the case. For example, news outlets responded when he used the murder of a young woman named Mollie Tibbetts by an undocumented immigrant as a rationale for building his proposed border wall.[45] His commentary on this murder showed the intersections of the mechanisms supporting crimmigration that we explore in this study. The emergence of social media has allowed for politicians to communicate directly with their supporters and constituents in ways that circumvent traditional modes of communication.[46] This study examines Trump's tweets for insights into how politicians may be using social media to spread narratives that support racial/political projects such as crimmigration and how they may be using dog whistle politics or group threat orientations to do so.

Methods

Data Collection

To examine Donald Trump's rhetoric surrounding immigrants and immigration in the U.S., we conducted a content analysis of original tweets posted to Trump's personal Twitter account. We gathered these data through the website www.trumptwitterarchive.com. This web archive of Trump's Twitter posts monitors his account and records his tweets in real time. Tweets deleted before September 2016 (when the archive was created) are missing from the archive. The archive began an automated collection of Trump's tweets in January 2017. Tweets written between these two points may also have been deleted prior to daily tweet collections during that period. Tweets collected for this analysis were posted between January 1, 2015, and March 31, 2018. The start date for tweet collection was chosen based on the year that Trump announced his presidential candidacy. Tweets were collected using a keyword search of Trump's Twitter archive for any tweet including the terms "immigrants" and/or "immigration." We only included original content; retweets were excluded because they reflect the original opinions and thoughts of other users.

Within the chosen time span and under the conditions previously specified, the search returned 129 tweets for analysis. Our analysis included the entire population of tweets for this period, rather than choosing a random or stratified sample of tweets, as is done in larger Twitter data analyses.[47] Roughly 88 percent of the 336 million Twitter users have public accounts. Many scholars treat tweets and other forms of social media content as public data and possible sites of quantitative, ethnographic, and thematic analysis.[48] We follow these scholars' empirical approach in our content analysis of tweets from Donald Trump's public Twitter profile.

Data

In addition to the body of text included in each of the 129 tweets in the dataset, we collected metadata on the tweets. The metadata include the date and time the tweet was posted and the number of retweets and favorites the tweet received. Retweets occur when another Twitter user repost the original tweet. It is similar to a forward in an email, but if the account is public, the tweet is accessible to all Twitter users. Favorites occur when another Twitter user likes a tweet. Favorites on Twitter are similar to Likes on Facebook and essentially express support for the statement that was made in the tweet. Some of the tweets contain web links to news articles and other sources. While we do refer to the popularity of tweets via their favorite and retweet counts in some instances, the sources included in the tweet are not a part of the data analyzed for this project. Hashtags also were not a point of analysis in this particular study, although they have been used in other studies to examine the construction of collective identities.[49]

Data Analysis

Our data analysis strategy included three main modes of analysis. First, we coded all of the tweets according to the overall tone of the statement. Following tone coding, we assigned thematic codes to each tweet based on emergent themes from the data. Third, we analyzed the tweets within our theoretical framework and categorized them based on expressions of group threat and/or dog whistle messaging. The following sections provide a detailed overview of each phase of analysis.

Tone coding. The first step in our data analysis was coding the tone of the tweets as either positive, negative, or neutral. The tone was analyzed in connection to the characterizations of immigration or immigrants themselves and their impact on society. To achieve inter-coder reliability, each author coded the tweets in the dataset separately. A coding comparison revealed an initial inter-coder reliability rating of 55 percent. This low rate of agreement, however, was a result of a discrepancy in analytical approach. One coder was coding general tone of the tweet, while the other coder was coding the tone of the tweets specifically in relation to the characterization of immigrants as a group. After agreeing to use the former analysis strategy, a second round of coding yielded a 95 percent inter-coder reliability rating. To decide on tone coding for the remaining 5 percent of the tweets, two additional coders were consulted, and tone for the tweets was coded according to majority rule.

Thematic coding. In our second phase of analysis, we followed a grounded theory approach for thematic coding of the tweets.[50] Individually, both authors identified emergent themes in Trump's Twitter statements about immigrants and immigration. We then consulted to assign agreed-upon themes to each tweet. Tweets that did not contain any of the prominent emergent themes were given a thematic label of "Other." In this portion of the coding process, we came to consensus about all 129 tweets in the dataset without consulting any third parties. Tweets that fit multiple emergent themes were included in all of the applicable categories.

Theoretical framing. The last major form of coding and analysis involved our theoretical framework. Each of the tweets was reviewed to determine whether the language signaled expressions of group threat, use of dog whistling, both, or neither. This mode of analysis speaks to the motive behind the specific rhetoric Trump uses when discussing immigrants and issues of immigration.

Results

Tone of Tweets: Trump Lacks Positivity

As shown in Table 1, tweets were coded positive, negative, or neutral. Of the 129 tweets, 60 (46.5 percent) were neutral, 69 tweets were negative (53.5 percent), and 0 tweets (0 percent) were positive. The most retweeted (47,818 times)

Table 1: Tone of Trump Tweets about Immigration (N=129)

	Number	Percentage
Positive	0	0.0%
Neutral	60	46.5%
Negative	69	53.5%

negative tweet stated, "Great to see how hard Republicans are fighting for our Military and Safety at the Border. The Dems just want illegal immigrants to pour into our nation unchecked. If stalemate continues, Republicans should go to 51 percent (Nuclear Option) and vote on real, long term budget, no C.R.'s!" This tweet was posted on January 21, 2018. This tweet also had the highest number of favorites (178,941). In fact, the nine most retweeted tweets from Trump's Twitter account were coded as negative in tone.

Trump's negative tweets focused on everyone and everything, including businesses. On January 12, 2015, Trump tweeted the following about Macy's, the retail store: "Macy's was very disloyal to me bc of my strong stance on illegal immigration. Their stock has crashed! #BoycottMacys." In this tweet, Trump is asking for his supporters to boycott the store because of his stance on immigration. Trump's reaction is in line with a part of crimmigration that aims to alter the lives and social experiences of individuals who support immigrants. Reports indicated that Trump was upset after Macy's dropped his clothing line from their stores. However, this did not come through in Trump's tweets. Instead, he never mentioned this. He simply stated that Macy's was upset because of his stance on illegal immigration. On July 6, 2015, Trump followed up on this attack of Macy's: "Thx to all the people who called to say they are cutting their @Macys credit card as a protest against illegal immigrants pouring into US." According to an article published in *Fortune* on July 6, 2015, Macy's stock dropped .5 percent, and Trump was taking credit for the drop and stating that it was related to his supporters cutting up their credit cards.

The most retweeted neutral tweet stated, "My Administration has identified three major priorities for creating a safe, modern and lawful immigration system: fully securing the border, ending chain migration, and canceling the visa lottery. Congress must secure the immigration system and protect Americans." This tweet was retweeted 37,373 times and had 119,333 favorites.

Nonetheless, even Trump's neutral tweets may be viewed as negatively implicating others. On July 5, 2015, Trump stated, "Flashback—Jeb Bush says illegal immigrants breaking our laws is an "act of love" He will never secure the border." However, this tweet is different in tone from the following tweet:

"Remember that Carson, Bush and Rubio are VERY weak on illegal immigration. They will do NOTHING to stop it. Our country will be overrun!" This tweet was coded as negative and speaks to Trump's approach. Trump rarely says anything positive about others. If he does, he takes credit for it. Instead, his approach is to negatively attack others directly and indirectly through the usage of verbs and adverbs that implicate that others are to blame for certain outcomes. Later we discuss the themes that developed from the tweets.

Trump Twitter Themes: Safety and Crime

Table 2 contains a breakdown of the themes of tweets in the dataset. In our analysis, we discovered a total of eight themes. The themes prevalent in Trump's discussion of immigration include: mentions of DACA (4.65 percent), bashing others (e.g., politicians, corporations, news anchors) (40.31 percent), discussion of different modes of immigration (chain migration, lottery systems, and merit-based immigration) (15.5 percent), lack of safety and crime (55 percent), building a wall and border security (26.36 percent), zero-sum resources (13.2 percent), and high levels of illegal immigration (17.8 percent). Tweets that did not fit into these themes were coded as Other (about 14 percent).

DACA represented the smallest percentage of tweets per theme. However, given its relevance to the immigration debate, we included it as its own theme. DACA refers to the Deferred Action for Childhood Arrivals Act, which is a policy aimed to allow children brought to the United States illegally to receive a two-year deferral to prevent deportation. Unlike the Dream Act under President Obama, DACA does not currently provide a path to citizenship. On December 29, 2017, Trump made the following comment about DACA: "The Democrats have been told, and fully understand, that there can be no DACA without the desperately needed WALL at the Southern Border and an END to the horrible Chain Migration & ridiculous Lottery System of Immigration etc. We must protect our Country at all cost!" This tweet actually stated that DACA staying in place was possible if Democrats supported building a wall in between the U.S. and Mexico, ending chain migration, and the immigration lottery system. On February 1, 2018, Trump tweeted, "DACA has been made increasingly difficult by the fact that Cryin' Chuck Schumer took such a beating over the shutdown that he is unable to act on immigration!" Once again, we see Trump's strategy to deflect blame away from himself and on to someone else. Trump's comments about DACA are interesting considering that he rarely, at least in his tweets, anyway, seems to overtly bash DACA. Rather, he seems to use DACA as a political pawn to draw attention to other immigration policies and bash political opponents. On February 6, 2018, Trump

Table 2: Distribution of Themes in Trump's Tweets

Themes	Distribution
Emergent Themes	
DACA	6 tweets (4.65%)
Bashing	52 tweets (40.31%)
Modes of Immigration	*20 tweets (15.50%)*
Chain Migration	7 tweets (5.43%)
Lottery System	8 tweets (6.20%)
Merit-Based	6 tweets (4.65%)
Safety & Crime	*71 tweets (55.04%)*
Safety	39 tweets (30.23%)
Crime	32 tweets (24.81%)
Border/Wall	34 tweets (26.36%)
Zero-sum Resources	17 tweets (13.18%)
High Illegal Immigration	23 tweets (17.83%)
Other	18 tweets (13.95%)

aimed to align a majority Americans with his positions. He tweeted, "Polling shows nearly 7 in 10 Americans support an immigration reform package that includes DACA, fully secures the border, ends chain migration & cancels the visa lottery. If D's oppose this deal, they aren't serious about DACA-they just want open borders." Trump went on to tweet that Congress needs to consider merit-based immigration as they come up with a solution for DACA. His tweets actually suggest that he was fine with losing on DACA, but he wanted to make sure that immigration polices strengthened.

Bashing represented the second most prominent theme in our analysis. Bashing refers to Trump tweets that demean or highlight flaws in others. Other politicians, mostly Republican presidential primary opponents along with President Obama and Secretary of State Hillary Clinton, were the main culprits of Trump's Twitter attacks. One of the most retweeted tweets coded as bashing stated, "Senators should focus their energies on ISIS, illegal immigration and border security instead of always looking to start World War III." This tweet also highlights the theme of building a wall and border security. Another tweet stated, "Paul Ryan should spend more time on balancing the budget, jobs and illegal immigration and not waste his time on fighting Republican nominee." A tweet on December 12, 2017, in support of former Alabama Senate Republican nominee Roy Moore, who was defeated by Democrat Doug Jones, stated, "The people of Alabama will do the right thing. Doug Jones is Pro-Abortion, weak on Crime, Military and Illegal Immigration, Bad for Gun Owners and Veterans and against the WALL. Jones is a Pelosi/Schumer Puppet. Roy Moore will always vote with us. VOTE ROY MOORE!" Moore ultimately lost the Alabama Senate race to Jones.

The following tweet by Trump represents Modes of Immigration: "We need a 21st century MERIT-BASED immigration system. Chain migration and the visa lottery are outdated programs that hurt our economic and national security." This tweet included references to chain migration, a lottery system, and a merit-based system. A merit-based system is Trump's preference for an immigration system. On January 16, 2018, Trump tweeted the following: "The Democrats want to shut down the Government over Amnesty for all and Border Security. The biggest loser will be our rapidly rebuilding Military, at a time we need it more than ever. We need a merit based system of immigration, and we need it now! No more dangerous Lottery." In the preceding tweet, Trump aimed to put support for immigrants as being against the military.

A majority of Trump's tweets about immigration focused on crime and safety. A tweet on April 18, 2017 stated, "The weak illegal immigration policies of the Obama Admin. allowed bad MS 13 gangs to form in cities across U.S. We are removing them fast!" This tweet was retweeted 17,597 times and has over 72,000 favorites. The narrative about immigrants increasing crime is a popular one, though empirical research actually shows that an increase in immigrants decreases crime.[51] We should also note that Trump used the word "weak" (typically referring to his perception that people lack resiliency, work ethic, or fortitude) nearly 30 times in these 129 tweets. Trump frequently would post any time that a person was killed by an alleged illegal immigrant. On August, 10, 2015, Trump tweeted, "Again, illegal immigrant is charged with the fatal bludgeoning of a wonderful and loved 64 year old woman. Get them out and build a WALL!" On December 1, 2015, Trump tweeted, "Jamiel Shaw was incredible on @foxandfriends this morning. His son, who was viciously killed by an illegal immigrant, is so proud of pop!" On May 6, 2015, Trump tweeted, "Just met with courageous family of Sarah Root in Nebraska. Sarah was horribly killed by illegal immigrant, but leaves behind amazing legacy." We could continue, but I think the point is made that Trump aimed to stoke the fear of immigration among Americans. These tweets allow for crimmigration as a racial project to be strengthened as more Americans fear the influx of mostly brown immigrants from South and Central America and the Middle East.

The theme of "Zero-Sum Resources" focuses on how Trump aims to establish a dichotomy that providing access to resources for immigrants subsequently takes away resources for U.S.-born citizens. On April 12, 2017, Trump stated, "Jobs are returning, illegal immigration is plummeting, law, order and justice are being restored. We are truly making America great again!" This tweet had nearly 140,000 favorites and speaks to research on how a sizable percentage of white Americans believe that whites are now more exposed to racial discrimination as blacks and Latinos are provided more access to resources.[52]

The theme "High Illegal Immigration" refers to Trump tweets that imply that illegal immigration is running rampant throughout the United States. On October 19, 2016, Trump stated, "Hillary has called for 550 percent more Syrian immigrants, but won't even mention 'radical Islamic terrorists.' This tweet also refers to safety and crime as well as bashing. Tweets coded as Other did not fit directly with the other seven emergent themes. For example, the tweet stating, "Nation's Immigration And Customs Enforcement Officers (ICE) Make First-Ever Presidential Endorsement" obviously references immigration, but it does not specifically refer to safety, the wall, or resources.

Theoretical Frames: Dog Whistles and Group Threats

The last part of analysis coded tweets according to major theoretical frames about dog whistle politics and group threat theory. As shown in Table 3, dog whistle politics only represented 15.5 percent of tweets, while group threat theory represented 43.4 percent of tweets. Only 6 percent of tweets included both types of theoretical frames, while slightly over one-third did not include either theoretical frame.

An example of dog whistling is the following tweet: "I look forward to working w/ D's + R's in Congress to address immigration reform in a way that puts hardworking citizens of our country 1st." This tweet implies that "hardworking" and "immigrants" are antonyms, while "hardworking" is synonymous with citizens. Another example of Trump's tweets coded as dog whistling is the following: "Do you believe that Hillary Clinton now wants Obamacare for illegal immigrants? She should spend more time taking care of our great Vets!" Once again, we see how dog whistling aims to establish dichotomies. Trump's tweet about Hillary Clinton implies that if she wants affordable health care for immigrants she does not care for military veterans. Regarding themes, this tweet was coded as zero-sum resources and bashing.

As stated in the theoretical background section, group threat generally addresses perceptions that outgroup members, which are typically minority in relative power and status, will increase crime, lower educational quality, and steal jobs. The following tweets epitomize these theoretical characteristics. Trump stated, "Democrat Jon Ossoff would be a disaster in Congress. VERY weak on crime and illegal immigration, bad for jobs and wants higher taxes. Say NO." Another Trump tweet said, "Notice that illegal immigrants will be given ObamaCare and free college tuition but nothing has been mentioned about our VETERANS #DemDebate."

A small number of tweets encompassed both theoretical frames. Trump's tweet sent on March 15, 2016, is an example: "Ohio is losing jobs to Mexico,

Table 3: Tweets by Theoretical Frame

	Number	Percentage
Dog Whistling (alone)	20	15.5%
Group Threat (alone)	56	43.4%
Both	8	6.2%
Neither	45	34.9%

now losing Ford (and many others). Kasich is weak on illegal immigration. We need strong borders now!" This tweet perceived Mexico, and Mexicans in particular, as taking jobs from U.S. citizens in Ohio. This is a dog whistle, but it also captures group threat because of the perception that Mexicans are stealing jobs. The following tweet is an example of a tweet that does not fit as dog whistling or group threat: "I will be in Wisconsin until the election. Jobs, trade and immigration will be big factors. I will bring jobs back home—make great deals!"

Conclusion

This chapter explored the relationship between Trump's tweets and his usage of dog whistle politics and group threat frames. Using data from the Trump Twitter Archive, we used every tweet that Trump made about immigration and/or immigrants. After a grounded theory content analysis, we found that a majority of Trump's tweets about immigration and immigrants are negative. Trump's tweets primarily focus on safety and crime as well as bashing others, primarily political opponents, whom he often labels as "weak."

It is very clear from this analysis how Trump aims to double down on crimmigration. Over 50 percent of all of his tweets about immigration and immigrants focus on crime and safety. In line with Provine and Doty, we found that Trump aims to implement harsher federal laws and policies regarding immigration.[53] However, he is only interested in focusing on certain parts of the world, including South and Central America (with a particular focus on Mexico) and parts of the Middle East. Trump's tweets aim to invoke fear of immigrants.[54] Interestingly, Trump's tweets about DACA were not negative in nature. Rather, he used DACA to engage in dog whistles with his base to bargain for stronger immigration policies.

Regarding theoretical frames, we found that group threat was more prominent than dog whistle politics. In the past, scholars noted that dog whistles were one of the main frames used by politicians to rally their base.[55] As a nontraditional politician who has not held political office before, Trump may be much more direct in engaging with his base to more concretely align his comments with individuals who hold racial resentment against immigrants, support the wall between Mexico and the U.S., believe in zero-one sums, and think that immigrants increase crime. While Trump may be much more direct and engaging more with the American people than politicians in the past, it is clear that he is using Twitter to his advantage to stoke fears about immigrants and immigration.

Notes

1. Paul Farhi, "'What a Stupid Question': Trump Demeans Three Black Female Reporters in Three Days," *Washington Post*, Nov. 9, 2018, retrieved Dec. 7, 2018, https://www.washingtonpost.com/lifestyle/style/what-a-stupid-question-trump-demeans-three-black-female-reporters-in-two-days/2018/11/09/272113d0-e441–11e8-b759–3d88a5ce9e19_story.html?utm_term=.9ad389abf4c6.

2. Peter Baker, "'Use That Word!': Trump Embraces the 'Nationalist' Label," *New York Times*, Oct. 23, 2018, retrieved Dec. 6, 2018, https://www.nytimes.com/2018/10/23/us/politics/nationalist-president-trump.html.

3. Rashawn Ray and Fabio Rojas, "Genuine Fear, Genuine Anger: Interview with Arlie Hochschild," *Contexts: Understanding People in Their Social Worlds* 17, no. 1 (2018):13–15.

4. Chandra Reyna, "Tear Gas? This Is America," *Contexts: Understanding People in Their Social Worlds*, Dec. 3, 2018, retrieved Dec. 7, 2018, https://contexts.org/blog/tear-gas-this-is-america/.

5. Patricia Hill Collins, *Black Feminist Thought: Knowledge, Consciousness, and the Politics of Empowerment*, 2nd ed. (New York: Routledge, 2000).

6. Collins, "Intersectionality's Definitional Dilemmas," *Annual Review of Sociology* 41 (2015): 1–20; Milton M. Gordon, *Assimilation in American Life: The Role of Race, Religion, and National Origins* (New York: Oxford University Press, 1964).

7. Eduardo Bonilla-Silva, "From Bi-Racial to Tri-Racial: Towards a New System of Racial Stratification in the USA," *Ethnic and Racial Studies* 27, no. 6 (2004): 931–50.

8. Ibid.

9. Bonilla-Silva, "Rethinking Racism: Toward a Structural Interpretation," *American Sociological Review* 62, no. 3 (1997): 465–80; Yarimar Bonilla and Jonathan Rosa, "#Ferguson: Digital Protest, Hashtag Ethnography, and the Racial Politics of Social Media in the United States," *American Ethnologist* 42, no. 1 (2015): 4–17.

10. Michael Omi and Howard Winant, *Racial Formation in the United States*, 3rd ed. (New York: Routledge, 2015).

11. Larry Bobo, J. R. Klugel, and R. A. Smith, "Laissez-Faire Racism: The Crystallization of a Kinder, Gentler, Antiblack Ideology," in *Racial Attitudes in the*

1990s: *Continuity and Change*, ed. Steven A. Tuch and Jack K. Martin (Westport, Conn.: Praeger, 1997).

12. Bonilla-Silva, *Racism without Racists: Color-Blind Racism and the Persistence of Racial Inequality in America* (Lanham, Md.: Rowman and Littlefield, 2018).

13. Omi and Winant, *Racial Formation in the United States*.

14. Antonio Flores, "How the U.S. Hispanic Population Is Changing," *Pew Research Center*, Sept. 18, 2017, accessed Dec. 8, 2018, http://www.pewresearch.org/fact-tank/2017/09/18/how-the-u-s-hispanic-population-is-changing/.

15. Veronica Montes, "Caravan, Invasion, Exodus: A Photo Essay," *Contexts: Understanding People in Their Social Worlds*, Nov. 27, 2018, accessed Dec. 8, 2018, https://contexts.org/blog/exodus/.

16. Nicholas de Genova and Ana Y. Ramos-Zayas, "Latino Racial Formations in the United States: An Introduction," *Journal of Latin American Anthropology* 8, no. 2 (2003): 2–17.

17. Bonilla-Silva, "From Bi-Racial to Tri-Racial."

18. Cirila Estela Vasquez Guzman and Gabriel R. Sanchez, "The Impact of Acculturation and Racialization on Self-Rated Health Status Among U.S. Latinos," *Journal of Immigrant and Minority Health* (2018); Nancy López, Edward Vargas, Melina Juarez, Lisa Cacari-Stone, and Sonia Bettez, "What's Your 'Street Race'? Leveraging Multidimensional Measures of Race and Intersectionality for Examining Physical and Mental Health Status among Latinxs," *Sociology of Race and Ethnicity* 4, no. 1 (2017): 49–66.

19. Edward Fergus, "'Because I'm Light Skin . . . They Think I'm Italian': Mexican Students' Experiences of Racialization in Predominantly White Schools," *Urban Education* 52, no. 4 (2017): 460–90.

20. Marta Maria Maldonado, "'It Is Their Nature to Do Menial Labour': The Racialization of 'Latino/a Workers' by Agricultural Employers," *Ethnic and Racial Studies* 32, no. 6 (2009):1017–2036.

21. Hana E. Brown, Jennifer A. Jones, and Andrea Becker, "The Racialization of Latino Immigrants in New Destinations: Criminality, Ascription, and Countermobilization," *Immigration and Changing Identities* 4, no. 5 (2018): 118–40.

22. Doris Marie Provine and Roxanne Lynn Doty, "The Criminalization of Immigrants as a Racial Project," *Journal of Contemporary Criminal Justice* 27, no. 3 (2011): 261–77.

23. Juliet P. Stumpf, "Introduction," in *Social Control and Justice: Crimmigration in the Age of Fear*, ed. M. J. Guia, M. van der Woude, and J. van der Leun (Netherlands: Eleven International, 2013), 7–16.

24. Maria J. Guia, "Crimmigration, Securitisation and the Criminal Law of the Crimmigrant," in *Social Control and Justice: Crimmigration in the Age of Fear*, ed. M. J. Guia, M. van der Woude, and J. van der Leun (Netherlands: Eleven International, 2013), 17–39.

25. Debora da Cunha Piacesi, "Crime and Immigration: The Discourses of Fear as a Theoretical Approach to Critical Evaluation," in *Social Control and Justice:*

Crimmigration in the Age of Fear, ed. M. J. Guia, M. van der Woude, and J. van der Leun (Netherlands: Eleven International Publishing, 2013), 157–75.

26. Shirley P. Leyro and Daniel L. Stageman, "Crimmigration, Deportability and the Social Exclusion of Noncitizen Immigrants," *Migration Letters* 15, no. 2 (2018): 255–65.

27. Collins, *Black Feminist Thought.*

28. Omi and Winant, *Racial Formation in the United States.*

29. Joe R. Feagin, "Imaging Mexican Americans: Rationalizing Oppression," in *The Latino/a Condition: A Critical Reader*, 2nd ed., ed. Richard Delgado and Jean Stefancic (New York: New York University Press, 2011), 189–93.

30. Charles Ramirez Berg, "Hispanic Stereotyping," in *The Latino/a Condition: A Critical Reader*, 2nd ed., ed. Richard Delgado and Jean Stefancic (New York: New York University Press, 2011), 183–88.

31. Mary Romero, "From El Bandido to Gang Member," in Delgado and Stefancic, *Latino/a Condition*, 194–96.

32. Steven W. Bender, "The War on Terrorism and Its Consequences for Latinas/os," in Delgado and Stefancic, *Latino/a Condition*, 204–7.

33. Jize Jiang and Edna Erez, "Immigrants as Symbolic Assailants: Crimmigration and Its Discontents," *International Criminal Justice Review* 28, no. 1 (2018): 5–24.

34. Amada Armenta, "Racializing Crimmigration: Structural Racism, Colorblindness, and the Institutional Production of Immigrant Criminality," *Sociology of Race and Ethnicity* 3, no. 1 (2017): 82–95; Armenta, *Protect, Serve, and Deport: The Rise of Policing as Immigration* (Berkeley: University of California Press, 2017).

35. Robert Koulish, "The Privatization of Immigration Control," in Delgado and Stefancic, *Latino/a Condition*, 101–5; Cecilia Menjívar, Andrea Gómez Cervantes, and Daniel Alvord, "The Expansion of 'Crimmigration,' Mass Detention, and Deportation," *Sociology Compass* 12, no. 4 (2018): 1–15.

36. Dana R. Fisher, *Activism, Inc.: How the Outsourcing of Grassroots Campaigns Is Strangling Progressive Politics in America* (Stanford, Calif.: Stanford University Press, 2006).

37. Ian Haney-López, *Dog Whistle Politics: How Coded Racial Appeals Have Reinvented Racism and Wrecked the Middle Class* (New York, NY: Oxford University Press, 2014).

38. Ibid., 4.

39. Stanley Feldman and Leonie Huddy, "Racial Resentment and White Opposition to Race-Conscious Programs: Principles or Prejudice?," *American Journal of Political Science* 49, no. 1 (2005): 168–83; Howard Schuman and Lawrence Bobo, "Survey-Based Experiments on White Racial Attitudes toward Residential Integration," *American Journal of Sociology* 94 (1988): 273–99; Schuman, Charlotte Steeh, and Lawrence Bobo, *Racial Attitudes in America: Trends and Interpretations* (Cambridge, Mass.: Harvard University Press, 1998).

40. Bobo and Vincent Hutchings, "Perceptions of Racial Group Competition: Extending Blumer's Theory of Group Position to a Multiracial Social Context," *American Sociological Review* 61 (1996): 951–72.

41. Jeff C. Dixon, "The Ties That Bind and Those That Don't: Toward Reconciling Group Threat and Contact Theories of Prejudice," *Social Forces* 84, no. 4 (2006): 2179–204.

42. Arlie Hochschild, *Strangers in Their Own Land: Anger and Mourning on the American Right* (New York: New Press, 2016).

43. Michael I. Norton and Samuel R. Sommers, "Whites See Racism as a Zero-Sum Game That They Are Now Losing," *Perspectives on Psychological Science* 6, no. 3 (2011): 215–18.

44. Ray and Rojas, "Genuine Fear, Genuine Anger," 15.

45. German Lopez, "Trump: After Mollie Tibbetts's Murder, 'We Need the Wall,'" *Vox*, Aug. 23, 2018, accessed Dec. 9, 2018, https://www.vox.com/policy-and-politics/2018/8/23/17771318/trump-mollie-tibbett-immigration.

46. Rashawn Ray, Melissa Brown, Neil Fraistat, and Edward Summers, "Ferguson and the death of Michael Brown on Twitter: #BlackLivesMatter, #TCOT, and the Evolution of Collective Identities," *Ethnic and Racial Studies* 40, no. 11 (2017): 1797–1813.

47. Brown, Ray, Summers, and Neil Fraistat, "Say Her Name: #SayHerName: A Case Study of Intersectional Social Media Activism," *Ethnic and Racial Studies* 40, no. 11 (2017):1831–46; Ray, Brown, Fraistat, and Summers, "Ferguson and the Death of Michael Brown on Twitter," 1797–1813.

48. Dhiraj Murthy, "Digital Ethnography: An Examination of the Use of New Technologies for Social Research," *Sociology* 42, no. 5 (2008): 837–55; Yarimar Bonilla and Rosa, "#Ferguson," 4–17; Catherine Knight Steele, "The Digital Barbershop: Blogs and Online Oral Culture within the African American Community," *Social Media + Society* 2, no. 4 (2016): 1–10.

49. Ray, Brown, Fraistat, and Summers, "Ferguson and the Death of Michael Brown on Twitter," 1797–1813.

50. Kathy Charmaz, "The Grounded Theory Method: An Explication and Interpretation," in *Contemporary Field Research: A Collection of Readings*, ed. Robert M. Emerson (Boston: Little, Brown, 1983), 109–26.

51. Graham C. Ousey and Charis E. Kubrin, "Exploring the Connection between Immigration and Violent Crime Rates in U.S. Cities, 1980–2000," *Social Problems* 56, no. 3 (2009): 447–73.

52. Norton and Sommers, "Whites See Racism as a Zero-Sum Game," 215–18.

53. Provine and Doty, "Criminalization of Immigrants as a Racial Project," 261–77.

54. Da Cunha Piacesi, "Crime and Immigration," 157–75.

55. Haney-López, *Dog Whistle Politics*.

9

Mirrors of Justice?

Undocumented Immigrants in Courts in the United States and Russia

Agnieszka Kubal and Alejandro Olayo-Méndez

A few days into office, the new President Donald Trump signed a number of executive orders in the area of immigration law in the United States. Aside from the headline-capturing ones like the "Border Wall with Mexico" (January 25, 2017) or "Muslim travel ban" (May 27, 2017), there was also this, equally far-reaching, though one that never really made it to front-page headlines: "Any undocumented person who has been in the US less than two years is subject to detention and deportation without a hearing unless they can show they have a credible fear of return to their home country."[1] To anyone even remotely familiar with immigration law enforcement in Russia, this brings to mind the notorious practices of the Moscow police "randomly selecting" Central Asian migrants for document checks near the metro[2] and pressing charges of immigration law offenses, the charges having deportation-related consequences.[3]

Prior to these dramatic immigration law changes in the United States, this type of comparative observation would, arguably by many, be considered adventurous; by some, plainly speculative. In this chapter, however, we suggest that the relative experiences of the U.S. and Russian immigration regimes at the everyday life level are not that different and highlight the punitive effects of the legal processes on migrant populations.[4] For the United States, we use the case study of Operation Streamline; for Russia, we rely on the most common immigration law offenses relating to migrants' residence and work status.

Operation Streamline (currently Streamline Initiative) started in 2005 as an initiative of the United States Department of Homeland Security (DHS) and the Department of Justice (DoJ) to expedite the criminal prosecution of individuals entering the United States illegally through specific geographic regions along the Southwest border between the United States and Mexico.[5] In practice, the initiative is a legal procedure that accelerates court proceedings and sentencing of defendants accused mostly of reentering the United States illegally. Large groups of defendants (sometimes up to seventy people) are brought to court, presented, and sentenced in a couple of hours. Defendants have very little pre-hearing time with attorneys assigned by the court, and the jail sentences could range from 30 to 180 days. The program has been called "assembly-line justice" and "conveyor-belt" or "*en masse*" immigration proceedings, emphasizing the mechanical and dehumanizing dynamics of the operation.[6] The aim of the program was to establish "zero-tolerance" immigration enforcement zones along the U.S.-Mexico border and to discourage illegal crossing attempts. U.S. Border Patrol sectors use Operation Streamline differently depending on resources, courthouse and jail infrastructure, geography, crossing population, and the prosecutorial priorities of federal authorities. Some Border Patrol sectors use Streamline for persistent border crossers, while others use it for migrants apprehended in specific target zones, regardless of crossing or criminal history.[7] While the program has changed in the past, it expanded significantly under the Trump administration.[8] Since May 2018, we saw how "zero-tolerance" policy gained a new and more sinister momentum, leading to the separation of children and families and prioritizing the prosecution of their illegal entry over attending to their potential asylum claims.[9]

There is no direct equivalent of Operation Streamline for Russia, mainly because there is a visa-free movement between Russia and the former Soviet Union "near abroad" republics (Kyrgyzstan, Tajikistan, Uzbekistan) from where most migrants arrive.[10] Anybody can board a plane or a train and, with their passport alone, cross the border with Russia. Upon arrival, migrants have a relatively short "grace period" to regularize their situation in Russia. If they want to work, they have to apply for a work permit (work license since 2015) and a residence registration.[11] If they happen not to fulfill one or both of these conditions, or sometimes simply fall through the cracks of the ever-changing and complex immigration rules, their stay in Russia becomes undocumented. For Russia, we therefore use a study of migrants' experiences of immigration cases, when they have been charged with offenses against Articles 18.8 and 18.10 of the Code of Administrative Offences (CAO)—lack of residence registration or working without a work permit, respectively. The number of immigration administrative cases increased by 100 percent between 2012 and 2013, demonstrating that the administrative prosecution of immigration law violations has become a popular tool of broader migration policy. The record year thus far was 2014, with 249,303 Article 18.8 and 18.10 CAO cases.[12] This translates into nearly 250,000 foreigners brought to trial, with potential expulsion orders issued against their names.

The questions we ask in this chapter focus on migrants' immediate experiences of the legal process and their "days in court" under two different jurisdictions: How similar and how different are these? How do these similarities and differences play out in everyday practice? Addressing these questions leads us to move beyond the civil-criminal dichotomy and demonstrates a number of similarities of the everyday experiences of justice despite structural embeddedness of these trials within the criminalized (Operation Streamline) versus administrative justice systems (Russia). First, both case studies demonstrate the limited role of the judge as a fact-finding figure and rather highlight his/her administerial role in delivering justice because of the *de facto* lack of discretion in making these judgments.[13] This is further amplified by the overwhelming feeling shared by the defendants in these processes that the decision "had already been taken" despite the decorum of the courtroom trial. Second, both case studies put into question the individualization of the justice principle—either by *en masse* "conveyor belt" justice in flip-flop courts[14] observable in the Operation Streamline cases or by the very short time within which the administrative cases and appeals are heard by the Russian courts. Taking a step back and thinking analytically, we put a mirror to *how* immigration and border control is practiced and theorized in Western and Northern American jurisdictions by bringing in its Russian counterpart. Ultimately, we concur with Mary Bosworth and Mhairi Guild, who have long argued that "the substantially harsher treatment of non-citizens flows naturally—some would argue inevitably—from the 'administrative' nature of immigration law."[15] *Why* does this happen? The observed similarities reveal that bureaucratic objectives—to deal with these "floods" of cases as efficiently and expeditiously as possible—override the initial divisions between civil and criminal and collapse the civil and criminal spectrum, especially when looked at from individual migrants' perspective.

This chapter proceeds as follows. We start with the review of the crimmigration thesis as the main prima facie distinguishing factor between how immigration cases are adjudicated in the United States (under Operation Streamline) and in Russia. Setting this context helps us to engage with the question of *how* immigration and border controls are practiced and experienced under these two jurisdictions. Upon presenting our methodology and the two ethnographies of the "day in court," we discuss the striking similarities between these two contexts and the repercussions these similarities have for further crimmigration theory and the criminal-civil dichotomy, especially addressing the second question as to *why* immigration control takes this specific shape at this specific time.

Why Compare?

The United States and Russia are two out of the top four countries worldwide that hold the largest share of migrants and refugees—23 percent of the world migrant population.[16] And yet there is no single meaningful, systematic, and disciplinary study—be it legal, historical, or sociological—that compares their immigration and refugee law regimes and migrants' and refugees' experiences of these wider legal environments. Perhaps this is not surprising. At face value, the United States and Russia (formerly the USSR) could not be more different—the former being the axiomatic immigration nation where the "huddled masses yearn to breathe free," the latter well-known for developing the restrictive *propiska* (residence registration) system and heavily controlled movement.[17] However, both global powers reached to their southern neighbors, either through colonization (Russia)[18] or labor recruitment programs (United States)[19] and created a set of structural interdependencies that have resulted in continued, sustained population movements (classified both as forced and economic migration, or mixed). Both countries have a large number of undocumented populations: 10.7 million in the United States[20] and 11 million in Russia.[21]

There is a massive scholarship on the immigration and refugee governance systems in the United States as well as their impacts, their everyday practices, and the experiences of those affected by them—largely Mexican and Latin American migrants and asylum seekers.[22] The current intense focus of immigration law seems to be the design of measures to combat "illegal" migration, where the various laws at federal, state, and local levels—also extraterritorially in Mexico and Latin America—seek to punish the behavior of undocumented (or would-be) immigrants, but at the same time push them to spaces outside the law, resulting in an overly criminalized immigration law system.[23]

There is also a burgeoning literature on immigration and refugee legal developments in Russia—everyday experiences of the law and migrant and refugees' access to justice.[24] Labor migrants come to Russia primarily from Central Asia (Uzbekistan, Kyrgyzstan, and Tajikistan). By virtue of being an important global political player, this country faces an increasing flow of refugees, most recently from Syria and Eastern Ukraine. However, Russia is almost uniformly portrayed through its hostile practices of migrant and refugee governance. Discrimination at work, routine denial of wages, failure to provide required contracts, unsafe working conditions, racial profiling for document checks, extortion of bribes by the police, and other extralegal strategies aimed at controlling migrants' movement are well documented.[25] There is a widespread view supported by empirical and scholarly evidence that state law, including immigration law, "does not work" in Russia.[26]

Notwithstanding the danger of portraying a too rosy picture of Russia, we suggest that the full picture is more complicated and that there are discernible logics according to which immigration law operates and how it is mediated by migrants' and legal professionals' variety of legal experiences and positionalities.[27] In Kubal's earlier work she discerned conditions under which migrants access justice and stand for their rights in Russia, but also what incites them to disengage from formal legal structures and, in some cases, deliberately subvert state agents, particularly those involved in law enforcement.[28] Kubal also ventured the first comparison of the everyday experiences of Russian and U.S. immigration law systems in the essay "Spiral Effect of the Law."[29] She based her observations on in-depth field research in Russia; as far as the U.S. was concerned she limited her findings to conceptual comparison drawing on existing scholarship, primarily the ideas of legal violence developed by Cecilia Menjívar and Leisy Abrego.[30] In this chapter we take this scholarship one step forward by bringing two empirical case studies into a dialogue with each other—the undocumented migrants' experiences of their "day in court" under Operation Streamline (for the U.S.) and migrants' experiences of the trial process when charged with administrative offenses against articles 18.8 and 18.10 COA (for Russia). The main aim that guides this comparison, aligned with the overall goal of this volume, is to critically engage with the different conceptual frameworks on crimmigration and discuss what a "discovery" of unexpected similarities between two contexts that rely on prima facie completely different immigration management systems can mean for future theorizing of immigration and border practices.

Criminalization versus Administrative Procedure: The Main Caveat?

We begin the comparative study by addressing the main critique that our endeavor may attract—namely, whether we are comparing apples and oranges. Is Operation Streamline directly comparable with the administrative adjudication of immigration offenses under Russian jurisdiction? To answer this question, we need to address the significant structural differences in how migration is governed and managed and how immigration law is enforced in the Unites States and Russia.

Operation Streamline has been conceptualized in the literature as one of the important pillars of criminalization of immigration law in the United States.[31] At the local level of its implementation it stands as a case in point of the prioritization of criminal enforcement in immigration law.[32] It demonstrates how criminal consequences (actual prison time) are being attached to immigration violations (irregular or "illegal" border crossing). Operation Streamline is a microcosm, where we can see how new immigration-related crimes are being created and prosecuted, how the increased minimum and maximum sentences for existing immigration crimes are being applied, and how more and more frequently, personnel in charge of implementing the criminal justice system are also in charge of enforcing immigration controls.[33]

This criminalization of migration—the transplantation of procedures and practices from criminal law into immigration law—has been hugely asymmetrical.[34] The enforcement of criminal law presumes a series of elements and rights that guarantee that the individual who committed a crime would be treated fairly. While the procedures of criminal law have moved into immigration law, there has not been a movement of the legal rights of alleged offenders into the immigration legal framework. For example, "the list of rejected rights includes double jeopardy [prevention to not be judged twice for the same offense], Miranda warnings, the privilege against self-incrimination, . . . right to counsel, and the ban on cruel and unusual punishment," which are not present in immigration law or in the enforcement of those laws.[35] The right to counsel has been partially remedied by the *Padilla* case law (*Padilla v. Kentucky* 2010), but only insofar as migrants or legal permanent residents who find themselves in criminal proceedings have to be informed about the imminent immigration consequences—deportation—of their guilty plea.[36]

The majority of recent theorizing of criminalization of migration converges around the crimmigration thesis.[37] In 1996 three pieces of legislation—the Illegal Immigration Reform and Immigrant Responsibility Act ("IIRIRA"), the Antiterrorism and Effective Death Penalty Act ("AEPDA") and the Personal Responsibility and Work Opportunity Reconciliation Act ("PRWORA") were passed by the United States Congress. Since these bills became law, the boundaries between immigration law and criminal law have become blurred in the United States, linking migration and criminal and security issues.[38] At the root of this convergence of criminal and immigration law is membership theory, which emphasizes a distinction between outsiders and insiders; its flexible nature allows the decision-maker to determine who is part of the community and which rights may apply.[39] The various conceptualizations of the crimmigration thesis seem to rest on a well-known argument: "Immigration law has been saturated with the punitive or coercive aspects of criminal law but has not absorbed the procedural protections of criminal law; the solution is to incorporate those protections," reverse this asymmetry, and reduce the vulnerability of the migrant population.[40] Weber and McCulloch, reviewing the different theoretical advancements around penal power and border control, applauded the crimmigration thesis as accounting for *how* immigration and border control "are being done" in the current era of border criminology.[41]

Russia—in contrast to the United States—has not formally criminalized its migration law.[42] The majority of violations of migration law that lead to migrants' "day in court" are of an administrative nature and follow administrative process.[43] The analysis of migrants' experiences in courts in Russia therefore invites a deeper reflection about the nature and the consequences of the civil and criminal labels in migration law.[44] The expulsion order that accompanies the administrative fines for immigration violations (working without a work permit or lack of residence registration) equates to *de facto* self-deportation. Migrants are given five days to leave the Russian territory; otherwise their stay becomes illegal, and in the event of a further document check and yet another administrative conviction, the state takes control of their expulsion (and detention). Because of changes in the law in 2013 (No. 207-FZ of 23.07.2013), the *de facto* deportation is a nondiscretionary part of administrative penalty in the places of the greatest concentration of migrants, like Moscow or St. Petersburg (and their respective greater administrative areas). It also suggests that the judges and courts have been called upon to be important enforcers of Russian immigration law through being designated a special role in the immigration management and control system. As in this chapter we focus on migrants' experiences in courts—interrogating the disruptive effects it has on immigrants' livelihoods—the *de facto* deportation definitely constitutes the most punitive aspect of the administrative justice system. It could be seen as one of the Soviet legacies of the current Russian legal system—an inclination to seek solutions to societal problems in repressive measures.[45] Examining Russia's legal tradition helps to explain this phenomenon: there was no need to criminalize Russian immigration law, as its repressive functions could be equally accommodated within the existing framework of historically punitive administrative law.[46]

The legal differences between the largely criminalized and administrative nature of immigration law in the U.S. and Russia, as pertaining to the structural nature of these immigration systems, have to be acknowledged.[47] We believe, however, that as we focus on individual migrants and their experiences, the structural and legal architectural conditions perhaps take a more peripheral role. The following sections show that migrants may experience administrative process in equally punitive terms, regardless of its formal classification.

Ethnographic Methods

In 2015, Alejandro Olayo-Méndez spent three months in the city of Nogales at the border region between Mexico and the U.S. state of Arizona. During those months, he not only observed the hearings of Operation Streamline at the Tucson courthouse, but also visited with the U.S. Border Patrol in Nogales, Arizona, a key actor in Operation Streamline. The stay at the border region and the visits to Arizona were part of a bigger research project that explores the dynamics of migration processes in Mexico, especially the role of humanitarian aid provided to irregular migrants, deportees, and asylum seekers.

Olayo-Méndez's research sought to understand the criminalization dynamics of immigration law involved in Operation Streamline, which range from detention, prosecution, and incarceration to removal. He held several meetings with U.S. Border Patrol aimed at better understanding of enforcement practices, including surveillance of different areas, procedures during apprehension, and processing during custody. The visits to the courthouse over the course of two months sought to witness firsthand the way in which the law is applied and justice delivered for prosecuted migrants. Additionally, the project sought to recognize the challenges faced by humanitarian organizations trying to deliver aid in the Sonoran Desert, as well as the process of identification and burial of dead and unidentified migrants. To this end, he met with humanitarian groups like the Samaritans and No More Deaths and visited the Pima County Office of the Medical Examiner-Forensic Science Centre and Evergreen Cemetery in Tucson, Arizona.

Operation Streamline is a comprehensive immigration process that includes more than the hearings at the courthouse. It starts with the apprehension of irregular migrants by the U.S. Border Patrol. Migrants are registered at Border Patrol stations where biographical and biometrical information is collected from them; they are also questioned and checked about their alleged criminal history. There, Border Patrol makes the decision whether or not to refer apprehended migrants to streamline prosecution.[48] Those migrants referred for prosecution are charged with illegal entry (8 USC § 1325). Cases are accepted and charges presented at the U.S. Court. At this point, often a couple of weeks after apprehension, a U.S. magistrate court holds the trials and sentences migrants. After the sentence, convicted migrants are taken into custody for the duration of their sentences. Once the sentence has been fulfilled, U.S. Immigration and Customs Enforcement (ICE) or Border Patrol takes back the custody of the migrant and processes their removal back to Mexico or another origin country.[49] Hearings at the courthouse are the most visible part of Operation Streamline and the most accessible to an outside researcher.

At the time of the visit, hearings for Operation Streamline were conducted twice a week. Normally, there will be a hearing every day. Defendants are assigned a lawyer to represent them. Often, these are Criminal Justice Act attorneys who are hired to represent a growing number of defendants. These attorneys counsel about four to six defendants at a time. They have brief consultations with their clients the morning before the trial. Thus, there is not much time to properly explain the charges and the consequences of the charges their clients face if convicted. Nor do they have time to address the particularities of each case, discuss the facts and the individual circumstances of the case, or prepare a strategy for the imminent trial. Similarly, the circumstances do not allow migrants to properly understand the legal process in which they are involved or to discuss with attorneys their cases to assess if any of them may have a rightful claim to asylum or to explore other legal avenues to remain in the country lawfully. In these circumstances, migrants face the U.S. legal system *de facto* alone.

Agnieszka Kubal spent over five months in Russia in 2014 collecting empirical data in a variety of settings. Her broader research project focused on human rights and access to justice for migrants in Russia. As part of this project, she conducted a three-month ethnographic study of a sample of low-level courts in Moscow (district courts, Moscow City Court, and Moscow Oblast Court). She entered the court building as a researcher and observed the cases once she had received permission from the judge presiding over these cases. She usually sat at the back of the room facing the judge, on the benches reserved for the audience. Normally she would be the only person not involved in the proceedings who would be occupying this place, as immigration cases are not particularly spectacular or known to attract a public audience.

The immigration cases in the Moscow City Court are organized so that the court's president allocates them to a selected number of judges who specialize in immigration questions. When Kubal was observing cases in the Moscow City Court there were two or three judges who, throughout the morning or the afternoon sessions of the court's working day, would be hearing only immigration law cases. Each judge would be allocated approximately five to seven of the 18.8 and 18.10 CAO cases per session. The judge usually heard the cases alone; there were no clerks or assistants present in the courtroom. As a result, the proceedings had to run swiftly, with about five to ten minutes spent per case. Sometimes, for one time slot, there were two or three cases allocated. The judge explained that this happens, as sometimes the parties do not show up in court, so these additional allocations help to reduce the judge's waiting time. However, the other side of the coin was that, when all the parties did actually show up, these overbookings led to delays in cases being heard and inspired derisive comments about the (dis)order of justice in Russia among the people who were waiting in the corridors for the trials to commence.

The courtroom proceedings were organized as follows. An usher normally called the party—consisting of the defendant, with or without legal representative—to enter the room. The usher directed the parties to take their place in front of the court's bench, facing each other. When required, this place would also be occupied by an interpreter—either ordered by the court or brought in by the defendant. Shortly afterward, the usher ordered the parties to stand, and the judge (dressed in a black robe) entered the courtroom from the adjacent office and sat on a raised platform behind the bench. The defendant or his/her legal representation usually kept silent until requested to speak by the judge. It was evidently the judge who was in charge of the room.

Every case hearing would follow a similar script. First, the judge would check all the documents submitted by the state immigration enforcement agents, the decision of the lower court, and the appeal, as contained in the case file, including the power of attorney (*doverennost'*) for the defense lawyer. S/he would inspect the passports of the defendant and his or her legal representative to confirm their identity. The judge then opened the proceedings by introducing him- or herself and asking the defendant if s/he trusted the judge to hear the case. Upon an affirmative response, the judge quickly read out the procedural rights of the defendant under an administrative process (including the right to an interpreter), which the defendant would be requested to acknowledge in writing. Only after seeing to these formal procedures would the judge move on to the facts of the case, hear the arguments of the defense, and finally render a judgment.

In the empirical section following, one of the authors of this essay focuses on typical cases that the court would hear and render judgments. We adopted a country-by-country rather than a thematic perspective to further highlight the striking similarities between these two immigration law systems, despite the different starting points.

"Migrants' Day in Court"—U.S. and Russian Perspectives

The Evo A. DiConcini U.S. Courthouse is located in downtown Tucson, Arizona. Almost every day about seventy people are tried and sentenced for crimes related to unauthorized entry or reentry into the United States. This courthouse is one of the places where the legal proceedings of Operation Streamline take place. After completing registration and passing the security filter at the courthouse lobby, one can access the room where the hearing will be held. The hearing is open to the public. Attorneys representing migrants and other visitors, often from humanitarian organizations, could be found outside the courtroom before the hearing. There are clear indications that no photography, recording, or use of mobile phone is allowed in the courtroom, although one is allowed to take notes. One member of a humanitarian group summarized the experience of attending these hearings by saying:

> One comes here to bear witness and to stand in solidarity with these migrants that experience the injustice of the legal system. At this point, there is nothing else one could do.

Upon entering the room, one should take a seat and remain quiet. There is an edginess that can be felt in the room as lawyers take their place and wait for migrants (defendants) to be allowed into the courtroom and for the judge to enter and officially begin the hearing. Each hearing can take between one and two hours, depending on the number of migrants whose cases are being heard on that day.

It has to be stressed that migrants do not appear in the court freely. They are led in by a U.S. marshal from a special pretrial detention. Their shoelaces and belts have been removed, and they arrive in handcuffs, along with chains around their waists, shackled by their ankles. They move slowly because of the chains and often stare at the floor. Their faces look confused, tired, and deeply sad. It is not too much of an epistemological stretch to compare the scene of people appearing, walking, and waiting in chains led by a court officer to the historical scenes from slavery times where slaves were sold or punished in open plazas. The defendants are asked to sit in rows at the center of the courtroom. The court officer announces that the judge is about to enter the courtroom, and everybody stands up. Then, migrants are called by name and told of the plea agreement and the charges brought against them. Since many migrants do not speak or understand English, they wear headphones and listen to the translations of the proceedings. An attorney mentions to the author that if the defendant does not speak Spanish or English there are no special accommodations made for him/her. Then, the judge asks the whole group if they understand those charges, if they are satisfied with their legal representation, and if their plea is voluntary. As a group, they respond "Sí" (Yes), and the court translator reports back to the judge the answer.

The judge then turns to individual migrants and asks them one by one how they plea to the charges. The answer is often "culpable" (guilty). After the U.S. Border Patrol has read the factual basis for the case (statement of facts), the judge asks the defendants if they have anything to say or to add. For the most part, for the remainder of the trial, the answer is "no" or simply silence.

However, during one of Olayo-Méndez's visits, Angela[50] stood up and said in Spanish:

> Your honor, I lived in this country for many years before I was deported. Since then I have been trying to get back into the country. I have a daughter that is a U.S. Citizen and she needs me. My only crime is wanting to be with her. So, you can deport me as many times as you want. I will continue trying to be reunited with her.

After listening attentively, the judge responded:

> I understand that these situations are complicated. And that occasionally there may be extenuating circumstances. However, my job is to impart justice according to the law. I am bound to do that and there is nothing I can do, but to work within those boundaries.

After that, the judge dictates a sentence to each of the defendants. One by one, migrants from Central American countries and Mexico hear that they will spend in jail thirty, sixty, ninety, or up to 180 days depending on their particular circumstances and how many times they have tried to enter the United States illegally. Angela is given a ninety-day sentence. At the end, the U.S. marshal asks everybody to stand up again, and the judge departs. There is more confusion now, as migrants do not know what is next. Many of them keep looking down, and, when possible, one can see a deep disappointment on their faces. Migrants have to get up again. Moving with difficulty and following the instruction from the court officer, they leave the courtroom to be handed into custody of other officers so they can be transferred to the prisons where they will complete their jail sentences, only to be handed once more to ICE officials for their removal. The particular hearing described here in detail took place in just under two hours. During this hearing, fifty-three migrants were tried and sentenced (leaving approximately two minutes per migrant defendant of an individualized justice process).

Upon the completion of their jail sentences, these migrants are deported. They travel handcuffed and in the company of a U.S. marshal across the border. Upon arrival, there is always confusion, as migrants return with few of their original belongings, without an I.D., and with no money. If migrants worked during incarceration, they receive their payment through an ATM card that charges high fees for any cash withdrawals in the country of origin

(Mexico or Latin American countries). In any case, migrants return in extremely vulnerable positions — economically, socially, and politically — often only to resume another attempt to enter the U.S. illegally.

Olayo-Méndez's subsequent visit to the courthouse was no different. Same procedure, same chains, same faces, same charges, same responses, same sentences given by the judge, and same fate for migrants. This time no one said anything at the end or challenged the judge's decision. Witnessing this scene and imagining playing it over and over every day, one can see why Operation Streamline is called "Assembly Line Justice."[51] At the same time, Angela's case and the judge's response show the moral dilemmas inherent in a legal procedure that aims to punish migrants regardless of any extenuating circumstance.

The detention process, the waiting, the uncertainty about what is going to happen — other than knowing that U.S. migration authorities had captured them — the chains, the trial, and the incarceration time are part of how Operation Streamline punishes and instills fear in migrants, hoping that they would not attempt another reentry, even when, for some of them, their only crime is entering the country illegally to be reunited with their U.S. family members. Often, the desire to be reunited with close family is stronger than any judicial system. As Angela said, "You can deport me as many times as you want. I will continue trying to be reunited with [my daughter]." Undoubtedly, these procedures have psychological effects on migrants as well as on their families, who rarely know of their whereabouts. However, the consequences and punishment involved in the legal system do not end with the removal of the person from the United States. Aside from family separation, there are always risks of losing custody of the children and being banned from returning to the United States through legal channels for prolonged periods.[52] At times, migrants are truly fleeing violence and may have a rightful claim to asylum. However, the hasty prosecutions of their illegal entry in flip-flop courts focusing on their *immigration crime*,[53] the subsequent removal, and the context for such removal do not allow them to access the legal means to put their claim forward and remain in the country lawfully.[54]

And what of migrants' experiences of their day in court in Russia?[55] Many of the cases that Kubal observed resulted from Federal Migration Service (FMS) raids on the premises occupied by migrants — either to allege that they were living there without the required residence permit (registration) or they were working there without the work permit.

One day a group of seven Central Asian men was brought into the B. District court following an FMS visit to a construction site in Moscow. The group was escorted to the court by two FMS officers on duty and charged with offenses against Art. 18.10 (part 3) of the CAO (working without a work permit).

The men were kept waiting in the corridor. Kubal happened to be in court at that time, as she had just finished observing a different case. The FMS officers were sitting next to the Central Asian men, reviewing the documents in the case file: the pictures from the raid, the protocols, and the printouts from the FMS database confirming the men's immigration record in Russia—when did they arrive, how did they cross the border, when did they apply for residence documents and/or work permit?

After some time, the FMS officers collected all the case files and submitted the bundles of documents, together with the passports of the Central Asian migrants, to the judge's assistant. The assistant took the files to the courtroom. Kubal did not have a chance to examine these particular case files in detail, but from observing the FMS officers, she concluded that the case files looked standard in content and size. The Federal Migration Service would normally supply the lower court with (1) protocols from the immigration raids, (2) a collection of photographs taken on site, and (3) elaborate affidavits, signed by migrants, confirming that they actually lived and/or worked at the raided addresses. This type of evidence was then debated and reviewed by the appeals court. This type of evidence served as the main reference for rendering a judgment.

After some time, the judge's assistant emerged from the room and asked if any of the men—Central Asian migrants—were married to Russian citizens or had close family members who were Russian citizens. They all responded negatively. The judge's assistant went back to the courtroom. The FMS officer turned to the Central Asian migrants and said, "Next time you have to do work permits, just do the work permits." The judge's assistant emerged again from the courtroom and asked if any of these men had small children who could be Russian citizens. Three of the men orally gave details of the gender of their children, together with their dates of birth. The judge's assistant, equipped with this information, went back into the courtroom. Then, the judge started calling the men into the courtroom one by one.

This interaction between the FMS officers, the defendants, and the judge's assistant—prior to the actual trial—made us think that the low-level district court judges act primarily as the auditors of the immigration case file. They know what the law is, and they know what documents should be included in the case file if the case is to be processed quickly and efficiently.[56] Prior to the trial, the judge must review (or audit) the written evidence supplied by the FMS, and the assistant's role is to make sure that all the procedurally required information is supplied and filed accordingly. The judge specifically asked whether the men had any close family members who were Russian citizens, as, given the fact that Russia is party to the European Convention on Human

Rights, Article 8 — the right to private and family life — could have been applicable to these cases. What this meant in practice was that the men were still found responsible for committing a particular immigration offense, but the expulsion (or self-deportation) would be excluded from the final judgment, given the men's strong family ties in Russia. In other words, the judge had to check these circumstances not necessarily from goodwill toward the migrants but to make sure that all the grounds that might have resulted in having the decision overturned on appeal were covered. About an hour later, all the defendants were handed written court judgments confirming that they have all committed administrative offenses working without a required work permit. The judgment specified the fine to be paid (5,000 rubles) and contained an expulsion order from Russia to be carried out "by independent means" (*samostoyatel'no*) within the next five days. With these court judgments in hand, the men were released from the custody of the FMS officers and allowed to leave the court building.

As Kubal already observed elsewhere, the main attribute of these everyday immigration law cases adjudicated in accordance with the administrative procedure was documentary evidence contained in the case file.[57] These cases, as "paper cases," were primarily decided according to what documents could be found in the bundle with which the FMS supplied the court. The judge very much scrutinized the material evidence contained in the case file, but did not venture further as to question to what extent these papers, protocols, and affidavits actually reflected the real facts of the case. The judge did not question the actual content of the file. Given the messy empirical reality and multiple possible scenarios of what really happened on the day of the raid at the building site (including the style of evidence-gathering by FMS), the written documents contained in the case file and signed by the defendants were the only "stable and solid" things according to which the judge seemed able to manage the reality and adjudicate the case. Dealing with complex legal rules and their haphazard enforceability by the FMS, the judge relied on the material evidence to take control over the volume of cases that still awaited decisions and deal with them in an efficient manner.

Given the nature of the administrative procedure, migrants had the right to appeal the decision of the lower court to a higher-instance court. Of course, not many migrants actually used this right. The right to appeal was primarily used by those migrants who were able to find legal representation. The quality of the legal counsel varied a lot; it ranged from excellent *pro bono* immigration lawyers who would passionately dispute the evidence presented by the FMS to lawyers who did not necessarily specialize in immigration cases and had taken the case because of the fee involved. At the appeals stage, the primary attention in the courtroom was again directed to the case file. As a result, migrants with whom Kubal spoke afterward quite often had the impression that "the decision has already been made" or "the judgment has already been prepared — the appeal trial is just a formality." The administrative case file logic meant that the judge once again turned to the papers before him or her, often at the cost of examining the witnesses and asking questions of the defendant. Migrant-defendants therefore directly questioned the discretion of the appeals judge in giving other judgment rather than just confirming (or rubber-stamping) the lower court's decision.

For example, M, a migrant worker from Tajikistan, was found guilty of working without a work permit on the basis of a photograph provided by the FMS in which he was sitting behind the steering wheel in a car, and an affidavit where he confirmed that he had been working as a driver. In the appeals city court M wanted to clarify this evidence, saying that in the picture taken by the FMS and contained in the case file, he, indeed, was sitting in the car, but he was waiting for a friend. That friend came with him to testify in court. The judge did not seem to give much credibility to this explanation, nor did he attempt to hear the witness brought before her. Instead, the judge brought everyone's attention to the signed affidavit already contained in the case file:

> But I have an affidavit signed by you, saying you were hired to work by company X., you were supposed to drive and deliver a package from this place to this place, it was an oral contract and you were to be paid 4,000 roubles per day. . . .
>
> M: [interrupting] But I have never earned that much, anywhere in Moscow. This is not a day's going rate of pay, it is far too high!

M was not trying to be disrespectful to the judge — he interrupted the judge but actually made an important observation about the artificiality of the affidavit-only-based evidence. He was genuinely astonished by the figure quoted in the testimony. He was attempting to challenge the affidavit for what it was: a piece of paper with all the correct signatures and official stamps to make it look like formal evidence but that was in no way connected to the reality of the situation. It did not account for what had happened on that particular day, nor was it true in general when it described the context of going wages for migrant workers in Moscow. The judge responded:

> But you have signed it. This is your signature. I have to expel you, as this is the minimum penalty.

The migrants, the defendants, the agents were rarely recognized *in* the people pleading before the judge who physically came to the court trying to clarify evidence and appeal the decision of the lower court. Instead, to the judges the agents were those *of whom* the documents contained in the case file spoke, who were portrayed in the photographs, or who signed the affidavits (sometimes *under duress* or without the working knowledge of Russian). The way the judges read and interpreted this documentary evidence in courts was crucial for the case file to attain the hyperbolic reality-mediating function: *Quod non est in actis, non est in mundo*—What is not kept in the case file does not exist.[58] This gives an impression that the trial indeed is only a formality, and the "real" decision has already been taken.

We do not want to portray the Russian judges as heartless. The perceived lack of discretion in how they arrived at the judgments and strict adherence to the formal legality of the case file could often be conflated with outward hostility toward the migrants themselves. We would argue that it is not so much a negative attitude to migrants as a bureaucratic and administerial approach to managing a docket full of immigration cases that makes the judges pay utmost attention to the papers before them.[59] They rely on the case file logic as a way of managing their workload in order to process these cases as quickly and as expeditiously as possible. In the breaks before the different cases, or even before the case has been formally closed, Kubal would often hear the judge saying:

> I cannot really change the decision—it was legally taken.
>
> I feel sorry for you, you work here, you live where possible, but Moscow has a different regime. I have to follow the law.

The oft-perceived rubber-stamping on the written evidence by the appeals judge leads to a conclusion that the delivery of justice does not seem to be related to hearings in a courtroom but is rather accumulated gradually through the various stages of pre-trial document gathering. It starts when the Federal Migration Service forms a suspicion and begins to investigate and continues through the several phases of the court proceedings.[60] The appeals courtroom in this administerial and bureaucratic model of justice is merely the final point in the chain. The collateral effect—particularly vocal in the corridors of justice immediately after the trial—is that the appeals court is often blamed for the procedural injustices of the pre-trial stage, and all the different (arguably autonomous) elements in the law enforcement hierarchy are conflated into one big, oppressive and unjust institution. "The judgment was ready before the trail had even taken place"—is an explanation I have heard from most of my respondents who were not successful in court.

Discussion

What can be said about the U.S. and Russian immigration justice systems? Are they indeed a mirror image of one another? Following the Cambridge Online Dictionary, "a mirror image" is "something that looks exactly the same as another thing but with its left and right sides in opposite positions."[61] This analogy strikes us as true if we compare many elements of the system, particularly taking the migrants-defendants' perspective; however, the full picture is more complex than the catchy mirror metaphor.

As mentioned earlier in this chapter, any comparative discussion between the United States and Russia in the domain of immigration law has to start with the initial structural and ideological differences: the U.S. immigration law system has been (largely) criminalized, while in Russia it still lies primarily within the administrative domain. The cases in Operation Streamline are criminal cases for illegal border crossings, while the cases heard before the domestic courts in Moscow follow the administrative law procedure for illegal residence or undocumented work. These differences can clearly be observed in the materiality of the trial and the court hearing. On the U.S. side Olayo-Mendéz documented the unkempt outlook of the defendants (some U.S. districts give defendants prison uniforms, but others do not) and the highly symbolic (though highly disproportionate and unnecessary) chains and shackles in which the migrant defendants appear in court for their cases to be heard. These experiences, particularly the visual and material decorum of the trial, are profoundly linked to the projected image of the criminalized immigration domain.

In Russia, by contrast, the migrant-litigants observed by Kubal were free to appear before the judge. Those migrant-litigants observed before the appeals court came because they disputed the verdict of the lower court—because they disputed their expulsion order, and because they hoped that the appeals court could reverse the judgment.[62] While there were no chains and shackles, the administrative procedure that applied in these immigration cases manifested itself in the sole reliance on written evidence: documents, photographs, protocols from the immigration raids, affidavits signed by the defendants. This materiality of the "trial by paper" was the most salient feature of the administrative immigration proceedings in Russia.[63]

Yet despite these initial differences, we may draw some analogies in how the two immigration justice systems were experienced by migrants.

The first analogy relates to the "on the ground" experience of the principle of individualization of justice, or rather how the actual experiences of the legal process put this principle into question. Many have dubbed Operation

Streamline the "conveyer belt of justice";[64] Olayo-Mendéz demonstrated that one two-hour hearing might involve up to seventy migrant defendants in the room. The judge at different stages of the trial attempts to make the process somewhat individualized by asking the defendants in turn about their plea and whether they have anything to add about the statement of the facts of the case. However, the convention and the decorum of the trial do not inspire the confidence to delve into personal extenuating circumstances that may pertain to an individual case. As Olayo-Mendéz documented, only the bravest or the most desperate migrant-defendants actually decide to speak to the judge and present the intricacies of their personal circumstances. Others quietly and passively accept the convention of the mass trial and limit their voice to monosyllables such as "guilty" or opt for submissive silence.

In Russia, while at face value, the migrant-defendants enter the courtroom individually and the judge listens to their cases one by one, the time difference between the consecutive hearings is sometimes as short as five to ten minutes. This is because of the high volume of the immigration cases and the need for the judge to process them quickly and efficiently. A ten-minute trial—which may result in a sentence affecting all future plans and livelihood in Russia—really puts into question how the individualization of the justice principle is experienced in practice. The individualization of justice in Russia is further put to question by deciding the cases on the basis of formal written documents with little or no time afforded to hear the personal stories of migrants appearing before the judge. That would lead to significant delays in the tightly knit schedule of processing these cases or, in the most serious scenario, could result in the judges losing control of their docket.

The second analogy we found striking when comparing our empirical material was how the justice by migrant-defendants in the United States and in Russia was perceived as a "done deal." Migrants in the U.S. sensed the inevitability of the guilty plea; this was reflected by their passive participation in the trial—they kept their heads low, they did not talk, they did not try to present "their version of events" or voice extenuating circumstances, even when requested to do so by the judge. The "done deal" nature of the trial was also confirmed by the attitude of the judge in Olayo-Mendéz's account; he seemed to be sympathetic to the plea by Angela about her U.S. citizen daughter, but at the same time had to "act within the remits of the law." The scope for discretion and a change of the judgment seemed significantly limited, if not outright nonexistent.

Similarly, in Moscow, because of the strict reliance on the formal, written evidence material contained in the case file, many migrants perceived the judge as simply rubber-stamping the evidence rather than delivering justice.

They did not feel like they had the opportunity to be heard or share "their side of the story." Sometimes, like in the case of M before the appeals court, they categorically challenged the written evidence for what it really was: a piece of paper with stamps and signatures but detached from everyday realities of "migrant Moscow."[65] This did not seem to make a difference or change the course of the trial; many migrants thereby rightly felt that they were left outside the justice system, that the decision had already been taken regardless of whether they showed up to the court or not. These experiences were tied to the structural position of the judge as bounded by strict immigration laws. Moscow and greater Moscow, as the capital city and the place of one of the greatest concentration of migrants, follow their own immigration regime, whereby any of the immigration administrative offenses attracts an expulsion order as the minimum penalty. This lack of discretion in delivering the judgment was echoed in the words of one of the judges observed by Kubal: "I have to follow the law. In Moscow we expel everyone."

Conclusion: Beyond Crimmigration

The main conclusion that stems from the comparative analysis of the everyday experiences of immigration cases under (largely) criminalized and administrative jurisdictions is that there are more similarities between them than there are differences. What looms large from our ethnographic data is a generally punitive experience of the immigration justice system whereby "the process is the punishment."[66] This has important repercussions for the crimmigration thesis.

Graham Hudson, in his recent controversial but extremely well-argued piece entitled, "Does Crimmigration Theory Rest on a Mistake?," proposed in relation to the punitive aspects of immigration law that "it is not necessary to invoke the concepts and organising divisions of criminal law to describe what is going on."[67] Expanding the notion of crimmigration or attributing the punitive aspects of immigration law solely to the encroachments of criminal law, where in fact these could easily be explained by coercive features inherent to administrative law itself,[68] is not the most productive way forward, either for analytical clarity or for the future of the crimmigration thesis. We agree with Hudson that "overreliance on criminal law as a heuristic device can harden faulty concepts and categories of thought into unalterable form, allowing accreted doctrine and underlying ideologies of exclusion to delimit constitutional aspirations."[69] Our comparative study illustrates more similarities with regard to *how* immigration control is exercised under (largely) criminalized and administrative jurisdictions than the uncritical reliance on crimmigration would perhaps permit.

Perhaps it is time to move beyond the criminal-civil dichotomy that crimmigration (unintentionally) reproduces.[70] In the various conceptualizations of the crimmigration thesis, one thing seems clear: the solution to punitive or coercive aspects of criminal law with which immigration law has been fused is the incorporation of protections inherent in criminal law.[71] Yet the proceedings for immigration law violations under Operation Streamline—we would say, "a bread-and-butter criminal law applied in the context of migration"[72]—demonstrate that bringing in criminal law–derived procedural protections does not necessarily sufficiently counterbalance the punitive elements inherent in the legal process. The counsel time afforded to defendants in the morning ahead of the court hearing does not make any difference to their legal representation and is not in any way outcome-determinative. The principle of individualization of justice is compromised in "conveyor belt" trials in flip-flop courts,[73] which see up to seventy defendants having their cases heard at once. The waiver of protections normally afforded to defendants in criminal justice proceedings might bring a significant downgrade of their "crime" from felony to the petty offense of illegal entry or a misdemeanor charge of possessing a fake I.D.[74] However, the outcome of these tradeoffs is the same: less time in prison only translates to quicker removal from the country. Deportation is a collateral consequence of a guilty plea. Given this evidence, we question whether the organizing principle of crimmigration actually sheds any light on what is going on here, as the procedural safeguards, tradeoffs, and assurances put in place seem to make no difference to the outcome of these cases. These cases rather seem to be predicated upon bureaucratic-administerial logic, serving the policy goal of processing them as quickly and efficiently as possible.

The Russian element of our comparative case study engages with and adds to the growing body of literature that further reveals the breakdown of the civil-criminal dichotomy in practice.[75] In Russia, the borders between criminal and administrative law and procedure have historically been rather porous: officers from the Federal Migration Service (which until 2016 was an administrative agency) cooperate with local police to enforce "civil" immigration regulations set by the very same administrative agencies.[76] Duress and social exclusion associated with an expulsion order, too often accompanied by the language of blame,[77] have been part of immigration law centered on "dispassionate management of population groups."[78] While migrants have the right to appeal their cases, and while some of them use this right and appear freely before the judge, these procedural assurances do not seem to counterbalance the highly punitive experiences of the justice process that emerge from our ethnography. We do not find the basic premise of crimmigration helpful here to account for these nuances, many of which are not specific to Russia.[79]

Indeed, the very features of the Russian immigration law trials that compelled us toward the comparative analysis of the cases churned out under Operation Streamline in the United States were the striking similarities: the perceived lack of individualization of justice principle, the inevitability of the outcome of the trial, and the lack of judicial discretion. *Why* does it happen? Our overall conclusion is that these immigration cases, regardless of the criminal or administrative jurisdictions under which they are heard, are overridden by the bureaucratic-administerial logic of efficiency. The judges in U.S. flip-flop courts and in Moscow are primarily concerned with processing these cases as quickly and expediently as possible—to clear their docket and make space for more cases that inevitably need to be decided the following day. The underlying bureaucratic efficiency, despite the formal procedural assurances of the court process, makes the experiences of these cases so uniformly punitive.

Notes

1. Executive Order 13768, signed January 25, 2017: "(c) Pursuant to section 235(b)(1)(A)(iii)(I) of the INA, the Secretary shall take appropriate action to apply, in his sole and unreviewable discretion, the provisions of section 235(b)(1)(A)(i) and (ii) of the INA to the aliens designated under section 235(b)(1)(A)(iii)(II)."

2. "Ethnic Profiling in the Moscow Metro," *Open Society Institute*, 2006, http://www.soros.org/sites/default/files/metro_20060613.pdf.

3. A. Kubal, "Refugees or Migrant Workers? A Case Study of Undocumented Syrians in Russia—LM and Others v. Russia," *ECtHR* (March 14, 2016), *Journal of Immigration Asylum and Nationality Law* 30, no. 4 (2016a): 265–82; K. Troiskiy, "Administrative Expulsion from Russia: Court Proceedings or Mass Expulsion?," 2016, http://refugee.ru/wp-content/uploads/2016/05/Doklad-o-vydvoreniyakh_pechat.pdf.

4. See for the U.S., C. Menjívar, and L. J. Abrego, "Legal Violence: Immigration Law and the Lives of Central American Immigrants," *American Journal of Sociology* 117, no. 5 (2012): 1380–1421.

5. "Streamline: Measuring Its Effect on Illegal Border Crossing," *Department of Homeland Security*, 2015, http://www.oig.dhs.gov/assets/Mgmt/2015/OIG_15-95_May15.pdf; A. Burridge, "From the Desert to the Courtroom: Challenging the Invisibility of the Operation Streamline Dragnet and En-Masse Hearings," in *Migration, Squatting and Radical Autonomy*, ed. P. Mudu and S. Chattopadhyay (London: Routledge, 2017), 35–39.

6. J. J. Lydgate, "Assembly-Line Justice: A Review of Operation Streamline," *California Law Review* 98, no. 2 (2010): 481–544; J. Slack, D. E. Martínez, S. Whiteford, and E. Peiffer, "In Harm's Way: Family Separation, Immigration Enforcement Programs and Security on the US-Mexico Border," *Journal on Migration and Human Security* 3, no. 2 (2015): 109–28.

7. "Streamline."

8. Attorney General Jeff Sessions Announces the Department of Justice's Renewed Commitment to Criminal Immigration Enforcement," *Department of Justice, Office of Public Affairs*, 2017, https://www.justice.gov/opa/pr/attorney-general-jeff-sessions-announces-department-justice-s-renewed-commitment-criminal.

9. J. M. Chacón, *Narrowing Asylum Grounds, Family Separations and Supreme Indifference at the U.S. Border*, 2018, Border Criminologies Blog, https://www.law.ox.ac.uk/research-subject-groups/centre-criminology/centreborder-criminologies/blog/2018/07/narrowing-asylum, accessed Jul. 9, 2018.

10. V. S. Malakhov, "Russia as a New Immigration Country: Policy Response and Public Debate," *Europe-Asia Studies* 66, no.7 (2014): 1062–79, http://doi.org/10.1080/09668136.2014.934140.

11. S. Abashin, "Migration Policies in Russia: Laws and Debates," in *Migrant Workers in Russia: Global Challenges of the Shadow Economy in Societal Transformation*, ed. A.-L. Heusala and K. Aitamurto (London: Routledge, 2017: 16–34); Kubal, "Spiral Effect of the law: Migrants' Experiences of the State Law in Russia—A Comparative Perspective," *International Journal of Law in Context* 12, no. 4 (2016): 453–68, http://doi.org/10.1017/S1744552316000215.

12. Kubal, "In Search of Justice: Migrants' Experiences of Moscow City Court," in *Sociology of Justice in Russia*, ed. M. Kurkchiyan and Kubal (Cambridge: Cambridge University Press, 2018).

13. M. Kurchiyan and Kubal, "Administerial Justice: Concluding Remarks on the Russian Legal Tradition," in *Sociology of Justice in Russia*, ed. M. Kurkchiyan and Kubal (Cambridge: Cambridge University Press, 2018), 259–77.

14. M. Lynch, "Backpacking the Border: The Intersection of Drug and Immigration Prosecutions in a High-Volume US Court," *British Journal of Criminology* 57, no. 1 (2017): 112–31.

15. M. Bosworth and M. Guild, "Governing through Migration Control: Security and citizenship in Britain," *British Journal of Criminology* 48, no. 6 (2008): 712.

16. "The International Migration Report 2017 (Highlights)," *UN Department of Economic and Social Affairs*, 2018, https://www.un.org/development/desa/publications/international-migration-report-2017.html.

17. M. Light, "Policing Migration in Soviet and Post-Soviet Moscow," *Post-Soviet Affairs* 26, no. 4 (2010): 275–313.

18. H. Pilkington, *Migration, Displacement, and Identity in Post-Soviet Russia* (New York and London: Routledge, 1998).

19. D. Massey, J. Arango, G. Hugo, A. Kouaouci, A. Pellegrino, and E. J. Taylor, "An Evaluation of International Migration Theory: The North American Case," *Population and Development Review* 20, no. 4 (1994); Massey and K. Espinosa, "What Is Driving Mexico-US Migration? A Theoretical, Empirical and Policy Analysis," *American Journal of Sociology* 102, no. 4 (1997): 939–99.

20. J. M. Krogstad, J. S. Passel, and A. C. D'Vera, "5 Facts about Illegal

Immigration in the U.S," *Pew Research Center*, 2018, http://www.pewresearch.org/fact-tank/2018/11/28/5-facts-about-illegal-immigration-in-the-u-s/.

21. Abashin, "Migration Policies in Russia," 16–34.

22. E. Aranda, C. Menjívar, and K. M. Donato, "The Spillover Consequences of an Enforcement-First U.S. Immigration Regime," *American Behavioral Scientist* 58, no. 13 (2014): 1687–95, http://doi.org/10.1177/0002764214537264; Menjivar, "Liminal Legality: Salvadoran and Guatemalan Immigrants' Lives in the United States," *American Journal of Sociology* 111, no. 4 (2006): 999–1037; Menjívar, "Immigration Law beyond Borders: Externalizing and Internalizing Border Controls in an Era of Securitization," *Annual Review of Law and Social Science* 10 (2014): 353–69.

23. Chacón, "Overcriminalizing Migration," *Journal of Criminal Law and Criminology* 102, no. 3 (2012): 613–52; A. G. Cervantes and Menjívar, "Mass Deportation: Forced Removal, Immigrant Threat, and Disposable Labor in a Global Context," *Handbook of Race, Ethnicity, Crime, and Justice* (2018): 527–46; Menjívar, Cervantes, and D. Alvord, "The Expansion of "Crimmigration," Mass Detention, and Deportation," *Sociology Compass* 12, no. 4 (2018): 1–15.

24. B. Davé, "Becoming 'Legal' through 'Illegal' Procedures: The Precarious Status of Migrant Workers in Russia," *Russian Analytical Digest* 159 (2014): 2–6; M. Reeves, "Clean Fake: Authenticating Documents and Persons in Migrant Moscow," *American Ethnologist* 40, no. 3 (2013): 508–24, http://doi.org/10.1111/amet.12036; J. Round and I. Kuznetsova, "Necropolitics and the Migrant as a Political Subject of Disgust: The Precarious Everyday of Russia's Labour Migrants," *Critical Sociology* (2016): 1–18, http://doi.org/10.1177/0896920516645934; Kubal, "Refugees or Migrant Workers?," 265–82; Kubal, "Spiral Effect of the Law," 453–68; Kubal, "In Search of Justice."

25. "Ethnic Profiling in the Moscow Metro."

26. A. Doolotkeldieva, "Conducting Interviews with Labour Migrants in Moscow," *CESR* 7, no. 2 (2008): 31–34; K. Hendley, "Varieties of Legal Dualism: Making Sense of the Role of Law in Contemporary Russia," *Wisconsin International Law Journal* 29, no. 2 (2011): 233–62; J. Kahn, "In Search for the Rule of Law in Russia," *Georgetown Journal of International Law* 37 (2006): 353–409; V. Ruget and B. Usmanalieva, "How Much Is Citizenship Worth? The Case of Kyrgyzstani Migrants in Kazakhstan and Russia," *Citizenship Studies* 14, no. 4 (2010): 445–59, http://doi.org/10.1080/13621025.2010.490038; R. Urinboyev, "Migration and Transnational Informality in Post-Soviet Societies: Ethnographic Study of Po Rukam ('Handshake') Experiences of Uzbek Migrant Workers in Moscow," in *Migrant Workers in Russia*, ed. Heusala and Aitamurto (London: Routledge, 2016); T. N. Yudina, "Labour Migration into Russia: The Response of State and Society," *Current Sociology* 53, no. 4 (2005): 583–606, http://doi.org/10.1177/0011392105052716.

27. Kubal, "Spiral Effect of the Law: Migrants' Experiences of the State Law in Russia—A Comparative Perspective," *International Journal of Law in Context* 12, no. 4 (2016): 453–68.

28. Kubal, "Entry Bar as Surreptitious Deportation? Zapret na v'ezd in Russian Immigration Law and Practice: A Comparative Perspective," *Law & Social Inquiry* 42, no. 3 (2017): 744–68.

29. Kubal, "Spiral Effect of the Law."

30. Menjívar and L. J. Abrego, "Legal Violence: Immigration Law and the Lives of Central American Immigrants," *American Journal of Sociology* 117, no. 5 (2012): 1380–1421, http://doi.org/10.1086/663575.

31. Burridge, "*Differential Criminalization under Operation Streamline: Challenges to Freedom of Movement and Humanitarian Aid Provision in the Mexico-US Borderlands*," *Refuge: Canada's Journal on Refugees* 26, no. 2 (2009): 78–91; Chacón, "Managing Migration through Crime," *Columbia Law Review Sidebar* 109 (2009): 135–48.

32. S. H. Legomsky, "The New Path of Immigration Law: Asymmetric Incorporation of Criminal Justice Norms," *Washington & Lee Law Review* 64, no. 2 (2007): 489.

33. Ibid., 476, 480, 496.

34. Ibid.

35. Ibid., 515–16.

36. A. Ortiz Maddali, "Padilla v. Kentucky: A new Chapter in Supreme Court Jurisprudence on Whether Deportation Constitutes Punishment for Lawful Permanent Residents?," *American University Law Review* 61, no. 1 (2011): 1–58.

37. K. F. Aas, "Crimmigrant' Bodies and Bona Fide Travelers: Surveillance, Citizenship and Global Governance," *Theoretical Criminology* 15, no. 3 (2011): 331–46; Menjívar, Cervantes, and Alvord, "Expansion of 'Crimmigration,' Mass Detention, and Deportation," 1–15; J. Stumpf, "The Crimmigration Crisis: Immigrants, Crime, and Sovereign Power," *American University Law Review* 56, no. 2 (2006): 367–419; Stumpf, "The Process Is the Punishment in Crimmigration Law," in *The Borders of Punishment: Migration, Citizenship, and Social Exclusion*, ed. K. Franko Aas and M. Bosworth (Oxford: Oxford University Press, 2013), 58–75; L. Weber and and J. McCulloch, "Penal Power and Border Control: Which Thesis? Sovereignty, Governmentality, or the Pre-Emptive State?," *Punishment & Society* 21, no. 4 (2018): 496–514.

38. Chacón, "Overcriminalizing Migration," 613–52; T. Golash-Boza, "The Criminalization of Undocumented Migrants: Legalities and Realities," *Societies without Borders* 5, no. 1 (2010): 81–90; A. S. Hartry, "Gendering Crimmigration: The Intersection of Gender, Immigration, and the Criminal Justice System," *Berkeley Journal of Gender, Law & Justice* 27, no. 1 (2012): 1–27; Stumpf, "Crimmigration Crisis," 367–419.

39. Stumpf, "Crimmigration Crisis," 412.

40. G. Hudson, "Does Crimmigration Theory Rest on a Mistake?," *International Journal of Migration and Border Studies* 4, no. 4 (2018): 307.

41. Weber and McCulloch, "Penal Power and Border Control," 3.

42. While illegal border crossing by presenting counterfeit documents is a

criminal offense in Russia (pursuant to art. 30.3 and art. 322.1 of the Criminal Code of the Russian Federation), it does not apply to a great majority of migrants in Russia because of a visa-free movement with Central Asia.

43. Kubal, "In Search of Justice."

44. A. Sarat, L. Douglas, and M. M. Umphrey, eds., *Law as Punishment*/Law as Regulation (Stanford, Calif.: Stanford University Press, 2011); C. Steiker, "Punishment and Procedure: Punishment Theory and the Criminal-Civil Procedural Divide," *Georgetown Law Journal* 85, no. 4 (1997): 775–819.

45. S. Pomorski, "Reflections on the First Criminal Code of Post-Communist Russia," *American Journal of Comparative Law* 46 (1998): 392.

46. Which Kubal did elsewhere; see Kubal, "Entry Bar as Surreptitious Deportation?"

47. We readily acknowledge that not all U.S. immigration law has been criminalized, and U.S. immigration is of course still largely an administrative law system. While we note that many immigration cases in the U.S. are civil, we used the Operation Streamline case study to critically engage with the crimmigration thesis and thereby make our point of comparison with Russia even clearer.

48. Lynch, "Backpacking the Border," 112–31.

49. "Streamline."

50. The name has been changed to protect the identity of the defendant.

51. Lydgate, "Assembly-Line Justice," 481–544.

52. C. E. Hall, "Where Are My Children . . . and My Rights? Parental Rights Termination as a Consequence of Deportation," *Duke Law Journal* 60 (2011): 1459–1503; M. Yablon-Zug, "Separation, Deportation, Termination," *Boston College Journal of Law & Social Justice* 32, no. 1 (2012): 63–117.

53. Lynch, "Backpacking the Border," 112–31.

54. Chacón, *Narrowing Asylum Grounds*.

55. An earlier version of this material has already been published as Kubal, *Immigration and Refugee Law: Socio-Legal Perspectives* (Cambridge: Cambridge University Press, 2019), Chapter 5, pp. 78–101.

56. See also K. Hendley, *Everyday Law in Russia* (Ithaca and London: Cornell University Press, 2017); V. Andrianova, "The Everyday Experiences of Russian Citizens in Justice of the Peace Courts," in *A Sociology of Justice in Russia*, ed. M. Kurkchiyan and A. Kubal (Cambridge: Cambridge University Press, 2018), 65–92.

57. Kubal, "In Search of Justice."

58. J. Kahn, "Adversarial Principles and the Case File in Russian Criminal Procedure," in *Russia and the Council of Europe: Ten Years After*, ed. K. Malfliet and S. Parmentier (Basingstoke: Palgrave Macmillan, 2010), 107–33.

59. Kurchiyan and Kubal, "Administerial Justice," 259–77.

60. Ibid.

61. See Cambridge Online Dictionary, https://dictionary.cambridge.org/dictionary/english/mirror-image, accessed February 1, 2018.

62. It has to be said, however, that this situation was particular for its time and

place—Moscow of 2014. Since then, and particularly since the disbandment of the Federal Migration Service in 2016 and making immigration matters a prerogative of the Ministry of Internal Affairs (MVD), more and more migrants upon receiving the expulsion order by the first-instance court are kept in administrative detention (Centre for temporary detention of foreign citizens, CVSIG), and their removal from the country is supervised and organized by the MVD local field office.

63. See also Kubal, "In Search of Justice."

64. Lynch, "Backpacking the Border," 112–31.

65. M. Reeves, "Living from the Nerves: Deportability, Indeterminacy, and the 'Feel of Law' in Migrant Moscow," *Social Analysis* 59, no. 4 (2015): 119–36.

66. Stumpf, "Process Is the Punishment in Crimmigration Law," 58–75.

67. Hudson, "Does Crimmigration Theory Rest on a Mistake?," 305.

68. Bosworth and Guild, "Governing through Migration Control," 712.

69. Hudson, "Does Crimmigration Theory Rest on a Mistake?," 305.

70. R. Nadadur, "Beyond Crimigration and the Civil-Criminal Dichotomy—Applying Mathews v. Eldridge in the Immigration Context," *Yale Human Rights & Development Law Journal* 16, no. 1 (2013): 141–75.

71. Bosworth and Guild, "Governing through Migration Control," 703–19; Legomsky, "New Path of Immigration Law," 469–528; P. L. Markowitz, "Deportation Is Different," *University of Pennsylvania Journal of Constitutional Law* 13, no. 5 (2011): 1299–1363; Stumpf, "Process Is the Punishment in Crimmigration Law," 58–75.

72. Hudson, "Does Crimmigration Theory Rest on a Mistake?," 308.

73. Lynch, "Backpacking the Border," 112–31.

74. Ibid., 112–31.

75. Hudson, "Does Crimmigration Theory Rest on a Mistake?," 303–25; Kubal, "Entry Bar as Surreptitious Deportation?," 744–68; K. Mann, "Punitive Civil Sanctions: The Middleground between Criminal and Civil Law," *Yale Law Journal* 101, no. 8 (1991): 1795–874; Nadadur, "Beyond Crimmigration and the Civil-Criminal Dichotomy," 141–75; Steiker, "Punishment and Procedure," 775–819; W. J. Stuntz, "Substance, Process, and the Civil-Criminal Line," *Journal of Contemporary Legal Issues* 7, no. 1 (1996): 1–42.

76. Kubal, "Entry Bar as Surreptitious Deportation?," 744–68.

77. I. Kuznetsova and J. Round, "Postcolonial Migrations in Russia: The Racism, Informality and Discrimination Nexus," *International Journal of Sociology and Social Policy* 39, no. 1/2 (2018): 52–67.

78. Bosworth and Guild, "Governing through Migration Control," 712.

79. Regarding the United States, see Nadadur, "Beyond Crimmigration and the Civil-Criminal Dichotomy."

III

Shoring Up Fortress Europe

10

Euroskepticism, Nationalism, and the Securitization of Migration in the Netherlands

Maartje van der Woude

> The West is suffering from an autoimmune disorder. . . . Part of our organism — an important part: our immune system, that which should protect us — has turned against us. We're being weakened, undermined, surrendered in every respect. Malevolent, aggressive elements are being smuggled into our social body in unprecedented numbers, while true causes and consequences are kept hidden. Police reports about violent incidents at refugee centers are not made public. The attorney general's office looks the other way when it runs into sharia courts.
>
> — THIERRY BAUDET, PARTY LEADER OF FORUM FOR DEMOCRACY WHILE ADDRESSING HIS PARTY'S CONGRESS IN JANUARY 2017

Not Just Another "Crisis"

These past two decades the European Union has been hit by two so-called "crises": the financial or "Euro" crisis of 2008 and the 2015–16 migration crisis. Whereas both crises have fed into Euroskeptic sentiments, it is safe to say that the response to the financial crisis at least seemed to be somewhat coordinated and uniform, with EU member states coming together to reinforce the monetary union through powerful new instruments and sacrificed control over their banking systems to save the Euro. The opposite has been true with regard to EU member states' response to the so-called migration crisis. Driven by a logic of renationalization, combined with the rise of xenophobia and identity politics, member states chose to sacrifice part of the functionality of the Schengen Agreement, also known as the Schengen acquis, rather than limit their national decision-making on migration and asylum. By falling back on national measures, such as border controls or fences, to contain the inflows of migrants and asylum seekers, member states chose to limit and monitor the cross-border mobility of people, and pronouncements became commonplace asserting that the Schengen Agreement—widely considered to be one of the paramount achievements of European integration—was effectively dead.[1,2] As Kmak describes it, a pressing urge was felt to be able to distinguish between "the Good," "the Bad," and "the Ugly" immigrant.[3] The group of migrants entering the European Union since 2015 would fall into the latter category: asylum seekers or undocumented migrants, a thoroughly unwelcome group of visitors "lumped together under one label, shunned by EU countries, which try to deter them by, among others, building physical obstacles at borders and introducing controls on their territory."[4] This lumping together of groups of migrants falls in line with the lumping together of migration and crime in discourse, laws, and practice. This process is also known as the process of crimmigration.[5]

Although the response to the 2015 "crisis" might seem extreme in terms of the measures that are taken and the duration of these measures,[6] concerns about the "open borders" between EU member states have been present from the very first moment in the deliberations about the Schengen Agreement. The viability of the principle of free movement was always questioned. While seeing the economic benefits of the lifting of border checks between member states, countries were also wary about the security deficit this would create because of strong concerns about the ability to secure the external border Europe so that it would become the protected and impenetrable fortress that it is often depicted to be. The migration "crisis" has painfully shown that it is not. Against a background of ever-growing concerns about terrorism and transnational crime and their relation to migration, for many countries the "crisis" has provided national governments with a classical window of opportunity to implement stricter migration policies, to implement a variety of measures to better monitor cross-border mobility, or, in the case of the United Kingdom, to, most likely, break with the EU altogether.[7]

As Lehne observed,[8] despite the fact that the acute crisis seems to have ended—the EU received 43 percent fewer asylum applications in 2017 than it did in 2016[9]—the sense of crisis around issues of migration is still deeply entrenched in public and political discourse and, most likely, will remain so for the unforeseen future. In many EU member states, nationalism and identity politics have gained ground, and views that used to be broadly criticized as xenophobic have become commonplace. Populist political forces—as well as some mainstream politicians and media outlets—are benefiting from anxieties about migration and doing everything they can to keep them alive. Can we conclude that with the erosion of the principle of free movement something has fundamentally been broken in the European Union, or are we just finally seeing what has always been present underneath the surface? If so, how do we move from here?

The aim of this chapter is twofold: First of all, it will argue that the principle of free movement in Europe was never meant to be all-inclusive and will show how this is illustrated by the ways in which member states can still police and monitor intra-Schengen cross-border mobility. Furthermore, illustrated by the case of the Netherlands as a country that is traditionally and internationally seen as tolerant, open, and lenient, the chapter will illustrate how, over time, discussions on migration and the functioning of the European Union have become securitized and politicized.[10] This securitization and politicization of migration in Europe have contributed to the fact that the objectives of border control in many countries, both inside and outside the EU, are increasingly inscribed into discourses about crime and punishment and into everyday practices of contemporary penal regimes. By drawing from literature on globalization, nationalism, and crimmigration, the chapter will reflect upon how (Western) European countries are trying to revitalize national identity and keep out the foreign and culturally different.

Globalization, Nationalism, and (New) Racism in Europe

Globalization is seen to produce new sources of insecurity, and in particular challenges to the security of states. Under conditions of globalization, the distinction between domestic and international is increasingly blurred, along with the line between internal and external threats. Irregular migrants are emblematic of the hybrid threat, characterized as a threat both to national security and sovereignty and to safety and order inside the state. Borders and mobility policing are therefore inextricably connected to state sovereignty. As will be discussed in the next paragraph, this reflection on the link between sovereignty and control of an individual's mobility is particularly striking in the case of the internal borders of the Schengen area. By policing the mobility brought about by the ongoing globalization of society, national—and even local—order and security regimes are created and shaped by national and/or local notions of social order and belonging. And this is where matters of state's responses to globalization link with the notion of nationalism.

Nations and nationalism propagate a sense of shared identity, solidifying a distinctive cultural heritage and personality for a given named population. Consequently, nationalism is used to maintain distance from others. The nationalist community strives to preserve the land, culture, language, political institutions, and way of life. Cultural differences are being seen as a threat to the existing way of life, and it is thus seen as rational to preserve one's culture through the exclusion of other cultural groups. Supposed cultural similarities and norms are grouped, necessitating the separation of those who do not "belong" from those who do. According to Ibrahim,[11] it is as a result of this obsession with cultural homogeneity that immigrants are linked with "the demise of the nation," an attitude that should be understood as racism. Whereas in many European countries — as a result of the atrocities of WWII — the term "race" is not openly used, it is important to see and to acknowledge that it has been replaced by the term "culture," the fear of cultural heterogeneity, and the wish to preserve cultural homogeneity — in particular by societies in the Global North.

The use of the "crisis" rhetoric in discussing the migration tragedy in Europe fits in seamlessly with the strong nationalistic sentiments in Europe, as it directly places an out-of-the-ordinary situation in a discourse that sees Europe as a continent under siege, a continent at war.[12] Within this discourse, refugees and other migrants are ambivalently, and sometimes interchangeably, portrayed as victims and dangerous invaders — posing a threat to "our" safety, economic well-being, cultural identity, language, and values.[13] Also, it is precisely through the idea of an invading outside that a distinguishable and coherent inside is reaffirmed. Thus, the nation is brought forth as if it were a subject — a subject that must dramatically stage control over its borders in order to remain safe, prosperous, and pure.[14]

Insofar as nationalism propagates a national identity and an ideal of a territorially bound community, it functions as an attempt to combine standardized notions of belonging with the desire to expel and exclude. It dictates terms of welcome into the state through the establishment of imaginary and physical borders. Significantly, both Carrington and Lueck et al. suggest that nationalist ideals thus support the enforcement of borders as they demarcate sovereign space.[15] Related to this, Sassen notes that to give up control of territorial borders is to relinquish one powerful instrument in the production of national cultures, as borders mitigate social pluralization and therefore a political challenge to the hegemony of state-sanctioned modes of national existence.[16] Nationalism supports the protection of territorially bound national communities and justifies the physical as well as psychological exclusion of those perceived as different.

In discussing the influence of globalization on the relationship between states, non-state actors, and the nature and meaning of territorial and temporal borders, the fact that globalization is serving both licit and illicit flows, including irregular migrants such as asylum seekers, refugees, "illegal" workers, and stateless people, is flagged as an important challenge for states. In pushing for stricter border control and migration measures, states tend to emphasize the illicit aspects of globalization in such a way that, according to Andreas,[17] "Illicit globalization has become the poster child for arguments that states are losing control," and therefore that measures need to be taken as soon as possible. As the concerns for and risks of illicit globalization resonate with the popular imagination and are confirmed daily in media stories and policy publications, it might seem hard to be critical about the measures that are taken in response to these concerns and risks. "Traffickers *are* routinely defying borders, mocking law enforcement and sometimes violently challenging the state. . . . It is clear that the same global transformations in communication, transportation and finance that aid legitimate business also aid illicit business."[18] Nevertheless, in the light of the far-reaching implications of nationalism that will be discussed in this paragraph, it is important to realize that the temptation to simply blame globalization for increased feelings of insecurity and unease is much too easy and convenient and that it can fuel calls to further escalate rather than reevaluate flawed policies and policing strategies. And, if there is anything we need in Europe right now when it comes to dealing with issues of migration and border management, it is a sense of distance and a critical assessment of the various (supra)national measures that have been put in place from 2015 onward. Rather, by looking at the outcomes of elections in various member states as well as on the EU level, it seems fair to say that the negative emotions and social fears of "the other" are still successfully exploited. European political populism is constantly growing and manifests itself mainly in the general rejection of the principle of equality of treatment and in the more and more overt hostility toward migrants and refugees.[19]

The objectives of border control in many countries, both inside and outside the EU, are increasingly inscribed into discourses about crime and punishment and into everyday practices of contemporary penal regimes. This illustrates how countries are trying to revitalize national identity and keep out the foreign and culturally different as well as fend off those who wish to take claim on the resources and protect welfare rights for citizens. The sorting between bona fide global citizens and the "crimmigrant others" by means of legal measures and practice is central to the growing body of scholarship on crimmigration—the merger of crime control and migration control.[20] The notion of borders is frequently discussed in the crimmigration literature. Scholars have pointed out that the merging field of crimmigration control functions as a clear gatekeeper in terms of membership and access. On the one hand, this has resulted in borders seen as "being everywhere"[21] as a wide range of nontraditional social control agents becoming pulled into the task of sorting between the deserving and undeserving migrant.[22] On the other hand, physical borders seem to become again viewed as major tools of exclusion "that can be strengthened and fostered to protect a community and a society against a phantasmic threat of otherness that tends to become flesh in the demonized and abject figure of a migrant or refugee."[23]

Free Movement for the Good, Not the Bad and the Ugly

The previous section presents a theoretical lens through which one could observe and analyze the situation in the European Union, in which member states — driven by the fears of globalization and the loss of the nation state, its safety, and its cultural homogeneity — increasingly tend to resort to restrictive hybrid measures of migration and crime control. This upsurge of nationalism and extreme right, anti-immigrant sentiments may seem at odds with the spirit of the European Union, a spirit of unity, solidarity, and harmony. Yet, looking at the extent to which migration law has been harmonized,[24] but also at the different ways in which member states have responded to the increased numbers of migrants entering the European Union since 2015, it seems safe to say that the continent is — rather unsuccessfully — trying to grapple with a new reality of increased mobility and the impossibility of controlling the expression of the freedom of movement of the human species on a global scale. The result is a mishmash of national measures, practices, and legal procedures that do not necessarily serve the broader purpose of the union. Also, when looking at the origins of the 1985 Schengen Agreement, it becomes clear that it is built on fears of crime and migration. Indeed, ironically, the establishment of an area without borders has effectively stimulated border control, since the notion that European integration via the opening of internal borders would lead to an increase in crime and more mobile criminal organized groups became the shared belief underpinning Schengen. In particular, third-country nationals and irregular migrants are increasingly seen as potential safety risks.[25] So, in response to the lifting of border checks between two Schengen countries — further referred to as intra-Schengen border checks — the signatory countries pushed for compensatory measures to counter the perceived risks of uncontrolled irregular migration and cross-border crime. Among these measures were the reinforcement of external border control as well as police and judicial cooperation, common visa and asylum policies, and the use of databases such as the Schengen Information System (SIS) or the European Dactylographic System (Eurodac) to keep track of intra-Schengen mobility.[26] The call for these compensatory measures seems to echo the more general sense of unease around immigration in Europe that can be traced back to the 1980s when immigration—and in particular asylum issues—started to become more and more politicized. It is from this moment onward that migration started to be identified as being one of the main factors weakening tradition and social homogeneity. These concerns were used to justify the need to protect the European community from the external enemy and build "Fortress Europe," a project that from the very start was aimed at keeping migrants—refugees especially—at bay by implementing legal and physical barriers to obstruct entry to Europe and facilitate deportation from its territory.[27]

A Closer Look at the Intra-Schengen Borders

Besides the aforementioned compensatory measures, the Schengen Border Code (SBC) sets out standards and procedures to be followed in controlling the movement of persons across internal Schengen borders. In other words, the SBC still acknowledges the necessity of mobility control between Schengen member states, which makes one wonder how "free" intra-Schengen movement was ever meant to be.

The most drastic way to "police" intra-Schengen cross-border mobility is by temporarily reinstating permanent border controls and thus breaching the principle of free movement. In Article 2(2) of the Schengen Convention and Articles 25–27 of the SBC, the Schengen acquis includes a procedure for the temporary reinstatement of internal border controls for the duration of thirty days in case of a serious threat to public policy or internal security. In order to assess whether there is indeed a serious threat, states must provide "all relevant data detailing the events that constitute a serious threat to its public policy." Articles 28–30 of the Schengen Borders Code provides for the possibility of a temporary reintroduction of control at internal borders "in exceptional circumstances where the overall functioning of the area without internal border control is put at risk." In this case, the internal borders can be closed for a period of up to six months—a period that may be prolonged, no more than three times, for a further period of up to six months if the exceptional circumstances persist. After September 2015, several Schengen countries—Germany, Austria, Slovenia, Hungary, Sweden, Norway, Denmark, and Belgium—reintroduced internal border controls because of an alleged "big influx of persons seeking international protection" or "unexpected migratory flow." All of the aforementioned countries (except Hungary) initially invoked the procedure under Article 27 of the SBC in 2015, which allows a member state to prevent foreseeable threats. In addition, two other member states—France and Malta—reintroduced internal border controls in line with the procedure under Article 28 of the SBC, which can be used to prevent a foreseeable "serious threat to public policy or internal security." Looking at the reasons that have been put forward by countries—and accepted by the European Council—to justify the reintroduction of border checks, it is clear that unexpected mass migration—described in whichever way—qualifies as an "exceptional circumstance" as referred to in Article 29 of the SBC.[28]

Although much of the international attention went to those countries that temporarily reinstated permanent border checks, it is important to realize that the SBC offers countries an alternative to this drastic measure. This alternative might be even more drastic in terms of monitoring mobility, as Article 23 of the SBC allows immigration and/or police checks to be carried out by national law enforcement agencies in border areas. By policing an area around the border, yet not performing checks at the physical border between two countries, these police or immigration checks are "Schengen proof." As argued more extensively elsewhere, this leaves a lot of room for discretion, not just for countries on how to interpret and implement Article 23 of the SBC, but potentially also for street-level officers that are tasked with performing these checks.[29] Article 23 of the SBC makes clear that lifting border controls does not mean giving up all forms of control and that there is a middle way between fully open and fully closed borders. Over the past couple of years, many member states have introduced these types of checks, mostly identity checks, some more structural than others. As a result of the use of these "scattered security checks," one could state that the Schengen Border Code allows for the border to be everywhere and nowhere at the same time. Whereas this could be seen as even more problematic in the light of the principle of free movement, in an attempt to avoid countries to too easily reintroduce internal border controls by closing their intra-Schengen borders, the European Commission issued a recommendation in May 2017 in which it "encourages Member States to better use their police powers and to give precedence to police checks before deciding on the temporary reintroduction of internal border controls." Almost all European member states are policing their intra-Schengen border zones in line with Article 23 of the SBC nowadays.[30] Yet, one of the countries that has used this form of intra-Schengen policing since the very beginning of the implementation of Schengen in 1994 is the Netherlands. This is not a surprise: As shown by Dekkers, van der Woude, and van der Leun in their discourse analysis of Dutch parliamentary debates, the opening of the internal borders had the Dutch parliament worried from the get-go.[31] As the last section of this chapter will illustrate, these worries seem to be indicative of the exclusive nature of the internationally renowned Dutch tolerance.

Rather than focusing on the legal and policy measures that have been taken in the realm of immigration, integration, and border control, the next paragraph will focus on the way in which these matters were addressed in political discourse. By, over the years, framing migration and integration along the lines of risk, danger, crime, and terrorism, political discourse has contributed to nationalist and nativist sentiments and the crimmigration laws and policies supporting these sentiments.[32] So, in other words, in order to understand the origins of crimmigration laws and policies, the *how* of immigration and border control, it is necessary to unravel its underlying drivers, the *why*.

Reflections from the Lower Countries

Several countries in Northern Europe have the international reputation of being leading examples on inclusion, equality, and tolerance. With strong welfare systems in place, countries such as Norway, Sweden, and the Netherlands are seen as countries that in general are taking good care of their citizens. Besides the aspect of social welfare, having relatively mild and humane penal climates also seems to be part of this grand narrative of hospitality and inclusion. Dutch criminal justice polices have long been characterized as "tolerant," lenient, and liberal: permissive toward many vices, foreigner-friendly and blessed with a mild penal climate, and perceived to be a beacon of moderation.[33] The centrality of tolerance and humanity in matters of criminal justice in the Netherlands seems to coincide with a strong emphasis on human rights. With Norway and Sweden, the Netherlands is often depicted as a so-called *gidsland* ("guiding country") and thus seen as the "conscience of the world" by setting moral standards in international relations and guiding other countries in the proper direction.[34] Whereas, compared to other countries, the Dutch prison and criminal justice system might appear to be more humane, when looking at the public and politic discourse around criminal justice, but in particular in relation to migration, the famous Dutch tolerance seems to be long gone. In the following section I will illustrate how, ever since the turn of the century, migration and crime, but also Europe's "open" borders, started to appear as key topics in the agendas of newly established and very successful populist—and nationalist—political parties in the Netherlands. In so doing, I do not intend to present a fully fledged and in-depth case study of the Netherlands, but rather will paint in fairly broad strokes the consistency in anti-immigrant sentiments and concerns about intra-Schengen mobility in Dutch political discourse.[35]

Post-War Political Correctness around Integration and Migration

In describing policymaking in the Netherlands, Lijphart highlights stability and calmness as some of the distinguishing features.[36] This, according to Lijphart and others,[37] could be explained by the coalition structure of Dutch governments that creates a necessity to bargaining and compromising. As Pakes notes, as a result, Dutch politics did not tend to be crisis driven, nor was it likely for radical shifts in policy to occur.[38] With politicians operating more or less "distant" from the electorate, partly because members of parliament only represent their party and not a town or region, and also because of traditional restraint in press reporting, they tended to be consensus-oriented and relatively shielded from criticism. As, again, Pakes observes, "Those circumstances in the post-war decades gave politicians a certain amount of breathing space that has served as a safeguard against radical populist changes in policy in the area of law and order."[39] Whereas this image of Dutch politics and policymaking might have been accurate in the 1970s and even in the 1980s, several authors have described how from the 1990s onward, crises in governance and in criminal justice and matters of immigration in particular became highly politicized.[40] The mid-1980s also seem to mark a shift in the political correctness around matters of integration and migration, matters that in the previous decades were not problematized at all. This dominant ideology of equality and antiracism in the 1960s and 1970s originated in the growing awareness of the atrocities of the Second World War, especially the Holocaust, the full weight of which was only acknowledged, after a considerable time lag, from the 1960s onward. Many people simply deemed it morally wrong to make migrants a plaything of political strife and societal discontent. Yet, although obviously a very important factor, it is not just the influence of the Second World War that stimulated this inclusive political climate in which any discussion along the lines of race or ethnicity was shunned. As Lucassen and Lucassen rightfully observe:[41]

> Added to this was indignation about apartheid in South Africa and—again belatedly—about the war crimes committed by European states in the postwar decolonization process by France in Algeria, the Netherlands in Indonesia, Belgium in the Congo. This created moral indignation and prompted international awareness, at least in the West, of the grave dangers of racism and discrimination and led to the wish to ban such barbaric behavior once and for all. In the Netherlands this "ethical revolution" was more intense than in other countries—with the exception of Germany, partially owing to the realization that the survival rate of Jews in the Netherlands had been much lower than that in neighboring countries.

From the mid-1980s onward, slowly but securely there is a shift in the debate on integration and migration. Both scholars and politicians are openly—yet very cautiously—critical about the integration policies at the time. It had become clear that the guest workers from Italy, Spain, Greece, and Yugoslavia, as well as from Morocco, Tunisia, and Turkey, that were brought to the Netherlands to temporarily help with the excess work as a result of the post-WWII booming economy would not return to their countries of origin at all. In fact, from the 1970s onward they used their worker rights to bring their families to the Netherlands, thereby quintupling the original number of guest workers. The lacking integration policies at the time are said to have caused the children of these first-generation guest workers to grow up torn between different cultures, which was said to contribute to delinquent behavior. With the political and public debate focusing on the criminal behavior of the "second generation" — the children of former Turkish and Moroccan guest workers — and to a lesser extent on lower-class colonial migrants from the Dutch Antilles, in the mid-1980s a turn is visible in which not only was crime placed within a law-and-order discourse over a penal welfarist/rehabilitation discourse, but in which migration — or the lack of integration — and crime were seemingly explicitly linked. Crime and migration are also no longer seen as concerns exclusively for professionals within the institutions of the criminal justice and immigration system, but rather as important matters of public concern that therefore needed to be addressed openly. In so doing, migration and crime are increasingly becoming politicized and placed within what can be called a cultural security complex. "Whereas crime in the previous wave was seen particularly to endanger personal security, in this discourse it is seen to threaten the cultural fabric of society. Over-offending minority groups are regarded to not only endanger victims, but also to violate the permissive and tolerant Dutch society as a whole. Their offending per se is part of that danger, but their perceived failure to adopt a Dutch tolerant way of life has increasingly become part of the same threat."[42] It was not until the mid-1990s and early 2000s that it became clear that anti-immigrant sentiments in the Netherlands were, for an important part, anti-Islam sentiments. With a large percentage of the former guest workers being Muslim, immigration and Islam were easily lumped together as one and the same.

A Multicultural Drama and the Rise of Anti-Islam Sentiments

When tracing the history of more openly and more populist anti-immigrant or, better said, anti-Islam debates in the Netherlands, a key moment seems to be the publication of an article in one of the country's national newspapers at the turn of the millennium with the title "A Multicultural Drama."[43] The article can be seen as a culmination of fears and concerns that were sparked by the publication of Rushdie's *The Satanic Verses* in 1988 and the outrage

Rushdie's work sparked among groups of Muslim immigrants in the Netherlands and other European countries. In calling for the banishment of Rushdie's work on religious grounds, immigration—and especially Islam—critics on both the political Left and Right were keen to point out that by protesting against Rushdie immigrants were showing their true "intolerant" faces.[44] Whereas the Left's discomfort with Islam can be found in the threat Islam was seen to be to the liberal and anti-religious values that were fought for and over for so long, the right-wing discourse on Islam was framed along the lines of assimilation and the impossibility of Muslim immigrants to integrate. Despite not openly wanting to admit this to each other, they saw their concerns seem to come together around the threat that the different cultural background of Muslims—as well as the process of European integration—would pose for "Dutch national identity."[45]

In "A Multicultural Drama," publicist Paul Scheffer expresses his grave concerns about the effectiveness of Dutch integration politics. According to Scheffer, by not taking integration seriously, the Dutch government has created dangerous disparities between different groups within society, with people from an ethnic minority background being clearly in a disadvantaged position. Scheffer warns that these disparities can lead to a deep polarization of Dutch society and thus to greater tensions between people from different ethnic backgrounds. Although debates over the alleged overrepresentation of ethnic minorities—in particular Moroccan youth and youth from the Dutch Antilles—in some of the petty crime statistics that date back to the mid-1980s, this article and the debates it spurred can be regarded as the keystone of the fierce criticism of political correctness, and the few remaining defenders of multiculturalism found themselves in the dock.[46] As various scholars have pointed out, this breeding ground, with increasingly openly voiced apprehensions about the Dutch multicultural society and concerns about immigration, integration, and crime, in particular in relation to the Muslim population, became only further fertilized by the unease that occurred globally in the aftermath of September 11, 2001.[47]

Whereas, as mentioned, crime was already creeping up the list of priorities in the 1990s, crime and security were the principal issues in the May 2002 general elections in the Netherlands. The key figure of those elections, Pim Fortuyn, was a minor public figure for years, but rose to prominence in 2001 as the leader of a political party called Leefbaar Nederland (Livable Netherlands), a party he left in February 2002 following a controversy concerning public statements on immigration. Soon after, he founded his own party, the List Pim Fortuyn. Fortuyn acquired notoriety for his fulminations against the Muslim faith and culture, which he called "backward."[48] He juxtaposed traditional Dutch values of tolerance to that of the Muslim culture and argued that Muslim immigration would jeopardize essential values of Dutch society. He called for a stop on immigration from Muslim countries and at one time called for a change in the Constitution to amend the ban on discrimination that is guaranteed in Article 1. His stance against Muslim culture, which for several years largely fell on deaf ears, met with increased public approval in the aftermath of September 11, 2001. Fortuyn primarily campaigned against the government in office—a coalition of labor (PvdA), liberals (VVD), and progressive democrats (D66)—that he accused of complacency, lack of ambition, and a failure to provide for governance in the areas of health and social care, education, and most particularly in the areas of immigration, integration, crime, and security, issues that Fortuyn regarded as inseparable. He criticized their "regentesque" attitude, which estranged the government from the population and served to perpetuate the position of those in power while enforcing policies that had gone stale. Fortuyn's persona and style of debating constituted a novelty in Dutch politics traditionally characterized by prudence, serenity, and compromise. With regard to immigration and asylum seekers, Fortuyn advocated a withdrawal from the Schengen Agreement and the reinstatement of border controls. He also advocated a reexamination of the UN charter on refugees from 1951. The aim was a reduction in the number and capacity of asylum seekers and a firmer policy on integration. Fortuyn, in passing, called Bush and Chirac's war on drugs idiotic and Bush's war on terrorism brainless.[49]

The anti-immigration and anti-Muslim feelings that Fortuyn had appealed to certainly did not disappear after his death in 2002, when he was shot dead by an animal rights activist in the country's first political assassination since the seventeenth century. Whereas Pakes pondered that it was perhaps "quite possible that List Pim Fortuyn will prove to be a flash in the pan," it has become clear that Fortuyn had introduced a new style of politics.[50] By openly voicing discontent on issues such as migration, immigrant crime, failed integration and immigration control policy, and multi-culturalism, Fortuyn had significantly—and permanently—moved the boundaries of political correctness, both on the left and right sides of the political field. It is safe to say that over the complete political spectrum a more populist strategy became visible, especially with regard to matters of crime and migration.

Anti-Europe, Oikophobia, and Anti-Establishment

After Fortuyn, politician Geert Wilders—often referred to as "the Dutch Trump"—would step into the "gap" of openly and viciously attacking the, in his eyes, left-wing naive cosmopolitan elite who had burdened the Netherlands with migration and integration politics and who were closing their eyes to the Islamization of Dutch society—the same so-called undemocratic elites who, by pleading their commitment to the European Union, were willingly sacrificing the nation's sovereignty and hence jeopardizing national security. Wilders founded his nativist party—the Party for Freedom (PVV)—in 2006, therewith breaking with the political party he had served for fourteen years, the neoliberal People's Party for Freedom and Democracy (VVD). Wilders has made political hay out of terrorism fears and Muslim integration in Europe, and his radical anti-Islam positions—he wants to shutter all mosques and ban the Quran—placed him far outside of the mainstream. Nevertheless, the PVV continued to gain electoral support over the years and even participated in the government coalition between 2010 and 2012.[51] With anti-immigrants only further fueled by a range of terrorist attacks in Belgium and France and populist, nationalist parties gaining political traction—and even winning elections—the PVV seemed bound to come out first during the 2017 national elections in the Netherlands. To the relief of many, the PVV failed to win the victory that some earlier polls had predicted. Still, it earned a record 1.4 million votes, coming in second with 20 of the 150 available seats, behind the neoliberal People's Party for Freedom and Democracy (VVD) of Prime Minister Mark Rutte, but far ahead of the social-democratic Labor Party, which was governing with the VVD and saw its support decimated. Wilders's loss was celebrated internationally, yet the critical observers were less optimistic: during the campaign for the elections it had become clear that most parties—on the Left and the Right side of the political spectrum—had shown a sharper and more exclusionary tone, adopting slightly softer versions of Wilders's positions, including Euroskepticism and thinly-veiled Islamophobia.

Apart from an overall shift "to the right," the 2017 elections also marked the rise of a new—and even more extreme—voice. After the onset of the European migration "crisis" in 2015, the Forum for Democracy (FvD) entered the Dutch political arena. FvD is a think tank that was reconfigured as a political party only six months before the March 2017 elections. Front man Thierry Baudet is said to be the Dutch face of the Alt-Right movement, and his flamboyancy and charismatic appeal are said to resemble that of the late Pim Fortuyn. In the 2017 national elections, FvD entered the Dutch parliament with two out of 150 seats—a modest but remarkable result for a party that didn't exist in the previous election.[52] Since then, Baudet has captivated the Dutch in the same way that Wilders benefited from the media's obsessive attention to his every move since he founded his party in 2006.

Like Wilders, Baudet is a so-called Euroskeptic. While immigration and multiculturalism have been "diluting" national values from below, he says, the sovereignty of the Dutch nation-state has been further undermined by its subservience to the European Union and other international bodies.[53] "Control over our lives is insidiously and increasingly taken away from us by devious acts of surrender that transfer our sovereignty to impersonal political megaprojects in which citizens have lost all forms of democratic control," he said at the party's congress in January of last year.[54] The FvD says it supports direct democracy and wants sharp tax cuts across the board. Whereas the PVV and FvD share the central themes of Euroskepticism and Islamophobia, the ideological grounding of the two parties seems to differ greatly. With the PVV lacking a clear ideological ground, the FvD likes to present itself as a party with an intellectual grounding in the notion of oikophobia, a term coined by Baudet used to express the notion of "fear of the home." Baudet defines this term, taken from the conservative British philosopher Roger Scruton, as a "pathological aversion" to the national home. Oikophobia, he insists, is destroying the nation-state through its concerted support for feminism, cultural Marxism, modern art, immigration, and the European Union, leaving the Netherlands open to the invasion of non-Western values.[55] It is in emphasizing the threat of non-Western values that PVV and FvD meet, as non-Western values are to be understood as Islamic values and traditions. Baudet's party has proposed a "Law in Defense of Dutch Values" that, among other things, would prohibit arranged marriages, demand that the Holocaust be taught in all schools, and ban any face-covering garments, including balaclavas and niqabs, from public spaces. Baudet has stated that cultural self-hatred has led to attempts to "homeopathically dilute the Dutch population with all the peoples of the world, so that the Dutch will cease to exist."[56] After a media firestorm, Baudet said he wasn't talking about race but about culture. And yet, this past February, when the party's second national deputy claimed that the connection between race and intelligence has "long been scientifically proven," Baudet remarked, "I don't see what the problem is."[57] Baudet's two-man party has, in recent polls, tied or even overtaken Wilders's PVV, drawing voters from among Wilders's supporters as well as the neoliberal People's Party for Freedom and Democracy (VVD), the party that came out first during the 2017 national elections. FvD has shown to be popular among new voters, but also with higher-educated people who always found Wilders too lowbrow or too coarse. FvD is diversifying the radical right by offering a more—seemingly—sophisticated tone of voice, while delivering apocalyptic messages about the loss of Dutch national identity and the dangers of Europeanization. During the provincial elections in March 2019, through which seats in the Dutch Senate are apportioned, the neophyte party won 13 of 75, taking votes from the

PVV as well as from the ruling People's Party for Freedom and Democracy. As a result, the current government coalition lost its majority in the Senate.

As mentioned before, FvD fits in with the broader trend of nationalism and nativism that seems to be sweeping through Europe, even in Europe's most progressive countries.[58] This leaves us to reflect on the question of what all this means for Europe and for those who are "on the move" for a multitude of reasons.

Concluding Reflection: Toward a Union of Nationalist Fortresses?

Despite the fact that the 2019 elections for the European Parliament did not lead to the expected overwhelming victory of nationalist, anti-immigrant, and Euroskeptic parties, on a *national level* these parties are still are gaining ground all over in the European Union member states.

The impasse with the Schengen Agreement, and more in general the impasse with regard to migration into the European Union, is pointing into a rather stressful and daunting European future: the German change of tone toward the Central and Eastern European states that refused to show real solidarity in the refugee crisis reflects a deeper divergence that will echo in the common European security agenda and migration policy. The difficulty of reaching an agreed plan with solutions for the so-called migration crisis, despite a series of several meetings in the European Council, reveals profound discrepancies in internalizing core European values and a different degree of attachment to the European project and idea. Europe needs to find its identity and unique voice, not many independent and divisive voices.[59] Europe's voice should include all citizens and newcomers alike, as being a refugee is respected through international and European standards. If Europe decides to move on in two speeds or, even worse, to compromise on Brexit, the whole castle will crumble; the long process of integration will disintegrate. Europe, in the context of many geopolitical and hybrid threats, cannot afford that, and each member state will remain weak on its own. However, to remain united, compromises must be agreed upon and implemented, and this has become increasingly difficult. The major challenge for Europe is to find the proper balance among all these conflicting needs: security, freedom, and unity.

What this chapter has shown is that it will be difficult to meet this challenge, as this would require countries actually wanting to balance these conflicting needs. While looking at the underpinnings of the European Project and the Schengen acquis in particular, it is clear that it is built upon false conceptions of unity and solidarity, with countries being concerned from the very beginning of Schengen about the security deficit that was created by the lifting of internal border controls. In a response to these concerns, countries were presented compensatory measures that focused on the fortification of the external borders of the European Union, but also with measures that enabled them to protect their national security and national identity and to filter between the "good," the "bad," and the "ugly" immigrant. In that sense, one could say that the foundation of the European Union has always left room for nationalism.

As the Dutch case study has illustrated, even in countries that are traditionally known to be lenient and tolerant, political and public discourse around matters of migration and crime has not only become intertwined but increasingly nationalized in the sense that the importance of controlling mobility into the country through (irregular) migration is framed as a threat to Dutch identity. Lucassen and Lucassen speak of "a seismic shock" hitting the Netherlands "that changed it almost overnight from an apparent leader in tolerance and multiculturalism into an anti-immigrant and anti-Muslim bulwark."[60] As van Houtum already rightly noted in 2010, the EU has failed in its agenda of "producing a zone of peace and comfort ruled by law and order" and is now an actor that engages in a "self-proclaimed war on illegal migrants and has created a border industry that constructs more, not less, 'illegality,' xenophobia and fear'"—an observation that only rings more true in the current day and age based on the way in which the European Union has dealt with the so-called migration crisis.[61]

Notes

This work is part of the five-year research project "Getting to the Core of Crimmigration" (project number 452-16-003), which is financed through the VIDI research scheme by the Netherlands Organisation for Scientific Research (NWO). The author is project coordinator and principal investigator.

1. M. A. H. van der Woude and P. van Berlo, "Crimmigration at the Internal Borders of Europe? Examining the Schengen Governance Package," *Utrecht Law Review* 11, no. 1 (2015): 61–79.

2. By November 2015 Germany, Austria, the Czech Republic, Slovakia, the Netherlands, Belgium, France, Italy, Spain, and Sweden had all begun to reintroduce temporary border controls; Nicholas de Genova, *The Borders of "Europe": Autonomy of Migration, Tactics of Bordering* (Durham, N.C.: Duke University Press, 2017), 11.

3. The phrase "The Good, Not the Bad and the Ugly" was taken from M. Kmak, "Between Citizen and Bogus Asylum Seeker: Management of Migration in the EU through the Technology of Morality," *Social Identities* 21, no. 4 (2015): 395–409, http://doi.org/10.1080/13504630.2015.1071703.

4. K. Witold, "Closing Gates to Refugees: The Causes and Effects of the 2015 'Migration Crisis' on Border Management in Hungary and Poland," *Yearbook of the Institute of East-Central Europe* 15, no. 3 (2017): 11–34.

5. J. Stumpf, "The Crimmigration Crisis: Immigrants, Crime and Sovereign Power," *American University Law Review* 56, no. 2 (2006): 367–419.

6. For the latest overview of temporarily reintroduced border controls, see https://ec.europa.eu/home-affairs/what-we-do/policies/borders-and-visas/schengen/reintroduction-border-control_en (last visited July 2019).

7. J. W. Kingdon, *Agendas, Alternatives and Public Policies* (New York: Longman, 1995).

8. S. Lehne, "The EU Remains Unprepared for the Next Migration Crisis" (2018), via https://carnegieeurope.eu/2018/04/03/eu-remains-unprepared-for-next-migration-crisis-pub-75965 (last visited on July 2019).

9. European Asylum Support Office, *Annual Report on the Situation of Asylum in the European Union 2017* (Luxembourg: European Asylum Support Office, 2017). The report can be obtained via https://www.easo.europa.eu/sites/default/files/Annual-Report-2017-Final.pdf.

10. K. Franko, M. van der Woude, and V. Barker, "Beacons of Tolerance Dimmed? Migration, Criminalization and Inhospitality in Welfare States," in *Contested Hospitalities in a Time of Migration: Religious and Secular Counterspaces in the Nordic Region*, ed. S. Bendixsen and T. Wyller (London: Routledge, 2019).

11. M. Ibrahim, "The Securitization of Migration: A Racial Discourse," *International Migration* 43, no. 5 (2005): 163–87.

12. N. Baerwaldt, "The European Refugee Crisis: Crisis for Whom?" (2018), available at https://www.law.ox.ac.uk/research-subject-groups/centre-criminology/centreborder-criminologies/blog/2018/03/european-refugee (accessed July 2019).

13. S. Dhaliwal and K. Forkert, "Deserving and Undeserving Migrants," *Soundings* 13, no. 61 (November 2015): 49–61; P. Gilroy, *There Ain't No Black in the Union Jack* (London: Hutchinson,1987). On the myth of black criminality, see P. Scraton, ed., *Law, Order and the Authoritarian State: Readings in Critical Criminology* (Milton Keynes: Open University Press, 1987), 118–32

14. S. Ahmed, "Affective Economies," *Social Text* 22, no. 2 (2004): 117–39, https://muse.jhu.edu/ (accessed July 6, 2019).

15. K. Carrington, "Law and Order on the Borders in the Neo-Colonial Antipodes," in *Borders, Mobility and Technologies of Control*, ed. S. Pickering and L. Weber (Berlin: Springer Verlag, 2006), 179–206; K. Lueck, C. Due, and M. Augoustinos, "Neoliberalism and Nationalism: Representations of Asylum Seekers in the Australian Mainstream News Media," *Discourse & Society* 26, no. 5 (2015): 608–29, https://doi.org/10.1177/0957926515581159.

16. S. Sassen, *Guests and Aliens* (New York: New Press, 1999).

17. P. Andreas, "Illicit Globalization: Myths, Misconceptions, and Historical

Lessons," in *Globalisation, Criminal Law & Criminal Justice*, ed. Valsamis Mitsilegas, Peter Alldridge, and Leonidas Cheliotis (Oxford: Hart, 2015), 45.

18. Andreas, "Illicit Globalization: Myths, Misconceptions, and Historical Lessons," 46.

19. A. Gliszczyńska-Grabias and W. Klaus, "'Governmental Xenophobia' and Crimmigration: European States' Policy and Practices towards 'the Other,'" *No-Foundations: An Interdisciplinary Journal of Law and Justice* 15 (2018): 74–100; G. Delanty, "Introduction: Perspectives on Crisis and Critique in Europe Today," *European Journal of Social Theory* 17, no. 3 (August 2014): 207–18, http://doi.org?10.1177/1368431014530922.

20. K. Aas, "Crimmigrant' Bodies and Bona Fide Travelers: Surveillance, Citizenship and Global Governance," *Theoretical Criminology* 15, no. 3 (2011): 331–46; Aas, "The Ordered and the Bordered Society: Migration Control, Citizenship, and the Northern Penal State," in *The Borders of Punishment: Migration, Citizenship and Social Exclusion*, ed. K. F. Aas and M. Bosworth (Oxford: Oxford University Press, 2013), 21–39; Vanessa Barker, "Global Mobility and Penal Order: Criminalizing Migration; A View from Europe," *Sociology Compass* 6, no. 2 (2012): 113–21; J. Stumpf, "The Crimmigration Crisis: Immigrants, Crime and Sovereign Power," *American University Law Review* 56, no. 2 (2006): 367–419; M. van der Woude and P. van Berlo, "Crimmigration at the Internal Borders of Europe? Examining the Schengen Governance Package," *Utrecht Law Review* 11, no. 1 (2015): 61–79.

21. E. Balibar, *Politics and the Other Scene* (London: Verso, 2002); P. Mutsaers, "An Ethnographic Study of the Policing of Internal Borders in the Netherlands: Synergies between Criminology and Anthropology," *British Journal of Criminology* 54, no. 5 (2014): 831–48.

22. V. Guiraudon and G. Lahav, "A Reappraisal of the State Sovereignty Debate: The Case of Migration Control," *Comparative Political Studies* 33, no. 2 (2000): 163–95; M. Ambrosini and J. P. van der Leun, "Introduction to the Special Issue," *Implementing Human Rights: Civil Society and Migration Policies, Journal of Immigrant and Refugee Studies* 13, no. 2 (2015): 103–15.

23. P. K. Rajaram and C. Grundy-Warr, *Borderscapes* (Minneapolis: University of Minnesota Press, 2007).

24. F. Trauner, "Asylum Policy: The EU's 'Crises' and the Looming Policy Regime Failure," *Journal of European Integration* 38, no. 3 (2016): 311–25, http://doi.org/10.1080/07036337.2016.1140756; M. Scipioni, "Failing Forward in EU Migration Policy? EU Integration after the 2015 Asylum and Migration Crisis," *Journal of European Public Policy* 25, no. 9 (2018): 1357–75, http://doi.org/10.1080/13501763.2017.1325920.

25. R. Cholewinski, "Criminalisation of Migration in EU Law and Policy," in *Whose Freedom, Security and Justice? EU Immigration and Asylum Law & Policy*, ed. A. Baldaccini, E. Guild, and H. Toner (Oxford: Hart, 2007), 301–36; G. Engbersen,

Joanne van der Leun, and J. de Boom, "The Fragmentation of Migration and Crime in the Netherlands," *Crime and Justice* 35 (2007), http://doi.org/10.1086/650189; A. De Giorgi, "Immigration Control, Post-Fordism, and Less Eligibility: A Materialist Critique of the Criminalization of Immigration across Europe," *Punishment & Society* 12, no. 2 (2010): 147–67.

26. D. Bigo, *Polices en réseaux: L'expérience européenne* (Paris: Presses de la Fondation Nationale des Sciences Politiques), 1996; Morten Jarlbaek Pedersen, "The Intimate Relationship between Security, Effectiveness, and Legitimacy: A New Look at the Schengen Compensatory Measures," *European Security* 24, no. 4 (2015): 541–59, http://doi.org/10.1080/09662839.2015.1014808.

27. J. Huysmans, *The Politics of Insecurity: Fear, Migration and Asylum in the EU*, New International Relations (London: Routledge, 2006).

28. Van der Woude and van Berlo, "Crimmigration at the Internal Borders of Europe? Examining the Schengen Governance Package," *Utrecht Law Review* 11, no. 1 (2015): 61–79.

29. Van der Woude and van der Leun, "Crimmigration Checks in the Internal Border Areas of the EU: Finding the Discretion That Matters," *European Journal of Criminology* 14, no. 1 (2017): 27–45; van der Woude and J. Brouwer, "Searching for "Illegal" Junk in the Trunk: Underlying Intentions of (Cr)Immigration Controls in Schengen's Internal Border Areas," *New Criminal Law Review* 20, no. 1 (2017): 157–79; S. Colombeau, "Policing the Internal Schengen Borders—Managing the Double Bind between Free Movement and Migration Control," *Policing and Society* 27, no. 5 (2017): 480–93.

30. "EMN Ad-Hoc Query on Intra-Schengen Border Monitoring and Border Control," Requested by NL EMN NCP on June 4, 2018, https://ec.europa.eu/home-affairs/sites/homeaffairs/files/2018.1303-intra-schengen_border_monitoring_and_border_control.pdf.

31. T. Dekkers, van der Woude, and van der Leun, "Exercising Discretion in Border Areas: On the Changing Social Surround and Decision Field of Internal Border Control in the Netherlands," *International Journal of Migration and Border Studies* 2, no. 4 (2016): 382–402.

32. For a discussion on crimmigration law in the Netherlands see M. A. H. van der Woude, J. P. van der Leun, & J. Nijland, "Crimmigration in the Netherlands," *Law and Social Inquiry* 39, no. 3 (2014): 560–79.

33. D. Downes, *Contrasts in Tolerance: Post-War Penal Policy in the Netherlands and England and Wales* (Oxford: Clarendon, 1988).

34. A.-S. Dahl, "Sweden: Once a Moral Superpower, Always a Moral Superpower?," *International Journal: Canada's Journal of Global Policy Analysis* 61 (2006): 895–908, http://doi.org/10.1177/002070200606100408; S. Engh, "The Conscience of the World?: Swedish and Norwegian Provision of Development Aid," *Itinerario* 33, no. 2 (2009): 65–82, http://doi.org/10.1017/S0165115300003107; Joost Herman, "The Dutch Drive for Humanitarianism: Inner Origins and Development

of the Gidsland Tradition and Its External Effects," *International Journal* 61, no. 4 (2006): 859–74, http://doi.org/10.2307/40204220.

35. For an in-depth case study of the Dutch discourse on integration and migration, see L. Lucassen and Jan Lucassen, "The Strange Death of Dutch Tolerance: The Timing and Nature of the Pessimist Turn in the Dutch Migration Debate," *Journal of Modern History* 87, no. 1 (March 2015): 72–101, https://doi.org/10.1086/681211.

36. A. Lijphart, *The Politics of Accommodation: Pluralism and Democracy in the Netherlands* (Berkeley: University of California Press, 1968).

37. R. B. Andeweg and G. A. Irwin, *Governance and Politics of the Netherlands* (Hampshire: Palgrave Macmillan, 2009); W. J. M. de Haan, *The Politics of Redress: Crime, Punishment and Penal Abolition* (London: Unwin Hyman, 1990).

38. F. Pakes, "The Politics of Discontent: The Emergence of a New Criminal Justice Discourse in the Netherlands," *Howard Journal of Criminal Justice* 43, no. 3 (2004): 284–98.

39. Ibid., 285.

40. Downes and René van Swaaningen, "The Road to Dystopia: Changes in the Penal Climate in the Netherlands," in *Crime and Justice in the Netherlands*, ed. M. Tonry and C. J. Bijleveld (Chicago: Chicago University Press 2007), 31–72.

41. Lucassen and Lucassen, "Strange Death of Dutch Tolerance," 80.

42. Pakes, "Politics of Discontent," 293.

43. P. Scheffer, "The Multicultural Drama," *NRC Handelsblad*, January 29, 2000.

44. Lucassen and Lucassen, "Strange Death of Dutch Tolerance," 72–101.

45. Scheffer, "Nederland als een open deur," *NRC Handelsblad*, January 7, 1995.

46. Lucassen and Lucassen, "Strange Death of Dutch Tolerance," 72–101.

47. I. Buruma, *Murder in Amsterdam: Liberal Europe, Islam and the Limits of Tolerance* (London: Penguin, 2006); van der Woude, "Dutch Counterterrorism: An Exceptional Body of Legislation or Just an Inevitable Product of the Culture of Control?," in *The State of Exception and Militant Democracy in a Time of Terror*, ed. A. Ellian and G. Molier, International Studies Library 36 (Dordrecht: Republic of Letters, 2012), 69–95.

48. P. Fortuyn, *De islamisering van onze cultuur: Nederlandse identiteit als fundament* (1997; repr. Rotterdam: Karakter/Speakers Academy, 2001); Fortuyn, *Puinhopen van acht jaar Paars* (Amsterdam: Uitgeverij Balans, 2002).

49. Fortuyn, *Puinhopen van acht jaar Paars.*

50. Pakes, "Politics of Discontent," 292.

51. A coalition government is a cabinet of a parliamentary government in which multiple political parties cooperate, reducing the dominance of any one party within that "coalition." The usual reason for this arrangement is that no party on its own can achieve a majority in the parliament. So, in this case, the PVV was one of

the political parties that formed the coalition. The other parties were the Party for Freedom and Democracy (VVD) and the Christian Democratic Appeal (CDA).

52. The Dutch electoral system is strictly representative, making it relatively easy for small parties to break through but almost impossible for any single party to win an absolute majority.

53. J. Chaffin, "Populists Seize the Moment as Dutch Fall Out of Love with EU," *Financial Times* (March 14, 2017), https://www.ft.com/content/4520bb4c-07e3-11e7-97d1-5e720a26771b (last visit October 2019).

54. S. Faber, "Is Dutch Bad Boy Thierry Baudet the New Face of the European Alt-Right?," *Nation*, April 2018, https://www.thenation.com/article/is-dutch-bad-boy-thierry-baudet-the-new-face-of-the-european-alt-right/ (last visit October 2019).

55. T. H. P. Baudet, "The Significance of Borders: Why Representative Government and the Rule of Law Require Nation States" (Ph.D. diss., Leiden University, 2012), https://openaccess.leidenuniv.nl/bitstream/handle/1887/19141/06.pdf?sequence=6.

56. Faber, "Is Dutch Bad Boy Thierry Baudet the New Face of the European Alt-Right?"

57. Ibid.

58. T. Kleinpaste, "The New Dutch Disease Is White Nationalism," *Foreign Policy* (2018), via: https://foreignpolicy.com/2018/03/20/the-new-dutch-disease-is-white-nationalism/ (last visited July 2019).

59. C. Postelnicescu, "Europe's New Identity: The Refugee Crisis and the Rise of Nationalism," *Europe's Journal of Psychology* 12, no. 2 (May 31, 2016): 203–9, doi:10.5964/ejop.v12i2.1191.

60. Lucassen and Lucassen, "Strange Death of Dutch Tolerance." 72.

61. H. van Houtum, "Human Blacklisting: The Global Apartheid of the EU's External Border Regime," *Environment and Planning D: Society and Space* 28, no. 6 (2010): 957, https://doi.org/10.1068/d1909.

11

Sorting Out Welfare

Crimmigration Practices and Abnormal Justice in Norway

Helene O. I. Gundhus

The Norwegian state devotes substantial resources to identifying, assessing, and deporting noncitizens. The country is, for example, one of the few deporting eighteen-year-old youths to Kabul. There has also been a remarkable rise in performance indicators related to forced returns, which have been strongly encouraged by both police management and politicians, and which involve several collaborators. In January 2018 the minister of Justice and Migration visited East African political leaders to facilitate agreements for forced returns. The numbers of those expelled from Norway because they have been convicted of an offense has increased almost exponentially over past decades. This practice relies heavily on targeting noncitizens for violations of criminal law and immigration law. In this chapter I will examine what this shows about the transformation of the border in a welfare state otherwise known for promoting an inclusive society and for limiting the use of penal power. This policy is particularly noticeable when it comes to young offenders. In Norway the age of criminal responsibility is fifteen, and there is a long tradition in criminal law of treating offenders under eighteen less severely than adults. The rights of children and young people in Norway are supported by the UN Convention on the Rights of the Child. The convention gives children under the age of eighteen, particularly unaccompanied refugee children, specific protections and rights. By looking at multiagency collaboration targeting young offenders, I will thus examine the different nodes making up the network of borders and border practices and the filters sorting out who belongs and who does not. Since Norwegian migration control is linked to changes in legal forms and practices, migration politics, and police strategies, it will be shown how different theoretical positions can be helpful in theorizing developments in this particular area.[1]

In contrast to crime policy toward nationals, official Norwegian asylum policy is claimed to be strict and fair, not relaxed and naïve. Immigration regulation concerns trump the welfare of nonnationals, especially in assessing compliance with the UN Convention on the Rights of the Child. As several observers have observed, asylum-seeking children have tested the limits of the principles in the UN Convention on the Rights of the Child.[2] The problem of treating children and young people humanely is seen as challenging because of immigration control and integration policies. Temporary resident status and a strong emphasis on deporting are seen as more effective and preventive and are designed to deter migrants from seeking asylum in Norway. For example, unaccompanied minor asylum seekers from Afghanistan only get temporary residence and must leave the country before their eighteenth birthday. The aim is to signal that Norway is strict about residence permits, and this approach seeks to prevent asylum seekers from coming to Norway. The temporary nature of minors' residence status has led to an increase in minors escaping from asylum centers and in the number of people helping those nearing their eighteenth birthday to leave the country.[3] The minister of Immigration and Integration has condemned those giving such assistance as immoral citizens, which has ratcheted up official rhetoric on this subject.

The Norwegian state thus devotes enormous resources to identifying and deporting noncitizens and has the highest deportation rate among European countries.[4] How is this possible in a country with high standards of human rights that is generally proud of being less punitive than other countries? The chapter draws on Franko's notion of the "crimmigrant other."[5] By the term "crimmigrant others" Franko points to the shift in the social perception of the immigrants: "They are no longer people in need of protection, or a potential source of labour; they have been turned into to rule-breakers and criminal offenders, or what can be termed "crimmigrant others."[6] In this chapter I look at the production of the "crimmigrant other" in a welfare state and the dilemmas, contradictions, and paradoxes involved in neglecting protection needs of vulnerable groups such as unaccompanied minors. It is the notion of the "crimmigrant other" that makes processes such as social exclusion of youth with temporary residence status and closing of borders a natural response. As Todd-Kvam argues in his recent analysis of penal populism in Norway, "Government representatives frame themselves as protecting individual security and prioritizing victims, whilst pursuing a bordered version of penal populism directed against non-citizens."[7] Because of the significance of the UN Convention on the Rights of the Child and the tradition of reintegrating young people and limiting the use of punishment, I will examine in particular crimmigration control of children and young people, highlighting the boundaries of the welfare state and the framing of "the other." My aim in using empirical data is to address in more detail the institutional logic of the agencies involved and the practices, norms, and ideas that make this possible. In so doing, the article charts the subtle ways in which the crime element in crimmigration becomes particularly important for enabling Norway to perceive itself as a country with a fair crime policy, although it is one featuring a markedly more exclusionary kind of justice for those labeled "foreigners."

I will first present broader moves toward crimmigration control in Norway, emphasizing the use of changes in legal strategies and practices. I will then point to weaknesses in ensuring the legally required duty of care to young people with uncertain residence status, for instance because of unclarified identity, which leads to the construction of crimmigrant young people. This is supported by the deployment of risk management as a prominent governmental strategy and reliance on high performance indicators on deportation figures. I will show how the lack of a child-sensitive approach helps merge crime and migration control and results in multiagency collaborations of a more coercive kind when young people without citizenship are being dealt with. It is the broad use of the concept of crime that makes this legitimate. I will conclude by exploring how the "crime" part of the term "crimmigration" makes it possible to treat nonnationals punitively and citizens inclusively while remaining a beacon of universal human rights and general social security.

Crimmigration Control in Norway

Norway and Sweden are known as humane and inclusionary welfare states. However, as Barker argues, welfare states are also Janus-faced.[8] For instance, Norway scores high on happiness and welfare, but is a world leader in deportation.[9] Several observers have pointed out that, within Norway, the border is everywhere, leading to increasing control of target groups.[10] As Jahnsen and Skilbrei argue, this policy also leads to a more punitive approach to migrant women involved prostitution in Norway, although such activity in itself is not criminalized.[11] The number of expulsions from Norway because of crimes committed has increased dramatically over the past decades. Those who have been ordered to leave the country because their asylum application has been rejected or their residence permit has expired can leave voluntarily or be forcibly returned by the police. There is also an increasing number of people who receive expulsion decisions because they have committed crimes, minor offenses, or misdemeanors such as shop-lifting, that under Norwegian law incur criminal justice sanctions, such as punishment and fines.[12] The expelled person must leave Norway either for a specified period or permanently. The sanction, then, is being expelled, expulsion being one of the penal sanctions available under the Execution of Sentences Act.[13] Although this is an administrative decision made by the Immigration Directorate, banishment is also a punitive sanction more broadly defined than in the strict definition of the penal sanctions in law.[14] The tools in use are designed to prevent crime and insecurity in the long term and to control unwanted mobility and maintain public order and security. The measures therefore have both actuarial and punitive aims. The Immigration Act, Section 108, third paragraph, letter e, which sets the penalty for anyone violating the entry ban after expulsion, was amended in January 2014, increasing the tariff to two years' imprisonment. Deportation orders, therefore, signal moral wrongdoing and are much more than a technical management tool.[15] They are seen as a better form of punishment, since they are more severe, with lower standards of proof, and also free up resources in the ordinary criminal justice system.

Success—Increased Numbers of Deportations

The number of forced returns has been determined by a remarkable rise in performance indicators, as set by the justice minister. This populist approach, convincingly analyzed by Todd-Kvam,[16] has been strongly supported by police management, immigration authorities, and the bureaucracy.[17] Increased organizational control over police discretionary practices has been used as a means to achieve this goal, while street-level police culture is regarded as an obstacle.[18] Efforts to professionalize the police have, therefore, in this sphere, a clear political objective. The approach relies heavily on targeting noncitizens for violations of criminal law and immigration law, using legal tools from both domains. In Norway, as elsewhere in Europe and the U.S.,[19] immigration law is therefore increasingly used in tandem with criminal law, both to fight crime and to control migration.[20] In Norway, the blurring of these two legal domains has been particularly noticeable because of the organizational integration of immigration police and ordinary police. The police are the main actor in migration control, there being no border agency.

The shift is a result of an increased political focus and of changes in European policy, domestic criminal justice systems, and, particularly, police leadership.[21] The police argument is that, through deportation, the police prevent crime from reoccurring, and the aims of both migration control and crime control include crime prevention. Moreover, as Todd-Kvam suggests, for the populist-right Progress Party, which took charge of the Ministry of Justice and Public Security in 2013, to "do populism" by focusing on "criminal foreigners" is easier than breaching the penal welfare consensus on citizens. Foreign wrongdoers are the main group that gets the label "criminal" in government discourse; citizens are "offenders."[22] This development, which in the literature has been known as the "crimmigration" process,[23] is related to intensified criminalization of immigration-related conduct, particularly illegal entry and reentry, together with the growing convergence of criminal law and administrative immigration enforcement and their support for each other. In addition to the crimmigration thesis, the notion of governing through migration control is helpful for understanding the changes in the policing of migrants in Norway.[24] It is striking how the risk management logic and deportation figures are interconnected in the governmental discourse.[25] The risk management logic is further strongly influenced by the New Public Management strategy, which sets out to achieve quantified goals.

Fear of the Foreign Criminal

What have been termed a bifurcation of penality[26] and bordered penal populism[27] are thus related to a risk-oriented and pre-emptive strategy. Police strategies are clearly aimed at neutralizing potentially harmful noncitizens as threats and security problems. This makes elements of the pre-crime thesis relevant for understanding why resources are put into the deportation of people with different residency status, including those judged to be over eighteen by the government.[28] The Police Security Service is also increasingly collaborating with the police and immigration directorate to target potential terrorist threats at an early stage.[29]

In Norway, state responses to migration have been driven by economic uncertainty and fear of "the other." The latter has been particularly significant since the refugee crisis of 2015. In Scandinavian countries, the fear has been strongly related to migration by such narratives as the notion of foreign abusers of social security and because of the fear of native citizens that they will lose their own welfare benefits, which is replacing the former fear of crime.[30] However, as Aas shows, a populist crime policy emerged in the 1980s, based on a distinction between law-abiding citizens and criminal outsiders.[31] In Europe, the criminology of the other has emerged from debates about immigrants and crime, especially now that crime statistics are going down, offenses like drug use have been decriminalized, and fear of crime in general is decreasing. It is the fear of the "foreign criminal" that is in the ascendant. As Barker argues,[32] in many Western countries and particularly in the Nordic ones, this points to how fear of crime is being replaced by concerns about the economy and immigration:

> Penal power at the border is routinely used to settle claims on access to material and symbolic values. It seeks to preserve these precious goods for those with the right set of attachments, identities, and citizenship.[33]

Like Todd-Kvam, Barker argues that popular attitudes tend to be more punitive toward nonmembers of a welfare state.[34] Debates in which migrants are seen as "the other" clearly include those on crime: they are "foreign criminals," while citizens are "offenders." As Ugelvik argues, the group has been given a radical otherness in Norway.[35] It is striking that public debate connects immigrants with crime, despite the fact that differences between Norwegians and immigrants are small, while those between different age groups, genders, and classes are much more significant. "They are not like us" is the usual argument in the debate on "immigrant crime," in Norway as elsewhere.

The combination of legal and political aspects and changes in the bureaucratic model toward New Public Management and risk management are making it relevant to draw on the crimmigration thesis, theories of governing through migration control, and the notion of a shift toward a pre-emptive state when seeking to understand how, why, and when changes are taking place.[36] As Huysmans has pointed out, the image of the criminal immigrant also plays a central role at the political level in the construction of a common European identity and of security strategies.[37] The difference in responses to foreigners and to citizens is particularly visible when it comes to managing youth crime, which I will turn to next.

Lack of Child-Sensitive Practice

There have been several research reports concluding that, in Norway, young people without a confirmed residence permit are discriminated against, and research on unaccompanied minors has pointed to several issues regarding protection of their rights and provision of adequate care arrangements.[38] This is particularly the case when it comes to unaccompanied minors between the ages of fifteen and eighteen. In contrast to what happens in Sweden, they are not cared for by the child protection services, as required by the UN Convention on the Rights of the Child, but by the state immigration services (UDI). Given Norway's high profile as a promoter of human rights in general and children's rights in particular, this fact indicates an ambivalent approach. Norway was the first country to appoint an ombudsman for children in 1981. The UN Convention on the Rights of the Child was ratified by Norway in 1991—it was one of the first countries in the world to do so. Although standards are high and cover all children, including those under eighteen without leave to remain in Norway, this is not followed up in practice. Norwegian policy on unaccompanied minors has been described as a gap between policy and practice.[39,40]

The challenges for unaccompanied minors in the asylum-seeking process are daunting. Despite the child-sensitive approach characterizing the UN

Convention on the Rights of the Child and the principle of "the child's best interests," they are subjected to countless tests and interviews and face a great deal of insecurity regarding their case during the asylum process. Caregivers work with young people who have been granted permanent residence alongside those waiting to be sent back to where they came from or to a third country.[41] Caregivers also have to carry out the controversial assessment of the child's age, which is crucial for children's rights to social support, and the outcome of asylum applications.[42] Age tests in Norway are particularly controversial, since so much weight is put on the result of medical age assessments, even though they are known to be inaccurate; excessive weight is also given to the subjective assessments carried out by the National Police Immigration Service to determine age.[43] In 2014, an assessment of the use of the medical test concluded that Norwegian practice violates UN guidelines:

> Norwegian age assessment practice does not comply with the Immigration Act and the UN's guidelines. More asylum seekers go through medical age assessment than what the Immigration Act and the UN guidelines provide for. Medical age assessments are given too much weight when age is determined. There is a lack of holistic age assessment examining both physical and psychosocial development. This is not in compliance with the UN guidelines, which is confirmed by UNICEF Norway.[44]

The doubt and suspicion alone are so stressful that investigation shows they harm children's mental health.[45] The medical age tests in use have also been criticized by Norwegian and international medical experts. The Medical Association refuses to use them because of the margin of error and lack of precision.[46] Although medical tests have long been seen as inaccurate by medical experts and have to be combined with psychosocial tests to be usable, as a rule the young person and his or her legal guardian are ignored, and it is decided that the young person is overage (eighteen or over).[47]

In 2015, the Immigration Act underwent a series of changes and limitations in response to the substantial increase in asylum seekers, including unaccompanied minors. Even if a young person has protection needs and refugee status, they are eventually internally displaced to a "safe place" in their country of origin after they turn eighteen:

> The assessment of what is a safe place should, according to the child-sensitive approach that is basic for the Immigration Act and to the Constitution Article 104, be carried out differently for children than for adults, with a special regard to the child's need for care and protection. Nevertheless, this particular change has led to an increase

> in limited permissions until 18 for applicants from Afghanistan, for then to be returned as internally displaced in Afghanistan.[48]

Trandum Detention Center was until recently the only detention center in Norway for irregular and undocumented migrants, rejected asylum seekers, and people who have been expelled but who refuse to return voluntarily, including children and young people. This was changed because the Norwegian Parliamentary ombudsman conducted several investigations in which the practice was criticized for being non–child-friendly, a view strongly supported by researchers and lawyers claiming that it is contrary to the human rights principle emphasizing a proportionate use of detention. Because of these criticisms, on December 30, 2017, it was decided this approach would be abandoned, and a new detention center for families is being built.

Taken as a whole, the restrictions that underpin immigration regulatory policies scarcely represent a child-sensitive approach. Some researchers have been particularly critical of temporary residence permits, blaming them for the increasing numbers of unaccompanied minors escaping from, for example, reception centers created for young people from fifteen to eighteen years old. Since the October 2017 ruling, which makes it possible to return people over eighteen to their country of origin, such as Afghanistan, where they can be internally displaced to a "safe place," voluntary groups have sprung up to help Afghan minors who are about to turn eighteen to escape from Norway. As mentioned, the minister of justice has officially condemned this voluntary activity as immoral. The Norwegian welfare system is based on universal provision and accords with the UN Convention on the Rights of the Child in covering all children under eighteen, regardless of their residency status. In principle, children who lack residence permits can also attend school, and education is free of charge. Asylum-seeking children are entitled to use the local health care system and child welfare services if necessary. However, there are several exceptions to this as regards both health and social services. Only asylum-seeking minors living in reception and care centers get economic support; those who disappear from care or reception centers lose social support. Despite the fact that the welfare model implies certain standards, values, and services, which help increase inclusion and integration and improve social engagement and health, research has concluded that:

> while children's asylum proceedings are underway, health institutions may be reluctant to start treatment for mental problems or chronic health problems due to the uncertain timeframe. Researchers have also found that local child welfare offices only follow up on grave problems involving UAM [unaccompanied minors](Lidén et al. 2013;

Paulsen et al. 2014; Tyldum et al. 2015). When UAMs are not granted a residence permit, they have access only to emergency health services.[49]

The issues faced by social workers are clear: it is difficult to treat young people humanely in the context of a strict migration policy.[50] The best interests of the child are trumped by immigration and asylum policies. As we will see, differences in the view taken of the young person's credibility are also found in the case of law-breaking and further challenge children's moral dignity.

Identification Problem

The inadequacy of the welfare state model in protecting the rights of children with uncertain residence status is particularly visible in approaches to juvenile offending. It is in such contexts that different trajectories of additional marginalization and social exclusion are particularly apparent. There are several reasons that a young migrant in need of support changes into a "criminal other," which will now be examined.

One reason can be that young people are not identified as such because of the environment they are frequenting. It is difficult to identify them among adults, and they may not be treated as children under eighteen because they have not been identified as minors.[51] They are perceived and managed as "crimmigrant others."[52] There is a lack of knowledge about identifying vulnerable young people and children in need of protection, particularly those involved in criminal networks.[53] It is also difficult for professionals to draw boundaries to do with human trafficking. This is reinforced by long lists of risk indicators that are not very helpful for recognizing victims of human trafficking. According to Tyldum et al., the risk indicator list developed for this work is too decontextualized to be of practical use.[54]

Among those with uncertain residence status, one particularly vulnerable group consists of those disappearing from ordinary reception centers. By leaving the municipality offering child and social welfare provision, they lose this support. From 2008 to 2015, 625 unaccompanied minors were reported missing. This is 1 percent of all applicants, and half of them disappeared from transit centers.[55] Since the creation of the stricter regime with temporary residence permits, there has been an increase in the number of those disappearing from both reception centers and care centers. According to Lidén, Gording-Stang and Eide, 143 UAMs disappeared in the first four months of 2017.[56] The new stricter approach has also caused further uncertainty and stress, which prevents integration, and mental health problems have increased.[57]

The difficulties of defining young people's need for protection have been analyzed from a crimmigration perspective by Gundhus and Egge.[58] Since then there have been several studies, mostly consisting of applied research, which look at specific aspects of unaccompanied minors' life situation in Norway.[59] They all confirm the difficulty of identifying vulnerable young people, particularly those in the grey zone, where they are forced into burglary, drug sales, or prostitution and are therefore victims of human trafficking. This is aggravated by how the credibility of asylum applications is assessed, given the aforementioned weaknesses of medical age assessment (which will be further explored later), and the difficulty of identifying young people when they are hanging around on street corners with adults in environments where drugs are sold.

The concern has been that young people disappearing from reception centers end up as victims of human trafficking.[60] The outreach youth workers in Oslo try their best to follow up young people they encounter and have brought to light the grey zone they live in as regards being a perpetrator selling drugs or being a victim of human trafficking.[61] This is a particular issue in the case of minor boys who are victims of forced labor.[62]

Belonging as Marker

The inability to protect young people without permanent residency permits who are involved in crime is exacerbated by the difference in the treatment given them by various agencies once they are identified as potential criminals. Traditionally, in Norway children are treated very leniently when convicted of crime. The age of criminal responsibility is fifteen, and it has been common practice for many years that those under eighteen are not given prison sentences. Instead, use is made of alternative options, such as community sentences, suspended sentences, follow-up teams, and, since 2014, youth follow-up and youth punishment for the most serious crimes.[63] These responses are designed to build upon the idea of restorative justice and require consent. In cases involving people under the age of twenty-three, inclusionary multiagency collaboration is supposed to be mobilized. Over the last twenty years, analyses of policy documents and discussion of crime prevention have focused on collaboration and partnership between different welfare services, such as schools, the child welfare services, and health and social services, with the aim of making early, knowledge-based intervention.[64]

In many municipalities in Norway (200 out of 422), crime prevention work is organized as a collaboration among various agencies, voluntary organizations, and the police; this is known as the Coordination of Local Crime Prevention Measures (SLT). The idea is that juvenile offending is best prevented in the community by multiagency partnerships consisting of the police, agencies such as schools and child welfare, leisure, cultural, and health facilities, and volunteers. The aim is to create interprofessional collaboration, led by an SLT coordinator. Young offenders who consent to "youth follow-up" or, for more serious crime "youth punishment," and who are residents of Norway and belong to a municipality are supposed to be supervised by interdisciplinary teams led by employees of the Office of Children, Youth, and Family Affairs and the correctional service. The cooperating bodies are connected with education or give support in finding work experience. The measures are adapted to the individual and involve close monitoring of the support system and control apparatus, with the aim of motivating and including young people who have dropped out of ordinary education and working life. For example, interventions such as mentoring schemes and the supervision of young prolific offenders are designed to bring about change and motivation and provide new opportunities.

The rate of success regarding social prevention is seen to depend on the individual's opportunities to be socially included. The essence of social prevention—including social *crime* prevention—is the assumption that society has a certain responsibility to facilitate integration, reconciliation, and participation. The main objective is to avoid social exclusion and marginalization by increasing inclusion through relationship building and community mobilization. For instance, the police and the correctional service do not have to be involved in less serious cases where youth supervision is used.[65]

These measures are all part of a preventive strategy that emphasizes inclusion. They follow a tradition based on the belief that crime prevention strategies have a clear impact on social prevention. Important social institutions such as education, health, and culture, together with general welfare and the welfare system, explicitly set out to level out differences and to protect those who are at risk of exclusion from ordinary social life by strengthening ties to social groups. The aim has been to assist young people who are identified as needing help, even if they have not asked for it, and also to help those actively avoiding assistance.[66] The police role ideally involves soft policing strategies, and the supervision teams and youth punishment depend on the youth consenting to alternative conflict solutions.

Control in the Grey Zone

If young offenders arrested in Oslo, Norway's capital, have no formal connection to the city, the police dispense an exclusionary and rough justice.[67]

The target group might be young people with home addresses outside Oslo or individuals without any address in Norway. Reports from the SLT multiagency collaboration in Oslo, entitled Salto, emphasize that crime prevention targeting such groups cannot employ the same methods as other SLT work because the young people do not have a network that can be made use of. Other measures and procedures therefore have to be developed. According to those involved, this has been challenging, and interviews with them reveal that they experience powerlessness.[68] The figures for juvenile delinquency in Norway show there is a concentration of young people without formal attachment to Oslo who commit offenses in the city center. However, juvenile delinquency statistics and reports from the outreach team working with these groups indicate there was a lower proportion of unaccompanied minors and visiting EEA citizens in the downtown of Oslo in 2015 than in previous annual statistics.[69] In view of the fact that increasing numbers of young people have been disappearing from asylum reception centers since 2015, researchers have suggested that more youngsters may be hiding from the authorities.[70] This state of affairs is reinforced by the barriers to acknowledging young people's vulnerabilities. As has been seen, there are difficulties in identifying young people in adult environments; the unreliability of age assessments makes it hard to recognize them; there are less satisfactory living conditions and care arrangements for children aged fifteen to eighteen; and there is increased use of limited residency permits for unaccompanied minors, meaning that the youth are being deported when they turn eighteen; previously, they had received permanent residency. All of these factors result in more children escaping before they reach eighteen.

Lack of belonging, a high degree of mobility, unknown identity, uncertainty about age, and uncertain residence status all contribute to the fact that crime prevention efforts directed at the group are different from those targeting young people with addresses in Oslo. The exclusionary cooperation that takes place goes beyond more inclusive multiagency collaboration and is aimed at milieus frequented by both adults and minors, targeting the crimmigrant other. These practices differ from the socially inclusionary multiagency collaboration targeting young people belonging to the area. In the inclusionary logic the police role is to identify risks and vulnerabilities, but the agencies are less involved in designing and accomplishing the efforts. Measures are carried out by actors practicing a more inclusive and social logic than the police. As we will see, this makes the belonging aspects of the governing through migration control thesis pertinent to understanding why this is happening.[71]

Criminalization of Identity

The cooperative effort involves the Oslo Police District, the Police Immigration Unit (PU), and the Immigration Directorate (UDI), which have been running a Joint Effort Against Open Drugs Scene, which specifically targets noncitizens. Since 2009, the aim of the Joint Effort on Open Drugs has been to develop targeted measures to limit overt drug sales in Oslo, thus making it difficult to recruit young people to the business. Geographically, the project has been limited to the area around the Oslo train station and the lower part of Akerselva. Operations have been directed at specific areas where there is a concentration of drug dealers of foreign nationality, and foreign dealers at street level have been expelled as quickly as possible. The practice has been portrayed as a success since 2010, and, as early as 2011, there had been 531 arrests. Although the arrests occurred in conjunction with drug-related activities, the most common sanction given was a deportation order, while criminal charges were brought against only nine individuals.[72]

Beyond this, the SLT/Salto coordinator in the city center has regular meetings with the UDI, the Oslo police, and the PU, as well as those engaged in social preventive efforts aimed at minors, such as child welfare workers, child welfare consultants, and outreach groups. Various issues concerning the target group, "young persons without a permanent connection to Oslo/Norway," are discussed, though few inclusive measures are in evidence. The view has been expressed, for example, that the local child welfare service does not follow up reported concerns.[73]

The aim of the crime prevention initiatives targeting noncitizens is not to change people, but to make their life situation worse. The action taken is based on an exclusive understanding of crime and is quite different from the inclusive approach to prevention described earlier. While the inclusive approach emphasizes social reasons explaining crime and its causes, exclusionary strategies increasingly invoke social disorder and security threats. A natural consequence of such a view is that social disorder must be met with control measures by the police to prevent it from developing into more serious crime.

Abnormal Justice

This shift from inclusion to exclusion means that the police's collaborative routines in these cases differ from established crime prevention practices. We also see that the distinction between short-term crime prevention and early intervention prevention is disappearing. Faced with these young people drifting into crime, police control takes precedence over interdisciplinary measures aimed at changing their life situations.

Immigration legislation gives the police wide powers to control those assumed to be foreigners. According to immigration law, police should have intelligence related to time, place, and situation to carry out an identity check, but how such intelligence is documented is not laid down in any further rules.[74] Increased territorial control is also seen as desirable both by politicians and by police managers in order to discover people's true identity and deport migrants with no residence permit, and a number of incentives have been put in place to encourage this. The argument is that intelligence, mapping, and analysis will provide a better overview of organized crime and help create suspicion profiles, which can also be used in street identity verification.[75]

The Oslo police district ensures that foreigners engaged in drug trafficking are arrested, imprisoned, and tried and not released before their sentence is pronounced. The Police Immigration Unit prioritizes this group for registration, identification, clearance, and expatriation and keeps the person in police custody until his or her departure, working closely with police investigators. The strategy assumes that the rapid processing of criminal cases, together with effective use of the means of expulsion provided by immigration legislation, will prevent and reduce crime.[76] Crime prevention should be achieved by "possible future offenders being asked to leave Norway."[77] The Norwegian Police Immigration Service cannot forcibly return a person to his or her country of origin without verifying and documenting the person's identity. To do so they use coercive measures available under immigration law. These include arrest and remand in custody, the seizure and search of a foreign citizen's personal belongings or dwelling, and traditional police methods such as surveillance and the tracking of his or her network. In criminal cases, particularly in larger cities, Norwegian police management is increasingly reliant on the use of coercive investigative powers given by immigration law.

In interviews, specialists spoke of "changing track" between criminal and immigration law and the advantages of being able to choose between these options as they wished, depending on their objectives and the resources available. This means that, whether a person is arrested for an offense involving drugs, pickpocketing, or burglary, the most common response is a deportation order.[78] A deportation order may then function as a substitute for punishment. The rationale behind such decisions is often based on *capacity concerns*, particularly for offenses unlikely to attract long custodial sentences. We see here how actuarial logic overlaps with the crimmigration perspective in the use of laws.

In other cases, criminal law and immigration law are mostly applied in a cumulative fashion, with deportation being added to (increasingly severe) custodial sentences. The *crime label* is important in carrying out deportation. The target group here is often EEA citizens, who are better protected against deportation than third-country nationals, who lose temporary residence permits for minor offenses such as petty theft, which normally incur writs or fines, not prison sentences. These policing strategies have had a profound impact on the Norwegian criminal justice system, where 33 percent of all prisoners and up to 56 percent of pre-trial detainees are now foreign citizens.[79]

If we look at the statistics from the Norwegian Directorate of Immigration, EU/EEA nationals are increasingly being deported from Norway with the crime label on their record. They are either sentenced for a major or minor offense or fined by the police for a low-level misdemeanor.[80] Consequently, although non-EU/EEA citizens — third-country nationals — are deported because they lack residency status in Norway, many poor EU/EEA citizens are also deported, losing their temporary residency permits as a punishment for minor offenses. As Franko and Mohn argue, "For a similar drug offense, a Nigerian man may be expelled, a Lithuanian citizen alike punished and expelled while a Norwegian citizen is only punished or expelled from the place."[81]

The convergence of border control and criminal law is therefore producing new forms of policing and criminal justice that are deeply "abnormal" in the sense that they radically depart from the policing and justice afforded to "domestic" citizens.[82] The strategies are clearly targeted and preventive, with suspicion directed exclusively at noncitizens as security threats, which points to pre-crime logic. Justice departs from the normal script, with deportation being the eventual outcome, and this helps to achieve the objective of deporting ever more foreign nationals who commit crime in Norway. Although this is not defined as punishment under the criminal code, it is made clear by managers, police officers, and politicians alike that the intention is to hand out harsher punishment. The discourse, however, invokes efficiency, improved security, pragmatism, and managerialism, not punitiveness.

Effective Capacity of the System

Combining the Immigration Act with the Criminal Code is promoted as being more convenient and easier to implement than prosecution. As was mentioned at the beginning of the chapter, this combination of tools is an outcome of the institutional set-up and division of labor between the police and immigration authorities in Norway, where immigration police are integrated into the police organization. It is resorted to because it is more effective and frees up police capacity by requiring less investigation. When interviewed, immigration police service specialists said that using the Immigration Act "reduces the burden of investigation," "increases capacity," "lowers the standard of proof," "is more serious," and "is more effective."

According to Sklansky, what he terms "ad hoc instrumentalism" is widespread; it uses legal rules and procedures as tools to achieve targets most effectively, including ones beyond the field of migration control.[83] This points to a nonsystematic, random, and unpredictable application of the law, involving extensive use of discretion on the legislation to be applied.[84] The danger is that the prosecution process becomes personal and arbitrary—you first identify the individual to target, in this case those without Norwegian citizenship, and then seek to identify which law, if any, is being contravened by the suspect.[85] The complexity of these practices and concomitant lack of accountability have therefore been described as challenges to the rule of law, in Norway and elsewhere.[86]

A different type of issue for the exclusionary approach is that of its efficiency in practice. Even if the expulsion case is settled quickly, this will not necessarily mean more people are deported. It has been found difficult to determine the identity of many of those arrested, particularly when they are third-country nationals, which is also why it is hard to tell how old they are. Indeed, the police consider lack of identification capacity to be a barrier to efficient deportation practice, except for Dublin cases.[87]

Exclusionary Inclusion of "the Other"

Asylum-seeking minors who have fled from asylum centers become public-order problems to be managed, sanctioned, and preferably deported rather than being seen as victims of poor social integration. The inaccuracy of age assessment facilitates exclusionary practice[88] and contributes to building up the production of the crimmigrant other.[89] However, when migrants are perceived to be a security problem, suspicion profiles increase the barrier to identifying the person's needs for protection. They are approached as threats carrying the future risk of uncertainty and thus making the enemy-penology outlined by Kraska in Weber and McCulloch an appropriate option.[90] Particularly since 2014, researchers and the Outreach group in Oslo have identified an increasing number of minors they define as victims of human trafficking in the drug business.[91] They have also expressed concern over the fact that children are treated as criminals rather than persons needing protection—and that they are not covered by the Children's Convention.[92]

This practice of selective suspicion regarding pre-crime means people get a dual identity of "criminal" and "migrant" combined; as mentioned previously, this is famously described as "the crimmigrant" by Aas.[93] Since only citizenship provides complete protection against expulsion, stricter practice in this area could also extend to people with strong ties and long residence in Norway who are not Norwegian citizens.

When there are political directives to streamline the process of forced return and increase the rate of expulsion and deportation, it becomes harder for the agencies involved to argue professionally for cooperation on inclusive crime prevention initiatives for "the stranger" and "the dangerous," regardless of age. "Foreign" and "dangerous" are indeed the adjectives that are increasingly applied to those produced as the "crimmigrant other,"[94] in Norway, as elsewhere. The links made among crime, security, and migrants have become stronger in the last decade, and they also figure in public debate and everyday talk. Formerly in Scandinavia and elsewhere in the Global North, there was an understanding that refugees were people in need of protection — asylum — but in the last two decades immigration and refugee policies have been increasingly described in terms of security, threats, and risks.[95] As mentioned, migration is increasingly framed as a security issue within the public debate,[96] and immigration to Europe has been presented as a threat in cultural, economic, and social terms.[97]

Welfare-Like?

The distinction I have described between inclusive and exclusionary strategies breaks with established welfare state principles: it is a process recently termed "welfare penalism" by Barker.[98] In a welfare state context, exclusionary means can also have an inclusive end. This applies not only to prevention, but also to repressive sanctions such as prison, which has inclusion as an overall aim.[99] "Young strangers" defined as belonging to "crimmigrant others," however, are categorized as merely excludable, at least in the long term.[100] Since many are in the country for a long time, their life situation involves exclusive inclusion — they are inside and outside at the same time.[101] Their plight is marked by a lack of welfare services and safety and their life situation with liminality.

As previously mentioned, through international conventions, Norway has committed to giving all children and adolescents under the age of eighteen living in Norway the same access to basic welfare benefits, regardless of origin, residence status, or other considerations. The UN Convention on the Rights of the Child, via the Human Rights Act, is incorporated into Norwegian law and takes precedence over any conflicting legislation. The Children's Convention contains a prohibition of discrimination, and the Children's Committee has interpreted the convention to mean that children without legal residence should normally have the same access to welfare services as other children. In Norway, this means entitlement to education (the right to elementary education and secondary education), child welfare, and social and health care, even if they do not have legal residence.[102]

The principle of equality is therefore not fulfilled as regards prevention or protection from vulnerabilities related to crime. The temporariness of their stay, uncertain age, and involvement in a criminal environment further weaken the view of them as young people with rights to special protection. Welfare services such as inclusive crime prevention involve measures that work for change by providing qualifications and building a sense of empowerment; but there are no such services for children and young people with temporary or nonexistent residence permits. Both the Children's Convention and European Convention on Human Rights indicate that inclusive approaches should be followed with children and adolescents. Just giving young people "a helping hand" on the road will in any case be more in line with the international conventions. Qualifications are something they can always carry with them and can be considered as harm- and trauma-reducing measures. They may also make young people less vulnerable to hazardous environments.

Control of Unwanted Mobility

Return-motivating measures bring reductions in social welfare benefits. Along with immigration control, this helps to strengthen the role of the police as a controller. When marginalized people with little affiliation to the community commit criminal offenses and misdemeanors, their life circumstances become a powerful tool for control.[103] When they are labeled "criminal aliens"/crimmigrants and this leads to expulsion, a logical consequence is that the police devote a lot of resources to exclusionary measures such as expulsion, crackdowns, and zero tolerance, even for the sale of small quantities of drugs.

When the symbolic dimension of the criminal justice system is directed particularly at foreigners, backed up by the moral weight of censure and sanction, their violations are seen as particularly "criminal." In that way it "divides the deserving from the wrongdoer," and only Norwegian insiders are treated as young people. The problem is that the police cannot tell just by appearance who are citizens and who are noncitizens. As specified in law, they need additional information about place, time, and situation. Although gathering such intelligence is supposed to avoid a general control of foreign-looking people, young people report that they are experiencing being seen and approached as threats by the police, particularly because of the increase in immigration checks.[104]

Officially it is claimed that controlling unwanted mobility by deportation helps manage, prevent, and control crime and is not punishment. However, the use of the criminal law toolbox also signals wrongdoing. Sanctions and censure involve harms and deprivations that lead to the criminalization of identity. It signals censure for suspected wrongdoing that might lead to punishment, such as detention, and may mean that the domestic police are tasked with border control and identity checks in the streets or expelling noncitizens on public order grounds. All these practices reveal the penal elements involved in border control.[105] The emphasis on the penal aspects makes it easier to make unwanted mobility into a crime and order problem by reinforcing the crime aspects of migration. Migration is not only regarded as a threat to social security because it signals crime and is managed as crime, but is also experienced as a more existential threat to our own well-being. Moreover, as Barker argues, it has less meaning if the reactions are, officially or not, defined as punishment. The merging of crime and migration into hybrid processes does the job.[106]

This analysis continues an established tradition within policing studies that has directed attention to how police suspicion and action develop at the local level and are embodied in local stop-and-search practices. In their seminal collection, Weber and Bowling uncover "a range of targets for stop and search practices, defined by race, religion, ethnicity and legal status, each able to be linked to specific local histories and perceptions of threat and belonging."[107] In her analysis of the policing of noncitizens in Australia, Weber outlines how migration control works in local contexts, such as shop doorways in inner-city streets, stores and warehouses, building sites, and other micro-circuits of control.[108] In such cases, where noncitizens are being targeted for social exclusion, it is possible to ask whether security rights are for all residents.[109]

As we have seen in the empirical examples from the city of Oslo, the convergence of border control and criminal law is producing forms of policing and criminal justice that are deeply "abnormal" in the sense that they are radically different from the forms of policing and justice afforded to citizens.[110] The police gaze, in these cases, is clearly targeted, directing suspicion exclusively at noncitizens; the dispensing of justice departs from the normal script, with deportation as the ultimate outcome. The framing of the "crimmigrant" can therefore explain the increase in the criminalization of migrants in public spaces in Norway. The rights of minors to care, health education, and education can easily be overshadowed by their presence in environments involving substance abuse and their categorization as immigrants without legal stay.[111] The political and symbolic attitudes that help to criminalize migrants also have an influence at the relational level and increase the vulnerability of young migrants.

Crimmigrant Youth

In this chapter I have argued that inclusive measures are becoming less important when "young strangers" have an unclear civil rights status and are perceived as nonmembers and belonging to the group of "the crimmigrant other."[112] This becomes particularly visible when we look at the situation of asylum seekers; integration-related measures usually have to derogate from regulation (deterrent) and return-related schemes.[113] In addition, we see that the convergence of crime and migration control is the expression of a new way of exercising social exclusion. Social control is thus different for members and nonmembers. Aspects of the global society, such as mobility, floating identities, and uncertain age because of lack of documentation, have consequences for help and control. A key aspect of globalization is that borders become tools for exclusion: they separate a homogeneous inside from a chaotic outside.[114] Not only administrative measures, but also access to welfare benefits become tools to control unwanted migration. Globalization also contributes to the expansion of the "social community" of children and young people beyond the national border, which affects the nation-state's responsibility for welfare services. The young "crimmigrant other" falls outside the responsibility of the welfare state and is not framed as belonging to the welfare state community.

Despite their constitutional rights, this group of young people find that social-preventive interventions are not implemented for them, and they stand outside the basic welfare state goal of "inclusive" inclusion. Internal border control can reinforce the perception of the "stranger" as dangerous and further legitimize a pre-crime approach to selected target groups. The question to be asked is whether rights, including the right to security, can only be granted to those who have a state that might protect them. The idea of security for all, in practice, can become unsafety for some.[115] Moreover, the considerable body of recent scholarship previously mentioned has documented the strength of exclusionary sentiments in Scandinavian societies that are directed particularly against nonmembers.[116] As Bosworth, Franko, and Pickering convincingly argue, both punishment and migration control rely on coercive measures, which vary according to membership:

> Central elements and characteristics of penal power including rights, institutional setting, reintegration and punitive sentiments vary by citizenship, adding and mixing with other, more familiar vectors of identity like class, ethnicity and gender.[117]

The police meet different expectations about their choices of strategy and method, depending on the target group's status. The collaborative networks the police participate in vary according to whether young people are defined as excludable or includable. Children and adolescents with temporary residency are excluded from the formal and informal social networks on which inclusionary measures are based. Policies to defend the national state against "dangers from abroad," so-called domopolitics,[118] also lead to children and young people with unclear residence status being treated largely as a security risk, despite the fact that they are covered by the Convention on the Rights of the Child, of which Norway is a prominent supporter.

It could be argued that inclusive strategies should be followed, even though the policy is not to give permanent residence to unaccompanied minors. There is good reason to think that room for maneuver is being ignored. Indeed, not even the specialist health service is available to this group. One of the UN Children's Committee's criticisms of Norway is that unaccompanied asylum-seeking minors do not receive adequate support from the child welfare services. In the current arrangement, child welfare services only have responsibility for unaccompanied minors under fifteen, which means that older children do not get the same assistance and protection. Children who have been in Norway for many years can be expelled even if they have strong ties to the country. Another criticism is that it takes a long time for authorities to decide whether someone can stay in Norway and that several unaccompanied minors have disappeared from asylum reception centers without enough being done to find out what has happened to them,[119] a criticism that is repeated by Aasen et al.[120]

When policing aimed at crime prevention carried out at street level involves a strategy of zero tolerance of deviant behavior and of crackdowns, this has unintended consequences for young people on the margins of these environments. One possible result is increased distrust between the police and the immigrant population. The dividing line between those defined as insiders and those considered outsiders is closely linked to nation building and how crime and penal welfarism are understood. If the prevention strategies used are not integrated into democratic social structures (education, employment, and housing), and if they are nurtured by an increasingly intolerant culture, the unintended consequences could damage such values as inclusiveness and reconciliation and strengthen social exclusion. The result for vulnerable young people may be an experience of being inside and outside at the same time.

Conclusion

Using examples from efforts to prevent juvenile offending, the objective has been to provide an insight into the complex and often volatile relationship between human rights, crime fighting, and security that marks migration control in a welfare state. Measures to foster integration give way to control (deterrence) and return-related schemes. The criminalizing discourse is fueled by security objectives that justify exclusionary policies and ultimately lead to banishment.[121] The convergence of crime and migration control thus represents a certain way of exercising social exclusion. Although it is not made explicit, such a change in logic can explain the difference in the treatment of nonnational juveniles who commit crimes and of those who are Norwegian citizens.

The official rhetoric is avowedly about managerialism, efficiency, and more long-term proactive crime prevention to increase safety—not about punishing migrants. Nevertheless, the link made between crime and migration will rhetorically emphasize that "criminals" are being punished, and migration will thus be criminalized. The tools and technology of crimmigration (*how*) amplify the governing of migration thesis (*why*), and vice versa, the tools and political context reinforcing each other.[122] The official narrative is that criminal aliens are expelled and that this is based on a logic of efficiency. This all helps Norway appear to be a humane country, despite unequal criminal justice policies that ensure that more repressive sanctions are applied to the crimmigrant than to the Norwegian citizen.

Discussions about "the other" seem prevalent in the area of crime,[123] particularly in the Nordic context.[124] The crime label puts moral value on control, and the use of terms from management and administration gloss over the fact that the immediate goal is public security. Moreover, as Zedner argues, this managementality is also linked to punitive practice:

> States have been quick to claim that if a coercive measure or detention regime is for prevention or regulation or administrative convenience it is not, by definition, punishment. Yet this privileging of purpose does not mitigate the pains imposed by coercive measures, so to re-label measures as non-punitive is often nothing less than a cynical subversion of the criminal process and its human rights protections.[125]

It therefore seems that the "crime" part of crimmigration makes it possible to be punitive toward nonnationals and inclusive toward citizens and at the same time remain a beacon of universal human rights and general social security. The framing of noncitizens as "crimmigrants" blurs the boundaries between the criminal and the administrative sphere. Because of different rule-of-law standards in immigration law and criminal law, using them in hybrid ways "determines who is deserving of certain penal rationalities, rights, inclusionary sentiments and the civilizational achievements of the rule of law and welfare provisions."[126] The fact that it is more cost-effective than prosecution also endangers basic legal principles of fairness, due process, and justice.[127]

Discourses about the "dangerous immigrant" therefore support strict expulsion practices and are helping to change the traditional system of prevention within the national state[128] toward a more preventative state.[129] The risk management logic is legitimized by the "crime" label, but fueled by the pragmatism and reduced legal protection resulting from the use of administrative legal tools. Given political directives aiming to strengthen the return policy, it also becomes harder to argue in favor of inclusive approaches to "young strangers." As the welfare services are seen as not applicable, police room for maneuver increases. As in other Western countries, the police are taking on a broader set of tasks and functions, including those traditionally carried out by welfare agencies.[130] The question is whether we are in the process of constructing a control device that is completely different from that used for the rest of the population without having discussed what direction this takes us in — what legal implications it has and whether it is something we can recognize as part of the welfare state.

Notes

I would like to thank the editors and anonymous reviewers, as well as Katja Franko and John Todd, all of whom gave me useful feedback on earlier versions of this chapter.

1. L. Weber and J. McCulloch, "Penal Power and Border Control: Which Thesis? Sovereignty, Governmentality, or the Pre-emptive State?" *Punishment and Society*, Online First (2018).

2. K. Eide and A. Hjern, "Unaccompanied Refugee Children — Vulnerability and Agency," *Acta Poediatrica* 102, no. 7 (2013): 666–68; H. Lidén, E. Gording-Stang, and K. Eide, "The Gap between Legal Protection, Good Intentions and Political Restrictions: Unaccompanied Minors in Norway," *Social Work & Society* 15, no. 1 (2017).

3. Verdens Gang Oct. 30, 2017, Dagbladet: "Nordmenn hjelper asylsøkere å flykte," https://www.vg.no/nyheter/innenriks/asyl-debatten/dagbladet-nordmenn-hjelper-asylbarn-med-aa-roemme/a/24174962/, available Oct. 10, 2019; Verdens Gang Jun. 6, 2017, "De flyktet fra Norge," https://www.vg.no/nyheter/utenriks/mindreaarige-asylsoekere/de-flyktet-fra-norge-yasin-18-sover-paa-gaten-i-paris/a/24172232/, available Oct. 10, 2019.

4. M. Bosworth, Franko, and S. Pickering, "Punishment, Globalization and Migration Control: 'Get Them the Hell Out of Here,'" *Punishment and Society* 20, no. 1 (2018): 34–53.

5. Franko, *The Crimmigrant Other: Migration and Penal Power* (London: Routledge, forthcoming).

6. Ibid., 7.

7. J. Todd-Kvam, "Bordered Penal Populism: When Populism and Scandinavian Exceptionalism Meet," *Punishment and Society* (2018): 1.

8. V. Barker, "Nordic Exceptionalism revisited: Explaining the paradox of a Janus-faced penal regime," *Theoretical Criminology* 17, no. 1 (2013): 5--25.

9. K. Franko and S. B. Mohn, "Utvisning som straff? Om grensesnittet mellom strafferett og utlendingskontroll," *Tidsskrift for strafferett* 2 (2015): 153–76.

10. S. Ø. Jahnsen and M.-L. Skilbrei, "Leaving No Stone Unturned: The Borders and Orders of Transnational Prostitution," *British Journal of Criminology* (2017); N.B. Johansen, T. Ugelvik, and K. A. Franko, eds., *Krimmigrasjon? Den nye kontrollen av de fremmede* [Crimmigation? The New Control of the Strangers] (Oslo: Universitetsforlaget, 2013); Gundhus and Franko, "Global Policing and Mobility: Identity, Territory, Sovereignty," in *Sage Handbook of Global Policing*, ed. B. Bradford, Beatrice Jauregui, Ian Loader, and Jonny Steinberg (London, Sage, 2016), 497–514.

11. Jahnsen and Skilbrei, "Leaving No Stone Unturned."

12. This could, for example, be a breach of the Immigration Act, the General Civil Penal Code, or the Medical Products Act. Another consideration is the seriousness of the crime committed. For example, it is a serious offense to provide false information about who you are or to present false documents. Being sentenced for a crime is also a serious matter. Drug offenses, domestic violence, and sexual offenses are particularly serious examples. Expulsion is considered to be an administrative sanction and does not admit of the usual legal safeguards in criminal law, either in terms of legal basis or legal aid; Franko and Mohn, "Utvisning som straff?"

13. The Courts of Norway, "Penal Sanctions," https://www.domstol.no/en/The-criminal-court-proceedings/penal-sanctions, available Oct. 10, 2019.

14. L. Zedner, "Penal Subversions: When Is a Punishment not Punishment, Who Decides and on What Grounds?," *Theoretical Criminology* 20, no. 1 (2016): 3–20.

15. V. Barker, "Penal Power at the Border: Realigning State and Nation," *Theoretical Criminology* 21, no. 4 (2017): 441–57.

16. Todd-Kvam, "Bordered Penal Populism."

17. K. Aas, "Bordered Penality: Precarious Membership and Abnormal Justice," *Punishment & Society* 16, no. 5 (2014): 520–41; H. O. I. Gundhus, "Discretion as an Obstacle: Police Culture, Change, and Governance in a Norwegian Context," *Policing: A Journal of Policy and Practice* 11, no. 3 (2017): 258–72, http://doi.org/10.1093/police/pax012.

18. Gundhus, "Discretion as an Obstacle," 258–72.

19. Aas, "Bordered Penality"; J. P. van der Leun, *Looking for Loopholes: Processes of Incorporation of Illegal Immigrants in the Netherlands* (Amsterdam: Amsterdam University Press, 2003); J. P. Stumpf, *The Crimmigration Crisis: Immigrants, Crime, & Sovereign Power*, Bepress Legal Series, Working Paper 1635 (2006); L. Weber and B. Bowling, "Valiant Beggars and Global Vagabonds: Select, Eject, Immobilize," *Theoretical Criminology* 12, no. 3 (2008): 355–75; J. M. Chacón, "Managing Migration through Crime," *Columbia Law Review* 109 (2009):135–48; M. A. H. van der Woude and J. Brouwer, "Searching for 'Illegal' Junk in the Trunk: Underlying

Intentions of (Cr)immigration Controls in Schengen's Internal Border Area," *New Criminal Law Review: An International and Interdisciplinary Journal* 20, no. 1 (2017): 157–79; van der Woude and van der Leun, "Crimmigration Checks in the Internal Border Areas of the EU: Finding the Discretion That Matters," *European Journal of Criminology* 14, no. 1 (2017): 27–45.

20. "Utlendinger og kriminalitet. Kontroll, metode og sanksjoner—veileder" [Foreigners and Crime: Control, Methods and Sanctions—Guideline] (Oslo: *Politidirektoratet*, 2010).

21. Franko and Mohn, "Utvisning som straff?," 153–76.

22. Todd-Kvam, "Bordered Penal Populism," 10.

23. Stumpf first coined the term "crimmigration" to describe the merging of immigration law and criminal law in both substance and procedure. However, Aas introduced a broader perspective on crimmigration as a combination of crime control and migration control, which also includes the social context of crimmigration; Stumpf, *The Crimmigration Crisis: Immigrants, Crime, & Sovereign Power*; K. F. Aas, "'Crimmigrant' Bodies and Bona Fide Travelers: Surveillance, Citizenship and Global Governance," *Theoretical Criminology* 15, no. 3 (2011): 332).

24. Bosworth and M. Guild, "Governing through Migration Control: Security and Citizenship in Britain," *British Journal of Criminology* 48 (2008): 703–19.

25. Todd-Kvam, "Bordered Penal Populism."

26. P. S. Smith and T. Ugelvik, "Introduction: Punishment, Welfare and Prison History in Scandinavia," in *Scandinavian Penal History, Culture and Prison Practice* (London: Palgrave Macmillan, 2017).

27. Todd-Kvam, "Bordered Penal Populism."

28. Weber and McCulloch, "Penal Power and Border Control."

29. S. Lid, M. Winsvold, S. Søholt, S. G. Hansen, G. Heierstad, and J. E. Klausen, "Kommunenes rolle i radikalisering av radikalisering og voldelig ekstremisme—hva er kommunenes rolle?," *NIBR* (2016): 12.

30. Barker, "Penal Power at the Border," 441–57; Bosworth, Franko, and Pickering, "Punishment, Globalization and Migration Control," 34–53.

31. Aas, "The Ordered and the Bordered Society: Migration Control, Citizenship and the Northern Penal State," in *The Borders of Punishment: Migration, Citizenship and Social Exclusion*, ed. Aas and Bosworth (Oxford: Oxford University Press, 2013), 21–39.

32. Barker, "Penal Power at the Border," 441–57.

33. Ibid., 447.

34. Todd-Kvam, "Bordered Penal Populism."

35. Ugelvik, "The Dark Side of a Culture of Equality: Reimagining Communities in a Norwegian Remand Prison," in *Penal Exceptionalism? Nordic Prison Policy and Practice*, ed. T. Ugelvik and J. Dullum (London: Routledge, 2012).

36. Weber and McCulloch, "Penal Power and Border Control?"

37. Huysmans, *Security Unbound: Enacting Democratic Limits* (Abingdon: Routledge, 2014).

38. Lidén, Gording-Stang, and Eide, "Gap between Legal Protection, Good Intentions and Political Restrictions."

39. Ibid.

40. "General Comment no 6: Treatment of Unaccompanied and Separated Children Outside Their Country of Origin, CRC/GC/2005," *Committee of the Rights of the Child (CRC)*, Sept. 6 1, 2005; "Consideration of Reports Submitted by States Parties under Article 44 of the Convention. Concluding observations," *Committee of the Rights of the Child (CRC)*, 2010; Norway, 2010: CRC/C/NOR/CO/4.

41. Eide and Hjern, "Unaccompanied Refugee Children—Vulnerability and Agency," *Acta Poediatrica* 102, no. 7 (2013): 666–68.

42. "Over eller under 18: Aldersvurdering av enslige mindreårige asylsøkere [Over or under 18: The Age Assessment of Unaccompanied Minors]," *NOAS Norsk Organisasjon for Asylsøkere (NOAS)* (2016).

43. G. Tyldum, H. Lidén, M. L. Skilbrei, C. F. Dalseng, and K. T. Kindt, "Ikke våre barn: Identifisering og oppfølging av mindreårige ofre for menneskehandel i Norge [Not Our Children: Identification and Following Up Victims of Human Trafficking]," *FAFO-rapport* (2015): 45, http://www.fafo.no/~fafo/images/pub/2015/20550.pdf.

44. "Over eller under 18," 12.

45. Ibid., 28.

46. There are further flaws in the process worth mentioning: "If the age assessment establishes minors as 'overage' (eighteen or over), contradicting their claims and those of their legal guardian, this might influence the immigration authorities' (UDI) credibility assessment of their asylum claims and thereby their case outcomes (Tyldum et al. 2015). This is the case even if confidence in the age assessment process is low. If assessed as overage, the minor will no longer get support from a legal guardian. Their case will be assessed like that of an adult"; Lidén, Gording-Stang and Eide, "Gap between Legal Protection, Good Intentions and Political Restrictions,"14.

47. "Over eller under 18."

48. Lidén, Gording-Stang, and Eide, "Gap between Legal Protection, Good Intentions and Political Restrictions," 5.

49. Ibid., 9.

50. Eide and Hjern, "Unaccompanied Refugee Children," 666–68; Lidén, Gording-Stang, and Eide, "Gap between Legal Protection, Good Intentions and Political Restrictions."

51. Gundhus and M. Egge, "Grenser for forebygging?: 'De unge fremmede' og kriminalitetsforebyggende politiarbeid," in *Krimmigrasjon? Den nye kontrollen av de fremmede*, ed. N. B. Johansen, T. Ugelvik, and K. F. Aas (Oslo: Universitetsforlaget, 2013), 210–25; Lidén and C. Salvesen, "'De sa du måtte': Mindreåriges erfaringer med menneskehandel [Minors' Experiences of Human Trafficking]," in *ISF rapport* (Oslo: Institutt for samfunnsforskning, 2016); Tyldum, Lidén, Skilbrei, Dalseng, and Kindt, "Ikke våre barn."

52. Franko, *Crimmigrant Other*.

53. G. Tyldum, H. Lidén, M. L. Skilbrei, C. F. Dalseng, and K. T. Kindt, "Ikke våre barn."

54. Ibid.

55. B. Aasen, E, Dyb, and S. Lid, "Forebygging og oppfølging av enslige mindreårige asylsøkere som forsvinner fra mottak og omsorgssentre" [UAM Disappearing from Care Centers/Reception Centers], *NIBR Report* (2016): 17.

56. Lidén, Gording-Stang, and Eide, "Gap between Legal Protection, Good Intentions and Political Restrictions," 10.

57. Lidén, *Barn og Migrasjon: Mobilitet og tilhørighet [Children and Migration: Mobility and Belonging]* (Oslo: Universitetsforlaget, 2017).

58. Gundhus and M. Egge, "Grenser for forebygging?"

59. These are, for instance, "living conditions, human trafficking and access to education and child welfare services. In recent years, doctoral-level research has added to the understanding of such issues as health and communication (Seglem 2012; Kjelaas 2016). Legal issues concerning refugee children have been assessed (i.e., Sandberg 2008; Stang 2012), particularly on their participation rights in hearings for UAMs, asylum interviews with UAMs, and hearings for children in appeal court cases (Lidén/Rusten 2007; Lidén 2012; Stang/Lidén 2014)"; Lidén, Gording-Stang and Eide, "Gap between Legal Protection, Good Intentions and Political Restrictions," 13.

60. Lidén and C. Salvesen, "'De sa du måtte': Mindreåriges erfaringer med menneskehandel," 45.

61. Gundhus and Egge, "Grenser for forebygging?," 210–25; L. R. Vollebaek, "Knuste drømmer: 'Mindreårige nordafrikanske migranter og gatelivets realiteter,'" in *Sommerfugl, fly! En artikkelsamling av barnevernspedagoger 2015*, ed. L. E. Bjørknes (Seksjonsrådet for barnevernspedagoger, FO, 2015), 104–17; Vollebaek, "Sosialt arbeid med irregulære migranter," in *Sosiologi i sosialfagene*, ed. B. Olsen, G. Farstad, and P. Stornaess Skotte (Oslo Universitetsforlaget, 2018); Vollebaek, *Sosialt arbeid med sårbare migranter: Mindreårige og voksne asylsøkere, papirløse, EØS-borgere og mulige ofre for menneskehandel* [Social Work with Vulnerable Migrants: Minor and Adult Asylum Seekers, Paperless, EEA Citizens and Potential Victims of Human Trafficking] (Oslo commune: Velferdsetaten, 2014).

62. Lidén and Salvesen, "'De sa du måtte': Mindreåriges erfaringer med menneskehandel"; Tyldum, Lidén, Skilbrei, Dalseng, and Kindt, "Ikke våre barn," 45.

63. M. Holmboe, "Norwegian Youth Punishment—Opportunity or Trap?," *Bergen Journal of Criminal Law & Criminal Justice* 5, no. 1 (2017): 37–58.

64. Egge and Gundhus, "Social Crime Prevention in Norway," in *Social Crime Prevention in Late Modern Europe: A Comparative Perspective*, ed. Patrick Hebberecht and Evelyne Baillergeau (Brussels: VUB Press, 2012), 255–77.

65. Holmboe, "Norwegian Youth Punishment?," 51.

66. "Oppsøkende og utadrettet arbeid overfor ingdom utenfor opplæring og

samfunnsliv," in *Ministry of Children and Equality, Rapport* (Oslo: Barne- og likestillingsdepartementet, 2009).

67. D. McCarthy, *Soft Policing: The Collaborative Control of Anti-Social Behaviour* (London: Palgrave Macmillan, 2014).

68. Gundhus and Egge, "Grenser for forebygging?," 210–25; Salto, *Salto handlingsprogram 2012–2015: Kriminalitetsforebygging blant barn og unge i Oslo* (Oslo: Oslo Kommune/Oslo Politidistrikt, 2011), 14.

69. Salto, *Barne- og ungdomskriminaliteten i Oslo: Rapport basert på data frå 2015* (Oslo: Oslo Kommune/Oslo Politidistrikt, 2016).

70. Aasen, Dyb, and Lid, "Forebygging og oppfølging av enslige mindreårige asylsøkere som forsvinner fra mottak og omsorgssentre," 17; Lidén and Salvesen, "'De sa du måtte.'"

71. Bosworth and Guild, "Governing through Migration Control"; Weber and J. McCulloch, "Penal Power and Border Control."

72. Aas, "Bordered Penality," 520–41.

73. Tyldum, Lidén, Skilbrei, Dalseng, and Kindt, "Ikke våre barn, " 45.

74. In 2010 the police were given the right to conduct territorial control in §21 (Utl loven) as a General Immigration Control, and this is the wording: "In connection with enforcing the provisions on foreigners' entry and residence in the state, the police may stop a person and require their credentials when there is reason to assume that he/she is a foreign citizen, and the time, place and situation justify such a check. In such cases, the foreigner must show proof of identity and, if required, provide information to confirm this identity and the legality of his/her stay in the realm."

75. "Til Politimestre, sjef saerorgan: Politiets utøvelse av utlendingskontroll på territoriet, herunder grenseområdene," *Police Directorate, Rundskriv* (2001).

76. "Utlendinger og kriminalitet. Kontroll, metode og sanksjoner—veileder."

77. Ibid.

78. Aas, "Bordered Penality," 520–41; Franko and Mohn, "Utvisning som straff? Om grensesnittet mellom strafferett og utlendingskontroll," *Tidsskrift for strafferett* 2 (2015): 153–76; Gundhus and Franko, "Global Policing and Mobility."

79. Gundhus, "Å målstyre skjønnsutøvelse: Profesjonalisering av politiets utlendingskontroll," *Sosiologi i dag* 46, no. 1 (2016): 54–79.

80. Gundhus, "Discretion as an Obstacle," 258–72.

81. Franko and Mohn, "Utvisning som straff?," 174 [author's translation].

82. Aas, "Bordered Penality," 526.

83. D. A. Sklansky, "Crime, Immigration, and Ad Hoc Instrumentalism," *New Criminal Law Review* 15, no. 2 (2012): 161.

84. Ibid.

85. Ibid.

86. Aas, "Bordered Penality," 520–41; Franko and Mohn, "Utvisning som straff?," 153–76.

87. Gundhus and Franko, "Global Policing and Mobility."

88. "Over eller under 18."

89. Franko, *Crimmigrant Other.*

90. Weber and McCulloch, "Penal Power and Border Control."

91. Tyldum, Lidén, Skilbrei, Dalseng, and Kindt, "Ikke våre barn," 45.

92. H. Lidén and C. Salvesen, "De sa du måtte'"; Vollebaek, "Knuste drømmer," 104–7; Vollebaek, *Sosialt arbeid med sårbare migranter.*

93. Aas, "'Crimmigrant' Bodies and Bona Fide Travelers: Surveillance, Citizenship and Global Governance," *Theoretical Criminology* 15, no. 3 (2011): 331–46.

94. Franko, *Crimmigrant Other.*

95. G. Brochmann, "Statsborgerskap, medborgerskap og tilhørighet," in *Sand i maskineriet: Makt og demokrati i det flerkulturelle Norge*, ed. Grete Brochmann, Tordis Borchgrevink, and Jon Rogstad (Oslo: Gyldendal akademisk, 2002).

96. Huysmans, *Security Unbound*; D. Skleparis, "(In)securitization and Illiberal Practices on the Fringe of the EU," *European Security* 25, no. 1 (2016): 92–111.

97. R. Koslowski, *Migrants and Citizens: Demographic Change in the European State System* (Ithaca: Cornell University Press, 2000), 156.

98. V, Barker, *Nordic Nationalism and Penal Order: Walling the Welfare State* (Abingdon: Routledge, 2018).

99. Ugelvik, "Imprisoned on the Border: Subjects and Objects of the State in Two Norwegian Prisons," in *Justice and Security in the 21st Century: Risks, Rights and the Rule of Law*, ed. S. Ugelvik and B. Hudson (Abingdon: Routledge, 2012), 64–82; Ugelvik, "Seeing Like a Welfare State: Immigration Control, Statecraft, and a Prison with Double Vision," in *The Borders of Punishment: Citizenship, Crime Control and Social Exclusion*, ed. Aas and Bosworth (Oxford: Oxford University Press, 2013).

100. Franko, *Crimmigrant Other.*

101. O. B. Lysaker, K. Fangen, and T. Sarin, "Inside and Outside Simultaneously: Recognising the Vulnerability of Irregular Migrants in Europe," *Policy Briefs* 5 (2011).

102. Gundhus and Egge, "Grenser for forebygging?," 210–25.

103. Zedner, "Security, the State, and the Citizen: The Changing Architecture of Crime Control," *New Criminal Law Review* 13 (2010): 382.

104. R. Solhjell, E. Saarikkomäki, H. M. Birk, D. Wästerfors, and T. Kolind, "We Are Seen as a Threat": Police Stops of Young Ethnic Minorities in the Nordic Countries, *Critical Criminology* (2018), Online First.

105. Barker, "Penal Power at the Border," 441–57.

106. Barker, *Nordic Nationalism and Penal Order.*

107. Weber and B. Bowling, "Introduction: Stop and Search in Global Context," in *Stop and Search: Police Power in Global Context*, ed. L. Weber and B. Bowling (Abingdon: Routledge, 2013), 3.

108. Weber, *Policing Non-Citizens* (London: Routledge, 2013).

109. Loader, "Policing, Recognition, and Belonging," *Annals of the American Academy of Political and Social Science* 605, no. 1 (2006): 213.

110. Aas, "Bordered Penality," 526.

111. Vollebaek, "Knuste drømmer," 104–17; Gundhus and Egge, "Grenser for forebygging?," 210–25; Lidén and Salvesen, "'De sa du måtte.'"

112. Franko, *Crimmigrant Other*.

113. M. Valenta, "Avviste asylsøkere, kamp mot uttransportering og livet utenfor mottakssystemet," in *Asylsøker i velferdsstatens venterom*, ed. I. M. Valenta and B. Berg (Oslo: Universitetsforlaget, 2012), 226.

114. Aas, "Ordered and the Bordered Society," 21–39.

115. Aas, *Ta vare på deg selv, lommeboka, mobilen og dine venner*, vol. 1, *Trygghet*, ed. T. H. Eriksen (Oslo: Universitetsforlaget, 2006), 73–95.

116. Aas, "Bordered Penality," 520–41; Barker, "Nordic Vagabonds: The Roma and the Logic of Benevolent Violence in the Swedish Welfare State, *European Journal of Criminology* 14, no. 1 (2017): 120–39; Barker, "Penal Power at the Border," 441–57; Barker, *Nordic Nationalism and Penal Order*; Ugelvik, "Imprisoned on the Border: Subjects and Objects of the State in Two Norwegian Prisons," in *Justice and Security in the 21st Century: Risks, Rights and the Rule of Law*, ed. S. Ugelvik and B. Hudson (Abingdon: Routledge, 2012), 64–82.

117. Bosworth, Franko, and Pickering, "Punishment, Globalization and Migration Control," 46.

118. W. Walters, "Secure Borders, Safe Haven, Domopolitics," *Citizenship Studies* 8, no. 3 (2004): 237–60; Aas, "Analysing a World in Motion: Global Flows Meet 'Criminology of the Other,'"*Theoretical Criminology* 11, no. 2 (2007), 283–303.

119. E. Gording-Stang, "Juss og praksis i behandling av mindreårige asylsøkere," *Materialisten* 38, no. 3/4 (2011).

120. Aasen, Dyb, and Lid, "Forebygging og oppfølging av enslige mindreårige asylsøkere som forsvinner fra mottak og omsorgssentre," 17.

121. D. Bigo, "Globalized (In)security: The Field and the Ban-Opticon," in *Terror, Insecurity and Liberty: Illiberal Practices of Liberal Regimes after 9/11*, ed. D. Bigo and A. Tsoukala (Abingdon: Routledge, 2008), 10–48.

122. Weber and McCulloch, "Penal Power and Border Control."

123. Aas, "Bordered Penality," 520–41.

124. Barker, *Nordic Nationalism and Penal Order*.

125. Zedner, "Penal Subversions," 4.

126. Bosworth, Franko, and Pickering, "Punishment, Globalization and Migration Control," 46.

127. Zedner, "Penal Subversions," 3–20.

128. Bosworth, Franko, and Pickering, "Punishment, Globalization and Migration Control," 45–46.

129. Krasmann, in Weber and McCulloch, "Penal Power and Border Control."

130. McCarthy, *Soft Policing*, 165.

12

The Fight against Terrorism in Belgium

Crimmigration Law as a Counterterrorism Instrument?

Lana De Pelecijn and Steven De Ridder

Several paradigms explain the shifting nature of crime and migration control in late modernity in relation to acts of terrorism. According to Beck,[1] the events of 9/11 have intensified the experience of living in a "terroristic world risk society." Despite the counterterrorism policy unfolded by nation-states worldwide, the perceived risk of terrorist events is omnipresent. A Foucauldian perspective puts more emphasis on how risk is being used through discourse and "*wielded as an instrument of disciplinary power through which populations are governed*."[2] This perspective also relates to the "governing through crime" thesis put forward by Simon explaining how the topic of crime and the fear of becoming a victim of it are used more generally to legitimize developments in the field of crime control.[3] A new conception of the baseline of the criminal justice systems and the development of actuarial instruments, dubbed "the new penology," were used to describe how particularly neoliberal governments in late modern society actually deal with crime.[4]

There are several resemblances between the emerging changes in the domain of crime control and the field of migration control.[5] When it comes down to the developing field of migration control, crimmigration scholars[6] have highlighted that under the umbrella of the acute necessity to prevent the nation-state and secure the citizens for further terrorist attacks, unseen policy initiatives, laws, and anti-terrorism measures are unleashed. According to Stumpf,[7] this fear of crime and terrorism became one of the main drivers of crimmigration law and led to the toughening of previous mechanisms for criminalizing migration and to the implementation of new ones.[8] As such, in order to protect society, a specific "law of the enemy" is created for those (foreigners, including refugees) who cannot be trusted and might pose a terrorist threat.[9] Characterizing this "crimmigration law" is the two-way exchange of legal provisions and procedures between criminal law and migration law targeting migrant groups as a whole rather than terrorism in particular. This observation raises the question of to what extent this increased collaboration aiming to control terrorism signifies a convergence of crime control and migration control as witnessed in other countries.[10] This question is particularly relevant for the Belgian case, as Belgium has evolved from a country building expertise on counterterrorism to foreseeing harsh counterterrorism measures.

Although the Belgian government had already been confronted with terrorism in the 1970s, the 9/11 attacks in the United States played an iconic role in the developments of the Belgian counterterrorism policy. Since then, the capabilities for dealing with terrorism were enhanced significantly.[11] Following the multiple Paris attacks in 2015 and the coordinated attacks in Brussels on March 22, 2016, the international community and media depicted Brussels as "the capital of European Jihadism." Also, the international media picked up the statement of the then Republican presidential candidate Donald Trump that living in Brussels is like "living in a hell hole." Being confronted with acts of terrorism for the first time in years and the perception by the international community of a malfunctioning judicial apparatus, Belgium launched a fierce fight against terrorism.

This contribution explores why, when, and how crimmigration law has become a counterterrorism instrument in Belgium. We explore why countries increasingly use crimmigration legislation to prevent terrorism and what underlying consequences this may have. Second, we examine when and how crimmigration became a counterterrorism instrument in Belgium by describing the evolution of the Belgian anti-terrorism policy and highlighting different recent developments in Belgian criminal law, prison policy, and migration law. Considering the different paradigms and theses explaining the nature of counterterrorism policy today, we highlight both the actual amendments of law relating to terrorism and as the discourse and rhetoric that was used in the aftermath of the Paris and Brussels attacks. This comprehensive overview is crucial for a good understanding of the national scope of crimmigration policy in Belgium. In addition, this contribution provides insight into the (emerging) relationship between crime control, migration control, and control of terrorism.

Evolution of the Belgian Counterterrorism Policy

In the 1970s and the beginning of the 1980s, Belgium became confronted with a movement of anti-capitalist terrorists called the *Cellules Communistes*

Combattantes. With the terrorist attacks in Paris in 1986 committed by the religiously inspired group "Fouad Ali Saleh" and the discovery of the support cells of the Algerian radical Islamist movement GIA in the mid-1990s, by the end of the twentieth century Belgium had already encountered a new form of terrorism called "Jihadi terrorism."[12]

Following the attacks of 9/11 in the United States, the Belgian government again began to add active legislative and judicial tools to combat Jihadi terrorism.[13] By the end of 2002, these new policy initiatives resulted in the so-called Plan Mosques, an action plan exclusively aimed at the phenomenon of "radicalization in relation to Jihadist Terrorism." In 2005—in the aftermath of the attacks in Madrid in 2004—this plan transformed into a strategic memorandum: the "Action Plan Radicalism," also known as "Plan R."[14] In addition to Jihadi terrorism, this federal plan focuses on other "statements of inflammatory language, fundamentalist ideas, racist, anarchist and extremist opinions." Based on specific vectors of radicalization and measures in the preventive, proactive, and reactive field, the government plan aims to tackle the initial forms of radical expression up to and including extreme forms of implementation. Plan R is currently the cornerstone of the Belgian federal approach to combating foreign terrorist fighters.[15]

Although radicalization was put on the political agenda in the aftermath of 9/11, it took about ten years after the introduction of Plan R before the preventive policy took shape on a decentralized level.[16] Because of the fact that the Belgian government did not consider radicalization an urgent problem, there was no decisive approach to tackle this phenomenon. Only after the departure of homegrown terrorist fighters from Belgium to Syria in 2012 were additional plans drawn up at the federal, regional, and local levels;[17] the terrorist attacks on Charlie Hebdo and the Hyper Cacher in Paris and the anti-terrorism campaign in the Belgian city of Verviers in January 2015 created the need to accelerate this fight against terrorism. As several perpetrators of the attacks had ties with Belgium, the Belgian approach to terrorism was strongly criticized by other countries and international media. The Belgian federal government launched its "12-point plan"[18] in the context of the fight against terrorism; the plan included a broad scale of repressive measures.[19] New terrorist crimes and a broadened list of offenses allowing the use of special methods of investigation were enacted into criminal (procedure) law. In the area of migration law, the rules for withdrawal of nationality, identity cards, and passports were eased. Policy documents and white papers on radicalization in society, in prison, and by foreign terrorist fighters were revised. A legal mechanism to identify persons involved in financing terrorism was installed. The capacity of the State Security Service was increased, and the information and data exchange procedures between federal actors such as the National Safety Council and local administrative and judicial administrations were optimized. The Belgian army was deployed for patrolling the streets and providing static protection of terrorist targets.

One of the goals of the 12-point plan was updating 2005's Plan R. The federal government approved the revised version in December 2015. The revision of Plan R emphasizes an integrated cooperation among policy levels (federal, regional, and local) in order to identify individuals and groups that can have a violent radicalizing effect on their environment. Additionally, this plan aims to reduce the impact of this phenomenon on society through administrative, judicial, and social preventive measures.[20] In practice, this approach is being outlined in a national task force, various working groups (permanent, thematic, or ad hoc), and local task forces. The intention at both the national and local level is to create collaboration among different services ensuring mutual exchange and exploitation of information.[21]

After the Paris attacks on November 13, 2015, the federal government added eighteen new measures against radicalization and terrorism. This federal *eighteen-point plan* promises intensified control and supervision by police and military personnel, extra funding in the budget for counterterrorism and security, criminal and administrative measures aimed at the deprivation of liberty, and a broadening of investigation possibilities:[22]

1. Extra budgetary effort—amendment to the 2016 budget: EUR 400 million for security and the fight against terrorism.
2. Strengthening police controls at the borders.
3. Deployment of 520 soldiers to improve safety.
4. Revision of the Code of Criminal Procedure.
5. Revision of the Constitution—administrative detention of 72 hours for terrorist acts. Amendment to Article 12 of the Constitution.
6. 24 hours a day—house searches for terrorist crimes.
7. Foreign fighters—deprivation of liberty. Principle: prison when returning to Belgium.
8. Registered persons—electronic supervision. Electronic band for persons who are registered with the threat analysis services: a contradictory procedure will be instituted to impose the wearing of electronic tape.
9. Belgian PRN—registration of the data of all passengers in means of transport. Without waiting for the European project, Belgium will carry out a systematic check on the registration of all passengers in means of transport (airplanes and high-speed trains).

10. Exclusion of hate preachers. Screening all preachers to put under house arrest, depriving them of their freedom or expelling anyone who promotes hatred.
11. Dismantling of unrecognized cult places that spread Jihadism.
12. Ending anonymous prepaid cards.
13. Molenbeek action plan—prevention and repression.
14. Strengthening the screening for access to sensitive jobs.
15. Expansion of the network of cameras for license plate recognition.
16. Shutting down websites that preach hatred.
17. Evaluation with a view to adapting the laws in connection with emergency situations. Possibility of temporary and exceptional measures to ensure public safety.
18. Participation on the international stage in the fight against ISIS.

On March 22, 2016, the coordinated attacks at Brussels Airport and the Brussels metro station took place, resulting in more than one hundred victims. Especially after these events, many of the proposals and measures in the context of the fight against terrorism were converted into laws. In order to combat terrorism and to protect Belgian citizens, various security services and federal authorities, such as the minister of justice, the minister of home affairs, the State Security Service, and the Coordination Unit of Threat Analysis (CUTA), started working more closely together. Consequently, the different measures appear to include both elements of crime control and migration control in order to facilitate this fight.

In the next section, we aim to explore *how* crimmigration law has become a counterterrorism instrument by discussing several recent amendments of Belgian criminal law, prison policy, and migration law.

Adjustments to Criminal Law and Prison Policy

Adjustments to Criminal law

TERRO I-Act

On July 20, 2015, the minister of justice implemented the "Terro I-Act" in order to make the fight against terrorism more efficient.[23] The Belgian anti-terrorism legislation had already been adopted on December 19, 2003.[24] However, with the new Terro I-Act the anti-terrorism legislation is augmented to cover a new terrorist crime.[25] According to Article 140 of the Criminal Code, anyone who leaves Belgian territory with a view to committing a terrorist crime, in Belgium or abroad, is punished with an imprisonment of five to ten years and with a fine of one hundred to five thousand Euros. The same applies to those who enter the country with a view to committing a terrorist crime. As such, a person can be punished regardless of whether the terrorist crime took place. As this amendment contains vague language, travel could be restricted even without evidence of the intention to commit or support terrorist acts.[26] From the time this crime was defined in law, it was clear that the burden of proof is far from evident.

In addition to adding a new terrorist crime to the Criminal Code, the Terro I-Act extends the possibilities of withdrawing nationality. According to Article 7 of the Act of July 20, 2015, to strengthen the fight against terrorism,[27] a judge can take Belgian nationality from someone convicted of terrorism at the request of the public prosecutor. This only applies to convicted persons who did not receive their nationality from their parents by birthright and who serve a prison sentence of at least five years. Contrary to the withdrawal of nationality in other crimes, it is not required for terrorist crimes that they have been committed within ten years from the day on which the person has acquired Belgian nationality.[28] The government justifies this amendment to the law by the effects that terrorism has on the entire country; an act of terrorism therefore can be interpreted as a form of rejection of the country, its institutions, and its values.[29] However, according to the Human Rights Watch's analysis,[30] the Act can lead to the perception that a category of "second-class citizens" is created on the basis of origin and ethnicity.

TERRO II-Act

According to the minister of justice, sharing information is of great importance in order to tackle terrorism. The correct assessment and the appropriate follow-up of a threat are only possible if all services have a good information position. The "Terro II-Act" of April 27, 2016,[31] creates a legal basis for a common database of foreign terrorist fighters. All persons who can be qualified as a "foreign terrorist fighter" are entered into this database. By establishing the database, all information available to intelligence agencies and police services, as well as to other partners, is centralized and shared in one place. In this way, relevant threat analysis can be made and follow-up can be organized of persons who can be considered foreign terrorist fighters. This follow-up may consist of police measures (e.g., introduction into the Schengen Information System) or judicial measures (e.g., opening a criminal investigation). The information in the database is provided by and shared with the CUTA, the State Security Service, the Military Intelligence Service (ADIV), the integrated federal and local police (including a permanent committee for local police), the Crisis Center-Directorate-General for Security and Prevention (FOD BIZA), the Directorate-General of Consular Affairs, the Federal Public Service of Foreign Affairs, the Public Prosecution Service, the Department of Financial Information Processing, the Immigration Service, the Directorate General of Penitentiary Institutions, and Penitentiary Institutions Investigation and investigation services of the General Administration of Customs and Excise.[32]

According to the minister of justice, investigators must receive adequate instruments in the fight against terrorism and serious crimes.[33] The Terro II-Act broadens the permission for telephone tapping in the context of illegal arms trade, and the illegal arms trade and certain violations of the Arms Act explicitly appear in the Code of Criminal Procedure as the basis for a telephone tap. This extension also applies to the external protection of nuclear material and other radioactive material.[34]

Last, the Terro II-Act enables the federal judicial police and the intelligence agencies to carry out house searches twenty-four hours a day. The exceptions to the prohibition to conduct a search in a home, a deprivation of liberty, or a search in a private place before 5 a.m. and after 9 p.m., are extended to target suspected terrorist crimes or criminal organizations when there are serious indications that firearms, explosives, nuclear weapons, biological or chemical weapons, or harmful or hazardous substances can be found (Art. 4, Act of April 27, 2016, concerning additional measures to combat terrorism, *BS*, May 9, 2016).

TERRO III-Act

With the "Terro III-Act" of August 3, 2016,[35] the penalties in the field of terrorist crimes are further extended. The first amendment concerns Article 140 of the Criminal Code, which makes *incitement to terrorism* punishable with imprisonment of five to ten years and a fine of one hundred to five thousand Euros. According to the minister of justice, incitement to terrorism plays a very important role in the spread of radicalization and terrorism.[36] Within this new act, the "burden of proof" has become less demanding, as only the "intention" to incite terrorism must be proven. This is an example of how the relaxed procedural norms of civil immigration proceedings are imported into criminal law[37] in order to combat terrorism.

The second amendment concerns Article 140 of the Criminal Code, which makes recruitment for terrorism punishable. Before the amendment, only recruitment for the commission of a terrorist attack or joining a terrorist group was made punishable. With the new act, recruitment to go abroad for terrorist purposes, for example to Syria or Iraq, is also made punishable, with imprisonment of five to ten years and with a fine of one hundred to five thousand Euros.[38]

The Terro III-Act also provides an amendment to the Act of July 20, 1990, concerning pre-trial detention.[39] For crimes with a punishment above fifteen years, the reasons for the imposition of pre-trial detention are "serious indications of guilt" and "the danger to public security." If the maximum applicable sentence does not exceed fifteen years (detention), the reasons for the risk of recidivism, absconding, or collusion also arise. Through the implementation of the Terro III-Act, the mere danger to public security suffices for terrorist crimes over which the legal maximum exceeds five years' imprisonment.[40] This distinction is justified by the federal government because of the specific nature and seriousness of these crimes, which are directed against individual victims as well as against the existence of society, the state, and its institutions.[41] We could question, however, whether this reduction of evidentiary requirements restricts the right to liberty.[42]

Temporary Withdrawal of the Identity Card, Refusal of Delivery, and Withdrawal of Passports

Besides the criminalization of foreign terrorist fighters under criminal law, additional measures were taken to limit the mobility of persons presumed to be involved in terrorist activities or networks. Since January 5, 2016, the minister of home affairs can temporarily withdraw the identity card of a Belgian citizen, can refuse to deliver it, or can choose to temporarily declare the identity card invalid.[43] This can only be done when there are well-founded and very serious indications that the person wishes to travel to an area where terrorist groups are active, that on his return to Belgium he can represent a serious threat to terrorist offenses, or that he wants to commit terrorist offenses outside the national territory. However, the minister can only apply these measures on the basis of a motivated advice from the CUTA. CUTA itself must first consult the federal prosecutor's office or the public prosecutor. In doing so, it must ascertain whether the application of the measures jeopardizes the execution of the criminal procedure. The withdrawal, invalidation, or refusal to issue the identity card by the minister of home affairs can initially be done for a maximum of twenty-five days. This period can be extended up to a maximum of three months, or six months in exceptional cases.[44]

The refusal by the minister of home affairs to issue the identity card or its withdrawal or invalidation automatically leads to the refusal to issue the passport or travel documents of the person identified as suspect by the minister of home affairs or the documents' withdrawal or invalidation; the two procedures are connected to each other.[45]

Adjustments to Belgian Prison Policy

Another priority in the context of the fight against terrorism is the approach to radicalization in Belgian prisons. The prison is regarded as a "breeding ground" for radicalization and recruitment, as potential recruits would be more receptive to radical thinking because of feelings of frustration toward society, their search for a religious or ideologically inspired sense of expression, group pressure, and their exclusion from society.[46] In this context, in 2015 the Flemish government launched the action plan "*Approach to Radicalization in Prisons*"[47] and the action plan "*Prevention of Radicalization Processes That Could Lead to Extremism and Terrorism.*"[48]

With a modified prison policy and the implementation of disengagement and deradicalization programs during detention, the government tries to prevent prisoners from radicalizing during detention (*preventive policy*) and provides a specialized framework for prisoners who are already radicalized (*reactive policy*). In this context, the federal government opted for a two-track policy. This means that prisoners are initially integrated into the general prison population as long as they do not pose a serious risk of radicalization, do not engage in an armed struggle from ideological motives, and their radicalization process is controlled. However, if there is a risk of radicalization, the detainee may be referred to a satellite prison in Lantin, Andenne, Sint-Gillis, Ghent, or Bruges. Here, the radicalized prisoner will be followed up more intensively with a maximum integration program within ordinary prison life. If the threat is too real or if there are signs that other prisoners are being recruited, the prisoner will be isolated and referred to a specialized department, called the Deradex (Hasselt or Ittre). In both the satellite prisons and the Deradex, two consultants in the context of deradicalization set up disengagement trajectories.[49] The consultants' guidance continues for some time after detention. When radicalized prisoners are released under conditions, a justice assistant will be appointed to verify compliance with the imposed conditions. For radicalized prisoners who are released without conditions, only a voluntary offer can be formulated. However, because of the Terro I-Act, prisoners that would normally be followed up with after imprisonment in the context of deradicalization can be removed from the territory, as a judge can take Belgian nationality from someone convicted of terrorism. This can be considered as a serious threat to realizing an effective deradicalization policy.

The Impact of Home-Grown Terrorism on Belgian Immigration Policy

The last substantial modification of the Belgian Foreigners Act before the terrorist attacks in Paris and Brussels dates back to implementation of the 2008 Return Directive issued by the European Parliament and the Council.[50] The implementation of the "Return Directive" by the Act of January 19, 2012,[51] was characterized by broader discretionary powers and relaxed procedural safeguards. These new decision-making standards resulted in a steep increase of entry bans attached to expulsion orders and a broader interpretation of being considered "a threat to the public order or national security." This amendment of Belgian migration law and policy was not related to terrorism. Instead, it was politically framed within a context of increasing efficiency of migration law enforcement.[52]

By the end of 2016, the secretary of state for migration policy had prepared several amendments to the Belgian Foreigners Act "aiming to protect the public order to strengthen the national security."[53] According to several memoranda,[54] the amendment of the Foreigners Act aims to make the expulsion policy more transparent, coherent, and efficient in order to preserve the public order and national security. It further refers to the fight against terrorism and radicalization initiated by the Belgian government in view of "*combatting any activity threatening the rights and freedom*" of the nation.[55] While a more transparent, coherent, and efficient migration policy had been a long-standing goal of the Belgian government,[56] the fight against terrorism suddenly became a new element in the political rhetoric for legitimizing changes in Belgian migration policy. Whereas the title of the act amending the Foreigners Act speaks for itself, the secretary of state legitimized in his political rhetoric this new legal initiative by explicitly referring to Salah Abdeslam, born in Belgium (but without Belgian nationality), for several months Belgium's most wanted terrorist, for his role in the coordinated attacks in Paris. One of the focal points of this amendment was relaxing the expulsion exclusion provisions in the Belgian Foreigners Act that heretofore protected residents based on their long-term residence in Belgian territory or having been born or having arrived in Belgium before the age of twelve. These provisions, applying to all foreign nationals, also applied to terrorist suspects such as Salah Abdeslam.

Moreover, the introduction of the Memorandum explicitly states that "*therefore, the government has committed itself to take all necessary and useful measures enabling the competent governmental institutions, to act efficiently, at all levels, including the administrative.*"[57] This quote directly links the modification of Belgian migration law and policy to a broader and more comprehensive national counterterrorism framework that includes changes in the area of crime control described in previous sections of this essay. Besides the emphasis on managerial concepts such as efficiency, the quote also clearly hints at a comprehensive approach to terrorism that includes criminal and migration law measures. What makes this finding noteworthy from a crimmigration perspective is that, until the creation of the Memorandum, the areas of crime control and migration control had been developing rather independently, without many cross-interferences.[58]

One very significant modification made by the Act of February 24, 2017, was the abolition of Ministerial and Royal Decrees of Expulsion enabling the Belgian Foreigners Administration to revoke residence rights with a standard expulsion order. Remarkably, these specific types of expulsion order had historically been the first measures under Belgian migration law enabling the Foreigners Administration to prohibit individuals from entering the territory. With the arrival of the entry bans under the Return Directive, the Belgian Foreigners Administration could already circumvent the more demanding legal procedure of the Ministerial Decrees of Expulsion. With the Act of February 24, 2017, every decision to revoke residence rights was made following the decision of a lone case processor of the Foreigners Administration. Before the Act of February 24, 2017, an independent commission, the Advisory Commission on Foreigners, evaluated the legal grounds and the motivation of the decision in light of the European Convention of Human Rights. The Act of February 24, 2017, also relaxed the conditions preventing foreign nationals from being eligible for expulsion or revocation of residence rights. Before the Act of February 24, 2017, foreign nationals residing long-term in Belgium and foreign nationals possessing residence rights for more than ten years had to commit a severe breach of national security in order to be eligible for expulsion. Notwithstanding some remaining legal safeguards, such as the consideration of the duration of their stay, these categories of foreign nationals became more susceptible to expulsion and revocation of their residence rights because of a less strict interpretation of the threat to the public order or national security clause.[59] Also, foreign nationals with asylum status or a subsidiary protection status were still prevented from expulsion and revocation of their status unless they committed an exceptionally severe crime or if there were reasonable grounds to believe that they were a threat to national security.[60] The Act of February 24, 2017, also included new legal provisions enabling the Belgian Foreigners Administration to implement entry bans to European citizens. Similar to the entry bans for third-country nations under the Return Directive, the entry ban for European citizens can exceed five years under the threat to the public order or national security clause.[61] These entry bans for European citizens would, however, only apply to Belgian territory.

Conclusion and Discussion

In recent years, the fight against terrorism and radicalism has become the cornerstone of the Belgian government's policy. Early experiences with radical Islam and Jihadi terrorism permitted Belgium to build up expertise and awareness of this phenomenon and can be considered the onset of Belgian counterterrorism policy.[62] The terrorist attacks of 9/11 in the United States functioned as a catalyst for the Belgian counterterrorism policy, which had pretty much been developing in the background up to then. Following the Paris attacks in 2015 and the coordinated attacks in Brussels in 2016, whereby terrorist suspects slipped past the attention of the criminal justice system and profited from the open borders of the Schengen area, Belgium's international image, with Brussels as the capital of Europe, was severely damaged. These developments urged the Belgian government to accelerate this fight against terrorism on a broad scale.

The different measures made it possible to raise financial and human resources for the fight against terrorism. For example, in order to guarantee the safety of its citizens, the government decided to deploy military personnel on the streets after the attacks in Paris in January 2015. New measures have also been taken to strengthen the means of action of the police, intelligence, and security services, as well as the work of the judicial authorities. With the extension of special investigation methods, the introduction in the Criminal Code of a new terrorist offense concerning transfer abroad for terrorist purposes, and the temporary withdrawal of identity cards of potential foreign terrorist fighters, the Belgian government also strengthened the legal means to combat terrorism.

Because of this increased cooperation among various security services and federal authorities, such as the minister of justice, the minister of the interior, the police, the state security service, and the Coordination Unit of Threat Analysis, 267 convictions for terrorist offenses have been issued since 2015.[63]

Similar to the developments in the U.S. after 9/11, the implementation of an anti-terrorist agreement in the aftermath of the Paris and Brussels attacks gave birth to a variety of measures affecting the nature of crime control and migration control. However, rather than the two-way exchange of legal provisions and procedures between criminal law and migration law as witnessed in the U.S.,[64] the nature of criminal law in terms of punishment and the administrative nature of migration law in terms border control remained relatively stable.

What is striking is that a sort of "exception right" has been created for terrorism-related cases and terrorist suspects. In this regard, it appears that the procedural safeguards of the Criminal (Procedure) Code are not affected as such, but a surrogate type of criminal law enforcement has been installed to deploy in terrorism-related cases. These modifications do not signify the incorporation of migration law enforcement standards as a crimmigration perspective would presume, but are inspired by the will to effectively fight terrorism through criminal law enforcement. In this context, human rights organizations warn that our fundamental rights and freedoms will come under pressure because of these anti-terrorist measures. According to Human Rights Watch's analysis, at least six of the new laws and decisions pose a threat to fundamental rights.[65]

The attacks in Paris and Brussels certainly brought Belgian migration law under the scope of counterterrorism policy as migration law was actively amended to deal with terrorist suspects under its scope. However, a significant revision of migration law relaxing procedural safeguards and broadening discretionary powers for the Belgian Foreigners Administration had already been initiated with the implementation of the Return Directive within the Belgian Foreigners Act in 2012.[66] Yet, using the terrorist suspect Salah Abdeslam as the ultimate example, the Act of February 24, 2017, in particular allows the Belgian Foreigners Administration to target foreign nationals with long-standing residence rights, and even those with Belgian nationality, under the "threat for national security" clause. As a result, the terrorist events in Belgium triggered the recent modification of the Foreigners Act and made it explicitly an active instrument not only to preserve national security but also to fight terrorism. As a result, Belgian migration policy fell prey to this "terro-turn"' in governance; no longer solely focused on the fight against illegal migration, it has become an active administrative piece of the Belgian counterterrorism puzzle. In this regard, the Belgian government goes down the path of media and politicians on the European level calling for tougher controls on migration into Europe and making it currently almost impossible to create a practical or conceptual division between the perceived threat from Islamist terrorism and migration.[67]

The impact of recent terrorist attacks on criminal law and migration law enforcement in Belgium can thus foremost be considered as a modification of law in order to act more efficiently in case of actual (suspicion of) terrorist attacks. Notwithstanding some similarities with popular theses in the literature, the described Belgian case provides a more pragmatic account of "governing terrorism" that doesn't totally align with what is often dubbed "governing terrorism through risk."[68] In this regard, there is a subtle difference between endorsing new terro-laws because the criminal code lacks certain provisions to prosecute accordingly compared to endorsing new terro-laws to reassure the public that a swift response to terrorism will be possible in the future or to make sure that prosecuting terrorism could occur according to less demanding procedural standards. As for the described developments in migration law, it remains to be seen to what extent actors deciding to appeal against migration law decision-making according to these new relaxed and more discretionary legal provisions follow the logics of Parliament and the secretary of state. The justification of the new provisions has more to do with reassuring that any necessary measure can be taken regarding terrorist suspects by implementing eased procedural and broader discretionary powers than that criminal justice norms are inserted in migration law,[69] which is a predominant aspect of the crimmigration process.

Although this contribution focused on the developments in the field of criminal law and migration law *stricto sensu*, one last reflection based on two other recent measures also provides a nuanced perspective on what "governing terrorism" involves in the Belgian case. Anti-terrorism measures such as the expansion of the network of cameras for license plate recognition and the registration of the data of all passengers in means of transport (Passenger Name Record) align more with the "governing terrorism through risk" thesis than the developments we described in the field of criminal law and migration law.[70] Yet, it would be too blunt to conclude that the terrorist attacks in Paris and Brussels have installed an active and vast strategy of risk governance and mass surveillance technology in Belgium for the purpose of counterterrorism. The PNR-law, for example, implements three European directives relating to the shipping (2010) and transport (2004) industries; and, of course, there is the most recent directive of 2016 on the use of PNR-data for the fight against terrorism.[71] Contrary to the directive of 2016, the directives applying to the shipping and transport industries relate far less directly to counterterrorism policy.[72] In the case of the so-called shield of license plate recognition, the Belgian government has foremost made resources available to create a national database for storage of license plate registration data. It should be noted that local police departments install many of the license plate registration cameras on Belgian territory. This has two main consequences: first, local mayors whose greatest concern is traffic safety and the fight against burglars and associated types of crime finance these cameras. Second, license plate registration cameras in the territory of local police departments are statically positioned in order to fight local crime rather than terrorism. Surely other actors than the local police can access and exploit the gathered data on license plates and passengers, particularly to combat terrorism. At the same time, however, as the example of license plate recognition cameras shows, even when measures were initially politically framed under the umbrella of counterterrorism policy and could easily be perceived in terms of risk assessment and surveillance, concluding that the governing terrorism through risk and surveillance theses are confirmed can be questioned.

Notes

1. Ulrich Beck, "The Terrorist Threat: World Risk Society Revisited," *Theory, Culture and Society* 19 (2002): 39–55.

2. Gabe Mythen and Sandra Walklate, "Criminology and Terrorism: Which Thesis? Risk Society or Governmentality?," *British Journal of Criminology* 46 (2006): 379–98.

3. Jonathan Simon, "Governing Through Crime," in *The Crime Conundrum: Issues in Criminal Justice*, ed. L. Friedman and G. Fisher (Boulder, Colo.: Westview, 1997).

4. Malcolm M. Feeley and Simon, "The New Penology: Notes on the Emerging Strategy of Corrections and Its Implications," *Criminology* 30, no. 4 (1992): 449–74.

5. Teresa A. Miller, "Citizenship & Severity: Recent Immigration Reforms and the New Penology," *Georgetown Immigration Law Review* 10 (2003): 611–62; Mary Bosworth and Mhairi Guild, "Governing through Migration Control: Security and Citizenship in Britain," *British Journal of Criminology* 48, no. 6 (2008): 703–19; Leanne Weber and Jude McCulloch, "Penal Power and Border Control: Which Thesis? Sovereignty, Governmentality, or the Pre-emptive State?," *Punishment & Society* (2018): 1–19.

6. Teresa A. Miller, "Blurring the Boundaries between Immigration and Crime Control after September 11th," *Boston College Third World Law Journal* 25, no. 1 (2005): 81–123; Juliet Stumpf, "The Crimmigration Crisis: Immigrants, Crime, & the Sovereign Power," *American University Law Review* 56, Lewis & Clark Law School Legal Studies Research Paper No. 2007–2 (2006): 367–419.

7. Juliet Stumpf, "Introduction," in *Social Control and Justice: Crimmigration in the Age of Fear*, ed. M. João Guia, M. van der Woude, and J. van der Leun (The Hague: Eleven International, 2013).

8. João Guia, "Crimmigration, Securitisation and the Criminal Law of the Crimmigrant," in *Social Control and Justice: Crimmigration in the Age of Fear*, ed. Guia, R. Koulish, and van der Leun (The Hague: Eleven International, 2013); Witold Klaus, "Security First—New Right-Wing Government in Poland and Its Policy Towards Immigrants and Refugees," *Surveillance & Society* 15 (2017): 523–28.

9. José Ángel Brandariz Garcia, *Política criminal de la exclusion: El sistema penal en tiempos de declive del estado social y de crisis del estado-nación* (Granada: Editorial Comares, 2007); Guia, "Crimmigration, Securitisation and the Criminal

Law of the Crimmigrant"; Robert Koulish, "Entering the Risk Society: A Contested Terrain for Immigration Enforcement," in Guia, van der Woude, and van der Leun, *Social Control and Justice*; Lucia Zedner, "Is the Criminal Law Only for Citizens? A Problem at the Borders of Punishment," in *The Borders of Punishment: Migration, Citizenship, and Social Exclusion*, ed. Aas and Bosworth (Oxford: Oxford University Press, 2013).

10. Guia, "Crimmigration, Securitisation and the Criminal Law of the Crimmigrant"; Boaventura de Sousa Santos, "Para além do pensamento abissal: Das linhas globais a uma ecologia de sabers," in *Epistemologias do Sul*, ed. B. S. Santos and M. P. Meneses (Coimbra: Almedina, (2009), 23–71.

11. Rik Coolsaet and Tanguy Struye de Swielande, "Belgium and Counterterrorism Policy in the Jihadi Era (1986–2007)," *Real Intituto Elcano, Working Paper* 40 (2007), http://www.realinstitutoelcano.org/documentos/WP2007/WP40-2007_Coolsaet- Struye_Belgium_Counterterrorism_Policy.pdf.

12. Ibid.

13. Ibid.

14. "Plan R: Action Plan Radicalism," *Federal Public Services Home Affairs*, 2016 https://www.besafe.be/sites/besafe.localhost/files/u18/brochure_radicalisme_nl.pdf.

15. Stef Wittendorp, Roel de Bont, Jeanine de Roy van Zuijdewijn, and Edwin Bakker, "Beleidsdomeinen aanpak Jihadisme," in *Een vergelijking tussen Nederland, België, Denemarken, Duitsland, Frankrijk, het VK en de VS* (Leiden: Universiteit Leiden, 2017).

16. Rik Coolsaet, "Het gevoel niet gewenst te zijn," *De Standaard*, Nov. 30, 2015, http://www.rikcoolsaet.be/files/art_ip_com/DS%20301115.pdf.

17. Stef Wittendorp et al., "Beleidsdomeinen aanpak Jihadisme," in *Een vergelijking tussen Nederland, België, Denemarken, Duitsland, Frankrijk, het VK en de VS* (Leiden: Universiteit Leiden, 2017).

18. For the complete overview of the 12-point plan, see https://www.premier.be/sites/default/files/articles/PPT_16012015_définitif.pdf.

19. "Fight against Terrorism — Measures," *Federal Government*, Nov. 19, 2015, http://www.premier.be/sites/default/files/articles/lijst%20van%20maatregelen%20 - %20veiligheid%20Pleniaire%20zitting%2019%2011%202015.pdf.

20. "Plan R. Action Plan Radicalism," *Federal Public Services Home Affairs*, 2016, https://www.besafe.be/sites/besafe.localhost/files/u18/brochure_radicalisme_nl.pdf.

21. Ibid, 11.

22. "Fight against Terrorism — Measures."

23. Act of July 20, 2015, to strengthen the fight against terrorism, *BS*, August 5, 2015.

24. Articles 137 to 141 of the Criminal Code.

25. Art. 2, Act of July 20, 2015, to strengthen the fight against terrorism, *BS*, August 5, 2015.

26. "Grounds for Concern: Belgium's Counterterror Responses to the Paris and Brussels Attacks," *Human Rights Watch*, 2016.

27. Act of July 20, 2015, to strengthen the fight against terrorism, *BS*, August 5, 2015.
28. Art. 7, Act of July 20, 2015, to strengthen the fight against terrorism, *BS*, August 5, 2015.
29. Memorandum of June 22, 2015, to strengthen the fight against terrorism.
30. "Grounds for Concern."
31. Act of April 27, 2016, concerning additional measures to combat terrorism, *BS*, May 9, 2016.
32. Art. 44/11/3, Act of August 5, 1992, on the police force.
33. Memorandum of March 21, 2016, concerning additional measures to combat terrorism.
34. Art. 90, Code of Criminal Procedure.
35. Act of August 3, 2016, concerning various provisions to combat terrorism (III), *BS*, August 11, 2016.
36. Memorandum of July 5, 2016, concerning various provisions to combat terrorism (III).
37. Jennifer M. Chacón, "Managing Migration Through Crime," *Columbia Law Review* 109, UC Irvine School of Law Research Paper), no. 2012–17 (2009): 138–48.
38. Art. 3, Act of August 3, 2016, concerning various provisions to combat terrorism (III), *BS*, August 11, 2016.
39. Act of July 20, 1990, concerning pre-trial detention, *BS*, August 14, 1990.
40. Art. 16§1, Act of July 20, 1990, concerning pre-trial detention, *BS*, August 14, 1990.
41. Memorandum of July 5, 2016, concerning various provisions to combat terrorism (III).
42. "Grounds for Concern," Belgium's Counterterror Responses to the Paris and Brussels Attacks," *Human Rights Watch*, 2016.
43. Act of August 10, 2015, amending the Consular Code, *BS*, August 24, 2015.
44. Art. 2, Act of August 10, 2015, amending the Act of July 19, 1991, on population registers, identity cards, foreigner cards, and residence documents, and amending the Act of August 8, 1983, on the regulation of a National Register of natural persons, *BS*, August 31, 2015.
45. Art. 5, Act of August 10, 2015, amending the Consular Code, *BS*, August 24, 2015.
46. "Action Plan: Approach of Radicalization in Prisons, March," *Federal Public Service Justice*, 2015, 11, http://justitie.belgium.be/sites/default/files/downloads/Plland%27actionradicalisation-prison-NL.pdf.
47. "Action Plan for the Prevention of Radicalization Processes That Can Lead to Extremism and Terrorism," *Flemish Government*, 2015.
48. "Action Plan: Approach of Radicalization in Prisons, March," 11.
49. Lana De Pelecijn, Wim Hardyns, Jelle Janssens, Stef Decoene, and Lieven Pauwels, "Waar een wil is, is een (uit)weg? Exit in de gevangenis: processen, programma's en aanbevelingen," *Panopticon* 39, no. 1 (2018): 18–33.

50. Some paragraphs of this section are based on Steven De Ridder, "Crimmigratie en gedetineerden zonder verblijfsrecht in België," *Panopticon: Tijdschrift voor Strafrecht, Criminologie en Forensisch Welzijnswerk* 38, no. 5 (2017): 338–59; Directive 2008/115/EC of the European Parliament and of the Council of December 16, 2008, on Common Standards and Procedures in Member States for Returning Illegally Staying Third-Country Nationals in Belgian Law, *Pb. L.* (December 24, 2008): 348/98.

51. Act of January 19, 2012, modifying the Foreigners Act of 1980, *BS*, February 17, 2012.

52. Steven De Ridder and Maartje van der Woude, "Changing Practices Regarding the Pmplementation of Entry Bans in Belgian Migration Policy since 1980," in *Immigration Detention, Risk and Human Rights: Studies on Immigration and Crime*, ed. M. J. Guia, R. Koulish, and V. Mitsilegas, 171–83 (Cham: Springer, 2016).

53. Act of February 24, 2017, modifying the Act of December 15, 1980, on the entry, stay, settlement, and expulsion of foreigners, aiming to protect the public order to strengthen the national security, *BS*, April 19, 2017.

54. Memorandum of December 12, 2016 (DOC 54 2215/001); Memorandum of February 2, 2017 (DOC 54 2216/002); Memorandum of February 3, 2017 (DOC P2215/003): 4.

55. Memorandum of December 12, 2016, on the Act of February 24, 2017, modifying the Act of December 15, 1980, on the entry, stay, settlement, and expulsion of foreigners, aiming to protect the public order to strengthen the national security.

56. K. Bergans, W. Cruysberghs *et al.*, "Het verwijderingsbeleid," in *Migratie- en migrantenrecht*, ed. M. C. Foblets and and D. Vanheule, Recente ontwikkelingen (Brugge: die Keure, 2010), 89.

57. Memorandum of December, 12, 2016, on the Act of February 24, 2017, modifying the Act of December 15, 1980, on the entry, stay, settlement, and expulsion of foreigners, aiming to protect the public order to strengthen the national security (DOC 54 2215/001): 4.

58. Steven De Ridder, "Foreign National Prisoners Facing Expulsion: The Percolation of Migration Law Enforcement into Sentence Implementation Decision-Making in Belgium" (*Unpublished Ph.D. thesis in Criminology, Vrije Universiteit Brussel*, 2016).

59. Article 22, Foreigners Act.

60. Art. 55/3/1, Foreigners Act.

61. Art. 44, Foreigners Act.

62. Coolsaet and de Swielande, "Belgium and Counterterrorism Policy in the Jihadi Era (1986–2007)," *Real Intituto Elcano, Working Paper* 40 (2007), http://www.realinstitutoelcano.org/documentos/WP2007/WP40–2007_Coolsaet- Struye_Belgium_Counterterrorism_Policy.pdf.

63. Press release, prime minister of Belgium, June 8, 2017.

64. Stumpf, "The Crimmigration Crisis: Immigrants, Crime, and the Sovereign Power," *American University Law Review* 56 (Lewis & Clark Law School Legal Studies Research Paper No. 2007–2): 367–419; Stephen H. Legomsky, "The New Path of Immigration Law: Asymmetric Incorporation of Criminal Justice Norms," *Washington and Lee Law Review* 64, no. 2 (2007): 469–528; J. M. Chacón, "Managing Migration Through Crime," *Columbia Law Review* 109 (UC Irvine School of Law Research Paper No. 2012–17 (2009): 138–48.

65. "Grounds for Concern."

66. De Ridder, "Crimmigratie en gedetineerden zonder verblijfsrecht in België," *Panopticon: Tijdschrift voor Strafrecht, Criminologie en Forensisch Welzijnswerk* 38, no. 5 (2017): 338–59.

67. Hindpal Singh Bhui, "Understanding Muslim Prisoners through a Global Lens," in *Race, Criminal Justice and Migration Control: Enforcing the Boundaries of Belonging*, ed. Bosworth, A. Parmar, and Y. Vázquez (Oxford: Oxford University Press, 2017), 201.

68. Mythen and Walklate, "Criminology and Terrorism," 379–98.

69. Legomsky, "New Path of Immigration Law," 469–528.

70. Claudia Aradau Rens van Munster, "Governing Terrorism through Risk: Taking Precautions, (Un)knowing the Future," *European Journal of International Relations* 13, no. 1 (2007): 9–115.

71. Council Directive 2004/82/EC of April 29, 2004, on the obligation of carriers to communicate passenger data, 261/24, *Pb. L.*, August 6, 2004; Directive 2010/65/EU of the European Parliament and of the Council of October 20, 2010, on reporting formalities for ships arriving in and/or departing from ports of the Member States and repealing Directive 2002/6/EC, 283/1, *Pb. L.*, October 29, 2010; Directive (EU) 2016/681 of the European Parliament and of the Council of April 27, 2016, on the use of passenger name record (PNR) data for the prevention, detection, investigation, and prosecution of terrorist offences and serious crime, *Pb. L.*, May 4, 2016.

72. Laure Lemmens, "Strijd tegen terreur: België gestart met analyse van passagiersgegevens luchtvaart," https://legalworld.wolterskluwer.be/nl/nieuws/in-het-staatsblad/strijd-tegen-terreur-belgie-gestart-met-analyse-van-passagiersgegevens-luchtvaart/.

13

How Does Crimmigration Unfold in Poland?

Between Securitization Introduced to Polish Migration Policy by Its Europeanization and Polish Xenophobia

Witold Klaus

The literature on the securitization of migration and criminalization of migrants as individuals is relatively abundant. What it is missing, however, is the focus on the countries of Central Europe. Their history, whether that of migration development or the development of law and migration policy, is often significantly different from that of the other countries of the Global North. Or rather was significantly different, since in a lot of respects they have very quickly caught up, both as regards the evolution of anti-immigration sentiments of their societies and in addressing the issue of (anti)immigration by politicians (mainly from right-wing and populist parties) and with the resulting changes in legislation. I aim to discuss these changes with the example of Poland, with special emphasis on the period after 2015, which in the European Union was dominated by the so-called Refugee Crisis. In Poland the time was additionally marked by increasing nationalist attitudes instigated by the new right-wing government, formed in the late autumn of 2015 by the Law and Justice Party [Prawo i Sprawiedliwosc].

In this essay I will be relying on the approach proposed by Leanne Weber and Jude McCulloch, which combines three mid-level theories—Juliet Stumpf's "crimmigration," Mary Bosworth and Mhairi Guild's "new penology," and Susan Krasmann's critique of "enemy penology." Using Poland as the case study, I would like to demonstrate how these three doctrines complement one another to create a suitable tool to analyze the fragment of social reality that is the current migrant policy.

Before I discuss specific examples of controlling and criminalizing migrants in Poland, I would like to briefly outline the Polish migration state of affairs. Throughout most of its history Poland was a country of emigrants—far more people left the country than arrived in it. Only around 2016 did the trends begin to shift, when the inflow of immigrants from Ukraine began to reach over one million people per year. However, it is to a large extent a temporary circular migration, and it is difficult to foresee whether and for how long the trend will last. Another characteristic feature of immigration to Poland is geographical proximity—that is, cultural and ethnic likeness of the new arrivals, with the dominant share of Ukrainians.[1]

The mainly emigration-oriented profile of Poland is very well reflected in the country's policy on migration or, more accurately, its absence—that is, the nonexistence of a document that would describe the policy. Although the policy itself manages without it, the lack of interest of decisionmakers in migration, leaving the policy without official guidelines, could be understood as a form of policy. Additionally, the policy is in fact run on the administration level by street-level bureaucrats.[2] It should be stressed that from its conception in the mid-1990s Polish migration law was subject to a heavy process of Europeanization. EU legislation determined the directions of Polish institutions of migration law and, most of all, the assumptions behind them. Sadly, they were based on the idea of securitization, closing borders, and treating foreigners with suspicion and reluctance. Poland adopted the regulations, which were necessitated by the desire of the country to access the EU and later the Schengen Area, even though they were often maladapted to the Polish migration context or openly detrimental to migration policy and international policy, as was the case with introducing visas for Ukrainians.[3] Naturally, the Europeanization of Polish migration policy brought about positive developments as well—in the initial stages it increased social rights and procedural guarantees, particularly of asylum seekers or individuals in return procedures. The influence of the EU also imported the concept of integration of migrants, based on ideas and premises developed at the EU Community level and executed largely with the money provided by the EU.[4]

Development of Fear and Anti-Immigrant Attitudes in Poland

Since the slow inflow of migrants to Poland mostly consisted of ethnically similar individuals who did not stand out from Polish society,[5] for a while public opinion seemed uncertain of what to make of migrants and migration. Since the 1990s there has been (at least as declared) an increased openness of Poles to representatives of other nations, along with friendliness toward them, albeit mainly with regard to people coming from the richer countries of the Global North. The nationalities that came lower in the friendliness poll were the ones whose representatives lived in Poland—that is, Ukrainians, the Vietnamese, and Russians. The lowest position belonged to Arabs — in other words, Muslims, who suffered the highest level of declared aversion. Regardless of the fact that immigration of the followers of Islam to Poland has always been marginal, in 2009 almost half of Poles believed there were too many Muslims living in Poland. The attitudes may be explained by anti-Islamic rhetoric that made its way to Poland from the West following the terrorist attacks of 9/11. Nevertheless, migration itself was perceived by Poles as a largely positive phenomenon benefiting the society, which was a reflection of how migrants were presented in the media at the time.[6]

The situation changed dramatically in the summer of 2015. The so-called Refugee Crisis in Europe affected Poland in one and only one way — it drastically changed the public debate around migration, moving it to the mainstream, while politicizing it and giving it a populist slant. Poland saw hardly any Syrian refugees — between the years 2011 and 2018 only 889 Syrians applied for international protection in Poland. There had been none as part of the relocation or resettlement schemes. Despite that, the election campaign of the spring and summer of 2015 featured the subject heavily. It was then that "the process of othering" of the group occurred.[7] Not only were refugees or, more broadly speaking, migrants — both terms were used interchangeably in the media — depicted as aliens, as strangers, as not belonging,[8] but also as threatening and dangerous. They supposedly posed physical threat (as perpetrators of crimes, including crimes against women, and as terrorists),[9] economic threat (scrounging off the "world famous" Polish welfare system or stealing jobs from Poles), and a symbolic threat — to Polish (that is, Christian) religion and culture.[10] The term "migrant" finally gained substance in the Polish public awareness.

Consequently, while 70 percent of Poles believed refugees should be welcomed when polled in May 2015, in April 2016 only 33 percent of the society expressed this sentiment. These attitudes have only solidified, even though Polish politicians raise the issue less frequently these days. Between the years 2017 and 2018 two-thirds of Poles expressed reluctance toward refugees, with one-third of respondents associating the word "refugee" only with a "terrorist" or an "Islamist." Likewise, the fear of terrorism had increased — in 2016 almost 60 percent of the polled group considered it a legitimate threat.[11] Aversion toward migrants is closely linked with Islamophobia. It's difficult not to notice a paradoxical pattern — Polish anti-Semitism with very few Jews actually living in the country, and Islamophobia toward nonexistent Muslims.[12] Both phenomena are invariably linked; according to Kinga Wysieńska-Di Carlo in her interpretation of the European Social Survey data for Poland, resentment toward migrants is a sign of societal xenophobia and the general reluctance toward all "others," where "otherness" is mainly defined by ethnicity and non-Christian religious denomination.[13]

Polish xenophobia had remained latent for many years. With their European aspirations, Poles knew to keep their excluding attitudes hidden as incompatible with the image of Europeans. And yet, victimhood nationalism nurtured by right-wing political parties and elevated to a national virtue after 2015 unleashed Polish xenophobia. Holding such views was no longer embarrassing. What is more, nationalism was built around the notion of unspecified "others,"[14] who are intent on obliterating Poles as a nation, thus exacerbating xenophobic inclinations. As Peter Vermeersch observes,

> when nationalist ideas of victimhood are translated into a policy that seeks to establish both ethnocultural homogeneity and historical "justice," certain target groups run the risk of becoming the subject of further oppression and exclusion. In other words, the political power holders who think of themselves as representatives of a victimised majority seeking justice may become responsible for instigating new injustices themselves.[15]

This quote fits perfectly as a description of the processes of otherization of refugees and migrants in Poland, which laid solid foundations for legislative steps undertaken by the Law and Justice government.

Polish Eastern Borders—Solid or Porous Part of the Wall of "Fortress Europe"?

Since 2004 the Polish eastern border has been the eastern border of the EU, and, since the end of 2007, of the Schengen Area as well. An important element of Poland's accession to the EU was the strengthening of protection of external borders, supported in different ways, including financially by the German authorities and the EU. The process was called "sealing" or "civilizing" of the border, which was supposed to become a "velvet" rather than an "iron" curtain in the East. The idea was to adapt the border so that it meets all the requirements that governments have with regard to borders of countries, but also borders separating different worlds and their inhabitants.[16]

Indeed, the Polish eastern border is exceptionally tight, if one is to measure this feature with the number of people caught trying to cross it illegally. Annually, only around 2,000 to 2,500 cases are reported, and most illegal border crossers are identified and approached. Although the stretch between Poland and Ukraine is devoid of any physical barriers preventing the crossing (apart from a river at some point), the whole border is dotted with electronic systems able to detect any forms of unauthorized movement. The situation looks slightly different on the border with Belarus, where there is a barbed wire fence rendering the crossing impossible. However, the fence is on the Belarusian side and is guarded by the Belarusian military. This is a remnant of Soviet times, when so-called *systiema* — that is, heavily guarded fence — was erected along the full length of the border of the former empire.[17] Technology-wise, the Polish border looks tight.

Another form of the impenetrability of "Fortress Europe" pertains to the policy of limiting migrants' access to the EU by means of legal channels. Interestingly, Ukrainian nationals seem to be exempt from an otherwise closing policy of the EU. Polish policy toward Ukrainians has always been special and has favored this group of migrants, the biggest immigrant group in Poland. Until 2003 they have enjoyed the benefits of visa-free travel; then, as part of the process of accession to the EU, visas for Ukrainians were introduced, but they were granted on a very liberal basis, and they were free of charge.[18] Since 2006, as part of Poland's preparation for membership in the Schengen Area, a special mechanism was introduced further facilitating their arrival and legal documentation — namely, declarations entrusting work to a foreigner. This is a simplified employment procedure, working alongside a work permits system that allows citizens of initially three (Ukraine, Belarus, and Russia) and now six (plus Armenia, Georgia and Moldova) countries to legally work in Poland for six months within a consequent twelve months. The number of people (mostly from Ukraine) taking advantage of this privilege has been gradually increasing over the years, gaining force in 2014 (after the Russian attack on Ukraine). As of 2016, over a million Ukrainians a year come to Poland using the declarations policy. By no means is it the total number of Ukrainians in Poland — with those who quote different grounds, for instance, there with job permits or as students, the number most likely totals 1.5 million Ukrainian migrants a year. The policy toward Ukrainians ensures that the doors to enter Poland are wide open for them.[19]

The different treatment of Ukrainians is not specifically Polish, though. Ukrainians are a group that is within the top ten migrant nationalities in Spain or Italy, and in the top three in most of Central and Eastern European countries, like Czechia, Hungary, and the Baltic countries.[20] It makes sense to say that the walls of "Fortress Europe" have various breaches, with each country using a slightly different strategy or legal tools to let Ukrainians in through wide or wide-ish open doors.[21]

Refugees, on the other hand, find themselves at the opposite end of the spectrum. Beyond any doubt, for them the fortress remains impenetrable.

Poland decided to apply the same policy after 2015. It is informal and contravenes the law (both Polish and international), but is consistent with the Law and Justice's Party views and ideology, which do not predict any space in Poland for refugees and Muslims. The Muslims that are at the receiving end of this treatment are mainly Chechens. Since 2000 they have been the most numerous group of individuals seeking international protection in Poland—over 100 thousand applied for it (and very few received it). Initially, Chechens escaped the war and its aftermath; later, they fled repression at the hands of the presidents of this Russia-subjected republic—Akhmad Kadyrov and, following his murder in 2004, his son, Ramzan. The authoritarian Kadyrovs have ruled with an iron fist and long enjoyed complete impunity. It is the people who were fleeing this regime in the summer of 2015 that the Polish border was at first only narrowly open for, and then almost completely shut.

The whole process is highly arbitrary in its nature. The Polish Border Guard on the border crossing in Terespol simply refuse to accept asylum applications from Chechens (and Tajiks, for a brief while) who arrive there to claim the status. The crossing is virtually the only facility of this type and has seen the vast majority of asylum seekers post-2000. The reason for refusal is the alleged attempt by applicants to abuse the procedure and gain "illegal" or "insidious" access to the EU territory, while their actual reasons, according to the border officers, are mainly economic. The guards also claim that the individuals never applied for protection in the first place. They pretend not to hear the requests because they choose not to hear them. Some people attempt to enter Poland several dozen times. Curiously, some of them eventually succeed. The remaining unlucky ones are sent back to Belarus. At the peak moment, there were 1,500 to 2,000 people waiting on the Belarussian site of the border, in the city of Brest, for their turn to apply for asylum in Poland yet and yet again.[22]

The events at the border are informal; Polish law has not changed and, according to NGOs' activists and courts, is violated by the officials refusing to process the refugee status applications. The scenario is hence similar to what is happening in Greece, where border guards do not accept asylum applications from certain refugees coming from Turkey.[23] In comparison, Hungary deals with migrants in accordance with the law, whereby several asylum seekers are accepted a day (currently a maximum of two people), while the rest of the applicants are just stopped or—if they succeed in reaching Hungary using other channels—are "lawfully" deported.[24] And yet the process of border closure happens with the blessing of or the political order of the Polish authorities. In 2016, Mariusz Błaszczak, then minister of the interior, commented on it in the following words:

> We will not succumb to pressure from those who wish to precipitate a migration crisis. Our policy is demonstrably different. The Polish border is sealed off completely. There is no war in Chechnya, unlike several years ago. . . . I perceive it as an attempt to create a new migration route for influx of Muslims into Europe. . . . As long as I'm the minister of interior, as long as Law and Justice is in power, we will not expose Poland to a terrorist risk.[25]

The quote is a perfect illustration of the attitude of the Polish government toward refugees, who are depicted as Muslim terrorists threatening Poland. It is also a clear (though informal) order for the Border Guard officers, subordinate to the Ministry of the Interior, to protect the borders from the menace by not letting in asylum seekers. It also provides an acute example of the language that Bosworth and Guild described as "punitive and fearful rhetoric . . . directed toward the most vulnerable, such as asylum seekers,"[26] especially the people who fled from their countries of origin to save their lives. In the previously described Terespol case, the asylum seekers are forced to wait in Belarus for months, oblivious to the fact that prolongation of their stay there is fraught with danger.[27]

State Security and Anti-Terrorism Legislation

Once the governing party had finally created "the other" and labeled migrants (and particularly refugees) as "enemy aliens"[28] and "dangerous enemies of the state"[29] or—to be more precise in the Polish case—enemies of the nation (because referring to the nation was one of the essential elements of this discourse), it was time to draft legislation reflecting this approach to foreigners. As a result, in 2016, the Act on Anti-Terrorist Activities was drafted and entered into force. Unlike in other countries, Poland had never had a separate anti-terrorist act. Looking at the theoretical groundwork behind the regulations (though it is unlikely their creators ever did that themselves), one can discover that the fear created by the government served as a solid basis to work on the securitization of the state. In this context the security of the society is treated as a "super right," and all other rights, especially individual human rights, should be surrendered to this one, even when they potentially happen to collide with security.[30] Adopting such an approach provides a basis for passing the "enemy criminal law" advocated by Günther Jakobs and criticized by Susan Krasmann. It provides for an anticipatory approach—using sanctions (often disproportionately severe) aimed at people presumed dangerous and applying criminal law and its instruments before any criminal offense has been committed, while suspending procedural rights of the suspects.[31] In fact, the concept of "preventive justice" can be found behind most anti-terrorist laws.[32]

Poland followed in the footsteps of other countries and nominated Muslims to play the role of the enemy. Even though the content of the Act on Anti-Terrorist Activity itself and its explanatory memorandum do not refer directly to this group of people,[33] it features quite heavily in the catalogue of terrorist events that were construed as terrorist threats. According to this memorandum the threat comes from "Islamic radicals" (as referred to in the document) and includes, inter alia, visits by imams in Polish prisons (regardless of the fact that each prisoner has the right to meet clergy of his or her own faith) or plans to establish Muslim schools in Poland. The list also features all offenses committed by inhabitants of asylum seeker centers. The final version of the list was heavily amended, and a more neutral term, "international extremism" instead of "Islamic radicals," was adopted to describe the threats.

This linguistic adjustment does little to conceal the real intentions of the authorities. It is worth adding that the provisions were drafted just before World Youth Day, which took place in Poland in the summer of 2016, with the participation of Pope Francis. The religious dimension of the drafted provisions was therefore significant (the protection of the icon of Catholicism from Muslim radicals).

According to the Act on Anti-Terrorist Activity, every foreigner in the territory of Poland is potentially suspicious and dangerous. Hence, the head of secret services may authorize a series of surveillance activities, including the control of correspondence, phone tapping, or even recording and filming of day-to-day activities of the person in question, private life included. The operations are only supervised politically; there is no requirement for an independent court to approve them. The way the regulations are formulated means that the surveillance can be practically interminable. The information, including the DNA, on every foreigner can be collected and stored by secret service agencies.

In practice, not many people in Poland are prosecuted for terrorist activities. Europol's database reveals that three people were sentenced for the jihadist terrorist activities in 2017, while one person was acquitted; there had been no convictions prior to that. Unfortunately, it is not known what the incidents in question were. Two more people were arrested in 2017, one of whom was a Chechen man with refugee status who was charged with membership in a foreign military organization, which most likely means that the individual fought in Syria.[34] A similar detention took place in January 2019, which was thus explained to the press:

> The foreigner had links with terrorist organisations and was engaged in providing logistic support for such organisations. . . . The Chechen was also a member of an organised criminal group investigated by Internal Security Agency in 2018, consisting of Russian nationals of Chechen origin, which supported terrorist organisations.[35]

However, the fact that a foreigner is suspected of a threat to public safety is most vital in the context of migration law. It can form a basis for revoking practically every residence permit and results in the foreigner automatically being expelled from Poland. With the question of security at stake, the whole procedure is confidential, so the foreigner (or his/her legal representative) has no access to the files that hold the key to his/her expulsion, nor does the foreigner have access to the reasons for the decision. Only an administrative court will be authorized to review the confidential documents, and it could be done only after the decision has been challenged (which is extremely difficult without having access to evidence collected during the deportation procedure). Nevertheless, bringing the case before the court does not have suspensive effect—that is, it doesn't prevent the expulsion of the foreigner. The court can evaluate the classified material based on which the decision was made, but with the foreigner or his/her attorney deprived of this "privilege," it is impossible to comment on or challenge the decision. Nonetheless, the procedure was accepted by the Supreme Administrative Court of Poland as fulfilling international standards,[36] though the judgment raises serious doubts, as it does not account for recommendations from the European Court of Human Rights (ECtHR) (particularly those made in the judgment in *A. and Others v. the United Kingdom*, 3455/05 of 19.02.2009).

Foreigners are expelled, often without the court's knowledge, and frequently without being able to access legal counsel. The evidence sufficient to expel a person can be of a worryingly poor standard—a suspicion is enough—and is later practically impossible to verify by an independent court, or is verified inadequately because of a lack of access to confidential documents by legal counsels who could effectively challenge it before the court. Nevertheless, the practice is used by many countries of the Global North.[37]

Immigrant Detention—Does Poland Differ from Other Countries?

Individuals considered to be a threat to security are detained. One of the functions of the prison sentence, apart from the element of retribution (and rehabilitation, to some extent), is the isolation of perpetrators. But currently, the detention is stretched beyond the sentence itself and is used as preventive detention with regard to individuals who served the sentence but who are assessed as still being a threat to public safety. The practice is debatable at the very least, especially in the context of how reliable the risk assessment is, but is nevertheless used more and more often.[38] And yet, how do you assess the detention of individuals who cannot be considered as a legitimate threat and are not even undergoing risk assessment? This is exactly what is happening with migrants as part of administrative immigrant detention, whose aim is to facilitate administrative procedures (be it asylum or return procedures), not security issues (unless in the symbolic meaning of the word, as in separating dangerous "others" from society).

I don't want to dwell too long on the subject of detention of immigrants, since it has already been thoroughly covered elsewhere. What deserves emphasizing, however, is that regardless of where the study was done, the stories and emotions recounted by foreigners placed in detention facilities are in fact identical. They feel deprived of any rights, abandoned, unjustly locked up in places they call prisons. They report psychological torture, suffer from depression, and have suicidal thoughts.[39] To briefly summarize these experiences and show the scale of abuse, let's look at testimonies of several people who were detained at Polish detention centers:[40]

> *I've had enough of being here* [locked up]. *I thought that coming here, after all I'd been through, would be an improvement. Now I've lost everything. I've been detained for 5 months, I'm tired, I wanted freedom and you didn't give it to me. I've lost 16 kilograms. I've decided to die, so that I don't suffer any more.*

> *I always thought that it was in Africa that human rights were violated, but now I see that Europe is even worse. They traumatise us in silence, they are hiding it. Nobody knows what they are doing to us here. . . . I had a completely different vision of Europe when I came here. And I'm very disappointed. As for human rights—it's the same as in Africa. And so it is with justice.*

> *I've reached a point when I have to wonder if being a refugee is a crime. Nobody chooses to be a refugee. We are refugees, because we have reasons to.*

What seems to distinguish Poland from other countries, at least to some extent, is detention of children, which is gradually forbidden in an increasing number of states. In Poland, the only forbidden detentions are unaccompanied minors in asylum procedures (up to eighteen years old) and unaccompanied minors in other procedures, but only if they are under fifteen years old. If a child travels with his or her parents/guardians, the whole family will be placed in detention. Theoretically (and by law), the best interests of the child should be taken into consideration in every case, but this principle rarely works in practice. In 2018, Poland lost a case before the ECtHR,[41] and the court stated very clearly that detention should be treated as a measure of last resort and alternatives to detention should always be considered, especially when it comes to detaining kids. The court added that

> the child's best interests cannot be confined to keeping the family together and that the authorities have to take all the necessary steps to limit, as far as possible, the detention of families accompanied by children and effectively preserve the right to family life. (para 85)

Notwithstanding this, many children are still in detention centers, where they constituted 20 percent of all the detained in 2018. The number of children who were deprived of liberty in this way stood at 248 (including 19 unaccompanied), and they spent on average 115 days in detention. While in detention, children have limited access to education.

The second group of individuals who are detained in Poland, although they should never end up in detention centers, are violence and torture survivors. The mere suspicion that a person experienced abuse (physical, sexual, or psychological) should result in immediate release from the facility. Unfortunately, it isn't so. What is more, the Border Guard have internal rules on how to deal with foreigners who satisfy the conditions of abuse survivors (e.g., were tortured, raped, trafficked) while in detention, but the rules do not obligate them to release such foreigners immediately, which is a contravention of the provisions of the law. There's an absence of a system to evaluate the mental condition of people who are put in detention or to verify whether they experienced abuse. This is true both about the Border Guard and on the judiciary level where the decision whether to begin or end detention is made. The court rarely calls upon experts to assess the condition of a foreigner (which the Supreme Court pointed out as being anomalous in its verdict II KK 358/16 from 02.03.2018). The verdict has had little impact on the reality of detention.

Although Polish authorities use detention sparingly (e.g., in 2018, there were 1,152 foreigners in all the detention centers), in 2017 new regulations were introduced that provided for a new organization of such facilities and placing foreigners in shipping containers. The shipping containers are to be added to the premises of the existing six centers. Additionally, new facilities might be built, for instance, near the eastern border, consisting exclusively of shipping containers surrounded by a wall and barbed wire, resembling camps or gulags, as has already been done in Hungary, which established so-called transit zones built on the same principles.[42] The idea conjures up historic images of similar detention facilities employed by the totalitarian regimes (communist and fascist) of the twentieth century.

Furthermore, since 2016 the government has been planning to introduce a new accelerated form of asylum procedure called "border procedure" (the third draft of the amendment to the act on granting international protection to foreigners on the territory of the Republic of Poland was published in February 2019). According to this proposition almost every asylum application could be processed under this new procedure, which is very fast (it should last for a maximum of twenty days), has a very vague and low standard of legal protection, and provides just a few safeguards for asylum seekers. In addition, every person submitted to this procedure will be obligatorily detained. This new law mirrors the Hungarian approach to refugees and, if accepted, will create a full new set of problems, including a dramatic increase in the number of detained foreigners.

Conclusions

Most of the changes that are taking place now in the societies of the Global North with regard to migrants are based on the premise that only citizens have rights, and it's they and their well-being that the government is obliged to protect from the "invasion" of a group defined as "dangerous aliens" or "enemies."[43] Thomas Nail observes that "the figure of the migrant is a political concept that defines the conditions and agencies by which various figures are socially expelled as a result of, or as the case of, their mobility."[44] This labeling of migrants as nonmembers of society is a departing point for further practices undertaken by governments. And it is mentioned in all three theories discussed by Weber and McCulloch.[45]

Poland is an example of a country where the processes described by the theories quoted by Weber and McCulloch's happened more quickly and sometimes in reverse order than in other countries of west Europe. As I explained, first the country implemented the law underpinned by ideas of securitization imposed by the EU, while the openly anti-immigrant attitudes voiced by society and politicians followed only later. Still, because of the existence of latent xenophobia, politicians accepted the regulations willingly, and the regulations were not particularly frowned upon by society, either. In this way, a lot of measures such as detention centers or detention and deportation of individuals perceived as a threat to the state (national) security were introduced that Juliet Stumpf identified as part of the process dubbed "crimmigration."[46]

Simultaneously, the process of perceiving migrants as criminals was taking place, which was particularly visible in the activity of law enforcement agencies. Each foreigner was perceived primarily as a potential threat or a criminal in the making, and foreigners' residence status was the chief and main characteristic and a focal point of officials' interest. Protection and support for the migrant was of secondary importance, leaving the most vulnerable group within this group exposed. Human trafficking survivors, domestic violence survivors, victims of bias-motivated crimes all fell victim to this neglect. Migrants who found themselves in such circumstances do not perceive the police as the institution that is there to protect them from the aggressor, because they've always been treated with indifference or suspicion, as if they were the offender. The shared experience of migrants resulted in their reluctance to contact the police or cross paths with their representatives. It is a variation, of sorts, of the process described by Bosworth and Guild,[47] strengthened by Poland closing itself to refugees after 2015 and leaving them in precarious conditions and in danger outside the EU borders.

Finally, the idea of "enemy criminal law" or "enemy penology" reached Poland as well, in the shape of anti-terrorist regulations or attempts to change migration law.[48] All the aforementioned processes intertwine and complement one another, exerting mutual influence. Hence the deliberate idea to consider them as one greater phenomenon that is placed in both legal and political domains and that has a severe impact on liberal democracy. Weber and McCulloch warned that "the steady advance of the securitization agenda threatens the very foundations of the social and legal order."[49] But first and foremost, it undermines the human and humanitarian values of European society that are so proudly presented as the cornerstone of European identities.

Notes

This essay was prepared under the project entitled "Ensuring the Safety and Public Order as a Justification of Criminalisation of Migration," financed by the National Science Centre, Poland (grant number 2017/25/B/HS5/02961).

1. A. Górny, "All Circular but Different: Variation in Patterns of Ukraine-to-Poland Migration," *Population, Space and Place* 23, no. 8 (2017): 1–10, https://doi.org/10.1002/psp.2074; W. Klaus, "Between Closing Borders to Refugees and Welcoming Ukrainian Workers: Norms and Values in Polish Migration Law after 2015 at the Crossroads," in *Europe and the Refugee Response: A Crisis of Values?*, ed. E. M. Goździak, I. Main, and B. Suter (London and New York: Routledge, forthcoming).

2. T. Hammar, ed., *European Immigration Policy: A Comparative Study* (Cambridge and New York: Cambridge University Press, 1985); M. Lipsky, *Street-*

Level Bureaucracy: Dilemmas of the Individuals in Public Service (New York: Russell Sage Fund, 2010).

3. J. Huysmans, "The European Union Securitization of Migration," *Journal of Common Market Studies* 38, no. 5 (2005): 751–77; D. Mtchedlishvili, "Theorising Europeanisation in European Literature: Conceptualisation and Operationalisation," *Australian and New Zealand Journal of European Studies* 10, no. 1 (2018): 79–91; P. Vermeersch, "Victimhood as Victory: The Role of Memory Politics in the Process of De-Europeanisation in East-Central Europe," *Global Discourse: An Interdisciplinary Journal of Current Affairs* 9, no.1 (2019): 113–30, https://doi.org/10.1332/204378918X15453934506003.

4. M. Pawlak, "Imitacja w tworzeniu polskiej polityki integracji," *Studia Migracyjne–Przegląd Polonijny* 39, no. 3 (2013): 97–122.

5. The Vietnamese are an exception. The number of Vietnamese people in Poland stands at thirty to forty thousand. They are grouped in two main locations in Poland, with most of them living in Warsaw and neighboring areas. They have mainly dominated two niches: Asian street food and semi-wholesale of cheap goods, mainly from China. Despite being ethnically different from Poles, they are hardly visible in the public space, relying on the strategy of separation. Their "hassle-free" presence is accepted by the Polish society in this form; A. Grzymała-Kazłowska, "The Role of Different Forms of Bridging Capital for Immigrant Adaptation and Upward Mobility: The Case of Ukrainian and Vietnamese Immigrants Settled in Poland," *Ethnicities* 15, no. 3 (2015): 460–90, https://doi.org/10.1177/1468796813518314.

6. W. Klaus, M. Lévay, I. Rzeplińska, and M. Scheinost, "Refugees and Asylum Seekers in Central-European Countries: Reality, Politics and the Creation of Fear in Societies," in *Refugees and Migrants in Law and Policy Challenges and Opportunities for Global Civic Education*, ed. H. Kury and S. Redo (Cham, Switzerland: Springer, 2018), 484–87.

7. A. Holslag, "The Process of Othering from the "Social Imaginaire" to Physical Acts: An Anthropological Approach," *Genocide Studies and Prevention: An International Journal* 9, no. 1 (2015), https://doi.org/10.5038/1911-9933.9.1.1290.

8. S. Ahmed, "Who Knows? Knowing Strangers and Strangerness," *Australian Feminist Studies* 15, no. 31 (2000): 49–68, https://doi.org/10.1080/713611918.

9. It only ever had a symbolic meaning because criminality of foreigners in Poland is marginal. In the years 2013–16 foreigners constituted a little over one percent of individuals suspected by the police of committing crimes (although this number and percentage have grown gradually). They were mainly responsible for petty crimes; 81 percent of those were offenses against transport safety (mainly drink driving), petty thefts and frauds, and forgery of documents; I. Rzeplińska, J. Włodarczyk–Madejska, "Przestępczość cudzoziemców w Polsce na podstawie danych policyjnej statystyki przestępczości za lata 2013–2016," *Studia Prawnicze*, no. 4 (2018): 137–163).

10. K. Jaskułowski, *The Everyday Politics of Migration Crisis in Poland: Between*

Nationalism, Fear and Empathy (Cham, Switzerland: Palgrave Macmillan, 2019), 77–98.

11. A. Defratyka, "19% Polaków kojarzy słowo 'uchodźcy' z terrorystami (sondaż)," Jun. 29, 2017, retrieved February 8, 2019, http://ciekaweliczby.pl/19-polakow-kojarzy-slowo-uchodzcy-z-terrorystamiakow-kojarzy-slowo-uchodzcy-z-terrorystami/; M. Feliksiak, *Zagrożenie terroryzmem*, Komunikat z badań 127, *Centrum Badania Opinii Społecznej* (2016): 14, retrieved from https://www.cbos.pl/SPISKOM.POL/2016/K_127_16.PDF; M. Omyła-Rudzka, *Stosunek do innych narodów*, Komunikat z badań 37 (Warsaw: Centrum Badania Opinii Społecznej, 2018), retrieved from https://www.cbos.pl/SPISKOM.POL/2018/K_037_18.PDF.

12. E. M. Goździak and P. Márton, "Where the Wild Things Are: Fear of Islam and the Anti-Refugee Rhetoric in Hungary and in Poland," *Central and Eastern European Migration Review* 7, no. 2 (2018): 125–51, https://doi.org/10.17467/ceemr.2018.04.

13. K. Wysieńska-Di Carlo, "Niechęć wobec migrantów: Rasizm i ksenofobia w Polsce na tle europejskim," in *Polska-Europa: Wyniki Europejskiego Sondażu Społecznego 2002–2016/17*, ed. P. B. Sztabiński and F. Sztabiński (Warsaw: Wydawnictwo IFiS PAN, 2018), 32.

14. Different groups could be labeled as such defined others: refugees and migrants, LGBT+ community, political opponents.

15. P. Vermeersch, "Victimhood as Victory: The Role of Memory Politics in the Process of De-Europeanisation in East-Central Europe," *Global Discourse: An Interdisciplinary Journal of Current Affairs* 9, no. 1 (2019): 125–26.

16. K. S. Follis, *Building Fortress Europe: The Polish-Ukrainian Frontier.* (Philadelphia: University of Pennsylvania Press, 2012); T. Nail, *Theory of the Border* (Oxford and New York: Oxford University Press, 2016).

17. Follis, *Building Fortress Europe*; W. Klaus, "Closing Gates to Refugees: The Causes and Effects of the 2015 'Migration Crisis' on Border Management in Hungary and Poland," *Yearbook of the Institute of East-Central Europe* 15, no. 3 (2017): 11–34.

18. Follis, *Building Fortress Europe*.

19. Górny, "All Circular but Different"; Klaus, "Between Closing Borders to Refugees and Welcoming Ukrainian Workers."

20. R. King and M. Okólski, "Diverse, Fragile and Fragmented: The New Map of European Migration," *Central and Eastern European Migration Review* (2018): 1–24, Online First, https://doi.org/10.17467/ceemr.2018.18.

21. I. Jóźwiak, "Mobility, Work and Citizenship in Uncertain Times: An Ethnography of Cross-Border Links at the Boundaries of the European Union," *CMR Working Papers* 95, no. 153 (2017): 1–15.

22. Klaus, "Closing Gates to Refugees," 11–34; M. Szczepanik, "Border Politics and Practices of Resistance on the Eastern Side of 'Fortress Europe': The Case of Chechen Asylum Seekers at the Belarusian–Polish Border," *Central and Eastern*

European Migration Review 7, no. 2 (2018): 69–89, https://doi.org/10.17467/ceemr.2018.08.

23. M. J. Alpes, S. Tunaboylu, and I. Van Liempt, "Human Rights Violations by Design: EU-Turkey Statement Prioritises Returns from Greece over Access to Asylum," *Policy Brief* 29, (2017): 7.

24. Klaus, "Closing Gates to Refugees," 11–34.

25. TVN24, https://www.tvn24.pl/wiadomosci-z-kraju,3/szef-mswia-mariusz-blaszczak-o-czeczenach-na-polskiej-granicy,672450.html.

26. M. Bosworth and M. Guild, "Governing through Migration Control: Security and Citizenship in Britain," *British Journal of Criminology* 48, no. 6 (2008): 715.

27. Szczepanik, "Border Politics and Practices of Resistance on the Eastern Side of 'Fortress Europe': The Case of Chechen Asylum Seekers at the Belarusian–Polish Border," *Central and Eastern European Migration Review* 7, no. 2 (2018): 69–89, https://doi.org/10.17467/ceemr.2018.08.

28. D. Cole, *Enemy Aliens: Double Standards and Constitutional Freedoms in the War on Terrorism* (New York: New Press, 2003).

29. J. van der Leun and M. van der Woude, "A Reflection on Crimmigration in the Netherlands: On the Cultural Security Complex and the Impact of Framing," in *Social Control and Justice: Crimmigration in the Age of Fear*, ed. M. J. Guia, M. van der Woude, and J. van der Leun (The Hague: Eleven International, 2013), 53.

30. T. Lemke, "The Risks of Security: Liberalism, Biopolitics, and Fear," in *The Government of Life: Foucault, Biopolitics, and Neoliberalism*, ed. V. Lemm and M. Vatter (New York: Fordham University Press, 2014), 59–74.

31. C. Gómez-Jara Díez, "Enemy Combatants versus Enemy Criminal Law: An Introduction to the European Debate Regarding Enemy Criminal Law and Its Relevance to the Anglo-American Discussion on the Legal Status of Unlawful Enemy Combatants," *New Criminal Law Review: An International and Interdisciplinary Journal* 11, no. 4 (2008): 529–62, https://doi.org/10.1525/nclr.2008.11.4.529; S. Krasmann, "The Enemy on the Border: Critique of a Programme in Favour of a Preventive State," *Punishment & Society* 9 no. 3 (2007): 301–18, https://doi.org/10.1177/1462474507077496.

32. A. Ashworth, L. Zedner, *Preventive Justice* (Oxford: Oxford University Press, 2015), 171–95.

33. "Rządowy projekt ustawy o działaniach antyterrorystycznych oraz o zmianie niektórych innych ustaw," *Sejm paper* no. 516 (2016), https://www.sejm.gov.pl/Sejm8.nsf/druk.xsp?nr=516

34. Europol, *European Union Terrorism Situation and Trend Report 2018* (The Hague, 2018), retrieved from https://www.europol.europa.eu/sites/default/files/documents/tesat_2018_1.pdf.

35. PAP, http://centrumprasowe.pap.pl/cp/pl/news/info/134779,,rzecznik-ministra-koordynatora-sluzb-specjalnych-nt-zatrzymania-obywatela-federacji-rosyjskiej.

36. Judgement II OSK 1710/18 of November 23, 2018.

37. C. Dauvergne, "The Troublesome Intersections of Refugee Law and Criminal Law," in *The Borders of Punishment: Migration, Citizenship, and Social Exclusion*, ed. Aas and Bosworth (Oxford: Oxford University Press, 2013), 76–90.

38. Ashworth and Zedner, *Preventive Justice*.

39. M. Bosworth, *Inside Immigration Detention* (Oxford: Oxford University Press, 2014); S. Khosravi, "Sweden: Detention and Deportation of Asylum Seekers," *Race & Class* 50, no. 4 (2009): 38–56, https://doi.org/10.1177/0306396809102996.

40. Klaus, "Cudzoziemcy niemile widziani: Detencja cudzoziemców jako przykład kryminalizacji migracji," in *Status cudzoziemca w Polsce wobec współczesnych wyzwań międzynarodowych*, ed. D. Pudzianowska (Warsaw: Wolters Kluwer, 2016), 170–90.

41. *Bistieva and others v. Poland*, application no. 75157/14.

42. Klaus, "Closing Gates to Refugees," 11–34.

43. M. Walzer, *Spheres of Justice: A Defense of Pluralism and Equality* (New York: Basic Books, 1983).

44. Nail, *The Figure of the Migrant* (Stanford, Calif.: Stanford University Press, 2015), 235.

45. L. Weber and J. McCulloch, "Penal Power and Border Control: Which Thesis? Sovereignty, Governmentality, or the Pre-emptive State?" *Punishment & Society* (2018), https://doi.org/10.1177/1462474518797293.

46. J. Stumpf, "The Crimmigration Crisis: Immigrants, Crime, and Sovereign Power," *American University Law Review* 56, no. 2 (2006): 367–419.

47. Bosworth and Guild, "Governing through Migration Control," 703–19.

48. Krasmann, "Enemy on the Border," 301–18, https://doi.org/10.1177/1462474507077496.

49. Weber and McCulloch, "Penal Power and Border Control," 13.

14

Migration Control, Citizenship Regime, and the Spectrum of Exclusion in Turkey

Zeynep Kasli and Zeynep Yanasmayan

On November 19, 2016, 123 asylum seekers in Kumkapi Deportation Center in Istanbul set fire to their beds and escaped from the center as their legal insecurity became insurmountable.[1] The maltreatment in the Kumkapi Deportation Center had previously been sanctioned by both the European Court of Human Rights[2] and the Turkish Constitutional Court.[3] Government chose to ignore the issues around legal uncertainty that impeded any kind of effective protection and instead responded to the overcapacity problems in Kumkapi by increasing the number of deportation centers. While the first recorded uprisings and hunger strikes in Kumkapi detention center go back to 2009,[4] terrible living conditions and prevailing legal insecurity are not germane to the deportation center in Kumkapi. Recent NGO reports cover instances from 2017, such as the one concerning the Harmandali Deportation Center in Izmir, where passersby reported hearing screams for help and food and statements such as "this is Guantanamo." There are also serious allegations that asylum seekers in these centers are subjected to maltreatment to coerce them to agree to a voluntary return, with their access to justice further curtailed.[5] Interestingly, Harmandali Deportation Center rebutted some of these claims in an internet statement by not only denying the accusations of maltreatment, but also accusing those who engender such news of being supportive of terrorist groups that aim to defame Turkey.[6] Their statement reveals how the discourse over terrorism and "enemies of the state" prevalent in Turkey, a country hosting the largest number of refugees worldwide for four consecutive years,[7] could so readily be mobilized not only against migrants but also against pro-migrant rights citizens by questioning their national loyalty and belonging.

Evidently, as this volume also showcases, the far-right populist discourse that targets and increasingly criminalizes migrants is globally on the rise. Studies on right-wing populist parties in Europe tend to see them as a divergence from the norm, but at the same time as agenda setters and a major challenge to liberal forms of politics.[8] One of the major implications of the populist anti-immigrant rhetoric has been to bring state sovereignty back into center stage in an increasingly globalizing era and make migration control an independent site of governance in which, as Bosworth and Guild's study of the UK case shows, citizenship and belonging are the primary considerations of government.[9] Similarly, looking at the overlaps among the substance, procedures, and enforcement of criminal and immigration law in the U.S., Stumpf coined the term "crimmigration" and showed how at the heart of this "marriage" lies the sovereign power of the state to define its membership through punishment.[10] With varying emphasis on the role of discourses, policies, and laws, scholars have underlined the state's expressiveness of sovereign power manifested in its desire to both govern mobility through crime and regulate its membership through migration control.[11] Bosworth and Guild further stress that contemporary political discourse is always ready to target the noncitizens as a source of potential risk and legitimate their confinement,[12] whereas Stumpf describes the continuity of exclusion both for migrants whose exclusion through deportability turns total and ex-felon citizens whose basic citizenship rights are retracted post-confinement.[13]

In the Turkish case, migration control, to the extent that it existed, has always been shaped explicitly in line with the state's definition of "insiders" and "outsiders" predetermined by the ethnoreligious bias of its citizenship regime. Immigrants with "Turkish descent" from Turkey's neighborhood have frequently received preferential treatment, and other noncitizens have routinely been criminalized and dehumanized. However, as we seek to show in this chapter, citizens also find themselves subjected to such exclusion because they happen to fall outside of the limits of ethnoreligious membership and the official ideology circumscribed by the Turkish state. Therefore, using Weber and McCulloch's terms, by addressing the *who* of the migration control, the Turkish case does not only unpack the category of noncitizens but also shows *how* it is intrinsically linked with the citizenship regime that prioritizes Sunni Turkish and the politically loyal majority.[14]

What is more, Turkey's border control measures and related cooperation with its neighbors also reveal that citizenship and foreign policy tools are heavily intertwined. The prime example of this is the controversial EU-Turkey statement that, in return for Turkey's cooperation on migration control with the EU, led to the EU's total disregard of Turkey's suppression of its dissidents at home. Hence, Turkey's willingness for such a deal becomes clear only when its migration control is examined in relation to the changing power relations in its neighborhood, which have implications on state-society relations at home.

Moreover, Turkey's migration control, as both citizenship *and* foreign policy tool, and its particular populist tone, are distinguished from the populist anti-immigrant movement in Europe. It is a ruling party populism that is a major catalyst for the emergence of competitive authoritarianism, especially in the developing world in the post–Cold War period.[15] It is widely agreed that contemporary Turkey has gone through such a regime transformation under Erdogan's (uninterrupted) political leadership since 2002.[16] Although neither populism nor authoritarianism are new phenomena for Modern Turkey, populism has recently gained in popularity as an explanatory force for the peculiarities of the incumbent Adalet ve Kalkınma Partisi (AKP).[17] Among other things, AKP's populism feeds itself from the grievances born from the suppression of Islamic cultural references over the course of the twentieth century by the Kemalist secular nationalist state and its reformers sitting at the high ranks of military and civilian bureaucracy.[18] With AKP's rise to power, virtues of conservative Islamic populism as "markers of an ummah-based political identity" came to the forefront. However, this did not imply that the idea of the "nation" was completely displaced.[19] As the incumbent AKP's neo-Ottomanist vision of modern Turkey shows, the power of nationhood can be conceived in terms of its links to the Ottoman precursors of the contemporary state, which plays the game of world politics with the lens of a neoliberal state of the twenty-first century.[20] The notion of "neo-Ottoman" historical, cultural, and economic drive was in fact first introduced after 1989 to describe Turkey's involvement in the post-communist space. However, with the former foreign minister and prime minister Ahmet Davutoglu's "zero-problems-with-neighbors" vision, it has become the core of AKP's citizenship and foreign policy. As we argue here, this neo-Ottomanist vision also has implications for the border regime. This is perhaps best exemplified in the then foreign minister Davutoglu's following statement: "We do all these with a sense of high responsibility as we regard our Syrian neighbors as our brothers and sisters with whom we share [a] long history and often a common fate."[21]

Indeed, as of January 24, 2019, Turkey is hosting 3,636,617 Syrians under temporary protection, 143,068 of whom are staying in camps run by Turkish authorities.[22] According to Türkstat data,[23] which covers the migration trends of 2016, 2017, and 2018, Syria, not surprisingly, is among the five top countries of origin and maintains a steady flow in the range of 25,000 to 38,000 migrants each year. Yet it lags behind Iraq, which "sent" almost triple the amount, reaching into the 90,000s in 2017 and the 110,000s in 2018. Migrants from

Afghanistan are also more numerous than Syrians in all three years, even if marginally in 2016 and significantly more in 2017 and 2018, coming closer to 45,000. This could be explained by the fact that of the 368,230 individuals registered with the UNHCR Turkey, 46 percent are Afghans and 39 percent are Iraqis.[24]

Ironically, while Turkey continues to be a source country for Europe, be it in terms of professional or family migration,[25] following the aforementioned coup attempt in 2016, asylum-seeking migration of Turkish citizens has also peaked. First-time applications from Turkey, which were around the 4,500 range between 2008 and 2015, more than doubled in 2016, reaching 10,105. It continues to remain at a higher level, with 14,655 applications in 2017 and 22,075 in 2018.[26] Moreover, very recent Turkish statistics provided by Türkstat shows that overall emigration shows a steady increase to 323,918 from 253,640 in 2017 and 177,960 in 2016.[27] Media reports support these statistics, often citing an increasingly oppressive political atmosphere, safety issues, and reduced job opportunities as push factors.[28]

Our chapter tackles this intermingling of border and migration control with citizenship regime and foreign policy and the ways they manifest themselves in an increasingly authoritarian regime. While trying to consolidate its economic and political power abroad, especially in a very fragile post-communist space, the incumbent AKP has extensively capitalized on the old secular-religious cleavage, continued the moralistic depiction of politics as a struggle between "us" the people and the "enemies" of the Turkish state within and abroad, and consolidated its hegemony by winning consecutive elections since 2002.[29] Moreover, we argue, in the Turkish context, that the (anti-)immigrant position and disenchantment with effects of globalization have been shaped through the same secular-religious cleavage that has its roots in Turkey's modernization history. In its current form, the government-led populist discourse claims to represent the interests of the people to be protected against any domestic or foreign "threat" to Turkey's unity in "one people, one flag, one homeland, one state"[30] underlined in President Erdogan's keynote toward the 2017 referendum, which consolidated change toward the presidential system. This imagery of the people sharing the four ideals of unity leads to a large outgroup in Turkey composed of seculars, Alevi, Kurds, Westerners, LGBTQs, feminists, and even anti-capitalist Muslims who, regardless of their nationality, are easily put in a suspect position, demonized, and criminalized for defying or challenging the unity of the "New Turkey." Therefore, what we have witnessed in the last few years is the contradiction between the growing number of Turkish nationals fleeing from an increasingly authoritarian regime on the one hand and a humanitarian state welcoming as "guests" (Sunni) Syrians fleeing the Assad regime on the other.

As the three following episodes depict, this contradiction is not a completely new phenomenon in Turkey's political history. Even though the republican ideal in theory promotes a civic identity, Turkish republican practice has been quite exclusionary of any ethnoreligious diversity.[31] Hence both minorities and migrants that are not considered part of "Turkish descent and culture" have rarely found a place for themselves in the public imagination and are easily othered and put in a suspect position. However, in the face of the ongoing Syrian conflict and the changing position of Turkey in both the regional and global political economy, rising authoritarianism and deteriorating fundamental rights have been veiled with and legitimized through the aforementioned ruling party populism, which expanded the scope of the "outsiders." The failed coup attempt, in July 2016, has reinforced this even further, as it legitimized a two-year-long state of emergency around a so-called anti-imperialist rhetoric that has allowed the incumbent AKP to maintain electoral power by framing any political demand as collaboration with enemies of the state from within or outside. Islamic populist discourse has also marked humanitarian aid—again by and for a selected group—as the only legitimate form of solidarity with migrants and asylum seekers by distinguishing between deserving (read obedient) and undeserving migrants and criminalizing the latter.

In other words, while populist anti-immigrant discourses have by now become very usual in politics in Europe, in Turkey, as we show in detail elsewhere,[32] it is embedded in long-standing societal divisions that continuously polarize and dominate Turkish politics, which in turn facilitate the categorization of *some* migrants as deserving of protection and basic rights according to the ethnoreligious cracks in Turkey's *Kulturkampfs*, in Kalaycioglu's words.[33] These differences in legal inclusion and exclusion therefore represent three distinct episodes of migration governance, rights' claims, and legal struggles that run parallel to each other. In the remainder of this chapter, we unpack the legal and political conditions that set these three episodes.

Episode I: Inclusive Exclusion through Ministerial Decrees

Turkey has been a country of emigration and immigration for decades. Non-Muslim populations who were forced to leave their hometowns since the foundation of modern Turkey, guest workers and their families who went to and eventually settled mainly in European countries since 1960s, and political asylum seekers who fled from the 1980 military coup to different destinations formed the majority of Turkey's emigrant population abroad.[34] There have also been various waves of immigration to Turkey, mainly of people of "Turkish ethnic descent and culture" moving from former Ottoman territories to the "Turkish homeland" who were able to acquire residency with a pathway to citizenship by appealing to clauses privileging ethnic descent in citizenship and settlement laws.[35]

From the 1980s onward and especially since the demise of the USSR and the regional political and economic restructuring in the 1990s, Turkey has progressively evolved into both an immigration and a transit country.[36] The nationality of migrants and patterns of migration have become much more diversified as Turkey attracted circular migration from neighboring countries as well as migrants with international protection needs from African and Asian countries, all of whom were accommodated in various sectors of its informal economy.[37] This partly explains why in the Türkstat data, the fourth and fifth places for migration flows are occupied by Azerbaijan and Turkmenistan in 2017 (around the 20,000 range) and by Iran and Azerbaijan in 2016 (around the 15,000 range).

Despite the growing diversification of mobility to Turkey, its migration and minority policies have continued to be shaped through a nationalist approach that aims to maintain the "people" as the Sunni-Muslim majority and selectively includes the newcomers as they fit into this ethnoreligious frame. Both the latest 2009 Citizenship Law and the 2006 Settlement Law maintain the distinction between "foreigner" and "*göçmen*" (denoting Turkish ethnicity) as well as the discretionary power of the Ministry of Interior, with the Cabinet as the sole authority deciding who would be awarded "*göçmen*" status. In line with this legal framework, the ruling political elite continued favoring migrants of Turkish descent (*göçmen*) such as Turks of Western Thrace, Iraq, Eastern Turkmenistan, Afghanistan, and Bulgaria through special regulations, such as the confidential addendum to the Cabinet decision 2009/14699 on February 23, which granted them a work permit waiver.[38]

This high level of discretion has not always worked to the advantage of even the most privileged migrant groups. The changing position of Turkish-Muslim immigrants from Bulgaria in the last three decades is a good case in point for such capricious ethnoreligious bias. Migration of the co-ethnics from Bulgaria have continued throughout the 1990s, the aftermath of the democratic transition, because no substantive change was foreseen in the economic and political position of the co-ethnic minority. Yet, unlike in the previous decades, and despite the existence of aforementioned exceptional clauses, Turkey no longer automatically granted residence permits through ethnic kinship with a pathway to citizenship.[39] However, in the first decade of the 2000s, the Turkish state offered temporary legalization to this specific group just before elections in Bulgaria, with the latent expectation that they would vote in the elections in Bulgaria, mostly likely for the Movement for Rights and Freedoms (MRF), the party that by and large represents the Turkish minority in Bulgaria. By providing temporary Turkish residence permits, the co-ethnic Bulgarian citizens would be allowed to visit their hometowns in Bulgaria without having to pay the fine for the days/years they overstayed in Turkey. Hence, just like pre-1990s co-ethnic immigrants, political elites have continued to maintain special ties with post-1990s co-ethnic immigrants and, through the "inclusive exclusion" of the latter, in Agamben's terms,[40] instrumentalized its migration policies so as to extend its sovereign power beyond Turkey's territorial borders.[41] This signaled a new level of populist strategy that was used first in 2001, right before the AKP came to power, and was repeatedly used in the following Bulgarian elections over the course of the 2000s.

Despite the fact that previous policies of immediate inclusion of co-ethnic immigrants have changed with the end of Cold War politics, people of "Turkish descent and culture" have maintained a privileged position compared with other migrants with irregular legal status. This has been achieved through ministerial decrees, utilized by the ruling political elite as both a citizenship and foreign policy tool.[42] Their relative privilege also reveals that migration governance, even when pursued by populist governments, does not frame *all* noncitizens as potential risks or threats to the nation and certainly not *all* the time. Even more, exclusive inclusion may also be an asset to bring political influence abroad.

Episode II: Absolute Exclusion with Impunity

As immigrants of "Turkish ethnic descent and culture" have begun to hold an ambiguous insider/outsider position, an increasing number of other migrants with irregular legal status have gotten stuck in a cycle of precarity in Turkey.[43] Since Turkey signed the 1951 Refugee Convention with a geographical limitation, asylum seekers arriving from anywhere but west of Turkey, which constitutes the majority of new arrivals, are not considered "convention refugees." Instead, they have to process their asylum application through the UNHCR and wait for resettlement in a third country.

From the perspective of the EU's expanding "remote" control of migration beyond its external borders since the 1990s,[44] Turkey has increasingly played an important role as a "transit" country, obtaining a label that was also internalized by Turkish governmental actors and bureaucrats.[45] For instance, the

Turkish Foreigners and International Law of 2013 was drafted in line with the 2001 and 2003 EU Accession Partnership documents and related national action plans for legal and institutional transformation.[46] Yet, as noted earlier, Turkey's migration policy has been shaped not only in relation to Turkey's EU membership but in Turkey's changing geopolitical and economic position regionally and globally.[47] As part of its goal to intensify economic relations, visa restrictions were lifted for nationals of various African countries in 2005, while a mutual visa exemption agreement was signed with Syria in 2009 with the aim to create "Samgen," a Schengen-type joint visa policy with Iran and Iraq.[48]

Moreover, migration control has again been used as both a citizenship and foreign policy tool despite legal changes toward a relatively more liberal visa regime. Migrants with irregular legal status have become pawns in international and domestic policy. Against the EU's requirement to abolish the geographical limitation clause of the Refugee Convention, Turkey has insisted on keeping it until full membership is granted and did not easily agree to the EU-Turkey readmission agreement, for which negotiations started in 2002 and became finalized in 2013.[49] Readmission talks were portrayed in Turkish mainstream media solely with reference to a visa exemption proposal for Turkish citizens, hence as an improvement in their right to mobility.[50] There was no mention of how the readmission to Turkey would affect non-European asylum seekers, whose only option is to become undocumented, in the presence of the non-refoulment principle and with no access to asylum or residency in Turkey. However, the "deportability" threat did not apply to *all* noncitizens and not *all* the time. It was dependent on the whim of the regime, which selectively activated deportability, rendering it a political, rather than a legal, decision. For example, in 2010, as a response to discussions concerning the recognition of Armenian Genocide in various European parliaments, the then PM Erdogan declared that 100,000 noncitizen Armenians living and working in Turkey are "managed," meaning their irregular presence is tolerated, but they could be deported if relations get tense.[51]

The Turkish Foreigners and International Law of 2013 was a step forward from the existing fragmented system, which contained secondary regulations, bylaws, and circulars, which were repeatedly criticized by migrant rights advocates and solidarity groups.[52] Based on the 2013 law, the Directorate General of Migration Management (DGMM) was established in April 2014 under the Ministry of Interior to replace the police as the main authority and become the primary and centralized civilian institution responsible for the whole process of registration, protection, detention, and deportation of all migrants. Human rights NGOs expected that having such a comprehensive law would help redress problems in access to international protection, ensure basic rights of asylum seekers in the application process, and overcome the security-driven mentality of the police. To the contrary, this law aimed primarily at categorizing regular and irregular migration movements with the national interest to better "manage" them through a centralized bureaucracy.[53] In the initial years of institutionalization and centralization, great variations were observed in how irregular and/or "transit" migration and asylum processes have been managed and experienced in different cities and borders of Turkey,[54] at times creating local conflicts.[55]

Importantly in this episode, irregular migrants have been overtly criminalized and subjected to police violence with a prevalent impunity. The harsh conditions in custody and detention accompanied by unknown detention periods and lack of legal assistance led to uprisings and hunger strikes as the vignette in the introduction portrayed.[56] We will introduce here one nationwide known case of police violence—the murder of Festus Okey in 2007 during his detention at a police station in Istanbul—in order to give an indication of the criminalization and impunity during this episode of migration control. Okey was a Nigerian migrant holding a UNHCR asylum application card for resettlement in a third country. The police officer, Cengiz Yıldız, who shot Okey, said in his defense that he thought Okey was hiding a gun in his shirt. Okey's shirt was mysteriously lost after he was brought to the hospital. During the first hearing in February 2008, three friends of Okey, together with the Nigerian ambassador, were present but did not dare to demand to be party to the legal action. The Progressive Lawyers Association's (ÇHD) intervention was also rejected with the reasoning that they were not directly affected by the crime. According to the ÇHD's accounts, the defense lawyer's statement offered an example of crimmigration par excellence: "This person is not called Festus Okey. He came here with an illegal visa, later on he called himself Festus Okey. I wonder, is he a terrorist?" While officer Yildiz was suspended briefly from his post, he was not even asked to hand over the gun with which Okey was killed for forensic investigation until 2009. Finally, ÇHD lawyers and members of Migrant Solidarity Network managed to reach Okey's family and requested that his brother, Mr. Ogu, be party to the legal action. In the sixteenth hearing in December 13, 2011, the court rejected this request and quickly sentenced the police officer to a four-year two-month prison sentence for "reckless killing." The Supreme Court of Appeals 1st Penal Chamber decided to overturn this prison sentence to have the police officer tried again, while the lower court insisted on its decision. On March 27, 2018, eleven years after Okey's death, the Supreme Court of Appeals Sentence Board decided that the brother Ogu's demand shall be considered and investigation shall be started again, first by checking the biological ties between Ogu and Okey.[57]

In other words, although liberal visa policies make entry easy and the new law offers the legal framework for a rights-based approach, ongoing geographical limitation to the Refugee Convention and exploitation in the informal labor market make access to basic rights and above all to justice close to impossible for migrants with irregular legal status. The first four years of no action and the last year's chain of decisions and appeals in Okey's case reveals, on the one hand, how migrants with irregular legal status are easily put in suspect positions, and, on the other hand, that the general tendency in the Turkish legal system is to slow down the process and delay due sentence when the defendant is a governmental official.

Episode III: Exclusive Inclusion under State of Emergency

The mass exodus from Syria has been a test case for the Turkish public and its officials in terms of how to legally and emotionally position these Sunni immigrants vis-a-vis other international protection seekers. Previous conflicts and regime changes in 1980s and 1990s in the region, such as the Iran-Iraq War and the first Gulf War, have also caused the arrival of many asylum seekers at the borders of Turkey. Although the seeds of the AKP's foreign policy reorientation toward the Middle East have been sown in the Özal era of the late '80s/early '90s,[58] Turkey approached asylum seekers composed of Iraqi Kurds and Turkmens more as a security threat and, despite ultimately offering shelter, made sure that their stay was temporary even by means of creating no-fly zones in conflict areas.[59] Turkey's policy toward mass movements from Syrians is similarly shaped by both the government's regional interests and concern over safeguarding territorial integrity and national identity, which once again put migration policies at the intersection of foreign and domestic policy.[60]

Once the civil war broke out in Syria in 2011, Turkey first pursued diplomatic channels to convince Assad in a peaceful transition, genuinely believing that it could play such a mediatory role in this conflict.[61] When these efforts failed, Turkey put a halt to the rapprochement policy of 2009 and radically altered its stance toward the Assad regime in 2011. Turkey not only cut all diplomatic ties and economic cooperation, but the then PM Erdogan also spoke out in various international and domestic forums about regime transition in Syria.[62] In the meantime, the open-door policy toward Syrians fleeing their country continued. Their arrival was portrayed by the AKP government as the living evidence of the atrocities of the Assad regime and allowed the government to gain international legitimacy. Initially, they lacked a legal framework within which protection claims could be assessed, and they were welcomed as "guests," "a term framed and justified in reference to the notion of religious fraternity as well as indicating a temporary stay."[63] The legal framework for these Syrian "guests" has somewhat improved with the introduction of temporary protection status in October 2011 based on an EU regulation,[64] putting them at a more privileged position in terms of securing basic rights compared to other non-European asylum seekers who, according to the geographical limitation maintained in the 2013 Law on Foreigners and International Protection, were still not allowed to apply for international protection in Turkey.

The Turkish state's stance toward the Syrian border has further been altered with the realization that the Assad regime would not be quickly overthrown and that Turkey would not receive the international support it desires for its staunch anti-Assad foreign policy. Moreover, the downing of Turkish jets by the Syrian regime in June 2012 and a number of "domestic" incidents, most prominently the bombing of the Turkish southeastern border town Reyhanli in May 2013 that claimed the lives of fifty-three people, increased the fear of a spillover of the conflict. The porous border intentionally maintained by the Turkish state in order to exert influence on the Syrian armed conflict changed, leading to a period of "gradual and partial securitization" of migration and border governance in 2013–14.[65] In terms of border-crossers, this implied an unofficial "closed-door" policy, although the border remained selectively permeable until mid-2015.[66]

Since 2014 the AKP government's humanitarian discourse via brotherhood has become harder to maintain. Turkey began to more systematically register Syrian refugees and to raise its voice about responsibility-sharing and international aid for accommodating refugees in Turkey.[67] The flight of Christian and Yazidi Iraqis as well as Kobanë Kurds from ISIS assaults disrupted AKP's narrative of Syrian "guests" as victims of Assad's despotism and revealed the selective nature of the Turkish asylum policy.[68] Amnesty International reports from that period of time show that asylum seekers from Kobanë were detained, questioned about their relations to PYG/YPG, and often convinced or forced to return.[69] Similarly, pro-government media reserved its humanitarian approach only for refugees fleeing from the Assad regime while turning a blind eye to atrocities committed by ISIS on these other groups.[70] Given their lack of confidence in Turkish authorities, asylum seekers from Kobanë mostly refused to take places at separate camps that the Turkish Disaster and Emergency Management Agency (AFAD) had organized and preferred to be hosted by local communities of the same ethnic/religious origin. Even though the effects of temporary protection status are not yet systematically analyzed, it also seems that this status is helping mostly Sunni and Arab Syrians to obtain access to rights.[71] In October 2014, the street protests that were organized in different cities in Turkey to draw attention to the atrocities in Kobanë turned into clashes between Turkish and Kurdish nationalists in some places, such as Antep, and were eventually suppressed by riot police with disproportionate use of force.[72] In the aftermath of these events, which ended with at least forty civilian casualties, the riot police's right to use firearms was expanded even further with the controversial 2015 "internal security package" that restructured the country's law-enforcement agencies, domestic security, and civilian affairs' authorities.[73]

Witnessing the side effect of blurring the boundary between domestic and foreign political interests, the incumbent AKP has ever since made national unity, territorial integrity, and border control its priorities. This national unity discourse has brought all opposition, except HDP, closer to the AKP's stance, marginalized Kurdish and leftist HDP and its vote base, and eased criminalization of any related groups, citizens and noncitizens alike. It also led to "full-fledged securitization" along the borders after mid-2015,[74] with the erection of a wall and cross-border military action becoming easily accepted by the majority of the Turkish public (e.g., Operation Euphrates Shield between August 24, 2016, and March 27, 2017, and the ongoing Olive Branch Operation since January 2018).[75]

Under this political turmoil within Turkey and across its southern border, the EU-Turkey Statement was agreed upon on March 18, 2016. The deal is built around the 1:1 principle, meaning that Turkey would accept the return of all new irregular migrants and asylum seekers whose applications have been declared inadmissible or unfounded after a fast-track asylum procedure in the Greek Aegean Islands, and, for every Syrian returned to Turkey, one Syrian would be resettled in the EU. The stakes are therefore higher for unauthorized crossers, who are faced with either being deported to Turkey, where they would have no access to international protection, or would be locked in the islands.[76] Although the movement has not stopped and the crossings have become riskier and deadlier,[77] these conditions have deterred a considerable number of migrants from undertaking the journey, lowering the number of arrivals to the Greek islands from 856,723 in 2015 to 173,450 in 2016 and to 29,000 in 2017 and 2018.[78]

Even though the total number of returns to Turkey remains far below the EU's expectations compared with the number of Syrians resettled to the EU from Turkey (1,896 to 8,834),[79] returns to Turkey began as early as April 2016. According to the press releases of the NGO Building Bridges, the returnees are received under extremely isolated conditions (e.g., authorities blocking volunteers from access to persons in the arriving ships) and are cut off from all human contact, including legal aid.[80] Returnees are directly placed in deportation centers, initially often in Pehlivanköy Center, and are veritably incarcerated, being held behind bars that are opened three times a day to allow returnees access to meals and very short recreation times.[81] They have no access to internet, phone, or TV, and often are unaware of the legal situation that they are in.[82] The report of the European Commission states that 57 returned non-Syrians applied for international protection in Turkey, while 831 of them have been returned to their countries of origin. These figures, which are already alarming, might not even be entirely true, as they are reported by Turkish authorities and are so far unverified by any nongovernmental agency. Additionally, NGOs such as Building Bridges and scholars on the ground show how access to international protection has been seriously hindered.[83] Legal aid is only provided to a few asylum seekers who can manage to get in touch with NGOs through personal contacts. Extreme legal uncertainty combined with prison-like detention conditions reduces returnees to what Agamben calls "bare life"[84] to the extent that they are rendered not significant enough to be addressed publicly by the European or Turkish authorities.

Things have only deteriorated since the failed coup attempt of July 15, 2016, and the ensuing state of emergency. According to Amnesty International reports, a series of executive decrees adopted have failed to respect even the reduced guarantees left in place under the state of emergency, such as the Decree Law of October 29, 2016 (KHK/675 and 676). While there were few instances of forced return of asylum seekers and refugees back to Afghanistan, Iraq, and Syria, where they would face a high risk of human rights violations,[85] Executive Decree 676 has basically removed significant safeguards against refoulement from the international protection regime in Turkey, extended the categories of foreigners against whom Turkish authorities can issue removal orders, and abolished the automatic suspensive effect of an appeal against removal orders for individuals, including a recognized refugee or a registered asylum seeker, who are considered to constitute a "threat to public order, security, and health" or are regarded as somehow associated with "terrorist organizations." In such cases, removal orders can be issued even when the person concerned is a recognized refugee or a registered asylum seeker.[86]

Since late 2017 and early 2018, Syrians who have thus far benefited from a comparatively secure legal status have been reported to experience hardship in registering their temporary protection status in ten provinces, including Hatay and Istanbul.[87] Even though Turkish authorities denied the suspension of registrations, NGOs report that only pre-registered Syrians, urgent medical cases, and babies were continuously registered. There are also more instances of refoulement and collective expulsion since 2017 from the eastern and southeastern border towns close to Syria, as well as cases of direct deportation of those apprehended at the Greek-Turkish border for unauthorized border crossing.[88]

The state of emergency in the aftermath of the failed coup and the aggressive fight against what is defined as "terrorist" activity put all newcomers in a suspect position, swinging the pendulum of victimization and criminalization of migrants to the criminalization end. The most obvious obstacle for both Syrians and other non-European refugees remains the exclusion from the right to citizenship in Turkey; meanwhile, the state of emergency executive decrees have extensively limited even basic rights of citizens by, for example, withholding the right to mobility of political dissidents.[89] The deportability of noncitizens, even though the practice is against the fundamental principles of international law, reinforces their absolute exclusion and makes it easier to completely disregard their political subjectivity, political demands, and basic rights.

Conclusion

By looking at the three episodes of migration governance in Turkey, we aim to contribute to this volume on populism and criminalization of migration by underlining the role of existing ethnoreligious divisions underlying a citizenship regime that might go unnoticed in general accounts in Turkey. Even though the flows of refugees from Syria since 2011 are indeed unprecedented in Turkey's history, our chapter has sought to situate this current migration within the historical and comparative perspective, which allowed us to underline continuities and ruptures more clearly. Significantly, it has shown how the intertwinement of citizenship regime and foreign policy interests has always been part and parcel of migration control. While the preferential treatment extended to "Turkish descent" migrants from Bulgaria described in detail in the first episode derives directly from the state-centric circumscription of Turkishness, which despite the official republican ideal is rooted in ethnicity, the open-door policy of the pre-1990s as well as the halt of the practice of automatic citizenship after the 1990s proves that the open-door policy was equally a foreign policy statement to communist Bulgaria in the Cold War era. The same lens can be applied to read the Turkish stance for the official welcoming of Syrian refugees, as explained in the third episode, which again shows the continuity of the amalgamation of foreign policy and citizenship regime while governing migration.

However, the episodes also enable us to demonstrate ruptures that came about most significantly during the authoritarian populist rule of AKP. Whereas the *how* of migration control—that is to say, the foundational elements of migration control—has not shifted significantly, the "packaging" of citizenship regime and foreign policy has gained increasingly Islamic undertones. To be sure, AKP has not invented populism or neo-Ottomanism; however, it made it a central piece of its citizenship *and* foreign policies. Again, following Hadiz,[90] this did not imply putting an end to the idea of nation, which was predicated in "Turkish descent," but rather adding Sunni majority references that were excessively mobilized in the reception of Syrian refugees. Even though AKP's brotherhood discourse did not find as much resonance within the Turkish public,[91] it was sustained by its hegemony over the parliament and the media, which failed to bring about a more rights-based discourse. Therefore, the *who* of migration control has become very significant. While some migrants were thus granted protection and rights on the basis of their putative proximity to the "imagined community" of Turkey, others, such as Festus Okey, who were not part of the national imagination, were legally disregarded and indisputably criminalized. The second episode shows us how the threat of deportability and criminalization is a Damoclean sword for non-Syrian and non-Western asylum seekers in Turkey.

Finally, throughout the episodes, but particularly in the third one, the criminalization of migrants along with citizens becomes the currency of the day, as Turkey's regional political and economic aspirations and migration control are shaped by AKP's Islamic populist politics transcending national borders. Constant fear of existential threats from within and outside paved the way for the imprisonment of all political dissidents, while military interventions in the neighboring countries, allowed by the emergency bill of September 23, 2017, and recent concerns for political (and economic) stability at home put all the new arrivals from the region in suspect positions. This is the new height of electoral authoritarianism, which easily suspends rights granted by the constitution and protected by international law, violates the right to mobility of its citizens and the principle of nonrefoulement for noncitizens, and shows its "benevolent" face only to its obedient citizens *and* migrants who fit into AKP's national imagery.

Notes

1. "Halkların Köprüsü Dernegi Kumkapı Geri Gönderme Merkezi Hakkında Basın Açıklaması" [Press release on the Kumkapi Deportation Center], Halklararası Dayanısma Köprüsü Dernegi, accessed July 15, 2018, http://www.halklarinkoprusu.org/2016/11/halklarin-koprusu-dernegi-kumkapi-geri-gonderme-merkezi-hakkinda-basin-aciklamasi-19-kasim-2016/.

2. Case of *Yarashonen v. Turkey*, June 24, 2014.

3. "Anayasa Mahkemesi'nden 'Kumkapı Geri Gönderme Merkezi' Kararı" [Constitutional Court Decision on Kumkapi Detention Center], Haberler.com, accessed July 15, 2018, https://www.haberler.com/anayasa-mahkemesi-nden-kumkapi

-geri-gonderme-8302451-haberi/; "AYM: Kumkapı Geri Gönderme Merkezi insan haysiyetiyle bagdasmıyor" [Constitutional Court: Deportation Center does not accord with human dignity], Haberler.com, accessed July 15, 2018, http://t24.com.tr/haber/aym-kumkapi-geri-gonderme-merkezi-insan-haysiyetiyle-bagdasmiyor,320719.

4. F. Genç, "Migration as a Site of Political Struggle: An Evaluation of the Istanbul Migrant Solidarity Network," *Movements Journal for Critical Migration and Border Studies* 3, no. 2 (2017): 115–31.

5. "Harmandalı Geri Gönderme Merkezi'nde yasanan hak ihlalleri" [Violation of Rights in Harmandali Deportation Center], Halklararası Dayanısma Köprüsü Dernegi, accessed July 15, 2018, http://www.halklarinkoprusu.org/2017/05/harmandali-geri-gonderme-merkezinde-yasanan-hak-ihlalleri-06-05-2017/; "Insanlık pencereden yardım istiyor" [Humanity Calls for Help from the Window], GazeteduvaR, accessed July 15, 2018, https://www.gazeteduvar.com.tr/gundem/2017/04/29/insanlik-pencereden-yardim-istiyor/.

6. "Harmandalı Geri Gönderme Merkezi Ile Ilgili Sosyal Medyada Çıkan Haberler Ile Ilgili Kamuoyu Duyurusu" [Declaration in Response to Social Media News on Harmandali Deportation Center], Izmir Governorate, accessed July 18, 2018, http://www.izmir.gov.tr/harmandali-geri-gonderme-merkezi-ile-ilgili-sosyal-medyada-cikan-haberler-ile-ilgili-kamuoyu-duyurusu.

7. According to the UNCHR 2017 report, 1 in 23 people in Turkey was a refugee, or a total of 3.5 million people. For details, see "Global Trends: Forced Displacement in 2017," UNHCR, accessed January 10, 2019, https://www.unhcr.org/5b27be547.pdf.

8. M. Minkenberg, "From Pariah to Policy-Maker? The Radical Right in Europe, West and East: Between Margin and Mainstream," *Journal of Contemporary European Issues* 21, no.1 (2013): 5–24; C. Mudde, "The Populist Zeitgeist," *Government and Opposition* 39, no. 4 (2004): 542–63; C. Mudde and C. R. Kaltwasser, eds., *Populism in Europe and the Americas* (Cambridge: Cambridge University Press, 2012).

9. M. Bosworth and M. Guild, "Governing through Immigration Control: Security and Citizenship in Britain," *British Journal of Criminology* 48 (2008): 703–19.

10. J. Stumpf, "The Crimmigration Crisis: Immigrants, Crime, and Sovereign Power," *American University Law Review* 56, no. 2 (2006): 367–419.

11. M. Bosworth and M. Guild, "Governing through Migration Control: Security and Citizenship in Britain," *British Journal of Criminology* 48, no. 6 (2008): 703–19, https://doi.org/10.1093/bjc/azn059; Stumpf, "Crimmigration Crisis," 367–419; M. van der Woude, V. Barker, and J. van der Leun, "Crimmigration in Europe," *European Journal of Criminology* 14, no. 1 (2017): 3–6.

12. Bosworth and Guild, "Governing through Migration Control," 711.

13. Stumpf, "Crimmigration Crisis," 367–419.

14. L. Weber and J. McCulloch, "Penal Power and Border Control: Which Thesis? Sovereignty, Governmentality, or the Pre-emptive State?," *Punishment & Society* (2018), https://doi.org/10.1177/1462474518797293.

15. S. Levitsky and J. Loxton, "Populism and Competitive Authoritarianism in the Andes," *Democratization* 20, no. 1 (2013): 107–36.

16. B. Esen and S. Gumuscu, "Rising Competitive Authoritarianism in Turkey," *Third Word Quarterly* 37, no. 9 (2016): 1581–1606; D. White and M. Herzog, "Examining State Capacity in the Context of Electoral Authoritarianism, Regime Formation and Consolidation in Russia and Turkey," *Southeast European and Black Sea Studies* 16, no. 4 (2016): 551–69; K. Akkoyunlu and K. "Öktem, "Existential Insecurity and the Making of a Weak Authoritarian Regime in Turkey," *Southeast European and Black Sea Studies* 16, no. 4 (2016): 505–27; A. Castaldo, "Populism and Competitive Authoritarianism in Turkey," *Southeast European and Black Sea Studies* 18, no. 4 (2018): 467–87.

17. See, for example, U. Bozkurt, "Neoliberalism with a Human Face: Making Sense of the Justice and Development Party's Neoliberal Populism in Turkey," *Science & Society* 77, no. 3 (2013): 372–96.

18. V. Hadiz, *Islamic Populism in Indonesia and the Middle East* (Cambridge: Cambridge University Press, 2016).

19. Ibid., 40.

20. F. M. Göcek, ed., "Introduction: Contested Spaces in Neo-liberal Turkey," in *Contested Spaces in Contemporary Turkey: Environmental, Urban and Secular Politics* (London: I. B. Tauris, 2018); E. F. Keyman, "Proactivism in Turkish Foreign Policy: The Global-Local Nexus," in *Another Empire? A Decade of Turkey's Foreign Policy under the Justice and Development Party*, ed. Öktem, Ayse Kadıoglu, and Mehmet Karli (Istanbul: Istanbul Bilgi University Press, 2012), 19–33; Öktem and Kadıoglu, "Introduction," in *Another Empire?*

21. "*Speech Delivered by Mr. Ahmet Davutoglu, Minister of Foreign Affairs of the Republic of Turkey at the UN Security Council, 30 August 2012, New York,*" *Ministry of Foreign Affairs,* accessed July 18, 2018, http://www.mfa.gov.tr/speech-delivered-by-mr_-ahmet-davutoglu_-minister-of-foreign-affairs-of-the-republic-of-turkey-at-the-un-security-council_30-august-2012_-new-york.en.mfa.

22. Turkish Directorate General of Migration Management, accessed January 28, 2019, http://www.goc.gov.tr/icerik3/gecici-koruma_363_378_4713.

23. "Vatandaslık ülkesine göre Türkiye'ye gelen ve Türkiye'den giden göç, 2016, 2017, 2018" [Migration to and from Turkey according to Country of Citizenship, 2016, 2017, 2018], Turkish Statistical Institute, accessed November 1, 2019, http://www.turkstat.gov.tr/PreTablo.do?alt_id=1067.

24. "UNHCR Turkey Stats," UNHCR, accessed January 28, 2019, https://www.unhcr.org/tr/en/unhcr-turkey-stats.

25. Z. Yanasmayan, *The Migration of Highly Educated Turkish Citizens to Europe: From Guestworkers to Global Talent* (New York and London: Routledge, 2019).

26. Authors' calculation on the basis of the Eurostat data: "Asylum and First Time Asylum Applicants by Citizenship, Age and Sex Annual Aggregated Data (Rounded)," Eurostat, accessed November 1, 2019, https://appsso.eurostat.ec.europa.eu/nui/submitViewTableAction.do.

27. See note 23.

28. See, for instance, "Turkey Brain Drain: Crackdown Pushes Intellectuals Out," *BBC News*, accessed November 1, 2019, https://www.bbc.com/news/world-europe-42433668.

29. K. Çınar, "Local Determinants of an Emerging Electoral Hegemony: The Case of Justice and Development Party (AKP) in Turkey," *Democratization* (2015): 1–23; S. Dinçsahin, "A Symptomatic Analysis of the Justice and Development Party's Populism in Turkey, 2007–2010," *Government and Opposition* 47, no. 4 (2012): 618–40; Hadiz, *Islamic Populism in Indonesia and the Middle East*; B. Yabanci, "Populism as the Problem Child of Democracy: The AKP's Enduring Appeal and the Use of Meso-Level Actors," *Southeast European and Black Sea Studies* 16, no. 4 (2016): 591–617.

30. "Tek Millet, Tek Bayrak, Tek Vatan, Tek Devlet Için Evet" [Vote YES for One Nation, One Flag, One Homeland, One State], accessed July 18, 2018, https://www.tccb.gov.tr/haberler/410/70982/tek-millet-tek-bayrak-tek-vatan-tek-devlet-icin-evet.

31. M. Yegen, "Citizenship and Ethnicity in Turkey," *Middle Eastern Studies* 40, no. 6 (2004): 51–66.

32. Z. Yanasmayan, A. Üstübici, and Z. Kaslı, "Under the Shadow of Civilizationist Populist Discourses: Political Debates on Refugees in Turkey," in *New Diversities SI: Populism beyond the West; Dissonant Diversities and Fragmented Politics* (forthcoming).

33. E. Kalaycıoglu, "Kulturkampf in Turkey: The Constitutional Referendum of 12 September 2010," *South European Society and Politics* 17, no. 1 (2012): 1–22.

34. N. Abadan-Unat, *Turks in Europe: From Guest Worker to Transnational Citizen* (New York: Berghahn, 2011); I. Atac, G. Heck, S. Hess, Z. Kaslı, P. Ratfisch, C. Soykan, and B. Yılmaz, "Contested B/Orders: Turkey's Changing Migration Regime; An Introduction," *Movements Journal for Critical Migration and Border Studies* 3, no. 2 (2017): 9–23; R. Hirschon, ed., *Crossing the Aegean: An Appraisal of the 1923 Compulsory Population Exchange between Greece and Turkey* (Oxford: Berghahn, 2003).

35. K. Kirisci, "Turkey: A Country of Transition from Emigration to Immigration," *Mediterranean Politics* 12, no. 1 (2007): 91–97.

36. A. Içduygu, *Syrian Refugees in Turkey: The Long Road Ahead* (Washington, D.C.: Migration Policy Institute, 2015).

37. A. Akalın, "Hired as a Caregiver, Demanded as a Housewife: Becoming a Migrant Domestic Worker in Turkey," *European Journal of Women's Studies* 14, no. 3 (2007): 209–25; M. Eder and D. Özkul, "Editors' Introduction: Precarious Lives and Syrian Refugees in Turkey," *New Perspectives on Turkey* 54 (2016): 1–8.

38. Z. Kaslı, "Who Do Migrant Associations Represent? The Role of 'Ethnic Deservingness' and Legal Capital in Migrants' Rights Claims in Turkey," *Journal of Ethnic and Migration Studies* 42, no. 12 (2016): 1996–2012.

39. A. Parla, "Longing, Belonging and Locations of Homeland among Turkish Immigrants from Bulgaria," *Journal of Southeast European & Black Sea Studies* 6, no. 4 (2006): 543–57.

40. G. Agamben, *Homo Sacer: Sovereign Power and Bare Life* (Stanford, Calif.: Stanford University Press, 1998).

41. Z. Kaslı and A. Parla, "Broken Lines of Il/Legality and the Reproduction of State Sovereignty: The Impact of Visa Policies on Immigrants to Turkey from Bulgaria," *Alternatives: Local, Global, Political* 34, no. 2 (2009): 203–27.

42. Ibid.

43. Eder and Özkul, "Editors' Introduction," 1–8.

44. William Walters, "Border/Control," *European Journal of Social Theory* 9, no. 2 (2006): 187–204.

45. S. Hess, "De-Naturalising Transit Migration: Theory and Methods of an Ethnographic Regime Analysis," *Population, Space and Place* 18 (2012): 428–40.

46. A. Içduygu, S. Erder, and O. F. Gençkaya, *Türkiye'nin Uluslararasi Göc Politikalari, 1923–2023: Ulus-devlet Olusumundan Ulus-ötesi Dönüsümlere [Turkey's International Migration Policies, 1923–2023: From the Formation of the Nation-State to Transnational Transformations]* (Istanbul: Mirekoc, 2014).

47. F. Genç, G. Heck, and S. Hess, "The Multilayered Migration Regime in Turkey: Contested Regionalization, Deceleration and Legal Precarization," *Journal of Borderlands Studies* (2018); G. Heck and S. Hess, "Tracing the Effects of the EU-Turkey Deal: The Momentum of the Multi-Layered Turkish Border Regime," *Movements Journal for Critical Migration and Border Studies* 3, no. 2 (2017): 35–57.

48. T. A. Börzel and D. Soyaltin, "Europeanization in Turkey: Stretching a Concept to its Limits?," *KFG Working Paper*, 2012, http://userpage.fu-berlin.de/kfgeu/kfgwp/wpseries/WorkingPaperKFG_36.pdf; N. E. Gökalp Aras and Z. Sahin-Mencütek, "The International Migration and Foreign Policy Nexus: The Case of Syrian Refugee Crisis and Turkey," *Migration Letters* 12, no. 3 (2015): 193–208; M. G. Özerim, "Stretching, Opening or Sealing the Borders: Turkish Foreign Policy Conceptions and Their Impact on Migration, Asylum and Visa Policies," *Journal of Balkan and Near Eastern Studies* 20, no. 2 (2018): 165–82.

49. K. Kirisci, "Syrian Refugees and Turkey's Challenges: Going beyond Hospitality" (Washington, D.C.: Brookings Institution, 2014).

50. See, for instance, the headline of a nationwide mainstream newspaper announcing the conclusion of readmission agreements: "AB ile kolay vize imzaya kaldı" [Easy Visa with the EU Is About to Be Signed], *Hürriyet*, accessed July 7, 2018, http://www.hurriyet.com.tr/dunya/ab-ile-kolay-vize-imzaya-kaldi-16872236.

51. "Erdogan: 100 bin Ermeni göçmeni sınırdısı edebiliriz" [Erdogan: We Can Deport 100 Thousand Armenian Migrants], *BBC Türkçe*, accessed July 7, 2018, https://www.bbc.com/turkce/haberler/2010/03/100316_bbc_erdogan_intw_update.shtml?print=1.

52. Helsinki Citizens' Assembly, Refugee Advocacy and Support Program, *Unwelcome Guests: The Detention of Refugees in Turkey's 'Foreigners' Guesthouses* (Istanbul: Helsinki Citizens' Assembly, 2007); Toplum ve Hukuk Arastırmaları Vakfı (TOHAV), *Göç Analiz Raporu [Migration Analysis Report]* (Istanbul: Toplum ve Hukuk Arastırmaları Vakfı Yayinlari, 2014); Mültecilerle Dayanısma Dernegi (Mülteci-der), Türkiye'de Mültecilerin Kabul Kosulları, Hak ve Hizmetlere

Erisimleri: Uydu Kentler Izleme ve Raporlama Projesi Raporu [Reception Conditions and Access to Rights and Services for Refugees in Turkey: Final Report for Satellite Cities' Monitoring and Reporting Project] (Izmir: Mülteci-Der, 2015).

53. Atac, Heck, Hess, Kaslı, Ratfisch, Soykan, and Yılmaz, "Contested B/Orders," 9–23.

54. A. Ikizoglu-Erensu and Z. Kaslı, "A Tale of Two Cities: Multiple Practices of Bordering and Degrees of 'Transit' in and through Turkey," *Journal of Refugee Studies* 29, no. 4 (2016): 528–48.

55. P. Senoguz, "Border Contestations, Syrian Refugees and Violence in the Southeastern Margins of Turkey," *Movements Journal for Critical Migration and Border Studies* 3, no. 2 (2017): 163–77.

56. See, for instance, "Ankara'daki Afgan mülteciler bir buçuk aydır oturma eyleminde" [Afghan Refugees in Ankara Are on Sit-ins and Hunger Strikes for One-and-a-Half Months], *BBC Türkçe*, accessed July 7, 2018, https://www.bbc.com/turkce/haberler/2014/05/140530_afgan_multeciler; "Kumkapı Geri Gönderme Merkezi'nde 123 sığınmacı firar etti" [123 Asylum Seekers Escaped from Kumkapi Deportation Center], *Ntv*, accessed July 7, 2018, https://www.ntv.com.tr/turkiye/kumkapi-geri-gonderme-merkezinde-123siginmaci-firar-etti,KY5_15pqfUm4pTDRXVXmyQ.

57. "Festus Okey davası 11 yıl sonra sil bastan" [After 11 Years, Everything from Scratch in Festus Okey Case], *Cumhuriyet*, accessed July 7, 2018, http://www.cumhuriyet.com.tr/haber/turkiye/951714/Festus_Okey_davasi_11_yil_sonra_sil_bastan.html. As a side note, the 2018 decision is quite symbolic in the sense that it comes at a time when many prosecutors and judges are suspended, including the 21st Assize Court, with the suspicion or well-founded links with the network of U.S.-based Islamic preacher Fethullah Gülen, referred to by the authorities as the Fetullahist Terrorist Organization (FETÖ). The members of this network have been accused of being behind a long-running campaign to overthrow the Turkish state by infiltrating state institutions, particularly the military, police, and judiciary.

58. P. Bilgin and A. Bilgiç, "Turkey's 'New' Foreign Policy toward Eurasia," *Eurasian Geography and Economics* 52, no. 2 (2011): 184–85; T. Oguzlu, "Middle Easternization of Turkey's Foreign Policy: Does Turkey Dissociate from the West?," *Turkish Studies* 9, no. 1 (2008): 3–20.

59. Gökalp-Aras and Sahin-Mencütek, "The International Migration and Foreign Policy Nexus."

60. A. Okyay "Turkey's Post-2011 Approach to Its Syrian Border and Its Implications for Domestic Politics," *International Affairs* 93, no. 4 (2017): 829–46; Senoguz, "Border Contestations."

61. Bilgin and Bilgiç, "Turkey's 'New' Foreign Policy toward Eurasia," Oguzlu, "Middle Easternization of Turkey's Foreign Policy."

62. Okyay, "Turkey's Post-2011 Approach"; Gökalp-Aras and Sahin-Mencütek, "The International Migration and Foreign Policy Nexus"; Özerim, "Stretching, Opening or Sealing the Borders."

63. Genç, Heck, and Hess, "Multilayered Migration Regime in Turkey," 6.

64. Council Directive 2001/55/EC of July 20, 2001, on minimum standards for giving temporary protection in the event of a mass influx of displaced persons and on measures promoting a balance of efforts between member states in receiving such persons and bearing the consequences thereof, retrievable from https://eur-lex.europa.eu/legal-content/EN/TXT/PDF/?uri=CELEX:32001L0055&from=EN.

65. Okyay, "Turkey's Post-2011 Approach."

66. Gökalp-Aras and Sahin-Mencütek, "The International Migration and Foreign Policy Nexus"; Okyay, "Turkey's Post-2011 Approach."

67. Bilgin and Bilgiç, "Turkey's 'New' Foreign Policy toward Eurasia," Oguzlu, "Middle Easternization of Turkey's Foreign Policy."

68. U. Korkut, "Pragmatism, Moral Responsibility or Policy Change: The Syrian Refugee Crisis and Selective Humanitarianism in the Turkish Refugee Regime," *Comparative Migration Studies* 4, no.2 (2016): 1–20.

69. http://m.bianet.org/bianet/toplum/159286-af-orgutu-nden-acil-eylem-Kobanëli-sinirdisi-edilemez, accessed July 7, 2018.

70. F. Göktuna Yaylacı and M. Karakus, "Perceptions and Newspaper Coverage of Syrian Refugees in Turkey," *Migration Letters* 12, no. 3 (2015): 238–50.

71. Korkut, "Pragmatism, Moral Responsibility or Policy Change."

72. Senoguz, "Border Contestations."

73. "Kobane Protestoları: Insan Hakları Ihlalleri" [Kobane Protests: Human Rights Violations], Amnesty International, accessed July 7, 2018, https://www.amnesty.org/download/Documents/EUR4420172015TURKISH.pdf.

74. Okyay, "Turkey's Post-2011 Approach."

75. As of 2017, like the EU member states Greece and Bulgaria's construction of fence along their land border with Turkey in 2012 and 2017 respectively, Turkey also constructed a 511m-long wall along the Turkish-Syrian border. A similar process is going on along Turkey's Iranian border.

76. Heck and Hess, "Tracing the Effects of the EU-Turkey Deal."

77. I. van Liempt., M. J. Alpes, S. Hassan, S. Tunaboylu, O. Ulusoy, and A. Zommers, "Evidence-Based Sssessment of Migration Deals: The Case of the EU-Turkey Statement," Final Report (Utrech: Utrecht University, Human Geography and Planning, 2017), retrievable from https://migratiedeals.sites.uu.nl.

78. "Sea Arrivals Dashboard," UNHCR Greece, accessed January 28, 2019, https://reliefweb.int/sites/reliefweb.int/files/resources/67184.pdf.

79. "Seventh Report on the Progress made in the implementation of the EU-Turkey Statement," European Commission, accessed January 28, 2019, https://ec.europa.eu/home-affairs/sites/homeaffairs/files/what-we-do/policies/european-agenda-migration/20170906_seventh_report_on_the_progress_in_the_implementation_of_the_eu-turkey_statement_en.pdf.

80. "Yunanistan'dan Türkiye'ye Geri Gönderilen Mültecilerle Ilgili Dikili'de Yapılan Basın Açıklaması" [Press Release in Dikili for the Refugees Who Are Returned from Greece to Turkey], Halklararası Dayanısma Köprüsü Dernegi, accessed July 15, 2018, http://www.halklarinkoprusu.org/2016/07/yunanistandan

-turkiyeye-geri-gonderilen-multecilerle-ilgili-dikilide-yapilan-basin-aciklamasi-4-nisan-2016/.

81. "Pehlivanköy GGM Basın Toplantısı" [Press Meeting on Pehlivankoy Deportation Center], Halklararası Dayanısma Köprüsü Dernegi, accessed July 15, 2018, http://www.halklarinkoprusu.org/2016/05/halklarin-koprusu-dernegi-pehlivankoy-ggm-basin-toplantisi-4-5-2016/.

82. "Pehlivanköy'den Izmir Isıkkent Geri Gönderme Merkezine Iskence Devam Ediyor" [Torture Continues inside the Deportation Centers, from Pehlivanköy to Izmir], Halklararası Dayanısma Köprüsü Dernegi, accessed July 15, 2018, http://www.halklarinkoprusu.org/2016/05/pehlivankoyden-izmir-isikkent-geri-gonderme-merkezine-iskence-devam-ediyor/.

83. Ibid.; Genç, Heck, and Hess, "The Multilayered Migration Regime in Turkey."

84. Parla, "Longing, Belonging and Locations of Homeland."

85. "Turkey: No Safe Refuge; Asylum-Seekers and Refugees Denied Effective Protection in Turkey," Amnesty International, accessed July 18, 2018, https://www.amnesty.org/en/documents/eur44/3825/2016/en/; "Europe's Gatekeeper: Unlawful Detention and Deportation of Refugges from Turkey," Amnesty International, accessed July 18, 2018, https://www.amnesty.org/en/documents/eur44/3022/2015/en/; "Turkey 'Safe Country' Sham Revealed as Dozens of Afghans Forcibly Returned Hours After EU Refugee Deal," Amnesty International, accessed July 18, 2018, https://www.amnesty.org/en/press-releases/2016/03/turkey-safe-country-sham-revealed-dozens-of-afghans-returned/.

86. "Refugees at Heightened Risk of Refoulement under Turkey's State of Emergency," Amnesty International Public Statement, accessed July 14, 2018, https://www.amnesty.org/download/Documents/EUR4471572017ENGLISH.PDF.

87. "Turkey Stops Registering Syrian Asylum Seekers: New Arrivals Deported, Coerced Back to Syria," *Harekact: Reporting on the Turkish-EU Border Regime*, accessed July 18, 2018, http://harekact.bordermonitoring.eu/2018/07/16/turkey-stops-registering-syrian-asylum-seekers/#more-2990.

88. "A New Nightmare: Picked up in the Aegean and Returned to Syria," *Harekact: Reporting on the Turkish-EU Border Regime*, accessed July 18, 2018, http://harekact.bordermonitoring.eu/2018/06/24/a-new-nightmare-picked-up-in-the-aegean-and-returned-to-syria/.

89. Z. Yanasmayan and Z. Kaslı, "Reading Diasporic Engagements through the Lens of Citizenship: Turkey as a Test Case," *Political Geography* 70 (2019): 24–33.

90. Hadiz, *Islamic Populism in Indonesia and the Middle East*.

91. See M. Erdogan, *Suriyeliler Barometresi: Suriyelilerle uyum içinde yasamanın çerçevesi* (Istanbul: Istanbul Bilgi Universitesi Yayınları, 2017).

Contributors

Ana Aliverti is an Associate Professor of Law at the School of Law, University of Warwick. She serves on the editorial boards of *Theoretical Criminology* and the *Howard Journal of Crime and Justice*.

Leonidas K. Cheliotis is an Associate Professor of Criminology in the Department of Social Policy, London School of Economics and Political Science. He is also Codirector of LSE's Mannheim Centre for Criminology, as well as an editor and book review editor of the *British Journal of Criminology*.

Lana De Pelecijn is currently a Ph.D. Researcher of the Research Foundation Flanders (FWO) affiliated with the Ghent University (research group IRCP).

Steven De Ridder is currently Director of Policy Development in a local Belgium police force and former postdoctoral researcher of the Vrije Universiteit Brussel (Belgium), Faculty of Law and Criminology, Criminology Department.

Simone Durham obtained both her Bachelor's and Master's of Arts degrees in Sociology from Morgan State University and is currently a doctoral student at the University of Maryland, College Park. Her current projects include a content analysis of politically polarized news coverage of the Black Lives Matter (BLM) movement and interviews with black millennials on their perceptions of BLM.

Helene O. I. Gundhus is Professor of Criminology at the University of Oslo and Professor II at the Norwegian Police University College. Her publications include *Technologies of Insecurity* (coedited with H. M. Lomell and H. O. Gundhus [Routledge-Cavendish, 2009]), and *Moral Issues in Intelligence-Led Policing* (coedited with N. Fyfe and K. V. Rønn [Routledge, 2018]).

Zeynep Kaslı is an academic researcher at the Erasmus School of Social and Behavioral Sciences at Erasmus University Rotterdam in the Netherlands. She has expertise in political sociology, sociolegal studies, migration, and citizenship with strong skills in qualitative methods and experience in quantitative research. She completed her Ph.D. in the Interdisciplinary Near and Middle Eastern Studies Program and received a Graduate Certificate in Law and Society Studies at the University of Washington, Seattle.

Witold Klaus is a professor at the Institute of Law Studies and a researcher in the Center of Migration Research at Warsaw University. He has a Ph.D. in law and is a lawyer and a criminologist. In 2009, he was awarded the Social Nobel Prize by the Ashoka Foundation.

Robert Koulish, a political scientist at the University of Maryland, is Director of the MLAW Programs in the BSOS College at UMD, Joel J. Feller Research Professor in the Department of Government and Politics, and Lecturer at Law in the UMD Carey School of Law. Koulish is a leading scholar in crimmigration law and is cofounder, in 2012, of the International Crimmigration Scholars Network (CINET). He is the author of *American Democracy: Subverting the Rule of Law* (Routledge, 2010) and coeditor of *Immigration Detention, Risk and Human Rights* (Springer, 2016).

Agnieszka Kubal is an interdisciplinary sociolegal and migration scholar with area studies interest in Central Eastern Europe and Russia. She joined the Department of Social Science at UCL from the Centre for Socio-Legal Studies and Russian and Eastern European Studies, both at the University of Oxford, where she held a research fellowship and a lectureship. She is the author of *Immigration and Refugee Law in Russia* (2019) and *A Sociology of Justice in Russia* (2018) *both* from Cambridge University Press.

Dario Melossi is Alma Mater Professor of the University of Bologna and Distinguished Affiliated Scholar of the Center for the Study of Law and Society (UC Berkeley). His most recent book is *Crime, Punishment and Migration* (Sage, 2015).

Alejandro Olayo-Mendez is currently a graduate student at the University of Oxford and is reading for a D.Phil. in International Development. He holds an M.Sc. in Migration Studies from the University of Oxford, a Master of Social Work from Loyola University Chicago, and a Master of Divinity (Theology) from Boston College.

Tony Platt is a Distinguished Affiliated Scholar at the Center for the Study of Law and Society, University of California, Berkeley. He is the author of numerous books dealing with issues of criminal justice, race, inequality, and social justice in American history, including *Beyond These Walls: Rethinking Crime and Punishment in the United States* (St. Martin's, 2019).

Doris Marie Provine is Professor *emerita* on the Justice Studies faculty in the School of Social Transformation at Arizona State University. She is the author of *Unequal under Law: Race in the War on Drugs* (2007) and coauthor of *Policing Immigrants: Local Law Enforcement on the Front Lines* (2016), both from the University of Chicago Press.

Rashawn Ray is Associate Professor of Sociology and Executive Director of the Lab for Applied Social Science Research (LASSR) at the University of Maryland, College Park. He is also one of the editors of *Contexts Magazine: Sociology for the Public*.

Juliet P. Stumpf is the Robert E. Jones Professor of Advocacy and Ethics at Lewis & Clark Law School. She has published widely in leading journals and books, including a series of crimmigration articles beginning with "*The Crimmigration Crisis: Immigrants, Crime, and Sovereign Power*," 56 *Am. U. L. Rev.* 367 (2006), and has coauthored the casebook *Immigration and Citizenship: Process and Policy* (8th ed. [West, 2016]).

Maartje van der Woude is Professor of Law and Society at Leiden Law School, the Netherlands. She is also affiliated with the Department of Criminology and Sociology of Law at the University of Oslo and the Center for the International Comparative Study of Criminology at the University of Montreal.

Sappho Xenakis is a Reader in Criminology and International Relations at the School of Law, Birkbeck, University of London, where she is also a codirector of Birkbeck's Centre for Political Economy and Institutional Studies and director of the M.Sc. program in Global Criminology. In 2018, she received the Critical Criminal Justice Scholar Award of the Critical Criminal Justice Section of the Academy of Criminal Justice Sciences.

Zeynep Yanasmayan is a Senior Research Fellow and Coordinator of the project "The Challenges of Migration, Integration and Exclusion." She holds a Ph.D. in Social Sciences from KU Leuven, Belgium. Before joining the Max Planck Institute for Social Anthropology in 2017, she worked as a research fellow at various institutions, including Humboldt University in Berlin, European University Viadrina, and the Max Planck Institute for the Study of Religious and Ethnic Diversity in Göttingen.

Index

Page references in **bold** indicate a table.

9 780823 287482

Printed by Libri Plureos GmbH in Hamburg,
Germany